A COMPANION TO E.M. FORSTER

Volume–1

Sunil Kumar Sarker

ATLANTIC

PUBLISHERS & DISTRIBUTORS (P) LTD

Published by
ATLANTIC
PUBLISHERS & DISTRIBUTORS (P) LTD
B-2, Vishal Enclave, Opp. Rajouri Garden,
New Delhi-110027
Phones : 25413460, 25429987, 25466842

Sales Office
7/22, Ansari Road, Darya Ganj,
New Delhi-110002
Phones : 23273880, 23275880, 23280451
Fax : 91-11-23285873
web : www.atlanticbooks.com
e-mail : info@atlanticbooks.com

ISBN 81-269-0748-7 (Vol. 1)
ISBN 81-269-0749-5 (Vol. 2)
ISBN 81-269-0750-9 (Vol. 3)
ISBN 81-269-0751-7 (Set)

Printed and bound in India at Syndicate Binders, Noida

DEDICATED TO

*The memory of my dear mother, **Nilima Sarker**, and my dear younger brother, **Subarna Kumar Sarker**, both of whom had seen the manuscript of this book, while in preparation, but before the manuscript could actually turn into this book, they suddenly departed from this earth.*

Preface

Edward Morgan Forster is one of the most read, most difficult, most controversial, and most discussed front-ranking twentieth century English novelists. Is he a modern novelist or a Victorian? Has he, in fact, written only a single novel and not six? Is he really difficult to read? Is he plain-speaking or enigmatic? Are his novels realistic, or is he fantasying in them as in his short stories? Does he have any message to deliver through his novels or is he just an entertainer? These are some of the questions that have been variously answered by critics, and this has made him all the more interesting. His novels apart, Forster is one of the major short-story writers of the twentieth century as well, astonishingly having not more than some two dozen extant pieces. In his short stories he is exactly fantastic as in his novels he is starkly realistic, and this should point to his wide range of literary peregrination. This is not all, Forster is a worthy and wise critic, commanding respect from other critics, writers and readers.

This book may be treated as an easy guide to Forster, the man, the novelist, the short-story writer, and the critic. After having read the works of a writer, hundreds of questions about the man that the writer is lurk behind us, and so to seek the answers to some of such questions about Forster in it I have dealt with his biography at a length that may seem to some readers rather inordinately expatiated, but then readers are not all of the same kind. For the biographical informations, frankly, I have heavily drawn on the official biographer P.N. Furbank's *E.M. Forster: A Life* and Nicola Beauman's *Morgan: A Biography of E.M. Forster*. I have narrated (or, rather, re-narrated) the starkly bare stories of all the five most popular novels of Forster—*Where Angels Fear to Tread, The Longest Journey, A Room with a View, Howards End, Maurice* and *A Passage to India*—again at some length, as I thought that for an understanding of a novel the bare story of it, which we can rarely recall in details after a lapse of time, particularly if we are voracious readers of fictions, is undeniably of some help. For the like reason, I have also narrated the 'stories' of his short stories. Forster is no less renowned as a critic and a theorist of the novel than as a novelist or short-story writer; as a novelist he can well compare with Henry James or Virginia Woolf, for instances, and as a short-story writer with Edgar Allan Poe or Katherine Mansfield, and, likewise, as a critic and theorist of the novel he stands in comparison with the novelists-cum-theorists-of-the-novel Henry James, Virginia Woolf and Percy Lubbock. It is for this reason that here I have discussed his *Aspects of the Novel,* freely quoting from the text.

I claim not even the least originality in this book, and no observation on, or criticism or appreciation of, Forster, here, is mine (except in a very few cases, and those only by the way); what I have done here is an orderly collocation of materials relevant to Forsteriana. This book may seem to be encumbered with quotations, at places even with long ones, but instead of paraphrasing them, instead of selling others' ideas and views as my own, I preferred to honestly do as I have done. Again, repetitions are here at places, but I have not shunned them keeping in mind the convenience of the reader. I have always had an eye not so much to the quality of my setting forth as to the quantity of materials essential to understand Forster.

My sons, Dr Suman Sarkar and Dr Sutanu Sarkar, had perseveringly collected books on Forster from diverse sources for me, without which certainly I could not have written this book, and my wife, Smt Manju Sarker, has typed the whole manuscript of it. My affectionate thanks I extend to them all. Lastly, I am grateful to Dr K.R. Gupta, Chairman, Atlantic Publishers and Distributors (P) Ltd., New Delhi, for publishing this book.

SUNIL KUMAR SARKER

Contents

VOLUME 3

Life and Works

1

(1)

Let us begin with what Lionel Trilling, the American critic and teacher of literature and the author of the excellent book *E.M. Forster* (1943), says about Edward Morgan Forster, the novelist: "E.M. Forster is for me the only living novelist who can be read again and again and who, after each reading, gives me what the writers give us after our first days of novel-reading, the sensation of having learned something" (Trilling, 9). But how the man E.M. Forster eventually came to be one of the great novelists of our time, wonderfully, with only six novels to his credit? The road from Forster, the man, to Forster, the novelist, will so provide an educative journey.

Martin Heidegger, the great German philosopher, in his article 'The Origin of the Work of Art,' very rightly wrote: "The artist is the origin of the work. The work is the origin of the artist. Neither is without the other" (Cazeaux, 80). Where on earth can the artist find both the content and the form of his art from if not from his own life, from his conscious mind, or from his sub-conscious mind? Forster himself said something like this, in his article 'The Raison d' Etre of Criticism in the Arts' (1948; reprinted in his *Two Cheers for Democracy* in 1951). "What about the creative state? He said: In it a man is taken out of himself. He lets down as it were a bucket into his subconscious, and draws up something which is normally beyond his reach. He mixes this thing with his normal experiences, and out of the mixture he makes a work of art" (Allott, 158). If we cannot psychoanalytically probe into Forster's subconscious, we can profitably learn about some of his normal experiences of life, which perhaps went into the creation of his literary works. The biography of an artist may work as an introduction to, as a horn-book of, the understanding of the thoughts, visions, fancies, ideas, ideals and emotions of an artist. Rejecting the need of reading the biography of an artist in order to enlarge and clarify one's knowledge of him, Forster himself wrote: "The personality of a writer does become important after we have read his book and begin to study it. When the glamour of creation ceases, when the leaves of the divine tree are silent, when the copartnership [between the writer and the reader] is over, then a book changes its nature, and we can ask ourselves questions about it, such as 'What is the author's name?' 'Where did he live?, 'Was he married?', 'Which was his favourite flower?', Then we are no longer reading the book, we are studying it and making it subserve our desire for information .... Study is only a serious form of gossip. It teaches us everything about the book except the central thing, and between that and us it raises a circular barrier which only the wings of the spirit can cross" (Beauman, ix). But we may humbly say that the 'everything' is not nothing, in that the 'everything' is in some way or other connected with the 'central thing,' and that the 'everything' is the condition in which the 'central thing' germinates and proliferates, and the truth of this we may come across in the course of this book.

However, our novelist, Forster, was born on the first day of January, 1879, at Melcombe Place in London. His father was Edward Morgan Llewellyn Forster (nick-named Eddie) and his mother was Alice Clara Whichelo (nick-named Lily). Forster belonged to the Forster family that was joined with the Thornton family when Charles Forster, jr, son of Charles Forster, sr, married Laura of the Thornton family. Edward Morgan Llewellyn Forster was a son of Charles Forster, jr, and Laura Thornton, and he married Alice Clara Whichelo, and was blessed with a single male issue—our novelist, Edward Morgan Forster. By contrast, Edward Morgan Llewellyn Forster's father, Charles Forster, jr, and his wife, Laura Thornton, were blessed with as many as ten sons and daughters, of which Edward Morgan Llewellyn Forster was one. The curious name 'Whichelo' is generally thought to be a corruption of 'Richelieu' (Furbank, 1).

Let us first take a rapid glance at the paternal side of Forster. Forster's paternal grandmother was, as we have already understood, Laura Thornton (1808-69). Laura was one of the nine issues of Henry Thornton (1760-1815) and Marianne Sykes (1765-1815), as Marianne Thornton (1797-1887) was another. So, Henry Thornton was Forster's paternal great grand-father and Marianne Sykes was Forster's paternal great grand-mother. Henry Thornton was "a remarkable man, not only an energetic reformer and philanthropist, but a pioneering theoratical economist, whose pamphlet on Paper Credit has a permanent reputation" (Furbank, 3). Marianne Thornton, eldest daughter of Henry Thornton, after the death of her father, became the head of the Thornton family. " Marianne was a downright, rather autocratic woman, distinctly pre-Victorian in her attitudes. She used to say she was the last survivor of the Clapham Sect, her brothers and sisters having all become high church and Tory; but if so, she was not noticeably marked by the Sect's pietism" (Furbank, 4). The Thorntons lived in the house known as Battersea Rise. The Thorntons were rich, pious, philanthropic and influential in the Evangelical circles. They were leading figures in the anti-slave-trade movement. Marianne's (affectionately called 'Monie') youngest sister Laura Thornton married Charles Forster, jr, and thus the name 'Forster' was attached to the ten issues of Laura and Charles—Edward Morgan Llewellyn Forster (our novelist's father) being one of the ten.

Now, the maternal side of Forster. Forster's mother came from a different family—the Whichelo family. Alice Clara Whichelo, Forster's mother, was a daughter of Henry Mayle, jr, (1826-67) and Louisa Graham (1827-1911). Louisa "was a sensible, breezy, witty woman, with a zest for life, and Forster eventually used her as his model for Mrs Honeychurch in *A Room with a View*" (Furbank, 2). The marriage between Forster's father Edward Morgan Llewellyn Forster and his mother Alice Clara Whichelo was an interesting thing. The Whichelos and the Thorntons were living at places far from one another, and Marianne (or 'Monie') and the Whichelos employed the same doctor, Tayloe by name, when necessities arose. Once Dr. Tayloe took Alice Clara Whichelo (or 'Lily') with him to visit the Thornton family. Lily was then twelve years old and was pretty to look at and charming in manners. On seeing her the ladies of the Thornton family liked her. From then on the doctor used to take Lily with him whenever he visited the Thornton family, and Monie fell in love of this little girl. In course of time Edward Morgan Llewellyn Forster (or 'Eddie') became enchanted by this girl. The name 'Morgan' derived from the name of Charles Forster's (sr) wife, Mary Morgan. Laura Thornton (1808-69) married the penniless son of Charles Forster (sr) and Mary Morgan. Thus our novelist Forster got his name 'Forster' from Charles Forster (sr) and his name 'Morgan' from Mary Morgan—the novelist's paternal great grandfather and great grandmother, the name 'Whichelo,' coming from his mother, being relegated to the limbo.

The love affairs between Eddie and Lily continued to run smoothly and warmly, and soon they pronounced their banns. Eddie (1847-80) was then reading at Trinity College, Cambridge. His father expected him to enter into the profession of the church or of the law, but Eddie wanted to be an architect. Ultimately Eddie enrolled himself as a pupil of the great architect Sir Arthur Blomfield. Before his engagement with Lily, Eddie already qualified as an architect and was earning a pittance. Though Lily belonged to the lower class of society, neither Marianne nor Eddie found any fault in the engagement because of the charming deportment and lively wit of Lily. Marianne was rather fascinated by the look of Lily, and nursed a motherly affection for her in the core of her heart. Marianne willingly took the charge of arranging for the education and aculturisation of Lily. Dr. Tayloe offered to bear a part of the cost of the education of Lily. When she was seventeen, Lily was sent to school where she "picked up a little French and some other mild accomplishments, and acquired social assurance" (Furbank, 5). After Lily's academic pursuit was over, Marianne procured for her the post of a governess in the palatial Abinger Hall in

Surrey, that belonged to Effe Farrer, a friend of Eddie's sister Laura.

The marriage between Eddie and Lily somehow happened on 2 January 1877, eight weeks after their engagement, without much of passion, joy or enthusiasm. Even Eddie did not show any sign of happiness in the marriage; he rather took a 'plunge' in it. This attitude of Eddie towards his marriage is reflected in what Mr. Elliot says, in *The Longest Journey,* about his marriage. "'I have taken a plunge' are the words Mr. Elliot in *The Longest Journey* (1907) uses to tell his family that he is to marry someone 'not impossible socially'" (Beauman, 12). Eddie was quite aware that his was a morganatic and half-hearted, passionless marriage, and Lily could promptly realise the insoucience of Eddie as regards the marriage, and took it to be a humiliation on her part. She could sense the apathy of all the members of Eddie's family, but only Marianne's, towards the marriage, and did not take the humiliation lying low: she burst forth in anger and held Eddie responsible for all the mess. Lily's strong, bitter reaction is reflected in Lilia's outburst at her first husband in *Where Angels Fear to Tread* "Do you think I'm a fool? Do you think I never felt? Ah! when I came to your house a poor young bride, how you all looked me over—never a kind word—and discussed me, and thought I might just do; and your mother corrected me, and your sister snubbed me, and you said funny things about me to show how clever you were!"

In mid-February of the year in which their marriage was solemnized (1877) Lily miscarried, but soon she once again conceived, may be due to "the rapaciousness of Eddie's sexuality" (Beauman, 13), and on 1 January 1879, she gave birth to her only child, a boy, our present novelist. Nicola Beauman has jokingly commented upon the promptness of Lily's second conception: "It seems that Lily, who was to be a strait-laced widow for sixty-five years, had once had a straightforward and eager attitude to sexuality of a kind that would, in different circumstances, have made her a mother ten times over like both her mother and her mother-in-law" (Beauman, 13). But the circumstances could never be different because Forster's father and Lily's husband Eddie died the very next year, *i.e.* in 1880. Forster was born at Melcombe Place "on a rainy, muggy day that became icy towards nightfall" (Beauman, 17). The new-born child was named "'Henry' after both Lily's Whichelo father and grandfather and Eddie's Thornton grandfather, and 'Morgan' after Eddie's Forster grandmother who had been called Mary Morgan" (Beauman, 17-18). On 15 February 1879, the child was taken to Holy Trinity on Clapham Common for christening. "And Eddie, having written the chosen names ['Henry' and 'Morgan'] on a bit of paper and handed them to his mother-in-law, who then refused to read them out because she suddenly 'became afraid of the sound of her voice in a sacred edifice,' gave the piece of paper to the vicar. He intoned them; but the names he read out were Edward Morgan (Beauman, 18). There was a confusion, there was a muddle. "And so Morgan Forster, whose work was to be constantly preoccupied with the idea of muddle, misunderstanding and mistake, began his life with a muddle" (Beauman, 18). However, our novelist is now known not so much as 'Henry' or as 'Morgan' but as 'Forster.'

Forster's paternal great grandfather Henry Thornton, though he died long ago, exerted a great influence on him. Henry belonged to the Clapham Sect who, "'laboured so abundantly for national righteousness and the conversion of the heathen, and rested not until the curse of slavery was swept away from all parts of the British Dominions.' The baby's [Forster's] great grandfather, Henry Thornton, was the linchpin of the Sect; and the influence of him and his circle was to make itself felt throughout the baby's [Forster's] long life" (Beauman, 19). The Clapham Sect was interested in two cardinal things: prayer to God and making money. Henry Thornton wrote two books which were as if the supporting pillars of Clapham Evangelicanism. Evangelicanism is, by the by, "one of the trends within *Protestantism,* closely related to the *Baptists.* Unlike the teaching of the latter, that of the Evangelican Christians is based purely on the *Gospels.* Evangelican Christians consider that *salvation* has been accomplished and that all those who have come to believe in Christ are saved: salvation is granted to man without any contribution on his part, purely on the strength of faith in Christ's redemptive sacrifice" (Progress Publishers, 189). However, the two books that Henry Thornton wrote were a collection of family prayers and *Enquiry into the Nature and Effects of the Paper Credit of Great Britain* (1802). Forster himself has left for us a graphic description of the mentality of Evangelican Christians of the Clapham Sect in his *Abinger Harvest:* "Riches, evangelican piety, genuine goodness, narrowness, complacency, integrity, censoriousness, clannishness, and a noble public spirit managed to flourish together in [their] ample bosom without mutual discomfort.... That they had no sense of art goes without saying, nor were they uninterested in literature unless it was an intellectual or formative character...indifference to the unseen seems to me the great defect in my great-grandfather's sect,and the reason why they have not made a bigger name in history.... Poetry, mystry, passion, ecstasy, music, don't count" (Beauman, 22). Therefore, the influence that Forster's great grandfather exerted on him was only negative. Forster, when he grew up attached himself with the Bloomsbury group which was quite at variance with the Evangelican Clapham Sect regarding beliefs, thoughts and attitudes. And yet Forster grew up for the first eight years of his life in the atmosphere of such a spirit of the Evangelican Clapham Sect.

Forster's maternal side was more intellectual than his paternal side. His maternal great grandfather Henry Mayle Whichelo (sr) was an artist of standing, and his maternal grandfather Henry Mayle Whichelo (jr) was also an artist of reputation. Forster's grandfather Charles Forster (jr), *i.e.* Eddie's father, was also an intellectual person, and he wrote some books among which were *Mohamedanism Unveiled* and *The Three Heavenly Witnesses*. So we may say that Forster was growing up in the confluence of Thornton, Forster, and Whichelo traditions. But Forster felt more inclined towards, and sympathetically attached to, the Whichelos, particularly to his maternal grandmother Louisa Graham Whichelo, about whom and the Whichelos he wrote: "'it is with her [Louisa]—with them—that my heart lies'" (Beauman, 27). Lily, Forster's mother, was "'lovely to look at, with a delicate complexion, and full of gaiety and charm,' the prettiest of the four Whichelo sisters, she was by nature more conventional than them. In later life, while she remained a kind of crystallised Victorian, her sisters would grow more bohemian. She was an obedient girl, responsible and anxious to please; she was by nature more Thorntonesque" (Beauman, 28). Eddie, Forster's father was also beautiful to look at: "Eddie seems, from his photograph, to have been a handsome young man, slightly petulant perhaps, slightly what we would nowadays call wet, but good-looking and with a romantically languorous figure" (Beauman, 28-29). And so it was not for nothing that at the time of Lily's engagement with Eddie, Louisa told her about Eddie: "'He is a man in 10,000'" (Beauman, 28).

(2)

The baby Forster was to Lily the most precious object in the world, particularly after the death of Eddie within around just one year. The baby was also an object of attraction to Louisa. But, unfortunately, the baby became a bone of contention, as to who would possess him solely, between Lily and her lifelong friend childless Maimie, the widow of Inglis Synnot and the daughter of an Indian Army Surgeon, James Blair Preston. "The infant Forster, Like Helen's baby in *Howards End,* was the lifeline for two shipwrecked women and their hopes haloed his head, and coloured his own sense of himself, all through his childhood" (Furbank, 11). Another tug-of-war developed, again on the infant Forster, between Marianne or, as she used to be called in the family circle, 'Monie' and Lily. P.N. Furbank writes in his the most authentic biography of Forster, *E.M. Forster: A Life* about the 'duel' fought over the infant Forster between 'Monie' and Lily: "As, too, with Lilia's baby in *Where Angels Fear to Tread,* a 'duel' soon developed over the possession of him [the infant Forster]. Monie, having lost two adored nephews, concentrated her affection on the infant Morgan [Forster] and wanted him and Lily wholly under her management" (Furbank, 11-12). However, the infant Forster was "a demonstrative child, prone to violent passions of love or fury, and Lily was accused of spoiling him, though Monie denied the charge" (Furbank, 14). And Lily was 'the most self contained woman,' at least as Monie thought, and she 'was able to support herself financially, was set upon independence.'

For some time past Lily was anxiously searching for a rented house and at last found one—the house known as 'Rooksnest'—not far from Stevenage. "'Rooksnest' was originally the name not of the house itself but of a hamlet including both it and the neighbouring farm" (Furbank, 15 f.n.). And 'Rooksnest' once in the past belonged to a family called Howard. It was "a charming house, with its rosy brickwork, its ancient vine, and its steep-pitched roof, pierced by dormer windows, sweeping down at the rear, in an odd way, almost to the ground. Forster evoked the house and his love for it in *Howards End* and wrote later, 'The house is my childhood and safety. The three attics preserve me. Only a little of my passion and irratinality was used up in *Howards End*'" (Furbank, 16). 'Rooksnest' was surrounded by apple-trees and paddock, and there was a garden in front of the house, and along the far side of the garden ran a meadow which Lily rented to the Franklyns who were farmers. The little Forster became very friendly with the Franklyns and respected their simplicity and affability and honesty, and later on recalled the Franklyn family as 'that honoured family.' "As a child, Forster spent half his days at the farm [of the Franklyns]. He would hasten nervously across the farmyard, which was always full of enormous and ferocious-looking pigs, and would play for hours in the great barns, scampering about and hunting for eggs in the mysterious twilight. In one of the barns lived a machine, with great wheels, for cutting oil-cake and hay. Young Frankie Franklyn used to spread himself out on the wheels and whirl round like Ixon, while Morgan [Forster] looked on admiringly, wishing he dared do likewise" (Furbank, 18-19).

Eddie's death—a sudden death—was a bolt from the blue to Lily, and she saw darkness in the blazing sun. After suffering from pulmonary consumption for eighteen months,

Eddie succumbed to death on 30 October, 1880, 'ten days before his thirty-three birthday when his son was twenty-two months.' Eddie died at 'Rooksnest'. After Eddie's death, Lily found herself shipwrecked with her infant son Forster. Even her mother, let alone anybody else, did not come to her rescue. And yet there was one who did her yeoman's service: 'Maimie' or the widowed Mary Preston. Money was not a problem, however, to Lily. "Eddie had left almost Pound 7000 (Pound 325,000), a sum that, together with the gifts and expectations Lily had from Marianne, ensured that she was not poor. She could afford to continue to rent Melcombe Place [at Rooksnest], at a cost of Pound 90 (Pound 4000) a year, and to employ two maids" (Beauman, 33).

The little Forster was now the lodestar of Lily's life. Forster was a 'delicate' child and so Lily was always 'morbidly anxious about Morgan's [Forster's] health and coddled him obsessively.' "All through his childhood he [Forster] was never allowed out if there were the slightest threat of rain, and in the mildest wind he had to be swathed in warm coats and mufflers. He imbibed the anxiety himself, and right up to middle age he thought of himself as extremely frail and likely at any time to develop consumption. In fact, as he came to realize late in life, he had an extremely sound constitution" (Furbank, 19). Forster was a "pretty child, at the age of three or four, with large expressive eyes. At Monie's insistence, he wore his hair in curls to his shoulders and dressed in Little Lord Fauntleroy suits with lace collars; he was, he said, one of the very last children to be tormented in this manner" (Furbank, 19). Forster was an 'extremely precocious' child. '"We have rather a life of it if we do anything baby [Forster] doesn't like,' wrote Lily to Aunt Monie, when he was three. 'He calls us "monstrous crows and rats," and when his grandmother asked him "not to do it" he said "I shall, Mrs piece of suet." I can't think what made him think of it. I suppose, 'the rhyme.' At the age of four, with the aid of the picture-books at 'East Side,' he discovered he could read, and he took himself very seriously in consequence. 'Tiresome to be interrupted in any reading when the light is so good,' he would say severely to

Aunt Monie's nurse. 'Can't you tell people I am busy reading, Havell?" (Furbank, 19). "Forster's favourite book during this time was *The Swiss Family Robinson* and he was interested in the book more because 'the boys in it were happy, whereas Robinson Crusoe was always worrying over savages.' Forster was not only a precocious reader but also a precocious writer; in fact the later great novelist, the oak, showed itself in the boy Forster, the acorn: "when he [Forster] was still only five, he began composing stories on his own account, 'long stories about things that have never happened except inside my head,' he [Forster] called them. They had sensational titles like 'Dancing Bell,' 'Chattering Hassocks,' 'Scream,' 'Scuffles in the Wardrobe,' 'The Earring in the Keyhole' and 'The Adventures of Pussy Senior.' In 'Chattering Hassocks,' fifty lions and fifty unicorns sat on hassocks and the lions made speeches in favour of tolerance and liberty of opinion; Monie declared it was better than *Alice*" (Furbank, 19-20). It was therefore very appropriate that Marianne called the little Forster 'the Important One.'

It was about this time that Forster's mother-fixation, his inordinate love for his mother and an instinct to remain always close to her, began to show itself: "a love-affair sprang up between Morgan [Forster] and his mother at this time. He wanted it to last for ever and became fearful at any threat of alteration" (Furbank, 21). And Lily was responsible for the development of the mother-fixation, for she was fond of being fondled by, and attached to, her son. The mutual affection between them began to grow into mutual passion, as is obvious from the recorded conversation between the two, during this time (Furbank, 21):

> *Morgan* [Forster]. When I grow up, my darling, I shall call upon you every day.
>
> *Lily*. You can live with me if you like.
>
> *M*. That will be best, and I will only sit with you and pay visits with you when you go with me.
>
> *L*. What shall I do when you marry?
>
> *M*. I shall only marry to you.
>
> *L*. You can't.

M. Why not? People can marry twice, so I don't see it will make any difference to you.

L. Boys can't marry their mothers.

M. What a bother. Well, I shall take care then never to go to any wedding in case I should be married and don't want it.

The idea of loveless marriage haunted Forster all through his life. In *A Passage to India* (chapter 29), for instance, Fielding (an alter-ego of Forster) tells Aziz: "Marriage is too absurd in any case. It begins and continues for such very slight reasons. The social business props it up on one side, and the theological business on the other, but neither of them are marriage, are they? I've friends who can't remember why they married, no more can their wives. I suspect that it mostly happens haphazard, though afterwards various noble reasons are invented. About marriage I am cynical." The seed of this cynicism may have grown out of the child Forster's frustration that, though he loved his mother the most, he was barred from marrying her, and that if he happened to marry he was to marry someone he did not either love her or love her as much. However, D.H. Lawrence was also mother-fixated, but perhaps his mother-fixation was not as strong as that of Forster.

During this time Lily and Forster were living in Stevenage. Lily did not much involve herself in the local society, and yet she made friendship with a few persons of the neighbourhood, among whom were Mr. Jowitt, the Rector, and his wife, the parents of the future Lord Chancellor. Lily was also in warm relationship with the Poston family. Mrs. Poston was very dear to Lily. In *Howards End* Forster held this Poston family as the model for the Wilcox family. The other persons with whom Lily and Forster mingled from time to time for gossips and courtesies were from their near relations: Georgie, Nellie and Rosie, the last one being Forster's favourite. Yet another person, with whom Lily was in frequent touches, was Maimie who had recently remarried. The "story of this second marriage [of Maimie] is worth a digression, as it exhibits the darker side of the Thornton clan-system and,..., contributed to the plot of *Where Angels Fear to Tread*" (Furbank, 27). "Maimie had gone to Salisbury to keep house for her young half-brother Willie Preston who had recently been ordained, and while there she received a proposal of marriage from her music-teacher, an elderly gentleman of the name of Aylward. Much as she cherished Inglis's memory, she was inclined to accept, partly to rescue the old man from a bullying daughter. However, as soon as the news reached Monie's ears, a most appalling storm broke over Maimie's head. For Mr. Aylward dropped his aitches, and he was in trade—he kept a music shop in the town—It was no good; in the family's eyes he could only be a fortune-hunter, and Maimie must be deranged in her mind to entertain any such scheme [of marriage]. Monie daily despatched letters in every direction, while Morgan's [Forster's] Aunt Laura begged that Mr. Aylward's name should not be mentioned in her presence; and as a result poor Maimie's mind did for a time become deranged, upon which Aunt Monie put the matter in the hands of lawyers and proposed to buy Mr. Aylward off" (Furbank, 27-28). However, the marriage ultimately happened and it proved to be a happy marriage.

At 'Rooksnest,' Louisa Whichelo, Forster's maternal grandmother, was the constant partner at play with the little Forster. Louisa detested women, and when Forster reminded her that she herself was a woman, she said: "Im not a woman, so I must be a mule." Later, when Forster was a schoolboy and about twelve, he composed the following poem on this theme, and Louisa delighted to read it (We do not know the exact date of the composition of this poem.):

The Opinions of Mistress Louisa Whichelo the Chastier of her Sex

'Here come the women! Out they walk
    In groups of two and three
To chatter forth their silly talk
    O'er filthy cups of tea.'

'They gulp the bread and butter down
    With shovellings and pecks,
They drop the jam upon their gown,
    I hate the female sex.'

'I hate their spaldering [?] wet feet;
    Why will they trail and roam?
If they must eat—well let them eat,
    But let them eat at home.'

The proper place for womenkind
    Is not to walk outside;
But see the house is clean and mind
    The men are well supplied.'

So spake Louisa, free and fair,
    Yet bowed not to her rule,
For Heaven's providential care
    Had classed her as a mule.

(Furbank, 29)

During this period of time Lily provided Forster with some garden-boys, as his companions, to make him feel that he was not a lonely boy. Among the garden-boys were Ray, William, Bible, Field, Chalkely and Ansell, the last being Forster's favourite. This name appears in *The Longest Journey,* which novel Forster said was his favourite.

(3)

In January, 1890, when Forster was eleven, Lily thought it high time for her son to go to school, and so got him admitted in the prep school called Kent House, 'on top of the cliff near Eastbourne,' not far from 'Rooksnest'. Here it may be worthwhile to dwell on Forster's passion for 'Rooksnest' where he and Lily had been living till 1893. 'Rooksnest' was attached to Forster's heart throughout his life; it was in it that his formative years began. "More than innocence, more than growth, what he [Forster] realised the decade at Rooksnest embodied for him for ever was *ordinary happiness,* the house remained throughout his life an ideal, a paradise. 'If I had been allowed to stop on there,' he would declare when he was in his mid-fifties, 'I should have become a different person, married, and fought in the war. And, twenty-five years later, 'The impressions received there remained and still glow...and have given me a *slant upon society and history*. It is a middle-class slant, atavistic.'" (the emphases mine) (Beauman, 37).

Forster was always happy with 'ordinary happiness' and a 'slant upon society and history' is there to be found in all his novels.

When Lily and Forster entered into 'Rooksnest', Forster was only four years old, and when they left it in 1893 he was around fourteen. The decade that elapsed through Forster's Rooksnest life left an indelible impression on him. 'Rooksnest' was a small house, having no mains water and electricity, and the house stood out on a vast pastoral scenario. Rural values prevailed in the surround and simplicity showed in every face. Everyone there showed no sign of want beside what little he had. Both Lily and Forster liked and enjoyed the country life in and without 'Rooksnest', and Forster, in particular, felt an empathy with the rural values which he regarded always with respect, and "concluded that life in the country is more 'real,' has more integrity, is more in touch with preceding and successive generations" (Beauman, 41). If we read his works closely we will find that Forster was always nostalgic for the Victorian rural life and values, and this was due to his most happy life at 'Rooksnest'. And yet it was here that his slant for philosophical attitude towards life and a tendency towards moribundity developed, and these two may be ascribed to his feeling of loneliness at 'Rooksnest'. Many of Forster's observations of the life in the rural environment around 'Rooksnest' loom largely in *Howards End,* and he could gather silently and intently those observations only because he was far from the 'madding crowd' of the urban area. However, during his 'Rooksnest' period Forster fast matured mentally, but of course not physically and emotionally. His look during this period he visualised long afterwards as something like this: "'a strange-looking youth, tall, prematurely aged, the big blue eyes faded with anxiety, the hair impoverished and tousled'" (*op. cit.,* 43). Being almost absolutely friendless at 'Rooksnest', Forster was gradually leaning towards his affectionate mother, as the mother also, having little connection with the outer world, was progressively slanting towards him. But "their relationship was not a love affair" (*op. cit.,* 44), as a few commentators of Forster prefer to fancy.

Now, to go back to Forster's schooling. As already told, he was enrolled in Kent House when he was eleven. The headmaster, Mr C.P. Hutchinson, was kind to him, especially when he heard that Forster was 'delicate'; the other masters were 'fussy but kind'; and "the music-master told him he had been very well taught" (Furbank, 33). Nevertheless, he was not happy in that school: after his first week there he wrote to Lily 'I am not happy' and asked her to 'send another Bible.' The reason of his unhappiness in the school was that he was being ragged by other students; "they called him 'Mousie' or jeered 'green-eye' or 'suck' at him" (*op. cit.*, 34). Forster tried to win their favour but failed. His only friends were Henson and the headmaster's nephew Haworth.

Forster's sex-consciousness began to grow when he was five or six. He wrote in 1935 diary: "'prepuce being very long I used to play with it'" (Beauman, 46). He was writing about himself when he was five or six. But he was not well acquainted with 'smut,' with sex-play or everything related to sex, even then. Forster's awareness of sex came to the fore during his Kent House days. The matter of sex played a great part, positively as well as negatively, in Forster's life, and so we should not, perhaps, shirk the oddities of sex in his life. And about Forster's awareness of sex we may better quote at some length from his most authentic biographer P.N. Furbank's *E.M. Forster: A Life:* "He had had no acquaintance with 'smut' till he came to Kent House, so he was rather mystified when he heard it in the dormitories. Not that so very much was talked, but he learned that there were queer things in the Bible; and an older, but virtuous, boy told him how he had seen a woman wringing out her bathing-drawers, and what a wonderful sight it had been, only Forster wouldn't understand—as indeed he didn't. He also learned the 'cock' from the other boys. One of them said, 'Have you seen Forster's cock? A beastly little brown thing,' which depressed him. His own word for his penis up till now had been his 'dirty,' and the fact is revealing. When, as a young child, he had discovered masturbation and announced the fact to his mother, she told him it was 'dirty·' She did not say it in an alarmist way, but he sensed her anxiety, and henceforth 'help me to get rid of the dirty trick' figured in his prayers. He also began to think of his penis as unique and as some kind of punishment—though, inconsistently, he used to look for the 'dirties' in Smith's *Classical Dictionary* and was annoyed when, in Kingsley's *Heroes,* they were covered up with drapery. He told his mother about this too, and she reproved him but did not take the books away" (Furbank, 36-37).

From the above passage we may get some knowledge about Forster's early unnatural idea about sex and about the disgust and horror entailing it. Now let us quote another passage from the same location to see Lily's attitude towards sex, which somehow influenced Forster's attitude towards it: "Lily's whole attitude to sex was that it was a dreadful subject and to be thought of as little as possible. She made no attempt at any stage to tell Morgan the 'tacts of life.' During his first term at Kent House he [Forster] formulated his own theory of them, which was that 'lying together' meant that a man placed his stomach against a woman's and it was a crisis when he warmed her; and on his return for the holidays, he told his mother he knew what 'committing adultery' meant. She looked worried and replied, 'So you understand now how dreadful it would be to mention it, especially if a gentleman was there.' For some years this remained more or less the total of his [Forster's] knowledge of the facts of life. Indeed he said later that it was not till he was thirty, by which time he had published three novels, that he altogether understood how copulation took place" (Furbank, 37). From all this we may guess, at least partially, the reasons of his being a homosexual later in his life—the ignorance of the natural joy of the opposite sex and the 'dirtiness' of sex may have contributed to his replacing the apparatus of the sex by the whole rest part of the beautiful human (particularly male) body.

The peculiar story of the early part of Forster's sex-life will remain incomplete without the 'sexual drama' through which he underwent during this time: "It is an interesting story and has some significance, I think, for his later development. One afternoon, in midwinter, he [Forster] was sent for a walk on the downs, and on reaching the summit he came on a middle-aged man, in a deerstalker hat and knickerbockers, urinating in full view. When the man had finished, he spoke to Morgan [Forster] and made him come and sit on his mackintosh, near some gorse-bushes, and after a moment or two of conversation he undid his own flies and told Morgan [Forster] to play with his penis. Morgan obeyed, being more puzzled than alarmed—though he was startled by the sight of the inflamed tip of the penis and was further astonished when he saw some white drops trickling out. This having taken place, the man quickly lost interest; he asked Morgan where he lived, and offered him a shilling, and when Morgan refused it, he let him go without more ado" (Furbank, 37 and Beauman, 48). Forster wrote about this incident simply 'Nothing' to remind him that it was something.

Kent House soon became disgusting to Forster, particularly due to some rowdy students there: they would harass him too much and too frequently. He reported once in a letter to Lily that such fellows "'last night kept on taking my pillow, and wetting my clothes; so I bore it for a long time and then when they began hitting me and hurting my face, I thought 'no more of this' and slapped their faces'" (Furbank, 39). Forster further wrote that he was 'threatened,' and this alarmed Lily, and she was thinking of taking him out of the school and get him admitted in another school. He was , academically, doing well in Kent House, inspite of all his harassments. In his Christmas examination of 1892, he "came out top of his form in classic, French and scriptures" (*op. cit.*, 38). Forster again wrote to Lily: 'I am in dreadful muddle.' Perhaps this was for the first time that he used the word 'muddle'—the word that he has been employed so frequently in his works. Not only Forster but Lily was also in 'dreadful muddle' as to what to do with her son's education. At last Lily decided to move her son to Tonbridge School, and in 1893 got him enrolled in that school. Unfortunately, from the frying pan of the Kent House Forster fell into the fire of the Tonbridge School. He went to the school as a dayboy and there he had to bear with teasing and all other sorts of torture from some other boys. He was then fourteen and a half, and so was quite conscious about his prestige. When he was devastatingly humiliated he became hysterical sometimes. His life was the most unhappy, the most wretched in the Tonbridge School—a public school. From the school he once wrote to Lily: '"...I feel utterly wretched, I would like to come away. Every one is against me... I have tried to keep from breaking down but I could not help it, and all the boys have noticed it'" (Beauman, 50). Tonbridge School was a respectable school, and yet in it such things went on. There were both resident students and dayboys in the school, and the former treated the latter, as if, as outsiders. There were in the school draconian disciplines and an emphasis on *esprit de corps*. No student was treated as an individual but as a part or block of a group or organisation. The school was rather pedestrian, and certainly it was uninspiring as regards academic matters. But here 'sporting ethic was supremely important.' The central objective of the school was to turn out heartless, hard, disciplined, most patriotic, and mechanical prospective rulers and administrators, and this is partially evident in the school's particular anthem that began with the lines: 'Here shall Tonbridge flourish, here shall manhood be, Serving God and country, ruling land and sea' (Furbank, 41). Tonbridge produced persons like Mr Turton and Ronny Heaslop (in *A Passage to India*), who had only heads and no hearts. The Tonbridge School was later caricatured and denounced by Forster in *The Longest Journey* where this school was the model of his fictional Sawston School ('Saw' plus 'Ton'/ Tonbridge?).

Whatever may be the motto and the spirit of the school, Tonbridge followed intensive and extensive curricula, and those very strictly. Forster "joined the classic side, and this still meant, at that period, a weekly diet of nineteen hours of classics, with not all that much else besides—at most a modicum of French and mathematics and a very little history and geography" (Furbank, 43). Throughout his stay in the Tonbridge School he was friendless, and so felt absolutely lonely, depressed, and his "depression made him stupid and torpid" (Furbank, 43). Nobody had any amount of sympathy for him, excepting one of his masters named Isaac Smedley, whom Forster used as his model for 'Mr Jackson' in *The Longest Journey*. When Forster reached the sixth form at the Tonbridge School, Aunt Laura decided to send him to a college under the Cambridge University, and her choice fell on King's College. With that aim in view, Forster sat for the scholarship examination of King's College in 1896, and though he failed to qualify for the scholarship, he got a chance to enroll himself in that college. In the later part of his stay at Tonbridge School, Forster made a small coterie of friends, enjoyed 'a reputation as a talker,' received some academic success, and won two prizes: one for his Latin poem, and the other for his English essay on 'The influence of climate and physical conditions upon national character.' In November, 1897, he was "awarded an Exhibition of Pound 40 for two years, presumably on the strength of his performance in the "Previous examination" (Furbank, 47). The Tonbridge School was authoritarian, tradition-bound, and prized *esprit de corps*, and Forster's bitter life in that school prompted him to become anti-traditional, anti-authoritarian and anti-racial, and made him respectful of individualism, and these remained with him till the end of his life. "It was the absurdity of the rules at Tonbridge, the almost manic longing with which some of the masters wanted to impose them but were, unable to do so, that first aroused Morgan's anti-authorian instinct" (Beauman, 57). And one thing positive about Kent House and Tonbridge must be said: "both institutions managed to instil in Morgan [Forster] his passionate and lasting love of the classics" (Beauman, 58).

The story of Tonbridge is not yet complete, for Forster's homosexuality began in his Tonbridge days. In his works and letters, and in his conversations Forster very carefully avoided a name: Reginald Tiddy. He slyly avoided this name because his relation with his close friend Tiddy was carnal, and therefore socially unacceptable: Forater "offered him a passionate romantic friendship of the type later described in *Maurice*" (Beauman, 61). Tiddy is also perhaps the model of Tibby in *Howards End*, and partially the model of Fielding in *A*

Passage to India. Tiddy was intelligent, more than Forster, gentle, charming in his 'owl glasses,' and was, like Forster, a devoted student of the classics. It was also during the Tonbridge period that Forster made friendship with Edgar Nicholas, whom he called simply Nic. Lily and he were in constant touch with the Nicholases. It may be that it was under the inspiration of the Nicholas family that Forster first tried his hand at novel-writing with his ever first unfinished novel *Nottingham Llace,* while he was in his third year in King's College, Cambridge. In the Tonbridge School Forster made another friendship with Goldie Lowes Dickinson whose biography he later wrote. In the school he was always in a depressing and morose mood, and only for a few days could he escape his nagging morosity. When he was around sixteen, he and Lily went on a tour to France in April, 1895.

(4)

In 1897 Forster entered into King's College, Cambridge, and stayed there till 1901. He was then eighteen plus. Let us have a glimpse of this youth of this time through the eyes of Nicola Beauman: "[Forster] was in the quiet unassuming manner: he, too, would not have wanted to be noticed. He by now walked in a slightly hunched way, neither with a self-confident amble nor with a purposeful stride. His clothes never looked quite right on him and never would: not that he ever gave them a great deal of thought, so one cannot assume that he minded. He was awkward, gauche and clumsy, not so appallingly that it was humorous but almost irritatingly; his was the kind of hair that looked thin from his earliest years, and which always looked mousey and greasy; ... "And yet, and yet. There was something attractive about the awkward, pale, seemingly unprepossessing young man that Morgan [Forster] had become by the time he was eighteen and a half, in the summer of 1897" (Beauman, 66-67). This peculiarly attractive youth virtually 'fell in love with Cambridge [*i.e.* with King's College]' and the college, or the Cambridge University quite 'transformed him.' Here his morosity, his loneliness, all went off him, and he "went for bicycle rides, attended Chapel, and drank coffee and played mild card-games with friends" (Furbank, 50), and continued to contribute to the Tonbridge School magazine *The Tonbridgian*. The King's College of the Cambridge University 'was the ideal place for him.'

In King's College Forster took classic and read under the loving care and guidance of, among others, J.E. Nixon and Nathaniel Wedd, the latter being his most favourite teacher. "Wedd was a young man: small thick-set and ferrety, a warm-hearted, pugnacious, hypochondrical character, militantly egalitarian, and with a passion for bad language" (Furbank, 55). Wedd told Forster that 'he had been very badly taught at Tonbridge,' and this was mostly true. In King's College Forster took up his study very seriously. "His reading list for his second and third terms includes *Paradise Lost, A Doll's House.*, Howell's *The Rise of Silas Lapham, Omar Khayyam,* some Kipling, and a good deal of Robert Browning and Christina Rossetti" (*ibid).* Meanwhile Lily was searching for another house to live in and ultimately got one at Tonbridge Wells. The influence of Wedd continued to pour over Forster. We know that in his early novels Forster was much concerned with 'the perils of 'aesthetic' attitude, and this was due to the influence of Wedd. Forster by now came closer to Goldsworthy Lowes Dickinson whose biography, as we have already said, he later wrote. During that time Dickinson was an important figure in King's College, and he stood for liberal virtues, such as reason, decency, good-will etc., and he wrote some such books as *The Greek View of Life* (1896) and *A Modern Symposium* (1905). Dickinson was a great votary of the ancient Greeks's view of life and of Hellenism. All these of Dickinson attracted Forster towards him. Cambridge, or King's College, was diametrically opposite to Tonbridge. For one thing, whereas Tonbridge strived to instil in its students the spirit of pride and lordship and *esprit de corps,* Cambridge valued the most such things as 'the cult of friendship,' individualism, and an interest in human beings. At the least in two of Foister's novels we find the influence of Cambridge on him: in the character of Rickie in *The Longest Journey* and in the character of Maurice in *Maurice.* In the King's College

Forster "fairly soon shed his lingering religious faith and any vestiges of conservatism" (Beauman, 72).

In King's College Forster developed a more keen interest in the classical masters, particularly in Sophocles and Theocritus. The brevity and clarity of his (prose) style may be due to his absorbing interest in the classics. Forster's intellectual awakening, in the true sense of the term 'awakening,' also occurred while he was in King's College, and occurred, he confessed, due to "'the tutors and resident fellows [of King's College], who treated with rare dexterity the products that came up yearly from the public schools. They taught the perky boys that he was not everything, and received education, often for the first time in their lives'" (*op. cit.,* 78). For his learning of the classics, Forster was most indebted to the thirty-five-year-old classicist teacher Wedd. In later years Forster declared that it was "'to him [Wedd] more than to anyone—that I owe such awakening [in classical literature] as has befallen me,'" (*op. cit.,* 79). For his career of a writer, Forster confessed, when he was eighty, that he was indebted to Cambridge (to King's College) and to one of its dons, Wedd: "'it was Cambridge that first set me off writing. And in this very room where I am now there was at one time my tutor, a man called Wedd, and it was he who suggested to me that I might write. He did it in a very informal way. He said in a sort of drawling voice 'I don't see why you should not write,' and being very diffident was delighted at this remark and thought, after all why shouldn't I write? And I did. It is really owing to Wedd and to that start at Cambridge that I have written. I might have started for some other reason'" (*op. cit.*, 80).

While in the King's College, Forster became a member of the 'Conversazione Society' of which the great philosopher G.E. Moore was the most influential member. The members of the society were called, among themselves particularly, 'Apostles' or 'angels,' perhaps because they thought themselves to be like them. In fact, it was Forster's friend H.O. Meredith who introduced him to the 'Conversazione Society.' When Forster was in his second year, there grew a deep friendship between himself and H.O. Meredith who was 'an intellectual romantic, always with some new key to the universe' but always, all at the same time, there ran through him 'a vein of cynicism, a shrugging conviction that nothing in the world was much good.' Forster thought him to be the most intellectual among all his friends. He did never have a deep faith in religion and Christianity, but till he made friendship with Meredith, a shaft of belief was embedded in his mind, and Meredith took it to be his very first duty to take it out of Forster's mind, and he promptly did it. The vacant space in Forster's mind left after the shaft of belief was extricated by Meredith was filled up with the moral or ethical teachings of G.E. Moore, the philosopher, who had been a teacher of philosophy at Cambridge University, from 1911 to 1939.

Moore's influence on Forster was enormous. He was a hard-boiled realist and was pugnacious to idealism. His most important work is *Principia Ethica* in which he strives to propound that goodness is the only thing man should ever aspire after, and not religious rituals, for he was an agnostic, and money-making business. "In *Principia Ethica,* goodness is seen as a non-natural quality of certain things or situations, that is, one not given in sense experience, but nonetheless directly experienced, by a kind of moral intuition. Goodness is the fundamental ethical concept which cannot be defined or analysed in terms of anything simpler. Our other ethical concepts, right, duty, etc., can be defined in terms of producing and preserving so far as possible whatever possesses this quality of goodness, which Moore himself found most obviously exemplified in the experiences of friendship and aesthetic enjoyment" (Flew, 238). In Cambridge, liberalism prevailed, as in Tonbridge conservatism did; in Cambridge individualism was respected, as in Tonbridge *esprit de corps* was worshipped; in Cambridge there was an environment for making friendship, as in Tonbridge there was an environment favourable for inspiring the herd instinct; and lastly, in Cambridge the atmosphere inspired intellectual growth, whereas in Tonbridge every attempt was made to instil into the pupils the cult of lording over. Psychologically, we may say that as Forster detested Tonbridge, he also detested all, or most of all, that were entailed to it; and as he loved Cambridge, he imbued himself with all, or most of all, that were associated with that institution. In Cambridge thus Forster's mental structure began to take shape—the structure that remained with him till his end. So, Cambridge may be called the cradle of the novelist E.M. Forster. It was while in Cambridge, again, that Forsater came under the salubrious influence of Moore's philosophy that he eagerly accepted and that gave the complete shape to his already growing Cambridgean view of life and ideals. G.E. Moore's influence on Forster was so immense that throughout the rest of his life he continued to argue for it in all his works, and, withal, continued to live under the sunshine of it till his death. We may, perhaps, suspect that Mrs Moore in *A Passage to India* is an incarnation of G.E. Moore's philosophy.

In his *Principia Ethica,* Moore upheld truth, beauty, and personal relation as the three *summum bona,* as the highest objectives of man's life, and rejected 'the mechanical and the socially divisive.' "Moore's work allowed Morgan [Forster] and his contemporaries [particularly those who belonged to the 'Conversazione Society'] to reject Clapham Sect values without feeling outcast; it allowed them to question religion, the money-making ethic, conventional morals, without feeling impossibly alienated from the society into which they had been born. This is why Cambridge, and later 'Bloomsbury,' mattered so much to Morgan: it became his value system and in this way his family, his background" (Beauman, 84). William Plomer described Forster, while at Cambridge, thus: "'In appearance he was the reverse of a dandy. Incurious fellow passengers in a train, seeing him in a cheap cloth cap and a scruffy waterproof, and carrying the sort of little bag that might have been carried in 1890 by the man who came to wind the clocks, might have thought him a dim provincial of settled habits and taken no more notice of him'" (*op. cit.,* 86). This appearance of Forster may suggest that he was not an uppish fellow concerned, solely, about personal aggrandisement, but one who deeply meditated, philosophically though, on life and its values, and ultimately came to the conviction that Moorean philosophy was the best philosophy of life—that 'one's prime objects in life were love, the creation and enjoyment of aesthetic experience and the pursuit of knowledge,' and that everything else were paltry, rubbish. This is radical philosophy, the philosophy of Moore, and it influenced not only Forster but also a good number of others, including Maynard Keynes, the famous economist.

In 1901 Forster walked out of the King's College for ever, taking a second class in classics Tripos and another second class in History Tripos, but more than that, taking with him the spirit of the Cambridge University, or, to be precise, the spirit of the King's College. In the college Forster won a Latin verse prize, and an English essay prize on the subject 'The Novelists of the Eighteenth Century and their Influence on those of the Nineteenth.' It was again here that he began to write his ever first but unfinished novel *Nottingham Lace,* when he was twenty-one. He also wrote half a dozen short essay pieces for *Basileon.* But his greatest achievement from Cambridge was gaining his sense of authentic individuality. "The pull between the conformity of Tonbridge Wells [and the Tonbridge School] and the individuality encouraged at Cambridge was to be the key to Morgan's [Forster's] life" (*op. cit.,* 89). Besides his sense of individuality, from Cambridge he also got his notion of human values—love, knowledge, and aesthetic enjoyment—all radical in nature. With such radical ideals Forster began his first novel *Nottingham Lace,* but dropped it in the middle, for fear that his intellectual rebellion in that novel might land him in impending dangers. But that was for the present moment only; throughout his works, later on, he continued to uphold the same radical values.

(5)

Coming out of the Cambridge University with some academic qualification, Forster found himself rather bewildered, puzzled: what to do now? Now it was time for him to take up the toil of life, but which sort of toil? He was thinking about teaching profession, but that required a first class which he did not possess. Of course he could submit a dissertation in order to become a don, but he mysteriously avoided this alternative door to the donship. By now, some of his contemporaries entered the coveted Indian Civil Service, but Forster thought himself physically inferior to them, and so thought he would not be able to successfully come through the interview, and therefore dropped the plan of sitting for the I.C.S. examination. By this time, Forster quite lost his faith in Christianity, partly because he found 'the personality of Christ unsympathetic' and partly because Christianity wants us to keep quite away from the material world, and so he became an agnostic for ever. His father once lost faith in Christianity, but soon regained it, but Forster could never retrieve it. He now imbued himself with Erasmus's and Montaigne's humanist philosophies of life—the former being an agnostic and the latter a sceptic, and both being anti-religious. In *Two Cheers for Democracy,* Forster wrote about his position regarding religion: '"My law-givers are Erasmus and Montaigne, not Moses and St. Paul'" *(op. cit.,* 92). He further wrote in the same book: '"My motto is: "Lord, I disbelieve—help thou my unbelief"'" (*ibid.*). Forster's agnosticism was bolstered up and fortified by HOM (he was known by his initials) who was a very intelligent and very skilled in making friends, and who later held the Chair of Economics at Belfast from 1911 to 1945 The friendship between Forster and HOM reached such a depth that, as Forster himself afterwards admitted, it was on the verge of 'love affair' in the sexual sense of the term. It was around this time that Forster first became quite aware of his own homosexual inclinations.

A graduate now, Forster was thinking about a job, as Lily was thinking about a refreshing tour to Italy and Greece, and, all at the same time, both were expecting a job for Forster in Italy. Money was no problem for them, because they kept in safety Eddie's seven thousand pounds and another eight thousand pounds of Marianne that they left for them at their deaths. On 3 October 1901, they crossed the Channel to France and then went to Italy. Forster had taken with him the growing manuscript of *Nottingham Lace,* and whenever he could find opportunities, he would sit down to write. In Italy, they visited Florence and Milan, among other places. Forster went to see the 'real' Italy, like Adela Quested in *A Passage to India* went to India to see the 'real India.' While in Florence, Forster 'first sprained his ankle and a few days later, perhaps as a result of his tottery steps, slipped on the steps of St. Peter's and broke his right, his writing, arm.' From Florence, they went to Cicily and then to Naples where, in the spring of 1902, Forster 'wrote, for the first time, a complete short story.' He liked Naples very much, and it was here that he found the 'real' Italy. He was delighted to see the Greek temples at Girgenti, and Taormina seemed to him to be 'the third most beautiful place in the world.' From Italy, they went to Ravello in Greece, where they stayed at Hotel-Pension Palumbo.

In September, 1902, Lily and Forster went to Germany and spent some time in Munich, Nuremberg, Heidelberg and Cologne, and then came back to Greece. In Greece, Forster came to understand that the "Greeks admired not only nudes but all the varieties of sexual pleasure that could be given and received by these nudes" (*op. cit.,* 143). His awareness of sex was bolstered up by his perceptions of the nudes, and now he could realise more clearly the fact that human consciousness is to a great extent informed by human sexuality—the fact which Sigmund Freud was then industriously working on, in Austria, to demonstrate. His Italian experiences were more stimulating than his Greek experiences, as regards his sexual awareness winch found outlets to show itself in his novels, later on: "It was Italy that began the slow process of his understanding of his sexual nature and it was his novels that completed it; without Italy, and without southern Italy in particular, he would have taken far longer to know himself and he would have been far less precocious a writer" (*op. cit.,* 115). In Italy, Forster found a place where there was the orgy of sex, the Dionysiac demonstration of sexual lust, and "Italy had been renowned, since the Renaissance, as the country where sexual pleasure was not confined to the conventional" (*op. cit.,* 114). The origin of his aversion to heterosexuality, and, contrarily, the origin of his homosexuality, may partially be found in his Italian experiences. It is not a fact that he never felt sexual drive, for he himself said that "lust was always lurking inside my head" and that "sexual images continued to spin around my brain like figures on a carousel" *(op. cit.,* 115). But in Italy he saw only lust, only the game of sex in which love was anathema, or at least love or friendship was unnecessary. This was an horrific experience of his, which subverted his heterosexuality, and led him towards homosexuality. And his month-long tour over Greece in 1903 reinforced his conviction of the importance of sex—the conviction that was generated in him while at Cambridge—and sharpened his intellectual awareness and added to his growing sense of happiness since leaving Tonbridge.

Perhaps due to his new knowledge of sex and to his sexual metamorphosis, while in Italy, Forster promptly, even while in that country, for ever abandoned his unfinished manuscript of the novel *Nottingham Lace* or *They are Nottingham Lace.* Explaining the reason of his jettisoning the on-hand project of the novel, Forster wrote to Dickinson: "'I've tried to invent realism, if you see what I mean'.... 'Instead of copying incidents & characters that I have come across, I have tried to imagine others equally commonplace, being under the impression that this was art, and by mixing the two methods have produced nothing'" (Furbank, 1, 91). He declared that since now, while writing fictitions, he would solely depend upon "'imagination pure and simple'" (*ibid.*), and soon decided to write a novel on some Italian theme, and in course of time the Italian theme grew into his 'Lucy' novel *A Room with a View.*

The tour to Italy and Greece over, Lily and Forster came back to England. In Italy, Forster could not find a job for himself; nevertheless the tour was not unprofitable for him because "Italy had warmed Forster and given him a vision, and ever afterwards he would think of it gratefully as 'The beautiful country where they say 'yes', and the place 'where things happen'" (*op. cit.,* 1, 96). During his nine months' tour over Italy and Greece, Forster grew in himself a great love of landscapes, that is noticeable in most of his novels. The beautiful scenarios of Naples and other places of Italy left an indelible impression on his mind and informed his aesthetic judgement about natural environments, particularly about landscapes, and grew in him the psychological conviction that landscapes have a part to play in the development of human characters. He began to believe, for instance, that the particular landscapes of Italy are to some extent responsible for the identity of the general Italian character, as the particular landscapes of England are to an extent responsible for the identity of the general English character. So, Forster was not really so much interested in the aesthetics of the form, content and colour of landscapes, as he was in the psychological effect of landscapes on human behaviour: "The effect of landscape on character was what was to matter to Morgan [Forster], not the abstract aesthetics of it: form, content, colour, geography of a place would always be less important to him than the feelings of those who lived in it" (Beauman, 125).

(6)

A job now became a necessity to Forster, who was now looking to his future. He dreamed of a job in the University of Cambridge, 'perhaps some unpaid post in the University Library,' but the dream did not come to be true. So, he was doing 'some university extension lecturing' and was taking weekly classes in Latin at the Working Men's College in Bloomsbury. Forster, during this time, came even closer to H.O.M. (H.O. Meredith), his all the best friend, and their relation now became noticeably homosexual; "they became closer than before—indeed, in some sense or other, they became lovers. It seems to have been an affair very much on the lines of that of Maurice and Clive in *Maurice*—that is to say, it was not a physical relationship, or at least went no further than kisses and embraces" (Furbank, 1, 98). But who of the two was the initiator of the relationship is not clear; perhaps it was Forster, for H.O.M. "had already had affairs with girls.' Howbeit, "it was Forster for whom the affair counted most. For him it was immense and epoch-making; it was, he felt, as if all the 'greatness' of the world had been opened up to him. He counted this as the second grand 'discovery' of his youth—his emancipation from Christianity being the first" (*ibid.*).

Forster now planned to write a 'novel or play' 'with three scenes or sections' in three locations: 'Rome, The Summit of Etna and Egypt.' And this project of his novel is now generally known as 'Old Lucy,' which he later abandoned in favour of the new novel which may be called the 'New Lucy' but which is now the novel with the title *A Room with a View*. But Forster was working on the 'Old Lucy' during the period in which he was giving extension lectures in the Working Men's College, along with taking weekly classes on Latin. A don of King's College, Reddaway by name, wrote about Forster as a lecturer: "'As teacher and examiner I saw a great deal of his work during the year which he devoted to History. His powers as a writer and thinker are considerable, and there is even a touch of real and rare distinction in some of his literary work—Forster is liked by all who know him and would never bring discredit of any kind upon the Extension [lecture] movement'" (Beauman, 130). It was also during this time that Forster came in touch with the Bloomsbury Group which comprised such celebrities as Leonard Woolf, Virginia Woolf, Maynard Keynes (the economist), Clive Bell, Lytton Strachey and G.E. Moore (the philosopher), the last being the most influential in the Group, so much so that he might be called the mentor of it. The other prominent members of the Group were Vanessa Bell, Desmond MacCarthy, David Garnett, Lady Ottoline Morrell and others. Though their association is known as a Group, "its members denied being a group in any formal sense, they were united in an abiding belief in the importance of the arts. Their philosophy can perhaps best be summerized in Moore's statement that 'one's prime objects in life were love, the creation and enjoyment of aesthetic experience and the pursuit of knowledge.' They were sceptical and tolerant, reacting against the artistic and social restraints of Victorian society" (Ousby, 96). The Bloomsbury Group was as a whole much influenced by G.E. Moore's *Principia Ethica*, and it is believed to have exerted a great influence on the *avant-garde* literature of the early 20th century. The Group was founded around 1905 and continued to exist till 1932, the year in which Lytton Strachey died, or till 1941, the year in which Virginia Woolf committed suicide. Forster's association with the Bloomsbury Group may have prompted the *avant-garde* quality of his novels, but it is certain that G.E. Moore's moral philosophy considerably influenced his vision of life. Moore argued for 'direct moral awareness,' and 'claimed that the contemplation of beauty and affectionate personal relations are the only supremely good states of mind.'

As the British Musium was in Bloomsbury, the venue of the Bloomsbury Group, not far from where he resided, Forster was a 'frequent visitor' to the Musium, perhaps to sit and write there the new novel, 'The New Lucy Novel.' He abandoned the 'Old Lucy Novel' in 1903 and began to work on 'The New Lucy Novel,' of course at a certain stage of his writing 'The New Lucy Novel' he finished one or two short stories as well. It may be kept in mind that after going through some length of the projected novel, 'The New Lucy Novel', Forster abandoned this novel also and started another novel on the almost same theme that was there in the old and the new 'Lucy' novels afresh, utilising some matters of the rejected 'The New Lucy Novel,' and this last projected novel he happened to finish and got published in 1908, as his third published novel, under the title *A Room with a View*. This means that *A Room with a View* may be supposed to have been written thrice between around 1903 and 1907. During this period, Forster's suppressed or repressed sexual drive began to surface: "Between 1904, when Morgan [Forster] wrote 'New Lucy,' and 1907, when he rewrote it a third time, his sexual awareness, previously suppressed, angry and bewildered, was changing into a far more mature understanding" (Beauman, 146). And this is the reason why '*A Room with a View* is... imbued with sexual imagery.'

By now three years elapsed since Forster came out of the Cambridge University, his carefree, idyllic, and sedentary, and also gossippy days now being only a memory. Nicola Beauman writes about the twenty-five-years-old Forster of this time: "He seemed not to care about his clothes, about his public persona, about living with his mother or being jobless and identity-less; inside he cared a great deal" (Beauman, 147).

And, nevertheless, he produced at least three beautiful short stories: 'A Day Off,' 'The Road From Colonus' and 'The Story of a Panic.' Lily and Forster were then living in Weybridge, and it was this place where Forster's life as a novelist began around the year 1902. In the autumn of 1904, Forster joined the newly founded Literary Society, and was looking forward to his future works, while Lily, who had so long feeling herself to be an *outre* in the previous places of residence, found herself sociable and comfortable in Weybridge.

(7)

In the late autumn of 1904, Forster completed his first novel *Where Angels Fear to Tread* when he and Lily were staying at Weybridge, in the house named 'Harnham.' Not only this novel but all Forster's six great novels were completed in the same house. So, this house is inseparable from Forster's life—from the happy portion of his life. Here in this house he entertained his friends—Dent, George Barger, Bob Travelyan, Meredith (H.O.M.) and others—but what he enjoyed the most was his 'inner life,' calm and happy. He wrote in his diary, during this period, about the inner workings of his mind or consciousness: '"self consciousness will do for me if I'm not careful—drive me into books, or the piano'" (*op. cit.*, 162). Music Forster enjoyed, and he and Lily often played on the piano. Forster's love of music may have been the reason why his novels are musical, as Benjamin Britten once opined about him: 'our most musical novelist.' Forster 'spent many hours playing [on the piano] peacefully in the drawing-room at 'Harnham,' and he 'went to concerts whenever he could.' Therefore, 'Harnham' perhaps provided him with his most favourable environment for writing novels, for which Nicola Beauman writes: "how appropriate that although he had made beginnings in other houses, other rooms, the house where he was to write all his six works of fiction was the one ['Harnham'] where he completed his first" (*ibid.*).

In 1905, Forster almost suddenly decided to go to Nassenheide in northern Germany (the village of Nassenheide is now in Poland and is called Rzedziny) to be the tutor to the three young daughters of Elizabeth von Arnim. This was the first time that Forster went abroad and stayed there for some time without Lily. The arrangement for Forster's tutorship there was made by his Cambridge friend Sydney Waterlow. Forster went there also with a view to learn German, and put up with Elizabeth's family, and began to teach the three daughters of Elizabeth: Evi, Liebet and Beatrix (Trix)—the first fourteen, the second twelve, and the third eleven. Elizabeth was an author of sentimental novels, but became famous for her *Elizabeth and her German Garden* (1898) which contains prescriptions for good gardening. She had an interesting personal history. She 'was the daughter of a self-made businessman who had made his fortune in Australia, and at the age of twenty-two she had married the Count von Arnim, a widowed Prussian landowner.' The marriage was happy at first, but soon it got overcast with mutual disinclination and dissatisfaction. She liked to make sudden dashes to England whenever she felt homesick, and he objected to this. More serious, he was set upon having a son, whereas further child-bearing did not appeal to her at all.'

Not long afterwards, a sense of urgent affection for Forster inchingly began to grow in Elizabeth, and once she proposed to him to write 'something in collaboration.' Forster "was aghast and was greatly relieved when he managed to wriggle out of it" (Furbank, 1,130). But there was no crack in their relationship: "Henceforth the two got on swimmingly. They played tennis together, and his peculiar action made her laugh so much that he sometimes won. He read *Emma* aloud to her, and *she* lent him *Erewhon" (ibid)*. Elizabeth was a cousin of Katherine Mansfield, and she wrote more than twenty novels, 'all bearing the same title "Elizabeth".' It was not unnatural, she being an intellectual, that she would like Forster. Afterwards, however, she married Bertrand Russell's brother Francis. Forster was a quite happy soul at Nassenheide. In July, 1905, the proofs of *Where Angels Fear to Tread* arrived at Nassenheide, and Elizabeth read, and expressed her mixed comments upon, the novel. Really, Forster liked the lady, though not aggressively; he wrote to Lily, afterwards, about her: "what a delightful character 'Elizabeth' was" (*ibid*). Forster did not stay at Nassenheide for long: he arrived there in March, 1905, and left the place in the July of the same year: "It had been agreed that his stay at Nassenheide should finish at the end of July, and he made plans to tour Rugen and various towns along the Baltic, on his way home. He left Nassenheide in glory. 'Elizabeth' told him he had been a most successful tutor; Steinweg gave him a copy of Goethe's *Faust* and as they saw him off on the train, the children produced gifts, all stuck over with flowers and ribbons. Evi's and Liebet's were poems and Trix, who hadn't been able to think of one, gave him gooseberries instead" (*op. cit.,* I, 134).

Forster did not, as told earlier, come back to England from Germany straight away, but made a detour through the Baltic coast, enjoying the 'genuine beauty blended with bourgeois values.' In North Germany (away from Nassenheide in what is now part of Poland) he 'bathed, sunbathed and continued to enjoy the sense of well-being that had been his at Nassenheide. 'His gladness was all the more because by then his short story 'The Eternal Moment' had appeared in the *Independent* and he was expecting to receive advance copies of *Where Angels Fear to Tread* any moment.

(8)

The detour through the Baltic coast over, Forster came back to England in 1907. 'Snow' Wedgwood or, rather, Julia ('Snow') Wedgwood was as though jumping in joy after she had gone through Forster's *Where Angels Fear to Tread* and invited the author for tea. 'Snow' Wedgwood, then in her seventies, was a family friend of the Forsters. She "was a daughter of Aunt Monie's great friend Fanny Mackintosh and of Hensleigh Wedgwood, a brother-in-law of Charles Darwin. Following in the steps of her grandfather, the celebrated Sir James Mackintosh, she had become a writer on ethics and philosophy, contributing heavyweight articles to the *Spectator* and the *Contemporary Review*. These had brought her into contact with Robert Browning, and for a year or two after his wife's death they had kept up a brisk exchange on philosophical topics: 'very high talk it would have been,' said Forster. "Then, for some unexplained reason, she broke off the friendship" (*op. cit.,* 1, 115). 'Snow Wedgwood told Forster that what was wrong with *Where Angels Fear to Trade* 'was that he hadn't made up his mind whether it was to be tragedy or comedy' and that 'he should have been more explicit about Gino's infidelities.' 'Snow' Wedgwood was also perhaps not quite satisfied with Forster's handling of love in the novel, and so "She begged him to fall in love before writing another novel, upon which he confided to her that he *was* in love—with Hamlet!" (*op. cit.,* 1, 136).

Recently Forster showed a brief fad for psychical researches under Victor Woolley, a fellow of the King's College and a demonstrator in physiology in the University of Cambridge. Woolley was a 'magnificent' friend of Forster in Venice. He was "a tall, moustached man with a rather dry manner, 'contentious in a pleasant way.' He collected books on sexology and psychical research and was thought of by his friends as a kind of wizard analyst" (*op. cit.,* 1, 168). Under the direction and instruction of Woolley, Forster "had tried putting himself into a trance, by repeating a name. He had had no success, and this suggested to him that he was growing more 'material'—'the beautiful veil has become thicker.' He was not very sorry" (*op. cit.,* 1, 137). Before all this, while he was out of England, touring along the Baltic coast, Forster "greeted the year 1906 with a poem, presumably one of his own.

We were not good enough for Heaven
Nor bad enough for Hell:
And therefore unto us was given
Unseen on earth to dwell:

To listen by the moonlit thatch,
By window-blinds to lurk,
To watch men on their knees and watch
Men go about their work.

We watch in hope to be forgiven:
But still we cannot tell
Whose deeds are good enough for Heaven,
Whose bad enough for Hell.

It is not a very good poem, but it is significant for what it says about the novelist's [Forster's] ghostly and *voyeuriste* role in life" (*ibid*). This poem (if it is his) and previously quoted one may assure us that Forster was not that ignorant about verse-building.

By the end of 1907, Forster was the author of two acclaimed novels: *Where Angels Fear to Tread* (1905) and *The Longest Journey* (1907). But before that, in the immediately preceeding year, he had a great encounter with a person, who was like H.O. Meredith, and with whom he had another long homosexual relationship, an impression of which may be found in the relationship between Fielding and Aziz in *A Passage to India*. The person is the seventeen year old youth named Syed Ross Masood. Forster was then around twenty-seven, ten years older than he. How Masood came to meet Forster, or the other way round, needs elaboration. In Weybridge, Lily found a friend in Mrs Morison, the wife of a distinguished Anglo-Indian officer and a member of the India Council that acted as an advisory body to the Secretary of State for India. Before returning to England from India, he was for some time a professor at the Muslim Anglo-Oriental College at Aligarh, and then became the Principal of the same college. The college was founded by Sir Syed Ahmed Khan, then the most prominent leader of the Indian Muslim community, in 1875, with British assistance. Theodore Morison (husband of Mrs Morison) was a close friend of Sir Syed Ahmed Khan, and "as a result of trouble in Syed's family, he had taken Sir Syed's grandson, Syed Ross Masood, into his own household [in England] and adopted him as his ward. He always referred to Masood as 'my son,' and the boy had come to feel closer to him than to his real father" (*op. cit.*, 1, 143). Nicola Beauman has described Masood thus: "In physical appearance Masood must have been like Antinous, tall, handsome, vigorous and with the most beautiful brown, melting eyes. He liked money, practical jokes and extravagant emotions, and had the vast self-confidence" (Beauman, 183). Masood was "'a little ultra-Mahommedan in some of his views and in his contempt of the mild Hindu'" (*op. cit.*, 184).

He had a 'sonorous and beautiful voice' and was 'full of nostalgia for the splendours of the Mughal past.' In short, Aziz of *A Passage to India* may well be taken to be a replica of Masood. Masood came to Weybridge in order to prepare for entrance to Oxford University.

Intimacy, and then friendship, soon grew between Forster and Masood, inspite of a wide gap between their ages, and in fact "Masood's arrival in his life was a major event for Forster" (Furbank, 143). The intimacy between the two, before long, turned into homosexual relationship. Forster, during this time was ashamed of his 'minorite tendencies,' but he failed to overcome it any way, and ao, while homosexually playing with Masood asked him to be 'dominant.' Masood was at first perplexed at such an extremely unnatural arrangement, particularly because of his traditional Indian conception of sex, but in the end, Forster's persuasions prevailed. Ofcourse it must be said that Masood's homosexual relation with Forster remained only on the psychological plane and did never descend to the physical. And, nevertheless, Masood was an energizing force, an *elan* of sorts, a *nisus* in Forster's life. "Masood, Forster was to say later, woke him up out of his suburban and academic life and showed him new horizons and a new civilization. The princely manner and good looks, the vividness and demonstrativeness, charmed and excited him; and gradually,..., he fell in love with Masood. It was his first affair of the heart since Meredith, and though it too was never fulfilled physically, it liberated him in other ways. It released him, or so he thought, from that negativity and defeatism with which Meredith had managed to infect all his friends" (*op. cit.,* 1, 146). Forster, when he was continuing to remain in the emotional closeness of Masood, was steadily working on *The Longest Journey* and planning for his third and even fourth novel. In 1906, he gave a series of lectures on Italian art and history for the Cambridge Local Lectures Board.

It is not a fact that as Forster was largely drawn to homosexuality, he did never meditate upon (heterosexual) marriage. But his experiences of marriage was not encouraging. For one reason, 'Lily had scarcely hinted at a blissful state of affairs with Eddie.' Secondly, he had a shattering experience of the married life of Mr and Mrs Poston at Highfleld near Rooksnest. Forster came across this experience thus. In August, 1907, after the publication of *The Longest Journey,* he went to Local Lectures Summer School to give a lecture on the novelist Samuel Richardson. On that occasion he took an opportunity to visit Rooksnest, and there at Rooksnest he grew a curiosity to visit the Poston family at Highfield, which was about a mile from Rooksnest. It was only this Poston family and the Jowitt family with whom Lily made rather close acquintance. On his visit to the Poston family, Forster found that Mr Poston remarried, but, he (Forster) most keenly and pitifully noticed that the replacement of Mr Poston's first wife by his second did not render even a slight change in the mode of functioning of the family. This experience of his "must have made Morgan [Forster] ponder the state of being a second wife, especially one who continued life in the same house as her predecessor, almost as if it was the house that was the stability and the harmony not a particular wife" (Beauman, 186). For these two, and for other undivulged reasons, if there were really such reasons, Forster began to doubt the authenticity of (heterosexual) marriage: "most marriages he knew about seemed to offer far less chance of happiness than was given to the unmarried dons at King's or to the young men he knew who lived in rooms in London" (*op. cit.,* 187). Forster concluded that (heterosexual) marriage was seeming happiness only sustained and guarded by tradition, and he dwelt on this theme in *Howards End.*

Howards End was published on 18 October, 1910, and Forster, with the publication of this novel and with his two earlier novels, almost overnight became a celebrity: 'friends flattered him, newspapers interviewed him, and letters and invitations poured in.' But Forster did never want popularity; he was always uneasy with it. Nevertheless, his popularity doubled, or rather redoubled, and he wrote to Dickinson on 21 November, 1910; '"I don't like popularity. It seems mad'" (Furbank I, 190-91). Almost all acclaimed *Howards End,* and yet there were a few who did not like it and Edmund Gosse was one of them. Gosse found at least three faults in the novel: an emphasis on the story, coarseness of the morals, and coruscation of the style. He said that the novel "' is sensational and dirty and affected'" (*op. cit.*, 1, 189). Forster's mother, Lily, also would not like the novel so much; she objected to Helen's pregnancy in *Howards End,* may be due to Helen's moral violation.

In spite of the joy of the success of *Howards End,* the year 1910 was not bright and inspiring to Forster. For one thing, in this year Lily's mother Louisa died. Secondly, now being around thirtyone, he was going through his 'mid-life crisis.' Thirdly, he expected that Lily would feel proud of the success of *Howards End,* but contrarily, she reacted with disgust to Helen's pregnancy in the novel. And lastly, he was plunged into depression by the decease of Ernest Merz on 8th July, 1909. On the previous day Forster dined with Merz, and in the night of that day the two friends ate their dinners, but the next morning forster found him dead, having hanged himself in his room in Albany. Merz was a contemporary of Forster in the King's College, and it was the memory of him upon which Forster invented the story and theme of *Maurice.* The foregoing factors may be the proximate and acute causes of Forster's depression in the year 1910, but the distant and chronic cause of the depression, according to the psychiatrist Anthony Storr, was the very early death of his father, that created a constant and inalienable void in his mind, which even Lily's anxious affection and ceaseless association could not eradicate. In his distress and despair, Forster had two comforts: Masood and Hugh Meredith—the first was his 'greatest comfort,' and the second "made love to him, kissing and embracing him passionately on the sitting-room at 'Harnham'" (*op. cit.*, 1,183). In the next year (1911) also Forster's depression did not leave him, and yet in that year he published six short stories under the umbrella title *Celestial Omnibus,* the six short stories being 'The Story of a Panic,' 'The Other Side of the Hedge,' 'The Celestial Omnibus,' 'The Other Kingdom,' 'The Curate's Friend,' and 'The Road from Colonus.'

(9)

During the years 1910 and 1911, Forster's depression and his feeling of isolation worked both negatively and positively: the negative effect of the two was his unhappiness, and the positive effect was his escape into fictional creations. Besides writing some superb short stories during this period, Forster began another novel—*Arctic Summer.* In it he wanted to "portray a young man who, he imagined, was what he himself might have become if he had married" (Beauman, 247). Forster wrote about 50,000 words for the novel, but then suddenly dropped the idea of finishing it, like his earlier novel *Nottingham Lace,* but while the manuscript of his earlier novel he destroyed, he could not be as cruel in the case of *Arctic Summer.* About cause of the fragmentary nature of *Arctic Summer,* which was never published, Forster later wrote: "I had got my antithesis all right, the antithesis between the civilized man, who hopes for an Arctic Summer, and the heroic man who rides into the sea. But I had not settled what was going to happen, and that is why the novel remains a fragment. The novelist should I think always settle when he starts what is going to happen, what his major event is to be" (*op. cit.,* 248-49). The other reason of abandoning *Arctic Summer* in the middle was that, Forster thought, it was rather going to be a repetition of his Italian novels.

Since sometime after his friendship with Forster, Masood had been urging upon him to turn to India his fictional gaze and write something about her, preferably a novel, but Forster always remained indifferent. Masood also tried to persuade him to visit India, but Forster produced reasons for remaining unmoved. In 1912, the joint pressure of Masood, Gaunt and Darling finally succeeded in diverting Forster's imagination towards India. Forster's interest in India was sharpened by his reading of another homosexual writer Edward Carpenter's essays on India. Carpenter abandoned the academic life of Cambridge, became an absolute free-thinker, formed a personal philosophy of life out of an assortment of Whitmanism, Tolstoyian ideals, Hindu mysticism, neo-paganism, Samuel Butler's theory of instinct, and homosexualism. Perhaps those essays of Carpenter attracted Forster the most because of the influence of all these on him, and consequently he readied his mind to prepare for a visit to India. Forster's interest was not in the geography and demography of India but, as he heard and read of, in the unsettled and shifting web of social relationships among the all too numerous stratifications of the Indian populace, and in the not-so-well-defined master-slave relationship between the Anglo-Indian or British rulers and the Indians or the natives who were ruled. In this regard, he may have been influenced particularly by C.F.G. Masterman. Masterman was a 'radical Liberal and East London MP' and he contributed a number of powerful articles in the *Independent* since 1904 expressing his deep concern about the disquiet caused by the rapid industrialisation of England. He had a 'social conscience' no less strong than that of Ruskin, and he deeply imbued Forster's consciousness with 'social conscience,' and he also inspired Forster "to write a novel that was not merely amusing, or perceptive, or critical of suburban values, or a plea for individual freedom: he made him want to write about English society at that moment" (*op. cit.*, 219). This inspiration of Masterman perhaps went into the making of *Howards End;* but the inspiration was not exhausted thereby—it spilled over into the writing of *A Passage to India* and, before that, it fired Forster's interest in the social panorama of India. Of course well before that he was pondering over writing a novel on some Indian theme.

In 1912 Forster was, along with Dickinson and R.C. Trevelyan, on board an India-bound ship which came all the way from England to India. After the long journey of twelve days they landed on the western-most part of India, and checked into the hotel called Pyrke's Apollo. Forster was not impressed by Bombay, but was certainly impressed by the Indian railway carriage, about which he wrote in the short-lived London magazine *Golden Hynde:* "'When the European enters his first railway carriage, he feels himself in a moving palace, so many are the luxuries that surround him. There are sofa beds, racks, hooks, washing apparatus, electric lights, a white lincrusta ceiling from which electric fans depend, and there are windows of which no Westerners has ever dreamed—shutters to keep out the glare, wire screens to keep out the flies, blue-grey glass to keep out everything. Meals are served on the train, or else the train stops while they can be eaten, gay little timetables and maps of India hang framed in the embossed wallpaper. Housed in such comfort, might one not travel for ever?'" (*op. cit.,* 257-58). Later on the vision of the train was, to Forster, a symbol of India. However, Masood received him at Aligarh station—Masood who was actually instrumental in alluring Forster to India, this time. Now they were friends for six years, since their days in Weybridge. The two friends for a week spent their time in the Anglo-Oriental College at Aligarh. Twenty years ago Edward Carpenter visited Aligarh and wrote about the place: '"the only place in India which I have visited where I have noticed anything like a cordial feeling existing between the two sections [the native Indians and the Britishers]'" (*op. cit.,* 258). But twenty years after, when Forster came to India, the situation drastically changed. Forster noted: '"The English staff complained that they were not trusted to give the help they had hoped to give, but would be turned adrift as soon as the Mahommedans could stand without them'" (*op. cit.,* 258-59). This distrust and stand-off between the two communities is to be found in Forster's Indian novel *A Passage to India.*

On 30 October, 1912, Masood and Forster went to Delhi, the new capital of India (upto 1911 it was in Calcutta), along with a doctor friend of Masood. Like Bombay, Delhi also failed to engage Forster's tourist attention, except that he to some extent enjoyed the country-side around the capital. In Delhi, he could suppress somewhat his homosexual drive, momentarily though, and opened his eyes to the attractions of the fair sex: on the last day of his visit to Delhi, for instance, he was beguiled by the songs and dances of nautch-girls, one of whom so much attracted the amorous notice of Forster that he confessed that he was 'never tired of looking at her.' From Delhi, he went to Lahore; but like Bombay and Delhi, Lahore also could not provide him with pleasure. Nevertheless, Forster could collect a plethora of photographic impressions of the divers walks of the Indian life, of the Indian mores, manners, sentiments, passions, beliefs, prejudices, taboos, personal and social relations, and particularly of the relation between the natives and the Britishers, during his first Indian visit, as is evident from his *The Hill of Devi* and *A Passage to India.* On top of all these, Forster had the rare opportunity, perhaps with the aid of Masood and through him of others, to peep into the private lives of the Indians. In Delhi also he gathered the experiences of Indian privacy, and he enjoyed it. He knew that "he was one of the few who had the rare privilege 'of dropping straight into native life"' (*op. cit.,* 260).

Forster visited India at a time (1912-13) when three-fifths of the country were being directly governed or ruled by the British, and the rest two-fifths were being ruled by around 500 Maharajas, with the assistance of British Residents, one for each state of a Maharaja, called a princely state. The princely states were pitifully suffering from despondency, particularly due to the utter inefficiency and 'lotos-eater' like life-style, combined with exuberant luxuriousness, of the Maharajas. Nicola Beauman writes about the perception of the Anglo-Indians of the Indian princely states: "Seventy-five years earlier the historian Macaulay had described Moghul India as a place where 'a succession of nominal sovereigns, sunk in indolence and debauchery, sauntered away life in secluded places chewing bang, fondling concubines and listening to buffoons.' This, alas, was still Anglo-India's attitude to much of princely India when Morgan [Forster] was there" (*op. cit.,* 261 f.n.). Regarding the three-fifths of India governed by the Britishers, three years before Forster's visit, some changes were introduced in the matter of governance. In 1909 the Morley-Minto reforms were introduced to curb the autocracy of the British Raj, and yet Forster was dissatisfied with the British style of governance and with the attitude of the British towards the natives. To him "the English position was untenable" (*op. cit.,* 261) In the British rulers he found, to his utter amazement and disgust, the echoes of the Tonbridge values: aristocracy, autocracy, tradition, and conformity. Reflection of all these is conspicuous in *A Passage to India.* In Lahore, Forster met a missionary named George Turner about whom he wrote: "'the only Englishman I have met [in India] who seems to care for the people'" *(op. cit.,* 265). Forster may have used Turner as the model of Mr Sorley, the missionary in *A Passage to India.* However, from Lahore, Forster went to Simla and there attended a Muslim wedding ceremony with Masood. P.N. Furbank writes about Forster's memory of that unforgetable wedding ceremony: "It was a curious scene: the bride, who was not veiled, sat with the bridegroom on a sofa on a dias, with the officiating *Moulvi* in an armchair beside them. The audience was restive, murmuring, 'This is totally contrary to Islamic law,' and a quarrel broke out between the *Moulvi* and the bridegroom's brother, who finally announced, in English, that the ceremony would begin with a verse from the Koran. After this a local poet recited verses in Urdu in praise of 'Conscience'—Conscience being a garden where the Bulbul of eloquence ever sang and the dew of oratory dropped continually. Having joined the couple, the *Moulvi* gave an address, saying that it was not important how one was married but how one behaved after marriage" (Furbank, 1, 233).

From Simla, Forster went back to Agra where Dickinson and Trevelyan were waiting for him, enjoying the beauty of the Taj Mahal, and after he met them there, they—the three friends—set out for Gwalior (in Madhya Pradesh), the fortress-city on rock. The Finance Minister of the State of Gwalior provided them with guidance and light treats with benignity and humiliation, and this impressed Forster so much that he wrote to Lily "'how wonderful is the oriental mind'" (*op. cit.,* 1, 234). From Gwalior, they soon went to Chhatarpur (Chhatrapur) where their royal host the Maharaja 'Vishnwarath' [Vishwanath] Singh Bahadur (1866-1932) had been beating time for them. This was the Maharaja who had appeared in J.R. Ackerley's *Hindoo Holiday.* P.N. Furbank has beautifully and interestingly described the person, the accoutrement, the deportment, and the intellectual inclinations of the Maharaja: "One should picture [the Maharaja] a little hobbling figure, dazzlingly dressed in a magenta frock coat, diamond earrings and velvet toque like Queen Mary's. He was excessively ugly, with a face like a Pekinese's, his nose being completely bridgeless and his tongue a nasturtium-colour from habitual betel-chewing. The passions of his life were philosophy, friendship and beautiful boys. As a young man, under Theodore Morison's tutelage, he had studied Plato and Herbert Spencer, and ever since had been wont to ask himself 'What is God?' 'Is there any Absolute?' and similar questions. He hoped to receive the answer from the West, and was perpetually angling for some Englishman to come and live with him and be his *guru*. Since he could not quite explain matters thus to the British authorities, he would say he was looking for a private secretary, or later on—as in the case of Ackerley—for a tutor for his son. But the truth was, or so Ackerley thought, he simply wanted someone to love him. (Once they were sitting together, watching the sun set in a blaze of pink and gold, and the Maharaja waved his hand towards it sadly, saying 'I want a friend like that.' While the perfect friend delayed, he occupied himself with his private theatre, for which he composed miracle plays. This entailed the recruiting of boy-actors, a great interest and a great trial to him" (*op. cit.,* 1, 234-35). This Maharaja warmly welcomed the English guests, including Forster, the Maharaja who is the model of Professor Godbole of *A Passage to India* (Beauman, 267, f.n.). However, Chhatrapur was enchanting to Forster; he wrote about the place "'The only idyllic place I have seen yet'" (Beauman, 267). Forster wrote about the Maharaja that he was a "'tiny and fantastic figure, incompetent, *ruse,* exasperating, endearing'" and that he was '"so sensible and shrewed, and so full of fun, that listening and talking to him are both delightful'" (*ibid*). The mind of the Maharaja harboured a blend of Western rationalism and Hindu mysticism—the blend that we find in the mind of Professor Godbole of *A Passage to India.*

While at Chhatrapur, Forster could understand India better. He understood the mutual hatred of the Hindus and the Mohammedans better from what the Private Secretary of the Maharaja told him one day on the top of his voice about the quarrel between the two communities. He said the wrangling 'might be laid if the one would give up Hindi; the other Cow

Killing.' Forster understood that in India religion was the most dominant factor in the social sphere, but what the Indians in fact did mean by religion he could not fully realise. One day, he went to see the temples at Khajuraho, 'in remote countryside twenty miles east of Chhatarpur,' but could gain from there only bewildering and nauseating impressions. The carved human and divine figurines on the walls of Khajuraho appeared to him to be "heavily heterosexual, the main impression being of bosoms, pouts and curving thighs with rather fewer penises and muscle." Forster later wrote about the Khajuraho figurines: '"I have never understood what they were about'" (*op. cit.*, 268). The temples of Khajuraho seemed to him 'very wonderful but nightmares.' Yet, though he could not discern the inner real meaning of the carvings—of the carved figures and figurines—of the temples, he somehow found out for himself a meaning, which was that the figures were individualistic, like the Cambridge fellows or scholars, not like the Tonbridge boys who were conformist, and that the figures bore, each one, sort of spiritual halloes, and also that there was some dark secrecy and deeper values around them. Forster later on wrote about them: '"Besides our war against totalitarianism, we have also an inner war, a struggle for truer values, a struggle of the individual towards the dark, secret place where he may find reality. I came away [from inside the temples] thinking,' 'Yes, the people who built these temples, the people who planned Khajuraho and Orissa and Madura—knew about that. They belonged to another civilization, but they knew, they knew that the community cannot satisfy the human spirit'" (*op. cit.*, 269).

From Chhatrapur, Forster and Co. went to Jhansi where the travelling party bifurcated itself—Goldie and Bob left for Benares, and Forster proceeded towards Bhopal, stopping on the way at Sanchi, for some whiles. To Forster, Bhopal looked 'barren and ugly,' and here he saw the 'Oriental hospitality plus Oriental confusion.' From Bhopal he went to Ujjain and thence to Udaipur which he called 'the Venice of the East,' and then turning towards the south he reached Indore, on 20 December 1912, where there was a large Anglo-Indian community. In Indore, he stayed with a friend of his friend Malcolm Darling, Major Luard, the Private Secretary of the Maharaja of Indore, sometimes mingling with the members of the English Club—the club that has fictionally been recreated by him in *A Passage to India.* "The Maharaja was then 24 years old and had been the active ruler of Dewas Senior for the last four years. He was a descendant of the Puars, a Rajput family of soldiers of fortune who, during the eighteenth century, had carved out a kingdom for themselves while in the service of the Mahrattas. The kingdom's first rulers, Tukoji Rao and Jiwaji Rao, having briefly attempted joint sovereignty, had agreed to divide the state between them; and possession of the twin states, now much shrunken, had been confirmed to their descendants by the British in 1818" (Furbank, I, 238). and as a result of that two lesser kingdoms were born: Dewas Senior and Dewas Junior. The Maharaja, we are talking about, was Tukoji Rao III who succeeded in 1899, "his aunt, the widow of the late Raja, having adopted him when her husband died without heir" (*ibid.*). "In physique Tukoji or 'H.H.' (His Highness), as Forster was accustomed to call him, was tiny, round-faced, with a long weeping moustache. He was vivid in manner, pulled one way and another by emotion: by turns kind-hearted and revengeful, confiding and secretive, regal and full of ridiculous schoolboy fun" (*ibid.*). With all these the Maharaja was an endearing personality to his Private Secretary Malcolm Darling as well as to Forster. But the geography of Dewas could not attract the attention of Forster, except the famous and sacred Hill of Devi—the locale of his *The Hill of Devi,* of which he wrote to his mother: "'There is a sacred hill above it [Dewas], covered with chapels, which makes scenary interesting'" (*op. cit.,* I, 240).

From Dewas, Forster went a long way back to Allahabad where the two sacred rivers, the Ganges and Jumna, meet, and they say that a third stream springs up from the confluence of the two rivers. "This notion appealed to Forster, suggesting an allegory of human relationship, and, with a Muslim friend of Masood's, Ahmed Mirza, he went to observe the miracle" (*op. cit.,* I, 245). But their curiosity and endeavour were all frustrated due to the tiredness of the boatman rowing in the high current and the risk of the boat's being capsized by the undertow and the waves. However, it was now time for Forster to go from Allahabad to Benares. In Benares, he had had a curious encounter with a fakir, 'Nrusinh' (Narasingha) Sharma "who lived in a charming house and talked excellent English. Nrusinh Sharma showed Forster his tea-things and a finger-painting by himself of Siva and Parvati. He compared Parvati to Queen Victoria, but Forster objected that the Queen would not have been sitting on her husband's knee but the other way round; the fakir laughed, and they rechristened them George and Mary" (*ibid.*).

On 10 January, 1913, Forster set out for Bankipore, some miles north of Patna, where Masood had been waiting upon his arrival there. It was then that on his way to Bankipore Forster saw "at a wayside station [a railway station not very far from Benares] a tablet inscribed RIGHT IS MIGHT. MIGHT IS RIGHT. GOD SI LOVE" (*op. cit.*, I, 246), which inscription partially appears in *A Passage to India.* Reaching Bankipore, he found the place 'horrible beyond words,' and yet Bankipore was the model of his fictional Chandrapore. Bankipore '"consists of a street 14 miles long edged with hovels,' he told his mother (15 January 1913), 'from which it is impossible to escape because the Ganges stops you on one side and rice fields on the other. I wouldn't believe it until I took a bicycle ride and tried.' From Masood's roof, however, as he discovered, the city appeared transformed, miraculously, into a palm and lemon grove. Some of these details were remembered in his portrait of 'Chandrapore' in *A Passage to India*" (*op. cit.*, I, 247). Bankipore might be a disagreeable place, but King-Emperor George V announced a plan to form a new province by uniting Bihar and Orissa and to make Bankipore, in Bihar, to be the capital of the new province. While at Bankipore, Forster saw the anger of the Indians there against the British. Now a call came to Forster from his friend Rupert Smith, an Assistant Magistrate stationed at Allahabad, to see the annual bathing-fair there, and Forster set out for Allahabad (this was his second visit to that place). On way to

Allahabad, he stopped at Buddh Gaya, about 70 miles south of Bankipore, and from there one day went to see the Barabar Hills, about 40 miles north of Buddh Gaya. Forster and Nawab Syed Imdad and also two nephews of the Nawab mounted an elephant and proceeded towards the Barabar Hills (the Marabar Hills of *A Passage to India)* and there in the Barabar Hills they saw the Crow's Swing (the Kawa Dol of *A Passage to India*). The echoes that Adela heard in the Caves of the Marabar Hills in *A Passage to India* reflect the echoes that Forster actually heard in the Barabar Hills near Bela.

Here we fail to follow the itinerary of Forster. After around a month since his visit to Allahabad (his second visit to that place) where he witnessed the annual bathing-fair, we find Forster emerge in Lahore once again. He went there on an invitation from a Brahmin member of the Brahmo Samaj, Mr Godbole, who was the model of Professor Narayan Godbole of *A Passage to India.* P.N. Furbank writes in this regard: "There is a gap in his [Forster's] diary at this point. When we catch up with him it is a month later, and he is once more in Lahore, where, one Sunday evening, he is invited to a reception by Brahmo Samaj and meets a Mr Godbole, a Brahmin. ('What a name!' he exclamed.) After the reception, the two strolled in the public gardens, and Mr Godbole sang to him. 'There are scales appropriate for all hours of the day,' he noted" (*op. cit.,* 1, 249). Now from Lahore Forster went to Patiala, the 'Sikh capital,' and from there he planned to visit Rajputana, but as he wanted to meet the Maharaja of Chhatrapur who was then in Delhi, he went to Delhi, met the Maharaja and said good-bye to him, as it was almost time for him to return to England. From Delhi he went to Jaipur and Jodhpur, and then from Jodhpur he proceeded towards Bombay state with the particular objective of visiting Mount Abu and the celebrated Jain temples that are there. And on the last leg of his first visit to India he next went to visit the Nizam's dominions in South India. He straight went to the city of Hyderabad where one May Wylde, whom he knew from childhood, had been running a school for Indian girls, 'the first of its kind in the subcontinent.' May thought that Forster developed prejudices against the British officials in India, and strived to drive away those prejudices, but he took these in good part.'

Forster went to Hyderabad not so much for taking a glimpse of the dominions of the Nizam as to see the cave-temples of Ellora in Aurangabad. One Abu Saeed Mirza, a younger brother of Masood's friend Ahmed Mirza, was a *munsif* or junior magistrate in Aurangabad. Abu Saeed was 'a dashing young fellow, with expensive tastes in horseflesh.' 'He had a distinguished career, eventually becoming a Chief Justice.' With Abu Saeed, Forster went to see the courts, and "in the sub-judge's court he heard a part of a murder-case, during which, at the end of the table, a *punkah*-boy sat pulling his rope with 'the impassivity of Atropos'" (*op. cit.*, I, 252). This *punkah-boy* was the model of the punkahwala of the trial scene of *A Passage to India.* One day, when Forster and Abu Saeed were discussing the relation between the Indians and the British, Saeed burst out in anger against the British and told Forster: "' It may be fifty or five hundred years,' he said, 'but we shall turn you out'" (*op. cit.*, I, 253). This anger of Saeed is echoed by Aziz to the hearing of Fielding at the fag end of *A Passage to India:* 'we shall get rid of you, we shall drive every blasted Englishman into the sea.' However, with Saeed, Forster went to the cave-temples, popularly known as Elephanta caves, of Ellora, but was not even the least attracted by them, though he was much amazed. "'The caves are cruel, obscene things, he told Masood, 'the work of devils, but very wonderful'" (Beauman, 279). However, now his 1912-13 India tour being over, Forster swiftly packed up for Bombay to return home at Weybridge, where Lily perhaps had so long been feeling a gap in her life for Forster's absence.

(10)

Back at Weybridge, in 1913, Forster wrote in his diary: "'I am with 3 unfinished novels on my hands'" *(op. cit.*, 284). These three novels are: *Maurice, A Passage to India,* and *Arctic Summer.* By now he was a famous novelist with four published novels—*Where Angels Fear to Tread* (1905), *The Longest*

Journey (1907), *A Room with a View* (1908) and *Howards End* (1910), the last being his mainstay yet. With the burden of three novels, he must have been all the while meditative, gloomy, and only tangentially attached to the world. Leonard Woolf has left for us a beautiful pen-picture of the Forster of this time: '"He was strange, elusive, evasive. You could be talking to him easily and intimately one moment, and suddenly he would seem to withdraw into himself; though he still was physically there, you had faded out of his mental vision, and so with a pang you found that he had faded out of yours—Lytton [Strachey] nicknamed him the Taupe, partly because of his faint physical resemblance to a mole, but principally because he seemed intellectually and emotionally to travel unseen underground and every now and again pop up excitedly with some subtle observation or delicate quip which somehow or other he had found in the depths of the earth or of his own soul'" (*op. cit.,* 282). However, of the three novels, he was then, most probably, most engaged with *Maurice* which he perhaps completed by August, 1914, just when the drumming of the First World War began to be heard.

Forster's response to the war was lukeworm; he was also not much concerned with it, for he was occupied with his novels. The director of the National Gallery, who lived in Weybridge, offered him 'a part-time cataloguing post' at a salary of Pound 100 (about Pound 5000 in 1993) a year. Forster joined the post, perhaps thinking that in the Gallery he could find time to finish the three novels on hand, in peace. Goldie by then had gone through the manuscript of *Maurice,* in part, and wrote a letter to Forster praising the novel and informing him that the twenty-five-year-old Masood had married. Hearing of Masood's marriage, he "was mournful but not unduly sad" (*op. cit.*, 286). During tins time, 'Forster and D.H. Lawrence tentatively began a friendship.' Lawrence invited Forster to stay with him and his wife Frieda, in Sussex, and he accepted the invitation. But the friendship never deepened any more, and rather soon began to thin out: "But the relationship, though intense, was too volatile to last: Morgan [Forster] was hurt by Lawrence's criticisms yet was too polite to say what *he* thought. He was also made angry by Lawrence's imputations against his sexuality, and the implication that Morgan needed someone like Frieda to loosen himself up. Uncharacteristically he wrote a sharp thank-you letter, saying that although he liked Frieda, and the Lawrence who was restful and wrote *The White Peacock,* he did not like the 'deaf impercipient fanatic who has nosed over his little sexual round until he believes that there is no other path for others to take, he sometimes interests & sometimes frightens & angers me, but in the end he will bore him merely, I know.' Lawrence respected the frankness of this approach. In any case, the day Morgan wrote his letter Lawrence had been writing one of his own to Bertrand Russell, describing Morgan sucking his dummy long after his age and being 'bound hand and foot bodily. Why? *Because he does not believe that any beauty or any divine utterance is any good any more....* Will all the poetry in the world satisfy the manhood of Forster, when Forster knows that his implicit manhood is to be satisfied by nothing but immediate physical action.' Morgan was intuitive enough to suspect Lawrence of penning letters like these, but he did not seem to resent it and the two men were to keep, slightly, in touch; in years to come Morgan was to describe Lawrence as 'most alarming and explosive but I like him' and to declare him to be one of the greatest novelists of the twentieth century; he began, although never finished, editing an edition of his letters" (*op. cit.,* 287). The Forster-Lawrence relation did not disintegrate quite soon, but, continued, sometimes warmly, sometimes lukewarmly, as, at any rate, Forster loved him. Once Forster even showed his gratefulness to him. In a letter to Reid, of 23 January 1915, he wrote that of late he was taken out of his gloom by Lawrence, and that Lawrence was 'really extraordinarily nice,' and also that Lawrence was 'so human, so personal.' Frieda Lawrence was delighted with *Where Angels Fear to Tread,* and both she and her husband invited Forster to lunch with them, and Forster accepted the invitation, and enjoyed more their conversation than the precious lunch.

However, after the publication of *Howards End* in 1910, as we have already said, Forster was working on three novels, all at the same time, *A Passage to India, Maurice,* and *Arctic Summer,* and he perhaps finished *Maurice* by August, 1914, but could not make a headway with the other two, and yet, by this time, to be precise in 1911, he finished his only play *The Heart of Bosnia.* The play, by Forster's "own account, was not good, although it almost reached the stage in 1914; plans for its production were abandoned at the outbreak of war [WW I] and the manuscript was lost by the producer" (Bradbury, 77).

(11)

The First World War [WW I] broke out in 1914, but before that unfortunate year a couple of very omenous years elapsed, and Forster very rightly wrote that the years between 1910 and 1914 were "'the sinister corridor of our age'," (*ibid.*). He was doubly disturbed by the war; for, firstly, he was a pacifist by birth; and secondly, he was a devoted member of the Bloomsbury Group which wanted to usher in, at least in England, a 'new age of tolerance and enlightenment' inaugurated by G.E. Moore's philosophy. The war, therefore, prevented him from concentrating his attention on novel-writing. So to stop the gap in the course of his creative writing, Forster decided to write a critical book on Samuel Butler who "had long been an interest of Forster's. *Erewhon,* he felt, was a book that he might have written himself; and in *Howards End* his handling of the money-theme, the Schlegel frankness about money that so shocks the Wilcoxes, owed much to Butler" (Furbank, II, 3). *Maurice,* which was not published till Forster's death in 1970, was circulated among his close acquaintances, and the novel received both adulating comments and scathing criticisms, and Forster tried to defend it. During this time he came more closer to the Bloomsbury Group; particularly to Virginia Woolf, whose *The Voyage Out* was published in the spring of 1915, and he announced that it was a 'masterpiece' of literature. However no sooner than the First World War broke out, in addition to his war-born perplexity, Forster had had a painful spell of chicken-pox.

About one year and four or five months after the breaking out of the First World War, Forster got a chance of staying in Alexandria, Egypt, by serving the Red Cross as a Searcher. He was then continuing to work in the National Gallery, his task being that of cataloguing, but he could no longer like the job, and so had been searching for an alternative employment. With the breaking out of the war the Red Cross's functions were accelarated. "With the war, Egypt had assumed great military importance for Britain. It was the supply base for the Dardanelles campaign, and a quarter of a million troops were stationed on its soil for the defence of the Suez Canal. Till then, Britain's position in Egypt had been very anomalous.... It was only with Turkey's entry into the war, on the German side, that Britain had declared Egypt a protectorate, proceeding to depose the Khedive and replace him by a puppet Sultan" (*op. cit.,* II, 21). Consequently, "Egypt, in fact, tended to be regarded as a rather second-rate part of the Empire" *(ibid.)*. The national spirit of the British made them interested in Egypt, particularly for medical care of the British soldiers stationed and fighting there. The activated British chapter of the Red Cross was searching for volunteers to work as 'Searchers' in the nursing establishments of the Red Cross in Egypt. At this time Forster felt an itch for the job of a 'Searcher,' especially because the job would provide him with a chance of seeing the fabulous Alexandria. But to get the job was not an easy matter, and he had to move from pillar to post to grab the job. Ultimately he could manage an interview with Gertrude Bell who was in charge of recruiting 'Searchers,' but Bell was not impressed by Forster. Then with the aid of Percy Lubbock, Forster somehow procured the job of a 'Searcher,' whose duty it was to interview "the wounded in hospital for information about fellow-soldiers reported 'missing'" (*op. cit.,* II, 19), and in October 1915, he, "wearing Red Cross uniform, embarked from England for Egypt expecting to be gone for three months" (*op. cit.,* II, 20).

Egypt, and for the matter of that Alexandria, were not to Forster's liking. Earlier he had visited India, and though then India could not steal his heart, she now seemed prettier to him than Egypt. Within weeks after his arrival in Egypt, he wrote to Masood (on 29 December 1915): "'I do not like Egypt much—or rather, I do not see it, for Alexandria is cosmopolitan. But what I have seen seems vastly inferior to India, for which I am always longing in the most persistent way, and where I still hope to die. It is only at sunset that Egypt surpasses India—at all other hours it is flat, unromantic, unmysterious, and godless—the soil is mud, the inhabitants are of mud moving, and exasperating in the extreme: I feel as instinctively not at home among them as I feel instinctively at home among Indians'" (*op. cit.,* II, 22). *A Passage to India* begins with Forster's experiences in Egypt, with 'mud moving' that he saw in the edges of the Nile—the mud that he associated with 'muddle,' or perplexity, and moral 'muddiness.' Soon he found his job not uninteresting. Though his status was that of an officer, he would unhesitatingly "play chess with the patients, take their watches to be mended, write their letters for them and act as unpaid solicitor" (*op. cit.,* II, 23). He made two friends of Robin Furness and Pericles Anastassiades; the latter engaged Forster as his tutor to teach him the English language. Through these two gentlemen, Forster made acquaintance with the poet Cavafy, an old friend of Anastassiades. Furness also introduced Forster to Aida Borchgrevink, with whom Furness had 'a passionate platonic relationship.' Aida "was an ebullient, romantic woman, who sang Wagner at the top of her voice as she drove.... She took a great fancy to Forster, whom she insisted on calling 'Rickie'" (*op. cit.,* II, 25). And this nick-name of Forster, 'Rickie,' appears in *The Longest Journey* as the nick-name of the protagonist, proving the possibility that the novel is almost autobiographical.

In Alexandria, Forster "found himself in the company of homosexuals and able to engage himself with them with a freedom he had not experienced previously. In his relationship with a tram conductor, Mohammed el Ad [Adl], he found a lasting love" (Edwards, 182-83). Like Italy, Alexandria freshened Forster once more. "Alexandria, prosaic, slightly debased, and less hag-ridden by the war than England, suited his mood. The weather was exquisite; he had taught himself to swim; and he was busy and useful" (Furbank, II, 25). He, on landing in Alexandria, almost hated the place, but now he was a different person—though at first he planned to stay there not beyond three months, now he showed no sign of returning home. The First World War was now raging fiercely, and so the British government promulgated conscription. Forster thought he would prove medically unfit, but to his consternation the medical board declared him otherwise. Being a pacifist, Forster declared himself a 'conscientious objector,' and so the military authority asked him to go to England and attend to a tribunal. The ship, on board of which he was to return, delayed, and the haggling meantime fizzled out, and he heaved a sigh of relief.

Forster went to Alexandria in October, 1915 and came back to England in January, 1919; that is he had been in Alexandria for over three years and not three months that he planned to spend there, before sailing, and this additionally proves his happiness in Alexandria, where, he perhaps delighted to recall, Alexander the Great is entombed and Cleopatra committed suicide, and, also, the great library Serapeum existed. In 1917, about two years after Forster's arrival in Alexandria, there was at that place a population of 450,000, of which one-sixth was non-Egyptian; and being himself a cosmopolite, Forster liked such a cosmopolitan place very much. There were there Greeks, Italians, the English, the French, Armenians and Syrians. He liked Alexandria also because it was the city of poets, where the Mediterranean breeze visited occasionally, and where such great and homosexual people as Theocritus and Callimachus had lived. It was in Alexandria, again, that Forster struck a friendship with the Greek poet and active homosexual Cavafy and shared the poet's sensibility.

In Alexandria, Forster had had homosexual encounters with at least two of his unforgetable homosexual friends: Frank Vicary and Mohammed el Adl. As we have said, as a 'Searcher,' Forser had to mix with wounded soldiers in hospitals and he did that freely. There in the hospital, he came across a young man, Frank Vicary, who had been serving as a steward in a battle ship. Vicary was 'small, vivid, rather gaunt and hollow-cheeked, but with bright blue eyes.' The first meeting between Forster and Vicary occurred in July, 1916, when 'Vicary talked charmingly and amusingly.' The two, psychologically, came too closer to each other and there everything of their relationship ended; and, consequently, Forster suffered from 'sexual frustration.' The frustration was overcomed by another homosexual incident with an anonymous person. "In October [1916] he [Forster] had a casual escapade with a soldier on the beach. It was his first full physical encounter, and he did not enjoy it greatly—not so much because he found it squalid, as because it was so anonymous. He reported it to Florence Barger [of whom Forster said 'my only woman friend'], remarking 'It is as if (in the novel [*Maurice*]) A [lec] had been ordered to come and then dismissed at once'" (*op. cit.*, II, 35).

Forster had had another homosexual relationship, this time, with Mohammed el Adl who was a tram conductor. Adl was a young and slightly negroid-looking Egyptian, and he frequently boarded the tram of which Adl was the conductor. Acquaintance grew between them, and soon also friendship. One day Adl took Forster to his poor home; 'they squatted on the bed and chatted amicably.' "On the next occasion, Mohammed [el Adl] came to Forster's room in Ramleh. They played chess and lay on the bed; and after a little while, they leaned towards each other and began to stroke each other's hair. Mohammed murmured, 'beautiful hair,' and they kissed. Things now went wrong, for Forster, growing excited, made too fierce a grab at Mohammed, and there was a scuffle, during which Forster hurt his hand and Mohammed hurt his eye. It was not a serious quarrel, and next day, encountering on the tram, they compared their injuries and laughed" (*op. cit.*, II, 38). The friendship deepened; Mohammed now addressed Forster as just 'Forster'; and they began to meet more oftener, mostly secretly, of course. For some time, nevertheless, Mohammed refused to go to bed with Forster. But after some time he overcome the pull, and since then "from time to time, they found the chance to spend a night together. Forster's happiness was now complete, and he determined to be grateful for his good fortune [of his homosexual relationship with Mohammed]. 'Wish I was writing the latter half of *Maurice*. I now know so much more,' he told Florence Barger. 'It is awful to think of the thousands who go through youth without ever knowing. I have known in a way before, but never like this. My luck has been amazing'" (*op. cit.,* II, 40). Forster, for one reason or another, could not respond to Alexandria, and for the matter of that to Egypt, imaginatively, and so he decided to respond objectively—he planned to write a book about Alexandria. And he wrote it, and it is *Alexandria: a History and a Guide.*

While in Alexandria, Forster was in touch with Bertrand Russell, and read avidly and with interest his recently published book *Principles of Social Reconstruction* (1917); with Siegfried Sassoon, and approvingly read his anti-war *Soldier's Declaration;* and with T.S. Eliot, and read his *Prufrock and Other Observations.* In the middle of 1918, he somewhat shockingly came to know of Mohammed el Adl's intention to get married and lead a family life. Adl first thought of marrying the widow of his brother, but later on found another match. "In July [1918], before the marriage, Forster came to stay with him [Adl] in the family house. It was a little slum dwelling, in a muddy lane overrun with ducks and chickens, and Mohammed had to let most of it; thus they had to live in one room—a room so crammed that, on entering, they had to jump strait on to the sofa. To wash, they stripped in a grimy stone-floored passage and poured tins of water over each other" (*op. cit.,* II, 50). Inspite of so much of his homosexual attraction towards Mohammed, "Forster felt happy for him and was not jealous of the coming marriage" (*ibid.*) which took place on 1 October 1918. But not long afterwards Forster felt very depressed to know that Mohammed el Adl had been suffering from confirmed consumption. He had to tell Adl that he was thinking of leaving Egypt in January, 1919, and he came back to England in the same month of the same year.

(12)

From Forster's letter to Masood written on 29th July, 1916, when the former was in Alexandria and the latter in England, we know that the Maharaja of Dewas Sr. invited Forster to come to his State, in India, and be his private secretary. Why did not Forster immediately respond to the call of the Maharaja we are not certain about, but one reason of it may be that he was at the time enticed by Egypt. However, sometime after his coming back to England, Forster was offered a job in Germany, the job being that of someone like a secretary in the Inter Allied Commission at a salary of Pound 600 (Pound 15,000 in 1993) a year, but he declined the offer because he did not like to leave Lily alone once again after his stay in Alexandria for three years leaving her in England, as Lily also could not bear with he idea of losing him another time. His experiences of the First World War made him quite cynical about war and averse to power—the power of one man over a multiple. Earlier he was a pacifist, but now he became a hater of war, and of the power that propels the engine that is the war. Forster now became more politically aware than before. In a letter to the war poet Siegfried Sassoon he vomitted his bile on war and power: "'I believe it's [the war is] the possession of power. Give a man power over the other men, and he deteriorates at once. The "troops" are decent and charming, I believe, not because they suffer but because they are powerless—and the devil who rules this planet has contrived that those who are powerless shall suffer'" (Beauman, 308). During the time when he was in Alexandria, he wrote about one hundred articles, most of them airing his anti-war sentiment, while during the whole year of 1914 he wrote only four articles. Why did Forster suddenly become prolific in Alexandria? Nicola Beauman surmises that it was all due to his absence from Lily. Forster's anti-power invective did not exhaust through those nearly an hundred articles, but continued to trickle into his last novel *A Passage to India.*

Forster's circle of friends now began to widen and his fame travelled farther. He was now in touch with Bertrand Russell, Leonard Woolf, Middleton Murry and such others, and was fiercely writing articles for Murry's *Athenaeum*. He was also continuing to write the yet untitled Indian novel *A Passage to India,* and was perhaps realising his dearth of data on India. Fortune now smiled on him and opened the gate to India for his required donnees. We have said that in 1916, the Maharaja of Dewas Sr. (of India) invited Forster to become his private secretary, but neither Forster nor Lily was prone to the idea of Forster's going to India once more making another gap in their lives. In 1920, the post of the private secretary to the Maharaja once again fell vacant, and so there grew another chance for Forster to go to India, but again the mother and the son felt disinclined, and thus the chance was missed. Fortunately For Forster (and also, of course, for us), a third chance for him to become the private secretary to the Maharaja came in 1921, this time the post was temporarily vacant. Both Lily and Forster counted upon and underlined the temporariness of the charge and agreed upon Forster's going to India. In the early part of March, 1921, Forster left England for India—for his second passage to India.

Forster's ship reached Port Said on 16th March, 1921, and there he met Sir Edmund Ironside, perhaps the model of Ronny in *A Passage to India.* Ironside had come to Port Said to be the Commander-in-Chief of the British troops in charge of safeguarding the British interests in the region of the Port. He was one of the model products of the Tonbridge public school, who fairly internalised the Tonbridge ideals of conformity with tradition, mechanisation, lack of emotion and sentimentality, draconian discipline, extreme nationalism, etc. Forster enjoyed the residual voyage to India, and ultimately reached Bombay where about eight years ago he landed for the first time. From Bombay he took the night train and eventually reached Dewas Senior to meet the Maharaja. The "extraordinary division of Dewas into two [Senior and Junior] meant that there was a 'Junior Branch' as well, complete with its own palace, court, army, flag and so on" (*op. cit.,* 313). Forster beautifully and faithfully depicted the Maharaja: '"a charming creature, gay, witty, affectionate, generous and with a strong religious element in him. I am tempted to call him a saint, but saints are supposed to be reliable, anyhow by the British, and the Maharaja certainly wasn't that. He loved intrigue, he could lie if he wasn't trusted, and since besides being deceitful he was unpractical, he made a tragic mess of his life in the end'" (*op. cit.,* 314). The Maharaja, 'bare-headed and capering with glee,' warmly welcomed Forster. "His first action was to dictate a cable to Malcolm Darling, and another to Forster's mother. He then handed Forster to the major-domo, who showed him his rooms. These were on the first floor of the palace and quite extensive, comprising three rooms and a bathroom. In the evening, courtiers fitted Forster out with Indian clothes, and he was taken to the Cavalry Barracks, where a visiting troupe of actors were performing" (Furbank, II, 71).

Next day, the Maharaja himself instructed Forster about the latter's charges and duties. Forster's "sphere of action was to be the palace garden and tennis courts, the Guest-House arrangements, and the garages and 'electric house;' in addition, all mail was to pass through his hands; and apart from this—and most important of his functions—he was to give the Maharaja as much of his company as was possible and sometimes read aloud to him. Forster, who had been picturing himself as some kind of high diplomatic aide or counsellor, was a little taken aback at his duties and not sure how he would cope with motorcars and electric generators. He was told that his predecessor, Colonel Leslie, had been a great expert in all such matters, as well as being fluent in several Indian languages; so he would hardly shine by comparison" (*op. cit.,* II, 71-72). But Forster's life in the Dewas was not that pallid, because there was an abundance of entertainments. The *Holi* came, and he was amused to see the reckless but innocent smearings of faces and bodies with ochre powder. That year (1921) the *Holi* and the April Fool's Day came jointly: "April Fool's Day arrived, reinforcing *Holi,* and Forster had to submit to exploding cigarettes and sofas that gave an electric shock. He was also, which pleased him more, given the chance to witness *Holi* observances in the country" (*op. cit.,* II, 73). During this period *of Holi,* Forster, along with one Malarao, went on an expedition along the bank of the river Sipra and to the villages, when he saw a crush of villagers stoning a shrub, taking it to be a snake, and at last realizing their mistake. He thought Indians sometimes failed to distinguish between appearance and reality. To Forster, this incident—the snake-tree episode—'seemed emblamatical of India.' But not only this confusing incident but his employing boss, the Maharaja, was also, perhaps emblamatic of India, to Forster. The geniality, magnanimity, saintliness of the Maharaja, beside his love of intrigues and all that—the co-existence of contrary aspects—appeared in the mind of Forster as a minuscule image of India, like a tiny image of the sun in the water of a dish.

Since his reaching Dewas, Forster had been dancing the attendance of Masood, and before long Masood arrived there at the invitation of the Maharaja himself 'attended by a private secretary and two servants.' Masood's "coming was quite an event, for he had never before been a private guest in a Hindu court, nor did Dewas often receive a Mohammedan visitor. The Maharaja was at his most gracious. It was almost like the meeting of two princes, and Masood told Forster that, in addition to the outward ceremonies, H.H. [the Maharaja] showed him niceties of respect that only an Indian could appreciate" (*op. cit.,* II, 75). For the entertainment of Masood and Forster, the Maharaja arranged an expedition to the sacred Hill of Devi. They mounted an elephant provided them by the Maharaja and saw the Hill of Devi; and another day they went to the holy city of Ujjain in a car arranged by the Maharaja, and there they saw on the riverside "a swarm of ash-coloured *saddhus* (fakirs), seated on spikes—some laughing, some quarrelling, others serving tea to one another" (*ibid.*). The Maharaja, whose wife, the queen, fled to Kolhapur due to quarrels between himself and the other Maharaja of the nearby Kolhapur state, whose daughter she happened to be, took a wife-cum-concubine whom he called 'Diamond Concubine.' The Maharaja introduced Forster to the concubine—an 'intelligent and amusing' woman, and since then Forster enjoyed from now and then her innocent company. The generality of the citizens of the state called the concubine 'Bai

Saheba.' The indulgent Maharaja addressed Forster as 'dear Morgan.'

In May, 1921, the Bai Saheba gave birth to her second daughter. According to the customs, the Maharaja would not see the new-born and her mother for five days, but loud and pompous celebration of the occasion continued for days together. "The court musicians played, there were fire-works, the army fired rifle-volleys, and *nautch* girls and boys in girls' clothing performed dialogues and dances. At night-time Forster came to join the Maharaja in his encampment [according to the custom the Maharaja, for those five days, would live in a make-shift camp near another such camp in which the Bai Saheba gave birth] and slept beside him, sometimes with his head propped against a bullock's flanks. The din was appalling and usually lasted till the small hours, but one night, at about 3 a. m. he was woken by music that he recognized as rare and beautiful, an endless *raga,* performed by a singer and a drummer, that seemed to him 'like Western music reflected in trembling water'" (*op. cit.,* II, 80). The festivities ended with 'an elaborate present-giving' from the Maharaja.

Forster came to India for the second time, with seventy pages of manuscript of his Indian novel—*A Passage to India*—with the implicit purpose of collecting donnees for the novel and, all at the same, to continue to write it further on, and not to serve the Maharaja, but what actually happened was that he "concentrated instead on his duties, only vaguely defined as that of Secretary, by trying to put to rights some of the intrigues, rescuing some of the palace contents from further decay, trying to stop money being frittered away" (Beauman, 314). Forster was now around 42 and yet unmarried. He was far away from Mohammed el Adl who was in Egypt; and though Masood was in India, he could avail of no free access to the palace compound where Forster lived. Sex can hardly starve and allow one peace. In the intense heat of Indian May, in his abundance of idleness allowed by his sinecure job, Forster's sex suddenly began to spring up in his moments of solitude, and so he was frantically searching for an object to let it out. But he was nervously apprehensive of being detected as an immoral and abject person, and of having to face the consequences thereof. As Forster was an incorrigible homosexual and his novels, particularly, were written under the abiding shadow of his homosexuality we should perhaps know more of this his abnormal sex and its ploys, deceptions, success stories, etc., and for that here we cannot do better than quote at some length from P.N. Furbank's *E.M. Forster: A Life,* the most elaborate and authentic biography of Forster, to show that, even in the restricted environment of the palace, Forster was on the try to satisfy his homosexual desires. Furbank writes: The heat was intense. It did not upset him, but its effect, combined with idleness and solitude, was to fill him with sexual desire: during the long seista period, especially, it became almost intolerable, and masturbation gave no relief. He began to feel he would be ill, and his good resolutions towards the Maharaja gradually weakened. He guessed that among the various palace hangers-on he could find someone he might have sex with. Two, he thought, had already guessed what he wanted: a young Mohammedan who acted as his postilion; and one of the palace workmen, a Hindu of about eighteen. When the Hindu salaamed him—very respectfully, using both hands—Forster would respond with his whole attention, and when the boy brought him a chair he would thank him with a smile. The coolie took his meaning and found an ingenious method of declaring himself: he took a leather strap and lashed the floor of the Hall with it, hard, startling Forster and making him look in his direction, he lashed the floor a second time, hard; and then a third time, gently, so that Forster would look round if he wanted to; and when he did so, the boy smiled. After that, for some days the two eyed each other in the corridors, and when the coolie disappeared round a comer, Forster could see from his shadow that he was waiting for him to follow. As he drove to Bai Saheba's, in the scorching heat, the other servant—the postilion—used various tricks to catch his attention. It was as if nothing existed except lust.

"His resolve [Forster, apparently, resolved not to proceed any further for fear of the Maharaja] held out no longer, and he sought some way of talking with the Hindu coolie. This was not an easy problem, for there were onlookers everywhere; however he hit on a solution. He let it be known that the *tattie* ['A screen made of grass-roots, kept wet as a form of air-conditioning.'] on his bedroom door needed watering, dropping a hint that the coolie should volunteer for the task. The hint was taken, the Hindu came, and, pretending to show him how to throw the water, Forster stroked his wrist. The coolie smiled happily, and Forster said meet me at 7.30 on the road near the Guest House.' Some ten minutes later, to his dismay, he heard two excited voices outside his door. The first said 'The *burra* (master) sahib has given orders to come at night.' 'At night?' said the other. 'Yes, and he will give me money.' Their voices then mingled with those of other workmen, leaving Forster in a panic of terror and shame. His thought was: 'H.H. [His Highness the Maharaja] has had me out from England because I am Malcolm's friend and as one of the few he can trust, and this is what I do.' To make matters worse, when he looked out of the window, he saw a flurry below and one of the senior clerks of the palace jumping into a bullock-cart. He felt sure the clerk had gone to report the scandal to the Maharaja; and when the H.H. himself returned an hour later, his manner—merry, but slightly malicious and hard—seemed to confirm it. As they passed a servant painting the wainscoting, H.H. exclaimed impatiently: 'everywhere—I cannot get away from them.' Forster sensed a sting in the words; and later that evening, in front of the assembled courtiers, the Maharaja said severely that he meant to banish all catamites from his court: 'What is the good of such people?' He was very silent when, late the same night, Forster joined him, and Forster was now finally convinced that he knew of his escapade. Worse, he felt sure that all the courtiers knew; he got the impression that they were mocking and no longer held him in respect.

For four days he swallowed his trouble, taking care to avoid or ignore the coolie, but at last he could bear it no longer and asked the Maharaja for a private interview. 'As I think you know, I am in great trouble,' he said.

> 'Tell me, Morgan,' H.H. replied. 'I have noticed you were worried.'
>
> 'I have tried to have carnal intercourse with one of the coolies and it has become known.'
>
> 'With a coolie-girl?'
>
> 'No, with a man. You know about it, and if you agree I think I ought to resign.'
>
> 'But Morgan, I know nothing about it,' said the Maharaja. 'This is the first I have heard of it.'

"Forster wished he were dead; he need never have confessed, and he guessed that the confession would do him no good in H.H.'s eyes. For a time, he thought the Maharaja must be lying, but H.H. found harmless explanations for all that had perturbed him. He questioned Forster further, kindly and seriously.

> 'Why a man and not a woman? Is not a woman more natural?'
>
> 'Not in my case. I have no feeling for women.'
>
> 'Oh but that alters everything. You are not to blame.'
>
> 'I don't know what "natural" is.'
>
> 'You are quite right, Morgan—I ought never to have used the word. No, don't worry—don't worry. I am only distressed you did not tell me everything before—I might have saved you so much pain. May I know all about this coolie now?'

"When he heard that nothing physical had actually taken place, the Maharaja was reassuring: there was nothing to fear, he said. 'Only always come to me when you are in difficulties like this. I would have found you someone reliable among the hereditary servants, and you could have had him quietly in your room. Yes, yes, it's true I don't encourage those people, but it's entirely different in your case and you must not masturbate—that's awful.'

"Forster was so touched and relieved that when he tried to appologize he broke down. The Maharaja nearly broke down too, crying 'Oh devil! Don't do that Morgan—the only way with a thing like this is to take laughing.' And he threw himself with zest into schemes for finding Forster a bed-companion" (Furbank, II, 81-84). And the Maharaja was not a lier: he really procured one—Kanaya, the barbar for the palace—and increased his salary for providing Forster with physical pleasure. Soon, one day, Kanaya arrived to shave Forster, and while he was doing his job, Forster drew Kanaya "to him and kissed him" (*op. cit.*, II, 84). Forster wrote about Kanaya: "'for a time all went well. I couldn't get from Kanaya the emotional response of an Egyptian [Forster here perhaps meant Mohammed el Adl], because he had the body and soul of a slave, but he was always merry and he improved my health'" (Beauman, 315). In the homosexual relationship between Forster and Kanaya, the latter was no less forward, advancing, aggressive than the former. Kanaya, in fact, took the abnormal sex as a means of his personal advancement, for, while the festival of Gokul Ashtami was being celebrated in August, 1921, one night he happened to be lying in a corner of the bed-room of the Maharaja, and after a while began to massage the Maharaja's feet while he pleaded for getting 'more employment,' and concluded his importunity by slyly telling the Maharaja that the 'Sahib [Forster] goes to bed with me.' The response of the Maharaja was: 'How dare you?'

The famous annual *Gokul Ashtami* festival of eight days arrived in August (1921) and Forster observed the festival from close quarters with his wondering eyes, sometimes himself participating in it, though he felt himself an insider in the it, and even '"walked barefoot in petticoats through the streets with black and red powders smeared over my forehead, cheek and nose'"(*op. cit.,* 317). We have said that Forster came to India for the second time with seventy pages of the manuscript of *A Passage to India* with a view to add further pages to these, but perhaps he could do either nothing or very little about the novel. Yet his pen did not lie idle, for he was writing long letters to Lily about whatever caught his attention—whatever, inside or outside the palace—about religious rites, social customs, smacks of politics, cities, people, and even about such trifflings as *itr* or *attar* (perfume) and *pan* (betel leaf). These letters constitute most of *The Hill of Devi,* published in 1953. Forster's experiences of the *Gokul Ashtami* festival was very important for him; for, as he thought, it comprised both spirituality and mundaneity; and so it was a complete ideal with its contrarieties, as against the fragmentary ideal of Christianity that allows only spirituality and ignores the other. The followers of Christianity, the English that is, he further thought, were an incomplete race: '"By sacrificing good taste,' he would write, 'this worship [of *Gokul Ashtami*] achieved what Christianity has shirked; the inclusion of merriment. All spirit as well as matter must participate in salvation, and if practical jokes are banned the circle is incomplete.' That is why, he now understood, for the English the circle would be—forever—incomplete" (*op. cit.,* 318). Forster understood that salvation can be achieved only through love in which spirituality and mundaneity mingle, and to him, the *Gokul Ashtami* festival was an exemplary demonstration of his conviction. And this may be one of the reasons why he wrote the Temple part of *A Passage to India* where the *Gokul Ashtami* festival looms large. Forster's observation of the festival was a big harvest of his six months' stay in Dewas.

Another great harvest of his from Dewas was his new realisation of Heraclitean flux, of eternal and all-pervading flux of the creation, which is also noticeable in *A Passage to India.* During his stay for six months in Dewas, he saw in and out of the palace continual "'building, decorations, repairs, drainings and diggings were going on in every direction'" (*ibid.*). "The inherent restlessness of life in the palace, of the very fabric of the palace itself, became, for Morgan [Forster] an image of India and of humanity. When, he wrote about *A Passage to India* that 'It's about something wider than politics, about the search of the human race for a more lasting home...,' he was not only defining the theme that had obsessed him throughout his life—'no resting place'—he was making the Maharaja and his home a symbol of eternal flux" (*ibid.*). In October, 1921, Forster witnessed another Hindu religious festival—the *Dessera,* which "traditionally, marked the return of the cold weather, when warfare might begin again, and it celebrated the nation's possessions and its military might" (Furbank, II, 96). But the *Dessera* is actually the celebration of the victory of god *Rama* over *Ravana* or the force of evil. In any case, Forster could not make anything very significant out of the *Dessera* festival. However, after spending a little more than six months—from March to October, 1921—Forster resigned his post, and "booked his return passage for early in January [1922], planning to spend a week or two with Mohammed [el Adl] in Egypt" (*op. cit.*, II, 103).

During his second visit to India, Forster very rarely moved away from Dewas, probably and partly because this time, unlike in the previous occasion, he was in service and not a tourist. He visited the old Mughal city of Mandu, about 250 miles south-west of Dewas. He then went to Hyderabad at the end of October, 1921, with the express wish of meeting his dear friend Masood, and there he passed a few happy days with him and his family. It may be said here that Forster liked to be close to the other members of the family of his homosexual partner. The January of 1922 came by and Forster boarded a ship bound for England, and on 23rd of the same month reached Port Said, and there at Helovan also passed a few happy days with Mohammed el Adl, his previous homosexual partner, and his wife Gamila, and eventually within a couple of days reached England to meet his mother Lily who must have been so long anxiously waiting for him. On the return voyage, Forster's ship briefly touched Marseilles in France, on the coast of the Mediterranean Sea, and he landed there and bought a copy of Proust's *Du Cote de Chez Swann* and read it with excitement on board the boat. Forster's second visit to India, compared to his first, was far shorter and far less extensive, but far more informing about India and far more contributive towards the making of his by far the best novel, *A Passage to India:* The "Court life at Dewas, the complexities of character of H.H., were not the inspiration; it was being in India, observing it as an insider" (Beauman, 317). And without being an insider he certainly could not write *A Passage to India* as it is.

(13)

Coming back to England, Forster felt the urgent and heavy burden of finishing the novel on hand: *A Passage to India.* His Indian experiences, on two occasions, made him confident about this novel, and yet he could not gather momentum to complete it: and so was feeling depressed for reasons better known to him, though certainly the death of Mohammed el Adl (who died of consumption) and the loss of the opportunity of frequently meeting with Masood (who was then in India with no sign of returning to England) added to his depression. Crestfallen, he went to Leonard Woolf for some vitalising effect, and Woolf wisely told him to complete the novel, arguing that though Forster was not sure about the fate of the novel yet he should finish it "regardless whether it could be published or not, for if he did not do so, he could never be sure it was a failure" (Furbank, II, 106). Leonard Woolf's advice worked, and Forster's writing slowly advanced. On another occasion, in the house of the Woolfs, Virginia Woolf advised him to read one or two novels by Proust. Forster took her advice too and was immensely benefitted thereby—the influence of Proust is quite noticeable in *A Passage to India.*

Forster's confidence about the prospect of his Indian novel, after the spell of his depression was over within months, was reinforced by "several admirers of Forster—testifying to their love and admiration for his books [his earlier novels]" (*op. cit.,* II, 107). *The Times* also paid him tribute. Consequently, he began to write the novel bravely and faster: "He pressed on doggedly with the writing, wanting at times to 'spit or scream like a maniac,' and by mid-May he was able to show some two-thirds of the novel to Arnold's [Edward Arnold, the publisher], who were enthusiastic" (*ibid.*). But all these could in no way abate his grief due to the death of Mohammed el Adl: he could not forget the line Mohammed wrote in a letter to him, 'I think we shall meet each other if not in the world it will be in the heaven.' During this time, *i.e* in 1922, Forster's *Alexandria: A History and a Guide* was published, which worked as a palliative balm over his lascerated heart. While he was assiduously trying to complete the novel, inspite of his sorrow for Mohammed, he was all the while haunted by the British empire's misdeeds and chauvinism in Turkey, India and other places, shadows of which misdeeds may be found in *A Passage to India.* In May, 1923, Forster's *Pharos and Pharillon,* which he wrote during his stay in Egypt, was published, and this added to his confidence as a writer, and to his fame.

It was an inborn trait of Forster to be happy to be of help to others, and during this period an opportunity came to him to help the twenty-six-year-old budding writer J.R. Ackerley ('Joe') who 'had fought on the Western Front as a junior officer, had been wounded and taken prisoner, and had subsequently been interned in Switzerland.' Ackerley was almost an unknown poet, and Forster published an article, about a poem of Ackerley's entitled 'Ghosts' in the *London Mercury* in April, 1922, and thereby promoted the poet's flimsy fame and reinforced his confidence. Forster went further in the way of Ackerley's advancement; he frantically corresponded with the authorities of Chhatrapur for the post of the private secretary to the Maharaja of Chhatrapur, as a consequence of which Ackerley got the opportunity of joining the post in October, 1923. Though there was a large gap between the ages of the two, they became like friends.

At this time, yet another person came to Forster to be his friend, though Forster, particularly after the death of Mohammed el Adl, desired no more friendship, at least for the time being. This person was Sebastian Sprott. "Sprott, the son of a country solicitor, was by now twenty-five and was studying psychology in Cambridge, having done some war-service before going to the University. Forster had got to know him through the Apostles [the members of the Cambridge Conversazione Society], and by the time that he did so, Sprott was already well known in Bloomsbury, the friend and lover of Maynard Keynes and an intimate of Lady Ottoline Morrell. Outwardly he was almost an 'exquisite': he fluttered, dressed elegantly and spoke in very Bloomsbury accents—the voice shooting up and down the scale or suddenly pouncing on some selected words. His style was, in a way, misleading, for his true wish was not for a 'gilded' Cambridge existence but for a hearty, egalitarian, sexually promiscuous low-life. A year or two later, being then a lecturer in psychology at Nottingham University, he had taken a house in a slum and had made for himself a largely working-class circle of friends, half of them regularly in and out of jail. "Sprott was a tender-hearted, loquacious and impractical young man, facing the world with a frown of pretended truculence. His comic insouciance made Forster laugh a good deal. There was never an 'affair' between them, but from the first Forster felt a kind of protectiveness towards him, regarding him as too harebrained to make a success of his career. Sprott, who was open-handed, was constantly hard up, and quite soon Forster was making him an allowance—something in the order of Pound 100 a year. Sprott developed a great loyalty and affection towards Forster and, to amuse him, would write him long picaresque accounts of his escapades and seductions: they were some of the few letters that Forster, an habitual burner of letters, never destroyed. One, belonging to the later 1920s, runs: 'And now for a warning, Forster old chap—don't you ever use a heap of chaff as a double bed. It is a long story...'"(*op. cit.,* II, 118-119).

As told earlier, Forster, during 1923, was frantically working on *A Passage to India,* with a determination to finish it at the earliest. In 1920 Masood wrote an article on 'Some Aspects of Urdu Poetry' and got it published in the *Athenaeum* through the help of Forster, and Forster 'drew on it' when he was writing in *A Passage to India* about 'Aziz and his friends and their love of flowery and melancholy verse.' "Forster had much trouble with the trial *scenes* in the novel. [*A Passage to India*], not being sure of his legal detail [because Forster had very little acquaintance with the procedures of the legal system] and doubting—with reason, as it turned out—whether a case as important as that of Aziz would have been tried in a subordinate court. He wrote about it to Masood, and Masood offered to check such details throughout the novel. When Forster finally sent him the typescript, however, his [Masood's] only reply was, unhelpfully, 'It is magnificent. Do not alter a word" (*op. cit.*, II, 119)." The final pages of the novel were assisted not only by Proust and J.R. ('Joe') Ackeriey, but by T.E. Lawrence's *Seven Pillars of Wisdom (ibid.)*. Proust, we may recall, Virginia Woolf advised Forster to read, and Forster, perhaps, always remembered Woolf while writing *A Passage to India,* as may be guessed from the brief dialogue between Mrs Moore and her son (Ronny) in chapter 3 of the novel. While the play 'Cousin Kate' was being enacted in the Bridge Party, Mrs Moore, not being able to enjoy the play, left the party and went to see the mosque. Finding her absent in the party at its close, and afterwards discovering her at a distance from the party, her son asked her when she went away from the party (while the play was being presented). Mrs. Moore replied: 'Between the acts.' Her answer of course refers to the interval between two succeeding Acts of 'Cousin Kate,' but her answer may also subtlety allude to Woolf's last novel *Between the Acts* (posthumously published in 1941). And though Forster was helped by Lawrence's *Seven Pillars of Wisdom,* after finishing his novel he sympathetically criticised Lawrence's style. However, *A Passage to India* was completed in January, 1924, and was 'due to appear on 4 June, 1924,' and Forster thought "an era of his life was over" (Beauman, 332).

Meanwhile news came from Abinger of the death of Aunt Laura, causing much grief to Forster. Coming out of the grief, he witnessed, 'with excitement' the trial of the Amritsar case in which Sir Michael O' Dwyer was charged with blindly massacring 379 innocent souls and wounding 1208 others at Jallianwala Bagh, through the agency of General Dyer, on 13 April, 1919. After the publication of *A Passage to India,* Forster 'had been assailed by doubts and despairs about this novel, but its reception removed all his fears.' Middleton Murry predicted that Forster would never write another novel, and the prediction proved true. *A Passage to India* was published in 1924 and Forster died in 1970, and during the long intervening period of forty-six years he did not write even a single novel. The reasons of his giving up novel-writing may be many, or it may be one—we do not know, let alone the reasons themselves. P.N. Furbank says that Forster "was of the type defined by Freud as 'Those wrecked by success': that he was one of those who, on realizing their dearest wishes, are afflicted and inhibited by superstitious fears—the fears in his case taking the form of a conviction of sterelity" (Furbank, II, 131).

But there may be some other and more potent reasons behind Forster's relinquishing novel-writing after *A Passage to India.* Firstly, Forster "himself sometimes gave a much more practical reason for giving up novel-writing: namely, that, being a homosexual, he grew bored with writing about marriage and the relation of men and women" (*op. cit.*, 132). Secondly, he felt frustrated when his *Maurice* was rejected by some publishers. Thirdly, he thought that his purpose, that of writing in favour of homosexuality, had quite been served through all his novels, including *A Passage to India,* and so he did not feel there was anything more to say about that subject. Fourthly and lastly, says P.N. Furbank, there is another 'consideration' "and that is that Forster was one of those who have 'only one novel to write.' I don't mean this in the vulgar sense that he repeated himself: I mean that he received his whole inspiration—a vision, a kind of plot, a message—all at once, in early manhood. He became an artist because of that early experience, an experience of salvation, and his inspiration as a novelist always harked back to that moment of enlightenment. For this reason he was content to use and re-use many of the same plot-materials: for instance the jaded traveller unable (for what reason he cannot tell) to respond to the scenes he or she has come to visit; or the picnic or party of pleasure invaded by panic forces. (Mrs Moore in *A Passage to India* is, again, clearly a reworking and elaboration of Mrs Wilcox in *Howards End.*) For the same reason, the social types and manners which ruled his imagination were those of his Edwardian youth. This was no small difficulty for a realistic novelist, though it would not have arisen for a poet. He already found it so with *A Passage to India,* and evidently it was bound to grow with every year or decade" (*op. cit.,* II, 132-33). Nicola Beauman writes that when Forster really stopped writing novels, critics, generally, were of the opinion that being fundamentally an Edwardian novelist, Forster could not write any more in the changed aspects of the new society and new *Zeit Geist* after the First World War. But, Beauman is of the opinion that all Forster's novels are essentially modern. In any case, no one should feel cock-sure about a single cause behind Forster's stopping of novel-writing. In addition to the supposed causes, we may add yet another and no less potent one. In May, 1922, Mohammed el Adl died, causing much grief to Forster, and this grief continued to lurk around him for a quite long time, changing his life and thoughts phenomenally.

(14)

Forster's homosexual drive did not abate yet, perhaps also never afterwards. During 1925, the relationship between Forster and Ackerley deepened: they became very intimate, though not lovers. Through Ackerley, Forster came to be friendly with Harry Daley, and their friendship "eventually became an affair [homosexual affair]" (*op. cit.*, II, 141). However, inspite of his acute and nagging homosexual drive, and inspite of his saying good-bye to writing novels, Forster could not keep him away from the field of literature. In the spring of 1926, he 'received an invitation from Trinity College in Cambridge to give the annual Clark Lectures.' He accepted the invitation gladly because it was a matter of prestige, and gave a series of eight lectures on novel between January and March of 1927. The lectures "were very much in a 'Bloomsbury' style—anti-academic, playful, full of odd, brilliant metaphoric flights—and he exploited his habitual simplifying technique, presenting complex matters in the homeliest and most 'bread-and-butter' terms. He was by now a very experienced platform-performer, and the lectures, and their manner—grave, charming, precise, but roll of little surprises of *nuance* and inflection—made a great hit with his Cambridge audience. Audiences grew larger and larger, and by the concluding lecture he was reporting to T.E. Lawrence that the series had been the greatestsuccess and his 'constant rise to fame' had impeded him from letter-writing" (*op. cit.*, II, 144). On the strength of the success of these lectures, Forster was offered by King's College a three-year fellowship, and he gladly accepted it. The eight lectures were published in the same year in book form with the title *Aspects of the Novel.*

In the autumn of 1928, Masood, with his two sons Anwar and Akbar, arrived in England and stayed at West Hackhurst. Recently he divorced his wife Zohra. Lily and Forster were much taken with the two charming boys of Masood—the elder aged thirteen and the younger eleven. With Forster's help Masood got them admitted in Perse School in Cambridge. Forster was now stand-offish with Cambridge, and even with literature—he was engrossedly reading Eddington's *The Nature of the Physical World* and was hazarding bizzare hypotheses as to some problems of physics and philosophy. "In a Commonplace Book, began a year or two before [*i.e.* around 1927 or 1928], he made on 5 January 1929 a long entry on Eddington, saying that he wanted to record, 'like the extra sounds one catches immediately after one's ear is squirted out,' his first sensations on realizing that matter was not solid, that one knew everything through measurements only, that his own 'spasmodic instincts and confusions about Time' had a value, and that one thing only—the quantum—had existence in the physical world" (*op. cit.,* II, 158). Sort of Leibnitzian philosophy of space and time, indeed; but does this have any relevance to Adela's (*A Passage to India,* chapter 22) speculation: 'In space things touch, in time things part'?

In 1929 an opportunity happened to Forster to go to South Africa. The British Association organised a cruise voyage for four to five hundred scientists, and it invited him to join the team, and he accepted the invitation hesitatingly, because he feared he would feel like a fish out of water, he being perhaps the singular non-scientist, in so large a crowd of scientists. The big party set off in late June, wanting to stop at the Cape, then in Johannesburg, then in Rhodesia, then in Zanzibar, and then in Kenya. Doing as they wanted, the party reached Florence in Italy. Throughout the tour Forster was deficient in spirit, and even his earlier wished-for Florence could not inject spirit into his soul: "though he loved Florence, he now, intermittently, found her a bore—too voluble, too appreciative, too high-minded and sentimental" (*op. cit.*, II, 160). Throughout the voyage, Forster had had only 'a few intense experiences', one of them being in St Helena. "This strange island, so rocky and inhospitable but inhabited by gentle birds and gentle people, captured his imagination" (*ibid.*). Africa, however, could not provide him with pleasure, because he was extremely saddened by the sorry plight of the peoples there; but, on his way back home, when the party stopped in France, he got some moments of pleasure—"he had an enjoyable sexual escapade with a French sailor, named Achille, in Toulon" (*op. cit.*, II, 161). Back home, Forster was passionately drawn to Bob Buckingham, and 'the two went to bed together,' and Forster was now 'confident that he had found a lasting friendship,' at last, in Bob Buckingham. Forster's love of Bob was the most intense, and this was so because Bob's love of Forster was also so.

(15)

The Forster family, the family that comprised only two closely knit souls—Lily and Forster—now settled in Hammersmith. Forster liked the green pasture around Abinger Hammer (in Hammersmith) which lies in the countryside in Stevenage, which place was later on very appropriately named 'Forster Country.' Forster was now a well recognised and respected literary figure, and this fetched him enviable invitations. He was associated with the B.B.C. since 1928, and now the B.B.C. invited him to broadcast fortnightly book-reviews, and since October, 1932, requested him to broadcast book-talks, 'alternating week by week with G.K. Chesterton.' For a quite long time back, Forster had been a 'temperate' member of the P.E.N. (association of Poets, Essayists and Novelists), and now he was invited by the P.E.N. for the third time to be its president, because of his being scandalised by some members of the association. In 1934, he was invited by the National Council for Civil Liberties to be its president, and he accepted the invitation.

In 1931, the Rumanian P.E.N. invited Forster to go to Bucharest, and he accepted the invitation and reached Rumania in the June of that year. The Rumanian P.E.N. gave a dinner in his honour, and in it he felt slightly low when he came to understand that "none of those present had actually read, or even, it seemed, heard of his novels" (*op. cit.,* II, 174). From Rumania he alone went to Cracow, where he met with a Polish lady, Mrs Myslakowska, who, in 1938, published a Polish translation of *A Passage to India.* She was "young, large and beautiful' and wanted to fall in love with Forster because she was contemplating a divorce with her draconian husband. Once she actually proposed marriage to Forster, but the mysogynist Forster avoided the proposal. A few weeks after this, Mrs Myslakowska came to England. "Forster was by now somewhat nervous, but he invited her to West Hackhurst; and during a walk in his wood, she vigorously repeated the marriage-proposal—also alarming him by suggesting they lie down under the trees. He found himself in an awkward situation; and it was made worse by the fact that Lily had taken a great fancy to their visitor. She sang her praises so loudly, Forster himself suggested she wanted to marry him off" (*op. cit.,* II, 175). The mysogynist Forster managed to extricate himself from that cumbersome situation honourably and all at the same time could continue his friendship with Mrs Myslakowska.

In 1932, Lowes Dickinson died, causing much grief to Forster. Forster paid his debt of friendship to Dickinson by writing his biography *Goldsworthy Lowes Dickinson* which was published in 1934. The year in which Dickinson died, Forster struck friendship with a number of young novelists, including William Plomer and Christopher Isherwood, and one day invited William Somerset Maugham and Herbert Read to have tea with himself and the young novelists. In April, 1932 Joe Ackerley's book *Hindoo Holiday,* that contained his experiences at Chhatrapur, came out of the press to receive warm welcome from Evelyn Waugh, who wrote about the book that it was "difficult to control one's enthusiasm and praise it temperately" (*op. cit.,* II, 180). The relation between Forster and Siegfried Sassoon also grew closer. In 1934, Ronald Kidd, a free-lance journalist, founded the National Council for Civil Liberties, perhaps a 'crypto-communist' organisation, and Forster was chosen as its first president. Not very long after the foundation of the Council, the National Government brought a Bill to ban circulation of communist journals among soldiers. The Bill contradicted the objective of the Council. Forster protested against the Bill by regularly writing articles in *Time and Tide* (in a series called 'Notes on the Way'). "Forster's *Time and Tide* articles had, in his own phrase, given him a 'pulpit' and from now on he was to be much heard and listened to on political and social issues" (*op. cit.*, II 190). Many supposed the Council to be an out-fit of the communists, and to drive away any such suspicion he tried to bring into the Council right-wing and non-committed persons, as members.

In the spring of 1935, Forster was invited to head the British deligation to an International Congress of Writers in Paris. Many writers of a number of countries were to attend the Congress: Gorki, Pasternak, Babel, Breton, Leonard and Virginia Woolf, Priestley, Lehmann, Gide, Malraux, Bernard Shaw, Aldous Huxley, and others. The five-day Congress was opened on 21 June at Palais de la Mutualite, and it was attended by 2,000 odd persons. Politics soon surfaced in the Congress, and divided the writers into two conflicting camps: the communists and the non-communists. Gide harangued to drive the audience to his point that "'individuals and their peculiarities can best flourish in a communist society' and prophesying a day 'when great literature could be made not, as till now, out of man's sufferings, but out of their joy'" (*op. cit.*, II, 195). The Congress, inspite of all its fanfares, was a sorry failure, mainly due to the political wranglings that it could only evoke. Bernard Shaw was averse to such futile, impotent, anarchist and anti-totalitarian intellectual fair.

(16)

Since their coming to Abinger, in West Hackhurt, Lily and Forster were leading a pastoral life of sorts, in all happiness—the two clinging to each other most of the whiles. They developed friendship with their neighbours of the sparsely populated area, particularly with one William King and his wife. Forster was a great lover of trees and pastures, and oftentimes used to undertake long walks through them with Ernest Read, a local butcher's son, with whom he became friendly. In 1934, the local village folk planned to stage a pageant 'in aid of the church-restoration fund' and 'under the auspices of the Farrers of Abinger Hall (the family with whom many years before Lily had been a governess).' A committee was formed for the pageant with Lord Farrer (Thomas Cecil Farrer, 2nd Baron) at its head, and the pageant was to be staged on the grounds of the Abinger Hall. Forster task was to write the speeches and the programme notes—which speeches were published in 1936 as *The Abinger Pageant*. The pageant was staged on July 14 and July 18 of the same year, under the direction of Tom Harrison and as per his conception. The principal scenarios or tableaux were: "ancient Britons in skins gathering fuel in the Abinger woods; a cry of 'Romans, the Romans!'; arrival of the Saxons and of the Normans; the news of the Spanish Armada brought to Abinger, and so on" (*op. cit.*, II, 198). Tom Harrison suggested, and Forster gladly accepted, that there should be a 'Pageant of Trees' (a tableau of trees) at the beginning of the whole Pageant, and the Woodman in the 'Pageant of Trees' began his prologue, written by Forster, thus: 'Welcome to our village and our woods.' This is ample evidence of Forster's deep love of pastures and trees.

The amiable relation between the Forsters and the Farrers did not continue for long but began to become inimical on point of property, as a result of which Lily and Forster had to face 'expulsion' from the Abinger Hall in West Hackhurst (a Surrey Ramble) by the Farrers. This bitter experience of Forster made him indignant for life about property itself. By this time Christopher Isherwood published his *The Ascent of F. 6* (co-authored by W.H. Auden) and *Mr Norris Changes Trains* and Forster was both appreciative and reservative of the latter novel. Forster sent *Maurice* to Isherwood, and 'this had helped cement their friendship.' On Isherwood persuasion, Forster went with him to Amsterdam in 1935, and there had had parlance with anti-fascist writers. In the autumn of 1935, he was selecting from his old articles for *Abinger Harvest,* with advices from William Plomer. During this time (1936) he was feeling physically weak, and went with his mother to Dover for convalescence. He was now about 57, and so age and hard work were telling upon his health. At Dover, Forster happened to be of considerable help to W.H. Auden. "Auden, the previous year (1935), had married Erika Mann, Thomas Mann's daughter, as a device to procure her a British passport, and he wanted other homosexuals to make similar marriages. ('What are buggers for?' he would say.) With Forster's help, he recruited John Simpson, arranging for him to marry a German actress friend of Erika's, Therese Giehse" (*op. cit.,* II, 213). The Second World War was now heaving up from hell. In January 1937, 10,500 Italian troops landed in Spain to trigger off the war. Forster disturbedly thought that the world was approaching the edge of hell. At home, his life was a mixed bag of devotion to, and exasperation over, his mother—exasperation, because "At eighty Lily had grown dumpy, solid and matriarchal—not a dragon, but someone whose wishes were to be obeyed" (*op. cit.,* II, 216).

The year 1937 was also an unlucky year for Forster, because in this year, within the space of only six months, he lost two of his sterling Indian friends: Masood, and Tukoji, the now-deposed Maharaja of Dewas. In the Urdu journal *Anjuman-e-Taraqqi-e-Urdu,* Forster, by way of paying tribute to Masood, wrote about him: "'There never was anyone like him,.'.. 'and there never will be anyone like him'" (*op. cit.,* II, 219). And in *The Times* Forster wrote about Tukoji (Sir Tukoji Rao Puar): "he possessed incomparable qualities as an individual: he was witty, gay, charming, hospitable, imaginative, and devoted, and he had above all a living sense of religion which enabled him to transcend the barriers of his creed and to make contact with all the forms of belief and disbelief. I am not the only English person who will mourn 'Bapu Sahib,' as we call him, and who will never forget his vivid and unique personality or cease to remember him with love" (*op. cit.,* II, 220-21).

Forster's illness, which ensued in 1936, did not leave him even in 1937, and so he resigned the presidentship of the National Council for Civil Liberties, and his works for the Permanent Bureau of Malraux's *Writers in Defence of Culture* slowed down. But inspite of illness, he 'agreed to take part in an *entretien* organized by the League of Nation's Committee for Intellectual Co-operation,' in the summer of 1937.' This was the body which Bernard Shaw had advised him to exploit; it had been conceived early in the 1920s by Henri Bergson, to be an expression of 'the deepest spirit of the League' and recently had been taken up with enthusiasm by Gilbert Murray, who had become president" (*op. cit.,* II, 221). In the summer of 1937, Forster delivered a speech written in French, in the Committee, on the theme of the special situation of the writer. His point was that the writer had a 'double duty': to 'promote general welfare' and 'to express his own personality.'

In the spring of 1938, Forster was invited by the *Nation,* of New York, to write a series of articles on the general theme: 'Living Philosophies.' He accepted the invitation and wrote some articles, the first of which was "originally called Two Cheers for Democracy' and later 'What I Believe'" (*op. cit.,* II, 224). The articles were 'a comprehensive statement of his beliefs.' Forster was not an academic philosopher, but he said that he was 'trying to construct a philosophy.' In the articles, or in 'What I Believe,' Forster made two very stunning and disturbing comments. The one runs thus: "I hate the idea of dying for a cause, and if I had to choose between betraying my country and betraying my friend, I hope I should have the guts to betray my country" (George Allen and Unwin, 43). And the other thus: "I believe in aristocracy though—if that's the right word, and if a democrat may use it. Not an aristocracy of power, based upon rank and influence, but an aristocracy of the sensitive, the considerate, and the plucky" (*op. cit.,* II, 47). These two comments, for the while, shook the comfortable foundations of both the nationalist capitalists and the Marxists, such that they could not immediately decide how to butt Forster. The European war (the Second World War) was now about to be kick-started, and Forster wrote to Isherwood that he 'was afraid of going mad,' but Isherwood wrote in his diary that Forster was 'the last person who'd ever go mad.' According to Isherwood, Forater was now 'a symbol and a hero.' Isherwood's description of the Forster of 1938, when Forster was around 59, and earned immense respect for himself, is striking. Isherwood wrote: "'Well—my 'England' is E.M. [Forster]; the anti-heroic hero, with his straggly straw moustache, his light gay blue baby-eyes and his elderly stoop. Instead of a folded umbrella or a brown uniform, his emblames are his tweed cap (which is too small for him) and the odd-shaped brown paper parcels in which he carries his belongings from country to town and back again'" (Furbank, II, 229).

(17)

The Second World War broke out in September, 1939, and Forster pessimistically took to journalism. He thought anti-Semitism as the worst of all evils. Like Forster, Isherwood also by now became a pacifist. Isherwood "under the influence of Heard and Heard's *guru,* the Vedantist monk Prabhavananda, (he had) began a conversion to Hindu mystical beliefs" (*op. cit.,* II, 237). But, inspite of Isherwood's nagging persuasions, Forster could not realise that there was any substance in mysticism. In 1941, he was engaged by the B.B.C. "to give regular weekly or fortnightly talks to India. Forster talked mainly about books; and, reflecting that Indians would have had English literature stuffed down their throats, he devoted as much time as he could to continental literature" (*op. cit,* II, 240-41). During 1942-43, many members complained that the National Council for Civil Liberties was being run by some disguised communist members of the Council, and Forster was, inspite of himself, drawn into the wrangle between the two categories of members. Forster was, in reality, a liberal, a pacifist, an egalitarian perhaps, but never a communist in the orthodox sense of the term. He felt bothered by the wrangling, and yet, after the death of H.W. Nevinson 'he briefly resumed the Presidency' of the Council in 1943.

In the same year Lionel Trilling, a great American critic, wrote a book on Forster, in which he lionised the novelist, and consequently there grew a considerable number of American friends of Forster. In the preceeding year, Forster did a little 'war work.' "He served on the Dorking Refugee Committee and, during most of 1942, attended each week at a local Searchlight Unit to lead discussions with the soldiers. For some time, too, he helped a friend, Mrs. King the builder's wife, give a weekly party for Italian prisoners of war" (*op. cit.,* II, 250). Forster's popularity in America continued to grow. The famous American actor William Roerick came to London in 1943 for a show called *This is the Army* and reverentially presented Forster with 'chocolate, soap, lemon-essence, American books and tickets for his show.' During the time, Forster and Max Beerbohm became fast friends, each being attracted to the other's writings. In the summer of 1944, German bombs fell on Abinger, but Forster and Lily remained unruffled, or rather remained stoical. Forster, even in that deadly situation, kept busy in literary affairs. But next year, *i.e.* in 1945, the greatest blow of Forster came to him: on 11th March of that year, Lily breathed her last. She was ninety and fell ill in the early days of March, 1945. "On 5 March she would not get up; a day or two later she had a fall from her bed; and then early in the night of 10 March she had another fall. Forster slept for the rest of this night in the passage outside her bedroom, and the next day they had a tender farewell conversation. Lily said: I shan't be long with you, to which he replied, 'But your love will.' At 1.30 p.m., as he was giving her some beef broth from a spoon, she fell back and was dead" (*op. cit.,* II, 255). Forster was certainly full of sorrow at the death of his mother, but all at the same time he felt for the first time a sense of freedom, and this was because there had been going on a love-hate relationship of sorts between the mother and the son. This is apparent from an entry in his diary. In the October of the year in which Lily died (1945), Forster came to India to attend a conference of PEN, and on his return voyage he wrote in the diary two astonishingly contradictory sentences: "The only first-class thing about me now is my grief." and "Thanks to her Lily's disappearance, (and my own fame,) I have had this outing at the age of sixty-six" (Beauman, 364-65). Both the sentences are saddled with bitter irony. Nevertheless he was drowned in deep despair, and to overcome it he resorted to 'erotic fantasies.'

(18)

In 1945, as told just now, Forster came to India for the third and last time, this time principally to attend a PEN conference in Jaipur. He set out on 5th October 'leaving a spray of honeysuckle on his mother's pillow' and in due course reached Bombay, and then from there went to Delhi where he put up with the novelist Ahmed Ali, author of *Twilight in Delhi* (1940) and a distant relative of Masood. Now, Forster was in India "a public figure, a famous Englishman, feted and interviewed, and expected to give talks and broadcasts, and to sign autograph-books, wherever he went" (Furbank, II, 260). He preached to the people the necessity of discarding *purdah,* like Aziz in *A Passage to India.* From Delhi he went to the Jaipur PEN conference which was attended by 'a thousand or more' literateures. "On the platform with Forster were the Prime Minister of Jaipur and Mrs Sorojini Naidu, famous as a poet and associate of Gandhi ('loveliest of toads,' Forster called her in his diary)" (*op. cit.,* II, 261). From Jaipur he came to Calcutta with Ahmed Ali and put up in the home of one Hashim Ali. He came to Bengal which "was the home of nationalist politics and also of the Tagore cult, neither of which attracted him" (*ibid.*). The city of Calcutta also could not attract him—Calcutta 'seemed to him quite desolating.' Forster spent ten days there 'attending official functions and meeting innumerable writers, half of whom he suspected to be gate-crashers.' But he enjoyed the paintings of Jamini Roy and Gopal Ghosh. He opened an exhibition of the paintings of Jamini Roy in London next year. While in Calcutta, Forster became friendly with Gopal Ghosh and Jamini Roy, and Ghosh 'gave him a drawing he much liked.'

From Calcutta, Forster went to Shantiniketan, the University (Visva-Bharati) or 'Home of Peace' founded by Tagore in 1901. Forster wrote about Shantiniketan that it 'really is an agreeable place,' but he was not impressed by the educational standard there. Alas! only four years ago Tagore died! To his hosts in Shantiniketan, Forster charmingly said: "I am not here to pass any verdict on India nor do I fortunately carry the white man's burden on my shoulder. All that I carry round my neck is the pleasant light burden of a lovely garland of marigold, which I feel, is the symbol of your love and friendship" (Dutta, 11). From Shantiniketan, Forster went to Hyderabad, and there he visited the famous Ajanta caves and enjoyed the Buddhist frescoes on the walls of the caves, about which he wrote: "the paintings have fused sadness with interest in the outer world,...The paintings (caves 1 & 2) have not been overpraised, and have gone further towards fusion than the Italian 14th & 15th cent art to which it is natural to compare them. They are not mystic—geese, Bhils, elephants eating lotus, do not go wispy. But they have found a connection (unconscious) between my two worlds" (Furbank, II, 262-63). And from Hyderabad he went back to Bombay to stay there for about a mouth in the house of Mrs Wadia, the Secretary of the All-India PEN. This time he was fascinated by Bombay of which he wrote to Sprott that the city was 'grand, fascinating and Levantine.' In Bombay, he attended several literary functions, including one of the Gujrat Vernacular Society in which he delivered a lecture. Inspite of all these and inspite of all warm receptions from India, he now felt himself no more worthy than an empty 'shell.' On 30th December, 1945, he took a plane bound for London, and on board the plane he 'meditated a little sadly: "I have failed to do what I might. The only first class thing about me now is my grief.... The day after tomorrow shall be 67 [he would turn 67]. O lovely world, teach others to expound you as I have not been able to do!" (*op. cit.*, II, 263).

Coming back home, Forster received an invitation from the Provost of King's College to receive an Honorary Fellowship. He was highly gratified, and in his acceptance letter he casually remarked that he 'would soon be homeless, so that it would be pleasant to feel he had some connection some where.' At this the college proffered him further honour: the college 'asked him if he would like to come and "reside" in the College.'

Forster gladly accepted this offer also, and accordingly moved to King's College to live there for the remainder of his life. In February, 1946, he was invited by the economist Keynes, 'who was the chairman of the Covent Garden Opera Trust,' to witness the *premiere* of *The Sleeping Beauty,* and he happily responded to the invitation. In 1947, Forster revived his connection with the Apostles Society, and also 'began a little college teaching in English literature' in King's College.

On 14 April, 1947, Forster boarded a plane to go to the United States, with two purposes: to deliver his Harvard lectures and to extensively tour over the whole of the American continent. His friend Roerick received him at the New York airport, and soon introduced him to the painter Jared French. Roerick read Forster's Harvard lecture and advised him to reconstruct it, and that Forster candidly did. The three-day Harvard symposium was to be held on 1st, 2nd and 3rd May, but before that Forster was interviewed by a journalist of the *New Yorker*. The journalist wrote about him: "'We found him a shy, apprehensive Edwardian gentleman of sixty-eight, with a long sensitive nose and tousled tan mustache,'" (*op. cit.,* II, 271). Forster told the journalist that the 'Americans had been "awfully kind" to his books.' He was the 'star performer and opening speaker' of the Harvard symposium, and he spoke on 'The Raison D' Etre of Criticism in the Arts.' At Harvard, Forster was the guest of Professor Finlay who gave a reception to him and T.S. Eliot in their honour, after the symposium. During the reception, the "two writers took up position in front of the fireplace, but very soon a vociferous group had collected round Eliot, and had pinned him down on a sofa, for questioning, leaving Forster more or less deserted. An eyewitness, George Martin, recalled that Forster was quite unabashed, looking on at the scene with amusement. Martin and he exchanged glances. He came over. And, while Harry Levin was grilling Eliot on his Theory of Language, Forster made mild chit-chat about travel in America" (*op. cit.,* II, 272).

And now actually Forster began his travel, and on his first leg he stopped in Colorado, and from there travelled to Berkeley, in California. He found the West 'makeshift and rootless.' From Berkeley he travelled a long distance by train, across the Rockies, the Salt Lake City, the Great Plains and the city of Chicago, and then reached Ontario, whose scenic beauty impressed him awfully. "He had been awed, too, by Boulder Dam, which had given him 'a vision of a transformed world'; and by a contrasting spectacle in the Arizona desert—an array of obsolete aircraft, thousand upon thousand of them, awaiting destruction. 'When you reflect that each plane carries a wireless set which will also be destroyed,' he wrote, 'you begin to realize the other side of the Spirit of America—the Spirit of Waste.' Certain oddities and surprises stayed with him as well: the five separate locks on his host's (Professor Morton Dauwen Zabel's) door in Chicago; a lady Saint reeling drunk in the streets of Salt Lake City: and the chambermaid in the hotel there, who told him, when he offered her a tip, 'I dont like to take your money, brother, you need it more than I do'" (*op. cit.*, II, 274).

There in the United States Forster responded to many other invitations. He also acquainted himself with the great American critic Lionel Trilling and his wife Diana, and by both of them he was much charmed. During this time, Forster came by some homosexual stories by the twenty-eight-year-old Donald Windham, a friend of the painter Paul Cadmus with whom he was earlier acquainted. Forster was impressed by the stories, and asked Cadmus to introduce himself to Windham who lived in New York. Some years afterwards Forster wrote an Introduction to Windham's collection of poems *The Warm Country*, in which he supported Windham's view about the essentiality of the flesh in love: "He knows that human beings are not statues but contain flesh and blood and a heart, and he believes that creatures so constituted must contact one another or they will decay" (*op. cit.*, II, 275). The Indian ambassador to the U.S.A., Asaf Ali, an old acquaintance of Forster, invited him to go to Washington and live with him for some days, and, accordingly, Forster spent five days in Ali's residence, in June, 1947. After spending three months in America, Forster came back to London, boarding a plane on 12th July. America pleased him much "He had felt he had 'had the America he wanted' and reflected, gratefully, how much he had been cosseted by his American friends—perhaps too much for his own good" (*op. cit.,* II, 276).

(19)

From America, Forster returned to King's College, Cambridge—his makeshift home—a 'home' for a rootless but famous and economically solvent person, with numerous friends but no family—no wife, no children.' In 1947, he was a bachelor aged about 68. As age advances, people generally and gradually relinquish their engagements. But Forster's case was different: on the one hand, his "daily post was enormous: there poured in invitations and requests for interviews, letters of praise or abuse from strangers, begging letters, business letters (for he employed no agent), theses on him sent for his comments, or books sent, unsolicited, for him to autograph" (*op. cit.*, II, 277); and on the other hand, he consented to write a libretto, *Billy Budd*, along with Eric Crozier, and he wanted to publish his Indian memoirs (*The Hill of Devi*) and his views about society politics and civics (*Two Cheers for Democracy*). Consequently, inspite of himself, he had to remain busy, perhaps more than before. For some years, Forster was not active in the National Council for Civil Liberties, for fear that, as his friends warned him, the Council might be a disguised podium of the communists, and ultimately in 1948 he resigned from it. In the summer of the same year Benjamin Britten invited Forster to give a lecture on George Crabbe in the first Aldeburgh Festival.

In the autumn, again of the same year, Forster fell into 'one of the acutest depressions of his life.' There were many factors in the aetiology: "He was nearly seventy, thus on the threshold of old age. He was still obsessed by his 'homelessness' and his 'expulsion' [by the Farrers] from Abinger. He felt unproductive and was living as it were, beggarly, intellectually. And, as happened from time to time, there was a hitch in his friendship with Bob Buckingham. "The perennial fear of his life, constantly dispelled and constantly returning, was that his imaginative life should dry up; but under this, and allied to it, lay a worse fear—that he should lose the power to feel about people or take interest in them. He had evoked this fear in *A Passage to India*, when depicting Mrs Moore's collapse after her visit to the Marabar caves, and it now took hold of him" (*op. cit.*, II, 282). However, the depression was quite ephemeral, and he soon got energised, particularly by Benjamin Britten's suggestion that he wrote an opera for the 1948 Festival of Britain. Forster accepted the suggestion hesitatingly, because he felt that he lacked in the theatrical technicalities, and with the help of Eric Crozier, 'an experienced librettist and man of the theatre,' ultimately wrote his only libretto *Billy Budd*, basing on Herman Melville's *Billy Budd* (1924).

In May, 1949, Forster made his second and last visit to America, with Bob Buckingham, this time the visit being very short He went there to receive an honorary degree from Hamilton College. In December, 1951, he underwent a prostrate gland operation, and after the operation Britten invited him to go to his home at Aldeburg and stay there for some time during his convalescence. Forster went to Aldeburg and lived there for some months. After that he went to Aldeburg several times and stayed with Britten. In one of these times—in June, 1951—when he was going to climb up the belfry of the parish church at Aldeburg, he fell down and broke his knee, and it took for him several months to come round. With his foot plastered, he walked on crutches: 'he was a bad invalid.' It was during this time that Forster was thinking of collecting his memories of Indian experiences and write about them, and the result was *The Hill of Devi* which was published in 1953. All at the same time, he was thinking of publishing some of his select reviews and essays in book form, and the result was *Two Cheers for Democracy* which was published in 1951.

Since 1951, there was, for some time, a spurt in his rising fame. Articles appeared about him in the *Spectator,* the *New Statesman,* the *Listener,* etc. He was being both appreciated and criticised, but appreciated for the most part. *The Concise Cambridge History of English Literature* honoured him by writing that he was 'at heart a scholar' and that he 'is the finest survival in literature, as Bertrand Russell in philosophy, of that liberal, humanist tradition of the early twentieth century against which some of the most acute intelligences of our time have directed their powers of denigration (Sampson, 869). In 1951, Forster was 72, pretty old, and Bob Buckingham, his homosexual partner, was 50, and yet the closeness between them did not go. Since 1951, the two gave a large party, each year, in which a great number of guests took part, filling the garden at Wendell Road. The curse of Forster's 'homelessness' visited him once again: 'he had to give up his rooms with the Wilkinsons in Cambridge. In lieu of them, the College gave him a bedroom.' Forster once more felt 'dispossession.' "I see my furniture everywhere, my home nowhere,' he lamented" (Furbank, II, 288).

At this time, in his advanced age, it was very natural to expect for Forster some national honours, and actually at least two or three came to him. In 1949, he was offered a knighthood, but he refused, "In 1952, however, he was approached by the Palace with the offer of a C.H. [Companion of Honour]. This seemed to him more suitable, and he accepted, remarking in his letter that he preferred honours that came after his name. The award was announced in the New Year's Honours for 1953, and he went to Buckingham Palace for the investiture the following month. It was quite a lengthy audience, in the course of which the Queen said how sad it was he had published no book for so long—upon which he politely corrected her. As he left, he brandished the insignia to an equerry, exclaiming brightly, 'Well, I got my little toy,' and was received with freezing glances. They failed to chill him, and he returned to Cambridge in a glow of loyalty, declaring that if the Queen had been a boy he would have fallen in love with her" (*op. cit.*, II, 288-89).

Forster completed the biography of his great grandmother Marianne Thornton (1765-1815), *Marianne Thornton,* by the end of 1955 and it was published in the next year. About this time, Leonard Woolf advised him to write his autobiography, but he declined to accept his advice. Forster's love of travelling did not go even in his advanced age: in 1953, he, along with P.N. Furbank, his biographer, went to Portugal for holiday making. In January, 1959, Forster turned 80, "and to mark the occasion King's College organized a large birthday luncheon in the College Hall, attended by more than a hundred guests—friends, relatives, writers and dons. Bill Roerick, Tom Coley and Edith Oliver came from France. Forster was happy and in high spirits. He heard himself referred to by the Provost, Noel Annan, as 'the greatest living Kingsman' and invited by him to 'ruminate and eminate' for long years to come" (*op. cit.,* II, 305).

In 1959, Forster paid his last visit to Italy. There he read the novel *Il Gattopardo* (*The Leopard*), by the Prince of Lampedusa, and read it in Italian and 'found it wonderful.' His activities now slowed down under the weight of age; nevertheless, in 1961, when he was 82, he wrote a review of Leonard Woolf's *Growing,* his very last reviewing, and it was published in the *Observer* on 5 November, 1961. Forster now had no doubt that his writing career was at its end, and that he had not many years to live; consequently, sadness began to settle down on him, and resignation ensued. His mental weakness also started: he found it difficult to concentrate. "He complained that his life was all in pieces and scraps, and the tone of these complaints, which were not new to him, was changing from self-rebuke to resignation" (*op. cit.,* II, 310). On 31 January, 1961, he wrote in an entry in his Commonplace Book the following very sad sentences under the heading 'Going to Bits': "This phrase describes me today and is indeed the one I have been looking for: not tragic, not mortal disintegration, only a central weakness which prevents me from concentrating or settling down. I have so wanted to write and write ahead. The phrase 'obligatory creation' has haunted me. I have so wanted to get out of my morning bath promptly: I have decided to do so beforehand, and have then laid in it as usual and watched myself not getting out. It looks as if there is a physical as well as a moral break in the orders I send out. I have plenty of interesting thoughts but keep losing them like the post cards I have written, or like my cap..." (*ibid.*).

Forster could realise, even as early as in 1961, that his days were numbered; perhaps even before that, to be precise since his falling from the belfry and breaking his knee in 1951, at the age of 72. He was so thinking about his biography, of course with much of *sprezzatura,* because he guessed that someone would attempt a *Life* [of his].' In 1960, Sprott suggested William Plomer as Forster's biographer, and accordingly Plomer began to question him about his life, and also he wrote some notes about his life for Plomer. In 1959, the Obscene Publications Act had been passed, and under this Act the Penguin Books was prosecuted for publishing D.H. Lawrence's 'unexpurgated' *Lady Chatterley's Lover,* 1960, at the Old Bailey court. Forster was summoned to appear as a witness, besides Helen Gardner and Richard Hoggart, and pleaded in favour of the novel. During the trial, when the defence counsel asked Forster 'where he would place Lawrence in literature,' he boldly replied: "'I should place him enormously high. When one comes to the upper ten novels, then one has to begin to think a little of the order, but compared with all the novels which come out, the novels he wrote dominate terrifically'" (*op. cit.,* II, 311). The Penguin Books won the case over D.H. Lawrence's *Lady Chatterley's Lover* (as in 1928 Radclyffe Hall had won in the prosecution suit over her lesbian novel *Well of Loneliness),* and Forster became elated.

William Plomer actually began writing the biography, but before long he ceased, because the 'close-knit alliance' between himself and Forster got fractured, for several reasons, the most potent ones among them being that Plomer "had grown by this time less in sympathy with some of Forster's attitudes. He had himself become religious, which created a barrier, also, he disliked Forster's indecent stories" (*op. cit.,* II, 312-13). Unfortunately for Forster, during this time Ackerley was also drifting away from him, for other reasons, including his critical and belittling views about Forster's works. Later on P.N. Furbank published a biography of Forster, his best biography, in 1977, about six years after the death of the novelist—with the title *E.M. Forster: A Life.* However, in April, 1961, Forster had had another fall and another suffering.

That month Ackerley returned from Japan and Forster went to see him in his flat at Putney when he fell on the threshold and broke his wrist at the age of 82. Three years later, he had yet another fall, or rather he collapsed due to alarming blood-deficiency. During this time he was perhaps quite sure that he was soon going to leave his 'mortal coil,' but yet he could not decide on his executorship.

(20)

Forster's last at last came, though slowly. His sight became blurred, and he became stone deaf in one year, causing much grief in him, for he could no more enjoy playing on the piano. Astonishingly, he was not afraid of his approaching end; he rather took it insouciently. Since 1962 he was almost thinking that he was no more existing in this world, that he was a stranger to himself, and perhaps this was the reason why since then he began "to try avoiding the pronoun 'I'" (*op. cit.,* II, 316). On the other hand, his generosity grew exponentially. He doled out largesses to friends and favourites. "He gave several thousand pounds to the Fitzwilliam Museum in Cambridge towards the buying of a Greek sculpture, and when the London Library, in need of funds, asked for gifts from members and well-wishers, to be auctioned at Christie's, he donated the manuscript of *A Passage to India*" (It fetched Pound 6,500, then a record price for a manuscript by a living author) (*op. cit.,* II, 316-17). In spite of all his ailments, Forster was a happy man, and was being, from time to time, 'plagued with sexual longings, but not too painfully.' In this regard, his senescence was quite contrary to that of W.B. Yeats: while there was no ebbing of the sexual drive in Forster's senescence, Yeats, disturbingly feeling that in his senescence he was going to be impotent and thereby to lose his poetic faculty, "underwent the Steinach rejuvenation operation, a kind of vasectomy supposed to restore sexual potency" (Sarker, 17).

However, there was at least one silent grief in Forster's heart: the grief due to the untimely death of his godson Robin Morgan Buckingham, son of R.J. ('Bob') Buckingham, policeman and his closest and enduring homosexual partner, who died in September, 1962. "Rob had grown a young man of much character: gentle, intelligent, and strong-minded. He had resisted all attempts to uproot him from the working class and had become a plumber. He had got married in 1953 and possessed two sons, and he and his wife Sylvia had become greatly attached to Forster, and he to them" (Furbank, II, 317). Two years after the death of Rob, Forster had two succeeding strokes within the space of about one year—the first one was mild and yet it left him 'with slurred speech and difficulty in writing'; and the second one was relatively hard and 'its effects lasted longer.' As a consequence of these two strokes, "for a month or two, Bob Buckingham had to write his letters for him; and his speech was slightly but permanently impaired—he would from now on momentarily grope for words or have difficulty in articulation. His memory also worsened, and he began to make muddles—forgetting faces and appointments" (*op. cit.,* II, 318). Forster was now certain that he was going to die. During this time he would feel some mysterious urge to show gratitude, but to whom he did not know. He wrote: "How odd is this feeling of gratitude when one isn't being grateful to anyone. Pleasanter than if there was someone e.g. God—which would entail a feeling of obligation" (*ibid.*). But he showed or expressed gratitude, nevertheless: "A habit was growing on him, also, of expressing gratitude—of exclaiming, during a meal perhaps, how lucky he was, how many things he had to be thankful for. Gratitude interested him as a sentiment" (*ibid.*). He was wishing now to die "in an odour of sanctity" (*ibid.*)—he was perhaps expiating, silently and sincerely in his soul. He was realising, perhaps, that he was to check out of the world, leaving behind his personal effects, and so was disengaging himself from his connections: "He was beginning quietly, to strip himself of possessions, pressing friends to accept books and pieces of his furniture" (*ibid.*).

In 1964, Forster went to Wiltshire to live for some time with William Golding, the novelist and author of the famous novel *The Lord of Flies.* In June of that year, they 'visited Figsbury Rings, the inspiration of *The Longest Journey.*' "As they walked the downs, they discussed the near-extinction of Chalk Blue butterflies, through pesticides, when one flew between them and settled on a tall grass stem, in the very entrance to the Rings. Forster, in a pantomime of the world's ruthlessness, danced after it, brandishing his walking-stick, with a cry of 'Kill! Kill!'" (*op. cit.,* II, 318-19). Ackerley now wrote letters for him. A new problem now arose for Forster. After his first stroke, he told Bob Buckingham that he loved him, and Bob, well-aware of their previous homosexual relationship, took the words of Forster with much of consternation. Bob, further, told his wife May what Forster had told him, and also that he did not know that Forster was a homosexual. May of course knew that Forster was a homosexual, but was in the dark about the homosexual friendship between her husband and him. Astonishingly, Bob now turned against Forster and would behave with him indignantly, but May took everything easily and told Bob that Forster "was their dear friend and benefactor and that so long as he lived, their house should be his home" (*op. cit.,* II, 320). But the matter did not end there, and Bob tried to forget Forster, though Forster continued to love him. In his most urgent need of friends, most unfortunately for Forster, his friends began to fall apart, with the single exception of Ackerley.

For reasons known to him, Plomer was very slow with his project of writing Forster's biography. One reason of Plomer's perhaps was that he thought Forster to be "too 'slippery' and establishment-minded" (*op. cit.,* II, 321). However, P.N. Furbank soon replaced Plomer as the 'official' biographer of Forster. The first thing about Forster that struck Furbank was Forster's "fondness for the word 'muddle'." At this time, Furbank was 'elected' by King's College as a research fellow, and from this time he was fast writing the biography. On 4 June, 1967, Ackerley died. His death was a great shock to Forster, who asked May Buckingham to read aloud to him some pages from Ackerley's *My Father and Myself.* 'Ackerley, a few months before his death, had written an obituary article on Forster, depositing it with the *Observer* for future use.' The 'climactic sentence' of the article ran thus: "'I would say that in so far as it is possible for any human being to be both wise and worldly wise, to be selfless in any material sense, to have no envy, jealousy, vanity, conceit, to contain no malice, no hatred (though he had anger), to be always reliable, considerate, generous, never cheap, Morgan [Forster] came as close to that as can be got'" (*op. cit.,* II, 323). Ackerley's article was published in the *Observer* on 14 June, 1970.

On the first of January, 1969, Forster was awarded an O.M. by the Queen, and the King's College arranged a luncheon for Forster's birthday. The College servants made a big birthday cake in the shape of a book, bearing the titles of Forster's novels. The Vice-Provost of the College presented Forster "with a copy, bound in green leather, of the symposium *Aspects of E.M. Forster,* just published by Edward Arnold & Co. under the editorship of Oliver Stallybrass" (*ibid.*) in which fifteen writers and authors, including Elizabeth Bowen, Patrick Wilkinson, David Garnett, K. Natwar-Singh, W.J.H. Sprott, William Plomer, Malcolm Bradbury, Oliver Stallybrass and others contributed their articles. In March, 1970, Christopher Isherwood came to see Forster at King's College. On 22 May of the same year, P.N. Furbank, who had been living in his rooms 'on the same staircase as Forster's,' heard, at about 6 p.m., two successive loud shouts of Forster. This was Forster's last stroke which left him paralysed in one leg, immediately, and then on the next day in the other leg. He was sure that he was dying, and yet was 'stoical and gay,' and only during the night would sometimes make miserable groans: 'Oh dear, oh dear.' On 2 June, Bob Buckingham took him to his house at Coventry. Next day, a number of sympathisers, including Eric Fletcher and his wife, visited him, and saw him 'perfectly serene.' Forster broke his 'lifelong habit of abstemiousness' and 'drank a great deal,' on the same day. But he had only about three days more to live. He died in the morning of 7 June, 1970: "On 6 June [1970], for most of the morning, he held May Buckingham's hand in silence, opening his eyes when she tried to take it away—till at last he fell asleep or unconscious. He died without recovering consciousness, early in the next morning" (*op. cit.,* II, 325). Forster "had left instructions that he was to be 'disposed of' wherever he happened to be at the time of his death, and without religious observances"(*ibid.*). His instructions were honoured; and according to the decisions of Bob Buckingham and his wife, his dead body was cremated near the Coventry chapel, while, at a distance, Beethoven's Fifth Symphony, from a record-player, was adding a counterpoint to the silent sorrow of all there present.

WORKS

It is true that Forster did not write very much, but then it is also true that he did not write very little. He is generally known for his five novels—two Italian, one English, one German and one Indian. But besides these he has a considerable amount of literary productions, which includes another full-scale novel (*Maurice*), three volumes of short stories, his 'Commonplace Book,' unfinished novels, essays, critical writings, two biographies, broadcastings, letters (most of which he destroyed), etc. Forster was a precocious writer; even when he was a boy of just six or seven, he wrote a few short stories which, unfortunately, have not come down to us: "He once told an interviewer 'indulgently': Of course, I had a very literary childhood. I was the author of a number of works between ages of six and ten. There were 'Ear-rings through the Keyhole' and 'Scuffles in a Wardrobe'" (Beauman, 67 f.n.). However, we are giving below a list of most of his published works.

Novels

1. *Where Angels Fear to Tread* (1905)
2. *The Longest Journey* (1907)
3. *A Room with a View* (1908)
4. *Howards End* (1910)
5. *A Passage to India* (1924)
6. *Maurice* (1971, posthumously)

Short Stories (collections of)

1. *The Celestial Omnibus and Other Stories* (1911)
2. *The Eternal Moment and Other Stories* (1928)

   (In 1947 Sidgwick and Jackson published the two volumes of the Collections in a single volume, with the title *E.M. Forster: Collected Short Stories.*)
3. *The Life to Come and Other Stories* (1972, posthumously)

Biographies

1. *Goldsworthy Lowes Dickinson* (1934)
2. *Marianne Thornton* (1956)

Play

The Heart of Bosnia (1911)

Pageant

The Abinger Pageant (written in 1934; published in *Abinger Harvest* in 1936)

Libretto

Billy Budd (with Benjamin Britten and Eric Crozier, 1949)

Essays. Histories and Travelogues

1. *Alexandria: A History and A Guide* (1922)
2. *Pharos and Pharillon* (1923)
3. *Aspects of the Novel* (1927)
4. *Abinger Harvest* (1936)
5. *Nordic Twilight* (1940)
6. *Two Cheers for Democracy* (1951)
7. *The Hill of Devi* (1953)

Extravaganza

The Deceased Wife's Husband

Pamphlets

1. *Anonymity: An Enquiry* (1925)
2. *What I Believe (1939)*

3. *Reading as Usual* (1939)
4. *England's Pleasant Land* (1940)
5. *Nordic Twilight* (1940)
6. *Virginia Woolf* (The Rede Lecture, 1941: published 1942)

Introductions and Notes (Trilling, 160)

1. Introduction and Notes to *The Aeneid of Virgil* (E. Fairfax Taylor's translation in The Temple Classics), 1906.
2. Notes on Egypt in *The Government of Egypt: Recommendations by a Committee of the International Labour Research Department,* 1920.
3. Introduction and Notes to *Original Letters from India,* by Mrs Eliza Fay, 1925.
4. Introduction to *Flowers and Elephants,* by Constance Sitwell, 1927.
5. Introduction to *The Life of George Crabbe, By His Son* (World's Classics), 1932.
6. Introduction to *Twenty Years a-Growing,* by Maurice O' Sullivan, 1933.
7. Introduction to *Untouchable,* by Mulk Raj Anand, 1935.
8. Introduction to *The Banned Books of England,* by Alec Craig, 1937.

In addition to the above list of publications, Forster did a good deal of editorial works and writing of prefaces. He also did a great amount of book-reviews and radio broadcastings on B.B.C. So, he was not joking when he wrote about his own literary production: "The longer one lives the less one feels to have done, and I am both surprised and glad to discover from this bibliography that I have written so much" (Edward Arnold, 155). The bibliography Forster referred to is *A Bibliography of E.M. Forster,* published in 1965 by Hart-Davis, London, which lists 516 contributions by Forster (*ibid.*).

Two of his unfinished (and unpublished) novels are *Arctic Summer* and *Nottingham Lace.* The former was "the abortive successor to *Howards End*" (Furbank, I, 170). In it Forster wanted to portray the hero, a young man, as his own self, provided he would have married, and to portray the heroine as a girl he would like to marry 'had he followed a more conventional pattern' of life. The story of *Arctic Summer* began thus: Martin Whitby, the hero, is a young civil servant. His childhood was prosaic, but there was in him dormant and unaroused aesthetic impulse which was aroused by his reading of appropriate books, perceiving of romantic pictures, and listening to sentimental music. But he married the wrong woman, Venetia, the daughter of the master of a Cambridge College. Venetia is a prosaic woman, but her sister Dorothea is a different kind of woman. A few months after their marriage, the love between Martin and Venetia began to cool down, and they 'produced a wedded love.' On their way to Italy (from England) they met a young man, Clesant March. The novel broke here. The reason for abandoning the novel at this point Forster explained thus: "I had got my antithesis all right, the antithesis between the civilized man, who hopes for an Arctic summer, and the heroic man who rides into the sea. But I had not settled what was going to happen, and that is why the novel remains a fragment. The novelist should I think always settle when he starts what is going to happen, what his major event is to be" (Beauman, 248-49). *Arctic Summer* was a fragmentary novel of Forster's mature period, but before it, when he was twenty-one, Forster had left unfinished yet another novel: *Nottingham Lace*. The novel breathed Forster's radical views, and bore testimony of his genius as a novelist. In it there were beauty and clarity, but it lacked in form and content. Forster broke off the novel, on its way, perhaps because he thought that his "intellectual rebellion would not be matched by action" (*op. cit.*, 89).

Forster wrote his only play *The Heart of Bosnia* in the spring of 1911 and published it the same year. It is a 'strange play,' and it was to some extent inspired by Bernard Shaw's *Fanny's First Play* which he saw staged in 1911. Of course he could not enjoy that play of Shaw's—he commented about it: 'Slipshod and bungling'—yet it shook off his present inertia and drove him to writing *The Heart of Bosnia.* Bosnia was then much talked about; because, for one thing, it was annexed by Austro-Hungary in 1908, and secondly in 1910 'a Serbian anarchist made an attempt to assassinate the Governor.' The action of the play *The Heart of Bosnia* "takes place in the British Consulate in Bosnia. The previous evening the consul, Mr Stevens, and his wife have given a ball, and their daughter Fanny, who has made a conquest of two of her Bosnian dancing partners, thinks it might be amusing to flirt with them. Her father warns her not to trifle with them: neither she nor he, he says, understands that unknown quantity—the heart of Bosnia.' But Fanny is bored, so when one of her admirers calls she grants him a *tete-a-tete.* Nikolai is all fire and passion; he lays his naked knife on the table, swearing to guard the house against all foes. Fanny plays with the knife and cuts herself, whereupon he plunges her bleeding hand under his shirt and kisses her. Pretending outrage, she orders him out of the house... Her morning's flirtation is proceeding briskly when there enters her other suitor, Mirko, who, it turns out, is Nikolai's bosom friend. Left alone, the youths embrace passionately, each informing the other that he is in love. They promise to exchange their souls' secrets that night, on the mountain; and meanwhile they dance and frolic, till there dawns on them the fatal *anagnorisis* that it is Fanny they both are in love with. Their horseplay now turns into a duel to the death. Re-enter Fanny, who seizes the opportunity, as an educated Englishwoman, to teach them a lesson... She confiscates their knives and returns into the inner room, leaving Mirko and Nikolai staring at each other in despair. All is over for them, they realize, and kissing each other once more—this time with the kiss of blood—they follow the only course left, which is to murder her. The servants look on impassively; they tell the distracted Stevens parents, when they arrive too late on the scene: 'We are sorry for you, who did not know our customs, but we can do nothing.' 'Call for the mayor,' cries Mrs Stevens. 'Telegraph for troops—this is neutral ground—we have a case for war—the British Consulate!' 'My dear,' replies her husband, 'we have a case, but she is dead'" (Furbank, I, 200-201). One may find a distant relationship between *The*

Heart of Bosnia and *A Passage to India,* but as a play *The Heart of Bosnia* has very little to be praised.

Forster began another play—'St Bridget'—in 1909, but ceased writing in the second Act of it. The motive of writing this play came to him from two sources: one, Herbert Trench asked him to write a play for his Repertory Theatre; and two, he was at that time reading Pastor's *History of the Popes.* 'St Bridget' is 'an historical drama, about St Bridget of Sweden.' " The play, such of it as he wrote, concerns the famous embassy of St Bridget to the court of Naples in 1371, to persuade the Queen Giovanna to bring the Pope back from Avignon. It was a promising subject, this encounter between the world-renouncing northern visionary and the profligate, art-loving queen, typifying the coming Renaissance; and Forster's handling of the opening scenes—the saint arriving with her bickering family in the scandalous southern court—is quite in the style of his Italian comedies. In the unfinished second act something odder develops. A little girl comes in, dripping wet, through an open window in the queen's apartments, lies down on the sofa, and dies. A guard explains to a lady-in-waiting: she is Virgil's daughter. The Palace, he says, was once the castle of Virgil, who built it on an egg and any day may crawl up, under the water, and break the shell. Mystery descends on the play at this point" (*op. cit.,* I, 178).

Forster wrote the libretto *Billy Budd* in collaboration with Benjamin Britten in 1949 (with the assistance of Eric Crazier), and the libretto was first performed in December, 1951, and it "became one of the few classics of twentieth-century opera" Beauman, 369).

Forster's third collection of short stories was posthumously published in 1972 with the title *The Life to Come and Other Stories* (the first and the second collections are *The Celestial Omnibus* and *The Eternal Moment*). *The Life to Come and Other Stories* contains short stories most of which are blatantly homosexual. "Morgan wrote the first of his erotic short stories in Switzerland in 1911; destroyed all of them in 1922 in the belief that they clogged me artistically' (and later rather regretted it); and wrote about a dozen more during the rest of his life" (*ibid.*). *The Life to Come and Other Stories* includes 'The Life to Come,' 'The Other Boat,' 'The Obelisk,' 'The Classical Annex' and some other short stories. The four mentioned are wonderfully beautiful short stories. The eroticity of the stories of *The Life to Come and Other Stories may* be compared with the stories or tales of Giovanni Boccaccio's *The Decameron*. Both of them—Boccaccio and Forster—had the same motive behind writing their stories: to provide vicarious erotic pleasure to the reader. But whereas Boccaccio's eroticity is heterosexual, Forster's is homosexual. The story 'The Life to Come' has a story behind it. In 1923, Mohammed el Adl died prematurely—Adl who was Forster's longest-term homosexual partner. Since his death Forster for many nights in tandem dreamed of Adl. In the entry of 20 December, 1923, in his diary, Forster wrote a detailed narrative of one of those dreams: "'I passed a young man in black with a slight but well defined moustache. He was and was not Mohammed [el Adl]—not he outwardly but he in the intensity, the quality of the emotion caused in my heart. I knew I ought to follow him but delayed—my character—and when I tried to do so my legs were weighted, I heard he was catching a train. Painfully I arrive, a bath being filled with hot water. I was in time, the train had not gone, others in the bath room left us alone, he lent against the edge of the bath, half sitting, half standing, entirely naked, his dark bush distinct, and he smiled. The effect was not physical nor was my awakening ghastly except that I awoke'" (Furbank, II, 114). This dream was perhaps the inspiration behind Forster's writing the short story 'The Life to Come,' because the story was written about the time when he had dreamt this dream, and also because the substance of the dream and that of the short story are almost identical, though the suggested underlying meaning of the story is different.

P.N. Furbank writes about the short story 'The Life to Come': "The story began merely as one of his [Forster's] 'indecencies,' but turned into something very different. It concerns a handsome young missionary who once sleeps with a young native chieftain, with the result that the chieftain takes their love to be that 'love of God' which is spoken of by

Christians and promptly announces the conversion of his tribe. The missionary is appalled but is too prudent to give up this brilliant conversion, so he cheats his uncomprehending disciple, who wishes to enjoy more such love, with shadowy promises. Years pass, and the chieftain, broken-hearted at the postponement, and finding himself robbed not only of his religion but of his lands and royal authority, falls mortally ill. The missionary, now dried-up and middle-aged, comes to visit him on his deathbed, finding him lying alone and naked on his house-roof. He feels it safe now to venture a Christian embrace and tells the dying Vithobai of the joys of life to come. 'And will there be love?' asks Vithobai. 'In the real and true sense, there will,' answers the missionary. 'The Life to Come,' shouts Vithobai. 'Life, life, eternal life. Wait for me in it'; and he stabs the missionary through the heart and hurls himself, victoriously, over the parapet" (*op. cit.*, II, 114-15). P.N. Furbank writes about Forster's motive in writing this story: "The story was written, Forster said, 'in indignation.' By which, he meant, partly, indignation against British imperialism; but he was hitting, too, at some suspected over-cautiousness in himself. It was a story, eloquent but over-romantic though it is, which always meant a lot to him" (*op. cit.*, II, 115).

'The Other Boat' is a short story that originated in the first chapter of an abandoned novel. Around 1915, Forster wrote the first chapter of a novel which was projected to be based on an Anglo-Indian family. This chapter was published in the *Listener* on 23 December, 1948, under the rubric of 'Entrance to an Unwritten Novel.' The narrative of that first chapter was about the returning on a boat from India of that Anglo-Indian family that consisted of a widow, Mrs March, and her young children. "The children, with their mother's grudging permission, take up with a half-caste playmate, called 'Coconut.' At first, being white *Sahibs,* they order Coco about which he rather enjoys. Then they let him lead them off on a mysterious game or errand of his own invention, and their mother catches sight of them on a distant deck, playing hatless in the mid-day sun. It is still the era of the solar *topi* and of the fear of sunstroke, and she rushes off to put a stop to their game, becoming involved in a curious little drama, full of confusion and cross-purposes. Suddenly, hot, tired and worried about the future, she becomes hysterical and vents her hysteria in rage against the half-caste: 'You're a silly little boy and I shall complain to the stewardess about you, 'she breaks out at him angrily. 'You never will play any game properly and you stop the others. You're a silly idle useless unmanly little boy'" (*op. cit.*, II, 301). Forster was forgetful of the manuscript of that first chapter of a projected but unfinished and untitled novel. Some years later, he came across the manuscript and thought of writing a short story on the material of that first chapter, giving a new direction to the material. Forster asked himself: what would have happened if the Anglo-Indian boy, Lionel, and the half-caste boy, Coco, would have been sexually attracted to each other, when grown up? This meant that Forster was going to place the two boys each on a different boat—on the other boat. This is the history of 'The Other Boat' in which Forster conceived of a homosexual relationship between the grown up Anglo-Indian and the grown up half-caste.

In the short story 'The Obelisk,' Forster has caricatured Sir Edmund Ironside. In 1921, on way to India for his second Indian tour, Forster arrived Port Said on the 16th of March, and there saw the ironside of the very tough British administrator Sir Edmund Ironside who seemed to him to be an obelisk. Even in this story Forster introduced homosexual ingredient 'The Classical Annex' is also a homosexual short story. It is "about a museum curetor whose son is seduced—eternally—by a statue of a Roman athlete" (Beauman, 369, f.n.). However, some of Forster's other short stories are: 'On Bicycling,' 'Albergo Empedocle,' 'The Rock,' etc. 'On Bicycling,' written in 1900, is an early story, sufficiently well-written with 'a better than average display of Forster's early satirical bent.' On the other hand, 'Albergo Empedocle,' written in 1903, is a moderately good story. 'The Rock,' written in 1906 and published in *The Life to Come and Other Stories* (1972), is a fully formed but not appreciable story. It is "about a man who, having been rescued by Cornish fishermen when his boat is wrecked on a rock on their coast, asks himself what he can give them in repayment, and eventually concludes that the only appropriate gift is his whole life—that is to say, he must give away all his possession and go to live on the charity of his rescuers. He felt such conviction of his own inspiration that, as a thank-offering, he put a sovereign in the Royal Lifeboat Institution's Collecting-box, being sure he would make the money over and again. The story turned out a complete flop and was turned down firmly by every editor, and he [Forster] had to conclude that his inspiration had been 'genuine but worthless like so much inspiration'" (Furbank, I, 139-40).

Forster has to his credit a good amount of writings, either not published in book forms or not at all published. In the volume of articles presented to Forster, on his attaining the age of ninety, George H. Thomson wrote the article 'A Forster Miscellany: Thoughts on the Uncollected Writings,' in which Thomson wrote: "Forster was twenty-one years old in 1900 when he began to write for the periodical press. He continued with such writing for the next sixty-five years, and the *Bibliography...*, by Miss B.J. Kirkpatrick, identifies 533 contributions to periodicals and newspapers. After seventy-one negligible items, mainly letters, have been subtracted, the meaningful figure is 462. Of these, Forster has reprinted 152: in *The Collected Short Stories* (11) *Pharos and Pharillon* (11), *Abinger Harvest* (62), *Two Cheers for Democracy* (65), *Marianne Thornton* (1), *The Hill of Devi* (1), and *The Longest Journey*, World's Classics edition (1). Forster has left 310 uncollected contributions, a substantial body of writing, comprising something over 300,000 words. At least one third of these stories, essays, reveries, and noes deserve to be rescued and made into a book" (Edward Arnold, 155-56). From this account of Miss Kirkpatrick, we may form an idea about the amount of literary works, done by Forster but not published, and if we take jointly into account both the published and the unpublished works of his, we may say that Forster's works are never little.

In 1907, Forster wrote his only extravaganza *The Deceased Wife's Husband,* to celebrate the occasion of the recently passing of The Deceased Wife's Sister bill. The extravaganza's "protagonist is the Rev. Paul Goodybrick, who, hitherto a happy widower, has responded to his country's command and, relinquishing his chaplaincy at Port Said, has hurried home to marry his deceased wife's detestable sister, Clara. Musing in Leicester Square on his fatal step, he falls into conversation with a stranger, a retired solicitor of the name of Flather, and relates the story to him. He has made an ill choice of confidant, for Flather is an ardent churchman—so much so that he has recently done time in Dartmoor for absconding with the securities of Agnostic Widows—and he receives the confession with indignation. The two nearly fall to blows, when Clara herself appears; and in the ensuing vicissitudes, Goodybrick and Flather discover that they are related, through their first wife's bigamy. The fatal news overcomes them, and they rush off in different directions to commit suicide. Clara soliloquizes: '... what am I to do now? Let me think. Which of these two gentlemen was my husband? Paul. Why had Paul to marry me? Because I was Lavinia's sister. Then surely, if Paul had a brother I shall have to marry him (*Rougishly*). We women are not so illogical as you think.' Waiting to hear no more, a policeman, who has been watching proceedings from behind the statue of Shakespeare, rushes from his concealment and handcuffs Clara. He has seen something of life's darker side, he says, but never in his gloomist experience has he contemplated quite so vile a case. England may permit murder, she may permit suicide, but there is one evil she will never permit—that the laws for women should be the same as for men" (Furbank, I, 158).

Forster wrote a good number of essays on divers topics, most of the good ones of which are included in *Alexandria: A History and A Guide, Pharos and Pharillon, Abinger Harvest, The Hill of Devi* and *Two Cheers for Democracy*. And some of those which are not included in those works are (some of these were published, others not): 'The Prince's Progress' (about the Prince of Wales' visit to India in November, 1921), 'Raison D' Etre of Criticism in the Arts,' 'Reflections in India, I: Too Late?,' 'What I Believe' (personal views), 'Society and the Homosexual: A Magistrate's Figures,' 'Woodlanders on

Devi,' 'We are not good enough for Heaven,' They Hold Their Tongues,' 'Luncheon at Pretoria,' 'The Last Parade,' 'Jew-consciousness,' 'Literature and War,' 'My Wood,' 'The Nine Gems of Ujjain,' 'The New Censorship,' "Notes on Human Nature Under War Conditions,' 'Our Graves in Gallipoli,' 'In My Library,' 'Influence of Climate and Physical Conditions Upon National Character'(school essay), 'A Flood in the Office,' 'Terney,' 'The Feminine Note in Literature,' 'Dr Woolacott,' etc. Besides essays, he has to his credit a number of published speeches. Forster has also written a good number of sympathetic 'Prefaces and Introductions' to other writers' workers; for instance in 1935, he wrote the Preface to the Indian novelist Mulk Raj Anand's novel *Untouchable. Anand's* novel had been rejected by seventeen publishers before Arnold Associates accepted it along with Forster's Preface for publication, and thereby Anand was saved from 'suicide,' as Anand himself confessed. Forster also filled a number of his diaries and his Commonplace Book with entries on personal affairs, experiences, sketches of projected works, comments about persons and works, etc.

Even a scanty reference to Forster's works should include a mention of his only pageant *The Abinger Pageant,* which was performed on 14 July and 18 July, 1934, 'in aid of the Abinger Church Preservation Fund.' Mr Tom Harrison was the producer of the pageant; DrVaughan Williams wrote the music if it; and Mr Wilfrid Grantham was the narrator, during the first performance. But the entire conception of the pageant was due to Forster. The pageant consists of six episodes, and begins with a Prologue and ends with an Epilogue (the second episode of the pageant is divided into two scenes). The Prologue is spoken by the Woodman. The first Episode presents a 'rapid imaginary survey' of select incidents that occurred in Abinger (in Surrey) From the beginning of history to the Norman Conquest [1066 A.D.],' while music is played. "When the Woodman has finished his Prologue, Ancient Britons appear, collecting fire-wood, hunting. 'The Romans, the Romans,' they cry, and the Roman legions enter, take possession, and make themselves at home. Soldiers, formed into a line, symbolize the strait Roman Road, then the bugle sounds retreat, and the Romans retire to Rome. "The Saxon invasion follows. The Saxons and Romanized Britons are hostile to each other at first, then fraternize. A priest arrives, Christianity is established. The Saxon leader moves with his men into battle, while women await the event. He is brought back dead. The priest comforts the mourners. "Finally the Normans enter with triumphant music. Grouping themselves round a Saxon scribe, they make the Domesday Survey and the episode closes" (Forster, 1955, 331-32).

As Episode I deals with the Anglo-Saxon period, so Episode II deals with the Middle Ages. Scene of Episode II refers to the year 1210, and deals with the king of England punishing the Lord of the Manor 'for sheltering an outlaw.' Scene ii of Episode II is not historical, like the rest of the text, but imaginative, and refers to the year 1220. The scene takes place in the Manor of Abinger, where villagers wait to welcome their beloved archbishop, the great Cardinal Archbishop of Canterbury, Stephen Langton. Pilgrims bring news of the Archbishop's approach. "Children play in the courtyard of the Manor, there is a mock tournament on hobby horses, and a miracle play on a cart. The Archbishop is seen in the distance, accompanied by a single novice, who is Giles de Braose of Paddington, but before they arrive the unpopular Bishop of Winchester appears with his monks; he converses with a crusader, since he will himself soon be going on a crusade. "Finally, the Archbishop comes and is received with joy. He and the Bishop greet one another distantly. A procession is formed and all start for the church, led by the monks, who sing a Latin Chant in Plainsong, appropriate to the dedication of a building. The first verse celebrates the Heavenly Jerusalem, the celestial model of all earthly churches, the second gives glory to the Father, the Son and the Holy Ghost" (*op. cit.*, 335).

Episode II over, the Woodman announces the coming in of the Elizabethan age by striking on the anvil and crying aloud: *Listen to the hammers at Abinger, Abinger Hammer*! Episode III refers to the Hammer Green in the year 1588. "Charcoal burners, apprentices, etc., enter, small boys play, a lady of position walks about." "Enter Lord Abergavenny's steward with a man who is dragged to the whipping post inspite of the protests of the villagers and the intercession of the Rev. Richard Dean, the Rector. But a hunting-horn is heard and Abergavenny himself arrives and has the man released. Quickly on this comes the news of the defeat of the Armada, and general rejoicing. There is a country dance, 'Gathering Peascods,' and the scene closes to the strains of ' Twankydillo,' and to the building of a bonfire" (*op. cit.,* 337).

Now the Woodman cries aloud 'off,' and Episode III goes off and Episode IV comes to view. Episode III brings in 'the troubled times of the seventeenth century'—the times between 1643 to 1660. As Episode III opens, "two villagers are about to be married by the Rector, the Rev. Anthony Smith, but the Puritans prevent them from entering the church, and marry them at a table instead, much to their bewilderment. The Rector is deprived of his living, and the Puritan and the villagers, now in black, sing the old metrical version of the 68th Psalm:

> Let God arise and then his foes will turn themselves to flight,...

While they are singing a solitary horseman—John Evelyn—rides slowly across the stage. When the Psalm is over, there is a sudden change in the music, to symbolize the Restoration of Charles II, and the villagers, glad enough of the change, throw off their black cloaks and reappear in colours. They sing a song of the period:

> Here's a health unto His Majesty
> Conversion to his enemies
> And he that will not pledge his health
> I wish him neither wit nor wealth
> Nor yet a rope to hang himself
> With a fa la la,

and follow it by a Country Dance, 'The Triumph,' during which the genuine Puritans retire. At the end of the dance they form a aisle up to the church. It is a second wedding. The Rev. Stephen Geree is now Rector of Abinger, and his daughter Elizabeth is marrying Mr. Francis Hammond from London.

The procession comes down the aisle, followed by guests... There is another Country Dance, 'Haste to the Wedding.' When it is over, a gardener hands John Evelyn [one of the guests] a small tree. He goes out to plant it in commemoration of the glad event,..." (*op. cit.,* 339). Here closes Episode IV which symbolises the days of John Evelyn.

Episode V 'introduces us to some rustic scenes of the eighteenth century, and to some changes in the woodland.' This episode shows us some scenes of village life, on a summer's day, outside the Inn at Abinger Hatch. A young woman is seen moving over the bridge and watching. "Then the Smugglers gallop on, and unload their casks. Excise men appear, the casks are hidden by various devices, but when all seems safe the excise men reappear, and John Lane is arrested, and taken off, to be deported." The casks are now opened, the neighbourhood of the Hatch Inn becomes gay and 'I'm Seventeen Come Sunday' is sung. "The quality now begin to arrive. Rousseau and his lady are actually stopping with Mr. Malthus at Westcott, but Mr. Spence is responsible for them in Abinger. The Countess of Donegal drives on last There is an entertainment of Morris Dances and of other Country Dances. Meanwhile the Curate of Abinger, who has a taste for philosophy, tries to have a little interesting talk with Rousseau. This ends badly, for Rousseau mistakes the Curate for a French spy, and finally dashes off in terror, to the concern of Mr. Spence. The gentry leave, and the villagers have another drink, and strike up the Surrey Falk Song, 'The Sweet Nightingale,' which has been sung in these parts for generations" (*op. cit.,* 340-41). When the singing is over, Episode V ends.

The Woodman cries out 'off' and Episode VI, the last episode, occurs. The scene of this episode is a place outside the Abinger Church, and the time is the nineteenth century. The stocks are being repaired, an Eton boy and a village boy squabble, the steward puts the village boy into the stocks, Dr. Riccabocca releases him and experiments with stocks himself until he can't get out Steward comes out of church with squire, and is much surprised. Meanwhile the rector arrives, with the farmers who are presenting a new porch to the church. They look at plans and sing some verses of the 84th Psalm... "While the Psalm is being sung all the performers of previous scenes assemble on the hill behind, and the hymn 'O God our help in ages past' concludes the active part of the Pageant The Woodman then comes forward to speak the Epilogue, and the sheep begin to return to the arena" (*op. cit.*, 342-43).

Before listening to the Epilogue, let us understand that the pageant is a rapid concatenation of symbolic scenarios of the different conditions of England and her people of the divers stages in the course of time, from the Anglo-Saxon period down to the nineteenth century. But there is an under-pinning with the pageant: there is a sense of frustration at the cutting down of trees, at the clearing of forests for making room for the industrialised and densely populated England, and concurrently there is an appeal to revert England to her former pastoral beauty. 'Cutting down of trees' is a sort of refrain throughout most of the pageant, and is a cause of concern and bewailing. The Woodman speaks the Epilogue: *Houses, houses, houses! You came from them and you must go back to them. Houses and bungalows, hotels, restaurants and flats, arterial roads, by-passes, petrol pumps and pylons—are these going to be England? Are these men's final triumph? Or is there another England, green and eternal, which will outlast them? I cannot tell you, I am only the Woodman, but this land is yours, and you can make it what you will. If you want ruin our Surrey fields and woodlands it is easy to do, very easy, and if you want to save they can be saved. Look into your hearts and look into the past, and remember that all this beauty is a gift which you can never replace, which no money can buy, which no cleverness can refashion. You can make a town, you can make a desert, you can even make a garden; but you can never, never make the country, because it was made by Time. Centuries of life amongst obscure trees and unnoticed fields! That is all our Pageant has tried to show you, and it will end as it began among country sights and sounds. Farewell! and take back its lesson with you to your houses, for it has a lesson. Our village and our woods bid you farewell (op. cit.*, 343-44).

As soon as the Epilogue is spoken out, the arena is again occupied by the flock of sheep.

The Abinger Pageant is superbly conceived and executed, and its appeal is insuperable. From this pageant, mostly, we understand that green fields, green hills, wide pastures, the antic village dances, the simplicity and the naturalness of places away from the humdrum of townships appealed to Forster as much as they did Wordsworth. The pageant is classic indeed.

A short essay, included in *Abinger Harvest,* deserves special mention, because it shows Forster's deep understanding of the practical philosophy of life that is there in the *Bhagavad-Gita,* one of the most revered books of the Hindus. The essay is only two pages long, but in it he has been able to capture the quintessence of the *Bhagavad-Gita,* whose subtle instructions the Westerners can hardly follow. The essay is very appropriately entitled: 'Hymn Before Action.' Arjuna is in a double-bind in the battle field: should he establish the right by destroying his enemies, or should he recile from the mortal action and thereby save their souls? On such a crossroad everyone is positioned almost every day. Krishna, the Lord, advises Arjuna to take the path of duty, relinquishing all desires to enjoy the fruits of his action and thereby escaping all potential sins consequent upon his action. In the short essay, Forster has masterfully presented all this. The advices of Krishna could successfully persuade Arjuna, and Arjuna "drives into the battle rejoicing, and wins a great victory" (*op. cit.,* 326). But, perhaps, the comment of Forster on the *Bhagavad-Gita,* in the last two lines of the essay, is unwarrented and inappropriate. Forster says about Arjuna's action: "But it is necessarily and rightly followed by disillusionment and remorse. The fall of his enemies leads to his own, for the fortunes of men are all bound up together, and it is impossible to inflict damage without receiving it" *(ibid.)*.

Forster also did some editing. For instance, being commisioned by Dickinson, he edited Virgil's *Aeneid.* We have said that for some time Forster read speeches, dialogues (for instance, his 'Conversations in the Train'), literary miscellanies, etc., all of which made him almost an 'anchor' of the B.B.C.

radio. Forster has also written a good number of essays in criticism, besides his *Aspects of the Novel;* we shall give a brief reference to them in the chapter 'Forster As A Critic.' And lastly, though he was not a poet, in the true sense of the term, perhaps he could show himself to be one had he wanted to, because that he had the sensibilities and fancies required of a poet is obvious from many places of all his novels, and because he wrote at least two poems, one of which has already been cited (p.13), and the other is being cited below—entitled 'Between the Butts and Figsbury.' In 1909, Forster was working hard on *Howards End,* during the summer time, "and then, in September, he went to stay with Maimie Aylward, to do some preparation for his next term's lectures. In this favourite scenary the mood of *The Longest Journey* returned powerfully, provoking him to write a poem, on the theme of possessing Wiltshire [the house at Wiltshire]" (Furbank, I, 177).

Between the Butts and Figsbury

The tints are here, to copy down
  Pale green, pale salmon, ochre pale,
Lifted above the creamy earth,
  Faint coronals of beech trees sail.

The air is here to breathe, the flowers,
  Fanned by its passion, rise and fall,
Knapweed and campion, feverfew,
  They garland me, I see them all.

And yet, when darkness comes, when sheets,
  And all the prison of a room,
Blots out the tints, shuts out the air,
  Withers the flowers with breath of tomb.

A richer treasure will be mine,
  For all the glory will have past,
Into my blood and ticking brain,
  And Wiltshire will be mine at last.

(Furbank, I, 177-78).

The Man and some of His Views

2

There is perhaps no better means today of having a vision of the person, and a conception of the manners, of E.M. Forster (photographs will not quite do, for they are dead things) than by looking at the dead novelist through the eyes of P.N. Furbank, who knew him personally, chatted with him, enquired of him personally for writing, with his consent, his most authentic biography, *E.M. Forster: A Life*. In the chapter 'E.M. Forster Described' of that biography (Bk II), Furbank has provided us with a fairly clear vision of the person and demeanour, and the personality, of Forster. Let us therefore quote at some length from Furbank for a vision of the person, manners, and personality of Forster. Furbank writes about Forster: "He was a fairly large and plumpish man, dressed ordinarily in a dowdy suit, cheap shirt and non-descript tie. Straggling hair, broad brow, a long reddish nose, and under it a wispy moustache; fine eyes, in steel-rimmed glasses, and a most expressive and sensitive mouth, by turns tremulous, amused, morally reproving or full of scorn. It was the mouth, one felt, of a man defending the right to be sensitive. Physically he was awkward, limp and stiff at the same time. He would stand rather askew, as it were holding himself together by gripping his left hand in his right. By contrast his gestures were most graceful; he had a beautiful blessing gesture of the hand, and a curious and charming habit, when drinking tea, of describing a little circling motion with the cup. On occasion, if he happened to be touched or grateful, he would kiss a friend's hand with great beauty of manner."

With a little pushing, on such a visit as I am describing, he could be got chatting freely, in a desultory way, his conversations would range widely—though always with lapses and hiatuses. Suddenly, he would let a subject drop, whereupon no effort could revive it. There would be a good deal of mild gossip, in exactly the same style whether one knew the characters in the story or not. These stories, dramatizing some absurd little scene or contretemps, were very funny and living, and, at the end, he would explode with laughter himself; he laughed as if it hurt him, convulsed, giving a wail from a mirthless face. Sometimes, after some ridiculous tale, he would bang his head in pretended despair, with a cry of 'Oh!'—meaning, 'What *was* there to be done?' Whatever the subject his talk had odd glints and tiny surprises in it, a queer precision of vocabulary, a perpetual slight displacement of the expected emphasis. The voice went into the air with charm and decision: a minute pause, and then a beautifully-formed, idiosyncratic phrase or just-hinted comic idea. 'Did you do any acting when you were young, Morgan [Forster]?' 'No never—I—no, that wasn't acting—I played the triangle once....'

There was a great quickness in his response: not so much quickness of wit, though he could be witty, but quickness in 'placing' someone else's remark, in instantly seeing its drift, its motive, its upshot. His mind would race so quickly round the remark, that the topic was exhausted as soon as began. As a part of this trait, he had a peculiar faculty for listening. Many acquaintances, throughout his life, remarked how intently he listened—seeming to attend not so much to what was said as to the underlying meaning or drift. It gave a special virtue to friendship with him, but for the un-self-confident it could be unnerving, and they would often find their words freezing on their lips.

He was at his best in a *tete-a-tete.* In company, even among close friends, he would be taciturn and would spark up only intermittently. He did not make much effort in general conversation; also he would never argue. Among strangers, though courteous, he could on occasion be very blank, shades of boredom and stimulated benignity flitting over his face as he spoke, very carefully, of trivialities. Sometimes strangers found him altogether disappointing; others were charmed by him but could remember nothing he had said.

He had certain rather oriental forms of courtesy. Once he called on me, carrying a large bunch of flowers intended for someone else, and when I prised the flowers he instantly felt bound to give them to me; whereon, of course, I was faced with the problem of finding him some more flowers. He would listen complaisantly to any suggestion, however preposterous, and only afterwards, by faint indications, convey that perhaps, just possibly, something might be urged against it. Similarly, he would gravely consider, or seem to consider, the most hackneyed remarks about his own works—for instance, that there were too many sudden deaths in *The Longest Journey*—as if he were hearing them for the first time. This courtesy of his went together, however, with some unnerving plain speaking. Once a fellow-guest at a party, having conversed with him for some time, remarked: 'But I mustn't keep you from more distinguished guests.' 'No, you mustn't,' replied Forster.

At any social gathering in these late days, he was exposed to much adulation and lionization. It was a phenomenon he understood very well, and he did not pretend to think it strange that people, especially the young, should reverence him or feel awe at meeting him. It could grow tiresome, however, and he developed ways of deflecting it. For instance, at a party, he might single out some stranger and spend most of the evening in quiet conversation with him. He would choose the stranger because he or she attracted him, or because the stranger looked lonely—and if the latter, it was done partly to shame his host or hostess. Whatever the motive, however, when he set out to please in this way, he did it wholeheartedly, occasionally getting snubbed for his pains—which enraged him greatly—but often making a new friend. These and similar habits of behaviour earned him a reputation for humility, and many anecdotes circulated of his 'humbleness' and unassumingness. It was in a sense a misunderstanding, for he had a very accurate idea of his own worth and was not slow to resent slights upon it. The truth was, rather, that he was modest—that is to say, had profoundly good manners, manners that were the fruit of his lifetime of moral self-cultivation.

The central preoccupation of his life, it was plain to see, was friendship, and he had a rather special attitude towards friendship. He never casually dropped friends, as most people do, out of forgetfulness or through change of circumstance—though, as has been seen, he might drop one with perfect deliberateness, if the friend had offended him in some vital way; and when this happened, he was unforgiving. Otherwise, if someone became a friend of his, he might expect to remain so for life, though perhaps gravitating over the years from one grade of his friendships to another. He believed—literally, and as more than a sentimental cliche—that the true history of the human race was the history of human affection. And for this reason it was a principle with him to keep his friendships in mind and to be continually reflecting on them. Also, to the end of his life, he was on the look-out for new friends and showed great enterprise in finding them.

He was frequently described as 'shy,' but this too was a misnomer. What was certainly true was that he was timid: that is to say, he did not like to be hurt and took elaborate precautions not to be hurt. He was, and wished to be, sensitive; and since sensitiveness made him vulnerable, he had equipped himself with innumerable defensive weapons, he could withdraw into himself, be evasive, be over-polite, be silent and let others flounder. On extreme occasions he could speak out angrily, and his anger was frightening—but it did not often come to this, for he was not easily cornered. And all these defences could be lowered; he was not encased in Edwardian courtesy and could play the fool and laugh delightedly at plain speaking. He did not avoid intimacies, indeed he courted them. On the other hand, he did remorselessly *manage* them and was not ready to 'give himself' undeservedly in friendship. For one thing, he greatly disliked being laughed at. He would swallow it sometimes, for friendship's sake, but for him it was no part at all of the pleasures of friendship, and he winced and bristled so visibly under teasing that people did not usually try it twice. Equally, as has been seen, he was bad at quarrels—that is to say, they assumed too vast proportions for him. He nerved himself up to a quarrel with painful effort and remembered it for years afterwards, still brooding about it at intervals and perhaps keeping a *dossier* on it. He had curious ways of describing a quarrel. If he were not involved personally, he spoke as though he were—'Tom got angry with Bill, and then we were all in trouble...' And if he were involved personally, he would put the whole thing between inverted commas. 'I have been *insulted*!' he might say, as if he had only just thought of the name for what had taken place. He could not conceive of quarrels as a natural part of a relationship, and when married friends, like the Buckinghams, had a quarrel, he felt sure their marriage must be breaking up. There was great sense of duty, and great loyalty and benevolence, in his relationships, but also something self-pleasing and managing; he was responsive, but never in the least pliable. Even with his closest friends, he took on the role of a mentor, he was a stickler, they could feel his eye on them, and sometimes, with those less intimate, his governessy side caused serious offence.

What was involved in this aspect of him was not bossiness but the determination to judge. A good way of visualizing Forster, I have found, is to imagine him being introduced to a dog or a cat. I never witnessed this, but can picture it. He would put himself on a level with the animal, approaching it tolerantly but non-committally. It *might* be a nice animal, but then again it might not; it was a mistake to have preconceptions on such matters; and at all events it didn't matter *much* what character an animal had—but it mattered a little. That would be his tone, I think, and he would shoot glances at the animal in the intervals of conversation, examining it from various angles till he had made up his mind about it. His mind was a vast breeding-ground for judgements and discriminations. He endlessly picked and chose and could distinguish one blade of grass from another. Similarly, no one ever made such *restrictive* remarks, giving and then drawing a limit to what was to be given. 'X—'with an intelligent face, fairly,' he might say; or 'I am devoted to Y—'s son, slightly.'

"One could imagine, knowing him, that he had a 'secret.' It is a sentimental notion, but one that occurred to many of his acquaintances. It had to do with the fact that, to a rather special degree, he lived the imaginative life and, whether in company or in solitude, was attending to imaginative impressions. He did this consciously, feared to lose the power of doing so, and rebuked himself for slackness in it. It was, to him, the rule and aim of his existence and was entwined with his sense for what—for want of a better word—he called 'life.' He felt as if, on occasion, he could see through to 'life': could hear its wing-beat, could grasp it not just as a generality but as a palpable presence. The feeling communicated itself. I remember him, once, describing Masood's children, and their love for their companion Cotter Morison, who was not quite right in the head. He spoke of it in a delighted tone, as if that was what life was made up of: the whole of life was present in it, and there was nothing beyond. I remember too, another even tinier incident. For some reason we were sharing a hotel bedroom, and as he undressed, the coins dropped out of his pocket, chinking as they fell, and he said, in a tone of mock-superstitious resignation: 'When they begin to sing, it's all over with them.' There was the same joyful note in his voice, and it was oddly ghostly and impressive, as if he truly had insight into the workings of Providence" (Furbank, II, 292-97).

The above excerpt is very apt, in the sense that from it we may form a sufficiently lively vision of Forster, the man, and can imaginatively follow his manners and moods. However, the most central and striking trait of Forster's personality was that he was an unflagging humanist. Whatever he thought or did relating to man or society or politics, or whatever he wrote in his novels, was surcharged with his love of humanity: man was his first love and man his last, all else were but an intermission. Before dwelling on the nature and quality and manifestation of Forster's humanism, let us try to clearly understand what is generally understood by the term 'humanism,' and then what Forster himself actually understood by it. The spring of all humanitarian thoughts was the Pythagorean dictum: 'Man is the measure of all things.' But well before Pythagoras the same opinion had been being held by the Sophists who wrangled with Socrates over the question whether there were universal and eternal moral principles (like the conception of a universal and eternal God) or each man had his own disparate opinion about morality, ratified by himself. Socrates stuck to the conviction that moral principles were universal and eternal, and this conviction of his was reinforced by religion, but the Sophists and the Pythagoreans disagreed with him and believed that each man is the best judge of his actions, that 'Man is the measure of all things' so that there was no universal and eternal moral principles. At the end of the medieval period, the dictum 'Man is the measure of all things' prevailed with all force, and consequently, with the dawning of Renaissance, God had to condescend to make room for Man. The revivified dictum of the Sophists and the Pythagoreans generated humanism—the belief that man, and not God, should be abiding at the centre of all man's thoughts and activities. But the term 'humanism' has been nebulous, ill-defined, and so we should know of which brand of humanism was Forster a votary. W.J.H. Sprott, in his essay, 'Forster as a Humanist,' writes about Forster's conception of humanism: "'The humanist,' he says, 'has four leading characteristics—curiosity, a free mind, belief in good taste, and belief in the human race'" (Edward Arnold, 75). And Forster possessed all these four cardinal virtues, which were comprised, according to him, in the single concept of humanism.

To begin with, Forster had a vast range of curiosity, about which Sprott writes: "Curiosity?... His range of literary criticism displays an inquiring mind. He ranges with ease from William Barnes to d' Annunzio. He is curious about music [He could play on the piano.] He is curious about places [He was an untiring traveller]..." *(ibid.)* Sprott writes about the second component of humanism, that was in Forster: "Forster has a free-ranging intellect, an unfailing readiness to consider new ideas, and a complete disregard for authority" (*op. cit.,* 76). The third criterion of humanism, according to Forster, was 'belief in good taste'—the belief that all human thoughts and actions were not equally appreciable, and that some human thoughts and actions were despicable, that is that some of them were good as some were bad. The discrimination between the good and the bad ones should be taken into account, and one should emulate the good ones and avoid the bad ones, and in any case one must, at least, believe in the discrimination, if he wants to practise humanism. Sprott writes about Forster: "He does not say that the humanist must *have* good taste [of thoughts and actions], but that he must *believe* in it [that there are good and bad thoughts and actions, and that the good ones must be discriminated from the bad ones]. He may possess it also, but who is to judge its 'goodness?' What is required is that he should value discrimination. The works of men are varied, and different people have their lives enriched by different things. What is important is that people should recognise what enriches their lives from what does not, and should help others to find their sources of enrichment.... We must discriminate between the good and the bad, and denounce the latter with boldness" (*ibid.*).

The fourth component of humanism, again according to Forster, was 'belief in the human race', that is the belief that the human race, inspite of all the hurdles before it, would be able to progressively refine its 'standard of moral values.' After the collapse of the authority of religion, since the ensuing of the Industrial Revolution and the growth spurt of scientific achievement, we were getting puzzled as to what was going to happen to the moral values, which were a starling possession of mankind: were moral values going to dwindle, and were we going to be immoral, or amoral like animals? Forster was not non-plussed like most people, because he believed that man had innate moral values which would sustain themselves without the props of religion. He believed that man had already achieved at least two things in the field of morality (without the blessings of religion). One, "the establishment and progressive refinement of moral values" (*ibid.*). And two, 'the production of works of art.' "For Forster this is, perhaps, its [humanity's] greatest achievement" (*op. cit.*, 77). For him, the ideal human being was one who was 'simple, kindly, unpretentious.' He did not value intelligence as much as we are wont to do, though he did never denigrate it. To him "Warmth of character is what really matters" (*ibid.*).

'Warmth of character' was the corner-stone or desideratum of Forsterean humanism—'warmth of character' or simply love. His humanism was not only magnanimously inclusive but also close-knit. Man could practise humanism only in the proximity of man. Spatially distant relationship between man and man was, to him, no sign of humanism; men must be naturally and closely drawn to each other by the force of love, and one must imaginatively posit oneself in the condition of the other and thereby realise the other, so that cohesion and empathy may sprout. This was what he termed friendship, which is a condition wherein a friend is an alter-ego. Forster's ideal society was that society where each and every member of it would be a friend to all the rest. But he was never utopian; he could never conceive of a large society of friends. He believed in, and desired, a small but close-knit society of (male) human beings, where all would be tied together with the bond of spiritual (and physical) love and where each would be a friend to all others irrespective of class, caste, creed, and even age. Philosophers have, down the ages, given us various models of the ideal society and divers means of achieving them, but they all have missed the most cardinal point that only true friendship can bring in the ideal society. This truism may have been thought of, casually though, but it was Forster who first spoke it out in clear terms, and emphatically.

Friendship was to him a matter of so great importance that he once wrote very boldly and bluntly in the collection of personal confessions of some great writers, entitled *I Believe:* "if I had to choose between betraying my country and betraying my friend, I hope I should have the guts to betray my country" (George Allen, 43). As has already been innuendoed before, Forster's conception of friendship was total, in the sense that by friendship he meant both spiritual and physical closeness or affinity (in the extreme case of friendship, of course), espicially between two males, which, in fact, means a homosexual relationship, to which we shall turn at the end of this chapter. But, in no case does this exclude the possibility of friendship between two non-homosexuals, or between a male and a female. This means that he could conceive of Platonic or spiritual friendship as well, in *A Passage to India,* the very warm relationship (or friendship) between Aziz and Mrs Moore, for instance. However, Forster's natural tendency of emphasising friendship was definitely reinforced by G.E. Moore's philosophy of goodness, i.e., of good behaviour. Forster was a votary not only of friendship but also of philanthropy. After the publication of *Howards End,* his capital increased phenomenally, and he happily gave away a great amount of money for charitable purposes.

Forster was a firm believer in the institution of democracy and in freedom in all fields, as is obvious, for instance, from his *Two Cheers for Democracy.* Though he valued republicanism more than democracy, he held the latter above all the other contemporary forms of government. In *I Believe* he wrote about democracy: "Democracy isn't a beloved republic really, and never will be. But it is less hateful than other contemporary forms of government, and to that extent it deserves our support" (*op. cit.,* 44). Conjoined with the concept of democracy is the concept of freedom: no freedom, no democracy. Freedom or liberty, again, is the first fruit of democracy, and freedom or liberty means individuality, and individuality, in turn, implies criticism, creative criticism, rather. Forster was a votary of freedom, individualism and criticism, because they sustain democracy. He wrote: "Democracy has another merit. It allows criticism, and if there isn't public criticism there are bound to be hushed-up scandals. This is why I believe in the press, despite all its vulgarity, and why I believe in Parliament. The British Parliament is often sneered at because it's a talking shop. Well, I believe in it because it is a talking shop. I believe in the private member who makes himself a nuisance. He gets snubbed and is told that he is cranky or ill-informed, has been mentioned, and very often an abuse gets put right just by being mentioned" (*ibid.*). Though he was not happy with the parliamentary system, as he saw it in England, and though he smelt hypocrisy in that system, because the parliamentarians or the law-makers only pretended to like freedom, he supported the system in the absence of a better one, only wishing that that system or custom, that had been bearing a tradition, assumed virtues. He thought that even with all its present faults, the parliamentary system was a sterling custom. He had to say to the parliamentary system only what Hamlet had to tell his 'erring mother:' "Shakespeare, whatever his personal opinions were—Shakespeare appreciated hypocrisy, and the words which Hamlet addresses to his erring mother might equally be addressed by us to the mother of Parliaments:

> Good night; but go not to mine uncle's bed;
> Assume a virtue, if you have it not.
> That monster, custom, who all sense doth eat,
> Of habits devil, is angel yet in this,
> That to the use of actions fair and good

He likewise gives a frock or livery,
That aptly is put on"

(Forster, 1955, 61-62).

Forster believed in democracy because he believed in the freedom of expressing personal views—personal ideas, opinions, thoughts and beliefs. He did not only believe in the right to express one's personal views, and in respecting other's personal views, but also acted according to his belief. In 1959, the new Obscene Publications Act was passed, and then D.H. Lawrence's *Lady Chatterley's Lover* was put on trial under this Act. Forster appeared as a witness in this case and boldly defended Lawrence, pleading vigorously that everyone should have the right to express his own ideas, especially when they belong to the realm of art. To the question of Jeremy Hutchinson, the defence counsel, as to the artistic merit of that work of Lawrence, he replied: "'I should place him [Lawrence] enormously high. When one comes to the upper ten novels, then one has to begin to think a little of the order, but compared with all the novels which come out, the novels he wrote dominate terrifically'" (Furbank, II, 311).

Forster did not belong to any political party and did not hold any well-defined political views. He was rather insouciant about politics, perhaps because he thought that not political jargons but only true friendship, in which good intention must be central, might work as the panacea for all social evils and might help establish an ideal society to live in. The little that we can say touching his political views is that he was a confirmed and unflagging liberal humanist (*A Passage to India* is the epitome of his liberal humanism) from the beginning to the end of his active life. What he disliked in politics and elsewhere was violence, hatred, tyranny and persecution, because these cannot bring in peace and friendship—the *summun bofnum* of human life. At the fag end *of A Passage to India,* we find alternations of friendship and hatred between Aziz and Fielding, showing no sure sign of true friendship between them. The earth, the temples, the jail, the palace, the birds, in short everything around them told them, 'in their hundred voices,' that so long as there would remain hatred and animosity, subdued and unconscious though, there would be no possibility of peace and true friendship between them. Everything around them, therefore, cried out: 'No, not yet.' Forster did not believe in God, but in man; again, he did not believe in machine, but in man; and, further, he did not believe in the immortal soul, but believed in the ontological authenticity of the conscious and independent being that is man. Man, he believed, could not be explained away as only an extremely complicated machine, nor could human relationship be explained in terms of transmitter, transponder and receiver. He very effectively mocked at the mechanistic-reductionist theory of man and human relationship in his short story, 'The Machine Stops.'

Though he was indifferent to politics, Forster was violently opposed to fascism, because it is opposed to 'creative actions' and 'all the decent human relations.' In *I Believe,* he wrote: "I realize that all society rests upon force. But all the great creative actions, all the decent human relations, occur during the intervals when force has not managed to come to the front. These intervals are what matter. I want them to be as frequent and as lengthy as possible and I call them 'civilization.' Some people realize force and pull it into the foreground and worship it, instead of keeping it in the background as long as possible. I think they make a mistake, and I think that their opposites, the mystics, err even more when they declare that force doesn't exist. I believe that it does exist, and that one of our jobs is to prevent it from getting out of its box. It gets out sooner or later, and then it destroys us and all the lovely things which we have made. But it isn't out all the time, for the fortunate reason that the strong are so stupid" (George Allen, 45).

Once Forster was, surreptitiously, being led to communism, but as soon as he realised his *faux paux*, he regressed. In 1934, the recently-founded National Council for Civil Liberties (N.C.C.L.) invited him to become its first President, and he indifferently accepted the invitation, perhaps being attracted by the declared liberal views of the organisation. As the President of the N.C.C.L., Forster, for some time, interested himself in political issues, and was writing for the *Time and Tide,* frequently. It was during this time that he wrote about communism: "'It would destroy nearly every thing I understand and like, and I want the present economic and social order to continue. If the present order breaks, communism seems the only hopeful alternative'" (Furbank, II, 190). On 21st June, 1935, the Popular Front organised in Paris a meeting of the International Association of Writers for the Defence of Culture (*Congres International des Ecrivains*) with a view 'to unite communists, socialists and liberals' for defending 'the cultural heritage.' Forster attended the meeting, and, in his speech, cried down facism; upheld justice, culture, liberty and freedom; and expressed his brinkmanship over communism and bourgeois stance. He said: "you may have guessed that I am not a Communist, though perhaps I might be one if I was a younger and a braver man, for in Communism I can see hope. It does many things which I think evil, but I know that it intends good. I am actually what my age and my upbringing have made me—a bourgeois" (Forster, 1955, 61).

Forster was definitely a pacifist, and he hated war desperately. In 1936, the gathering black cloud of the Second World War was invading the consciousness of Forster, gradually making him more and more depressed about the fate of mankind. He was afraid that the impending catastrophe would have left nothing on its march human beings had been living by and for. In the entry of 5th September 1936, in his Commonplace Book, he recorded his reaction to the oncoming wide-ranging pugnacity: "'...the collapse of civilization seems to eat up from below into any thing I do'" (Furbank, II, 214). Again, about five months afterwards, to be precise on 5th January 1937, when he came by the news that 10,5000 Italian troops landed in Spain, to aggravate the war situation, Forster wrote to Christopher Isherwood that it seemed to him that the world was 'close to the edge'. "In the present time, he said, the passage in literature which most satisfied him was the one in *War and Peace* about the Russians after the fall of Moscow: '...Those who were striving to understand the general course of events, and trying by self-sacrifice and heroism to take a hand in it, were the most useless members of society; they saw everything upside down, and all they did for the common good proved to be futile and absurd'" (*op. cit.*, II, 215). Forster hated war because he hated power, muscles and dictatorship, and these are the generators of war. But he was not daunted by them, for he believed that those who flaunted them were fortunately 'stupid.' His conviction was that "The dictator-hero can grind down his citizens till they are all alike, but he cant melt them into a single man. That is beyond his power. He can order them to merge, he can incite them to mass antics, but they are obliged to be born separately and to die separately and, owing to these unavoidable termini, will always be running off the totalitarian rails" (George Allen, 50).

But sometimes, and as regards some matters, he could not keep himself confined within the bound of his pacifist philosophy, particularly in the case of anti-Semitism. P.N. Furbank writes: "For Forster there was no doubt that anti-semitism was the worst and most shocking of all things. It was the one evil, as he wrote [in his article 'Jew-consciousness', first published in *New Statesman* on 7 January, 1939, and then reprinted in *Two Cheers for Democracy*], that no one had foreseen at the end of the First World War; and it dominated his attitude to the present one, making it impossible for him to be a pacifist, he detected Jew-consciousness in the air even in England. 'A nasty side of our nation's character has been scratched up—the sniggering side,' he wrote. 'People who would not ill-treat Jews themselves, or even be rude to them, enjoy tittering over their misfortunes.' When, in May of this year [1940], he heard that a young policeman friend of his and Bob's had been talking anti-semitism, he at once despatched him a stinging letter. He wrote that he was surprised that E— of all people should be anti-Jewish, pointed out the evil effect of such opinions, and ended with a list of the names of great Jews" (Furbank, II, 236).

P.N. Furbank says that "Forster, to the extent that he was a pacifist, was so by instinct rather than settled conviction" (Furbank, II, 1). But it is also true that his natural or inherent pacifism was reinforced by his association with the Bloomsbury Group, and particularly by G.E. Moore's philosophy of tolerance. Forster's pacifism was acid-tested in 1916. The Government issued conscription for the First World War, and the Red Cross sent him, among many others, for medical test with a view to his being conscripted. Forster thought he would not pass the test, and in the case of his failure he would be able to stick to his antiwar stance without any fuss. But even with his weak musculature he was declared fit. He was, nevertheless, determined not to 'attest,' i.e., not to sign his induction into the military service. As he was not an avowedly religious person, he could not be considered a true 'conscientious objector.' He therefore politely wrote to the Chief Red Cross Commissioner, Sir Courtauld Thomson, begging to the excused from attesting, whereupon Sir Thomson asked Forster to tell him the reasons of his not attesting. Forster replied that "It was a matter of instinct, 'a very profound instinct which he could only call conscience and which presented the taking of the life of a fellow-creature as the most horrible thing he could do.'" (*op. cit,* II, 26). As regards war, he advocated tolerance. W.J.H. Sprott, who in 1941 had been close to Forster during the Second World War, says that Forster was anxious about the behaviour of the English with the Germans. Sprott writes that Forster "pleads for tolerance: 'Don't try to love them: you can't, you'll only strain yourself. But try to tolerate them'" (George Allen, 80).

Forster failed to value money, contrary to the general habit of people. Nicola Beauman has written that to Forster possession of money was a sort of moral weight on the shoulders: "What is so much to Morgan's (Forster's) credit is that his money seemed to make so little difference to him—except, that is, as a burden of responsibility, as a moral weight on his shoulders" (Beauman, 34). Forster and his mother had always been more or less affluent, and this may be a reason why he cared so little for money. Nay, he even tended to hate money, particularly the ethic and ethos that are generally attached to the superfluity of money. Though he himself led a financially comfortable life on inherited property, that is on unearned money, he disliked the financially careless life based on unearned money. In *Howards End,* the theme is 'money ethic.' In this novel, Forster "was to try to resolve his ambivalent feeling about living on inherited wealth; to try to work out who had the greater integrity, the Schlegels for living on 'fortune' but being honest about its origins (and, in Helen's case, trying to give some of it away) or the Wilcoxes for earning it but refusing, honestly, to mention it; and to try to determine whether Leonard Bast would have been 'saved' had he accepted Schlegel money" (*op. cit.,* 168). W.J.H. Sprott says that Forster needed little money for his living and that he "dislikes spending money on himself" (George Allen, 79). He hated money because of the dangerous consequences that follow it, and he hated money so much so that he, inspite of his insouciance about communism and disgust about Christianity, partially liked the two creeds for their animosity towards money. In 1940, he wrote: "...The parts of Communism and of Christianity that interest me are *not* their boring egalitarianism, but their attempts to cut out money. I do think money is dangerous, and I know more about its dangers than you suppose, for my great grandfather was quite a famous banker, and some of his canniness runs in my blood, and tempts me to prefer money to the things it buys" (Furbank, II, 236).

Though he had small regard for money, Forster said that he believed in aristocracy. There is no contradiction here, for he said so only facetiously. In his article in *I Believe,* he wrote: "I believe in aristocracy though—if that's the right word, and if a democrat may use it. Not an aristocracy of power, based upon rank and influence, but an aristocracy of the sensitive, the considerate, and the plucky. Its members are to be found in all nations and classes, and all through the ages, and there is a secret understanding between them when they meet. They represent the true human tradition, the one permanent victory of our queer race over cruelty and chaos. Thousands of them perish in obscurity; a few are great names. They are sensitive for others as well as for themselves, they are considerate without being fussy, their pluck is not swankiness, but the power to endure, and they can take a joke" (*op. cit.*, 47). No, this is no 'right word' for what we generally understand by aristocracy, and if Forster called himself an aristocrat, in *his* sense of the word, we would rather be glad to welcome him, because his aristocracy would not offend or irritate us. In his sense of aristocracy anyone, irrespective of class, class or creed could be an aristocrat; and in his sense of aristocracy no muscular, monetary or intellectual superiority was necessary. His aristocracy, in effect, was the aristocracy of the heart.

And for the same reason, Forster distrusted great men. In *I Believe,* he ironically wrote against the so-called great men: "They produce a desert of uniformity around them and often a pool of blood too, and I always feel a little man's pleasure when they come a cropper. Every now and then one reads in the newspapers some such statements as, 'The *coup d'etat* appears to have failed, and Admiral Boga's whereabouts is at present unknown.' Admiral Boga had probably every qualification for being a great man—an iron will, personal magnetism, dash, flair—but fate was against him, so he retires to unknown whereabouts instead of parading history with his peers. He fails with a completeness that no artist and no lover can experience, because with them the process of creation is itself an achievement, whereas with him the only possible achievement is success" *(ibid.)*. But if there were no great men, according to Forster, what people did he like and respect, at least? He respected those people in whose hearts 'human spirit' did dwell. He wrote: "'The people I respect must behave as if they were immortal and as if society was eternal. Both assumptions are false: both of them must be accepted as true if we are to go on eating and working and loving, and are to keep open a few breathing holes for the human spirit'" (Furbank, II, 225). As we have said, Forster did not count any other possessions of man to be of as much worth as passion or love or a highly developed heart. Inwardly, he was a lonely man; because, being a homosexual, he was deprived of natural and heterosexual love; and because due to the over-protective care of Lily he had been growing up in a marooned situation; and also because in the Tunbridge School he was, so to say, forced to learn *esprit de corps* and not to be an individual. He grew up, as if, in the aridity of the world, and so he valued the sacred succuss of the heart as nothing else.

Forster did not believe either in the existence of God or in the belief that the rituals, recommended by religions, are of any efficacy in propitiating or pleasing God for deriving benefits from him. He may have been hesitant about politics and many other things, but regarding religion he was an orthodox unbeliever. Interestingly, he began his essay in *I Believe* by expressing his lack of faith—by declaring his disbelief in religion. In that essay he has written: "Faith, to my mind, is a stiffening process, a sort of mental starch, which ought to be applied as sparingly as possible. I dislike the stuff. I do not believe in it, for its own sake, at all.... My law-givers are Erasmus and Montaigne, not Moses and St Paul. My temple stands not upon Mount Moriah but in that Elysian Field where even the immoral are admitted. My motto is 'Lord, I disbelieve—help thou my unbelief'" (George Allen, 42-43). He did not believe, and more than that, he could not be persuaded to believe, that there was God and that he could help him in his needs. About 1940, Christopher Isherwood, through his close association and conversation with the Vedantic monk Swami Prabhavananda, was spiritually converted to Hindu mystical beliefs, and wanted that his friend Forster followed his suit. Isherwood was writing letters, now and then, to Forster explaining his new understandings and experiences, but received from him only 'discouraging response': "...Forster said he 'couldn't imagine' the belief that God could help him" (Furbank, II, 237). But though he did not believe in God even when he could well foresee his imminent end, he believed in the intrinsic value of such things as 'sanctity', negative attitude to worldly possessions, and 'gratitude'—three elements of religiosity: "It was clear to him that his remaining days must be a preparation for death. He had once said that he would like to die 'in an odour of sanctity,' and the wish made itself felt. He was beginning, quietly, to strip himself of possessions, pressing friends to accept books and pieces of furniture. A habit was growing on him, also, of expressing gratitude—of exclaiming, during a meal perhaps, how lucky he was, how many things he had to be thankful for. Gratitude interested him as a sentiment. He wrote in his diary for 16 May 1964: 'How odd is this feeling of gratitude when one isn't being grateful to anyone. Pleasanter than if there was someone e.g. God—which would entail a feeling of obligation"' (*op. cit.*, II, 318). In any case, Forster was against asceticism, which happens to be a component of most forms of religion. He would not like to sacrifice the body for any sublimer end. In *I Believe,* he wrote: "I'm against asceticism myself. I'm with the old Scotchman who wanted less chastity and more delicacy" (George Allen, 48).

Even if one does not believe in God or religion, one may have a graduated scale of preferences for religions. Forster's case was such; but his scale was not clearly notched and the graduations were shifting and complex, at some places. Christianity he could not obviously stomach, "but Islam and Hinduism have aroused mixed feeling in him" (Bradbury, 1983, 174). Of Islam, Forster wrote: "I do like Islam'" *(ibid.)*. The concept of equality in Islam was attractive to him. Frederick C. Crews writes about him; "Nowhere does Forster imply that he actually believes the dogmatic content of Islam; the point is that he is aesthetically gratified by a religion that is not grossly anthropomorphic. He is no more of a Moslem than he is a Christian, but Islam at least does not outrage his common sense and his love of modest form" (*op. cit.,* 175). Crews further writes: "Forster's opinion of Hinduism is more clearly a dual one: he finds Hindu ritual absurd but Hindu theology relatively attractive" (*ibid.*). In any case, He was never serious about religion, of whatsoever ilk it might have been.

Disbelief in religion was no hindrance to Forster's believing in morality, because he believed, like Wordsworth, for instance, that morality did not derive from belief in God. His view of morality was immensely influenced by G.E. Moore's moral philosophy, recorded in his *Principia Ethica.* Moore's moral philosophy was based on the concept (nebulous, though) of goodness, with a short prescriptive list of instructions or commandments relating to right, duty, etc. "In *Principia Ethica,* goodness is seen as a non-natural quality of certain things or situations, that is, one not given in sense experience, but nonetheless directly experienced, by a kind of moral intuition. Goodness is the fundamental ethical concept which cannot be defined or analysed in terms of anything simpler. Our other ethical concepts, right, duty, etc., can be defined in terms of producing and preserving so far as possible whatever possesses this quality of goodness, which Moore himself found most obviously exemplified in the experiences of friendship and aesthetic enjoyment" (Flew, 238). Forster believed that, contrary to the general belief, the more individuals would be set at liberty, the more ethically would they behave, and that "The more highly public life is organized the lower does its morality sink" (George Allen, 48). His philosophy of individualism is obvious here, and his belief in the individual, and not in the group, led him to moral relativism. This is obvious from the murmuring of the echo in the cave (in which Adela was losing her hold on life): '...Everything exists, nothing has value' *(A Passage to India,* chapter 14).

Forster's misogyny was perhaps a natural corollary of his homosexuality, and of his being a sort of hermaphroditic or androgynous person. Though in his novels females predominate and though he has been able to depict a good number of unforgettable female characters, women were, so to say, allergens to him. His aversion to womankind is obvious in his *en camera* conversation with the maharaja of Dewas (Sr), after his having a carnal intercourse with a coolie in the palace premises of the Maharaja. Believing that the Maharaja was quite in the know of the matter of the intercourse, Forster confessed to him: "'I have tried to have carnal intercourse with one of the coolies and it has become known.'

> 'With a coolie girl?'
> 'No, with a man....'
> 'Why a man and not a woman? Is not a woman more natural?'
> 'Not in my case. I have no feeling for women'"
> (Furbank, II, 83).

Forster did not only dislike women but also children. He liked cats but not dogs: "Morgan [Forster] and Lily had had cats all their life together" (Beauman, 365, f.n.). He was fond of tea, so much so that in all his novels and in a few of his short stories we come across talks about tea, tea-party and tea-things, not very infrequently. Even his style of writing novels has been termed 'tea-tabling' style. To him tea was a symbol of friendship and enjoyable moments of life. Forster also loved music, and could appreciably play on the piano. He "spent many hours playing peacefully in the drawing room at Harnham. He went to concerts whenever he could. In later years he listened to the gramophone. And he incorporated music into his novels, to such an extent that he was to be called by his future friend Benjamin Britten [who co-operated with him in composing *Billy Budd*] 'our most musical novelist':

from the opera scene in *Where Angels Fear to Tread* to the description of Beethoven's Fifth Symphony in *Howards End* to the more subtle musical imagery of the trial scene in *A Passage to India,* in all three and in the other novels music, as Morgan [Forster] himself put it, would be 'deep beneath the arts' and beneath his life" (*op. cit.,* 162).

Forster's another love was trees, and this is readily obvious from his *The Abinger Pageant,* in which he poured out his own love of trees and pastoral scenarios. P.N. Furbank writes about Forster's love of trees: "Forster, from childhood, had had a passionate fondness for trees, and such landowning instincts as he possessed were largely concerned with woods and trees. Adjoining West Hackhurst there lay a wood, of some four acres, called Piney Copse, and soon after he had settled there he had discovered that the wood was threatened, and on an impulse he had bought it, for the sum of Pound 450" (*Furbank,* II, 199). Furbank further writes about Forster in this regard: "From the beginning, he foresaw the effect the wood might have on him, depicting this satirically in an essay, 'My Wood,' published in the *New Leader* in 1926. In the first place (the essay ran) the wood made him feel heavy and laden and a 'man of weight,' like the one who failed to get into the kingdom of Heaven" (*ibid.).*

Travelling was a part and parcel of Forster's life: it was not a hobby, but a necessity, to him. He went to Italy, Germany, Egypt, India and some other countries; he wanted to mix with the peoples of those countries, to learn their lores, to know their imaginations, to feel their hearts. He perhaps loved the antic peoples more than the civilised—the peoples of sensibilities more than the peoples of rationality. He wished the two sorts of peoples connected with each other: his commandment was 'only connect!' *(Howards End,* section XXII)—only connect rationality with sensibility (only connect the Tunbridge motto with the Cambridge ideal; only connect the English civilisation with the Italian sensibilities, for instance). His wide-ranging love of humanity, of the variety of human beings and their manners attracted him to be a traveller and write travelogues. As a traveller, he was not only interested in sight-seeing but also in the big and small things of the people's daily and perennial life. During his brief period of stay in India, for instance, he got acquainted with almost everything that came in his way, from the Taj in a white night or the *Gokul Ashtami* festival to the Indian habit of chewing *pan*.

However, Forster was a shy, unassuming, introverted, sentimental and loving person. His look was gauche and his manners were girlish. He seemed to be always physically gathering himself up, and to be behaving as a poppet or puppet. For this reason, one of his two nicknames was 'Poppy' (perhaps a combined variation of 'poppet,' meaning 'puppet,' and 'popsy' or 'popsie,' meaning 'girl'). Forster was 'strange, elusive, evasive,' and for this reason his another nickname was Taupe' (a French word, meaning 'mole' or 'mole-hill'): "'Lytton [Strachy] nicknamed him [Forster] the Taupe, partly because of his faint physical resemblance to a mole, but principally because he seemed intellectually and emotionally to travel unseen underground and every now and again pop up unexpectedly with some subtle observation or delicate quip which somehow or other he had found in the depths of the earth or of his own soul'" (Beauman, 282).

Though of delicate physic, Forster suffered relatively fewer bouts of illness, and even fewer fatal diseases, before his last years, save "once or twice later in life in times of stress—he developed a kind of falling sickness [i.e. epilepsy] and had bouts of hurling himself against the furniture" (Furbank, II, 26). In his literary works (which are mostly social comedies), he was somewhat pessimistic, but in real life he was full of verve and jest—though not always noticeably. When Forster was an old man of 59 years, in 1938, Christopher Isherwood wrote about him: "'While the others tell their followers to be ready to die, he advises us to live as if we were immortal'" (*op. cit.,* II. 229). Again, in 1945, when he was returning home, on board a plane, after his third and last visit to India, Forster ejaculated in a Whitmanesque tone: "'The day after tomorrow [I] shall be 67. O lovely world, teach others to expound you as I have not been able to do!'" (*op. cit.,* II, 263).

****

Forster was a confirmed but rather secretive homosexual, without any feeling of sin or guilt or shame; he exalted and slyly canvassed for homosexuality, as he went on practising it most of his life. Throughout his creative writings underhand references to homosexuality are liberally strewn, and the central theme of the novel *Maurice* and of the ten short stories in *The Life to Come* (as well as of a good number of other short stories that he himself destroyed) is homosexuality. Even in his novel of cultural antagonism, *A Passage to India,* he found opportunities for referring to happy homosexual relations. For instances, Aziz and Fielding, in the first one-fifth of *A Passage to India* (chapter 7) exchange collar studs, a symbol of homosexual relationship, and at the fag-end of the novel (chapter 37) Aziz half-kisses Fielding. Sara Suleri Goodyear, in her article 'Forster's Imperial Erotic,' has justifiably given us an oblique suggestion that *A Passage to India* is a homosexual novel: "In place of the Orientalist paradigm in which the colonising presence is an irredeemably male as the colonised territory is female, *A Passage to India* presents an alternative colonial model: the most urgent crosscultural invitations occur *between male and male,* with racial difference serving as a substitute for gender" (emphasis added: Tambling, 152). It is therefore almost imperative that we learn at least a little about Forster's homosexuality to better understand the man, as well as the artist, Forster.

The term homosexuality derives from the Greek word or root *homos,* meaning 'same' (and not from the Greek word or root *homo* which means 'man') and the English word 'sexuality.' Homosexuality denotes sexual attraction or performance of sex between two partners of the same sex: between two male partners or between two female partners, the latter is specially called lesbianism—a term that derived from the name of the island of Lesbos, home of the first poetess Sappho who flourished between B.C. 611 and 592. In the homosexual activity between two persons of the same sex, generally one assumes the active role while the other assumes the passive role, but the roles may be exchanged between them from time to time. In the case of lesbianism, the active or dominant partner is, in homosexual parlour, called 'butch' and the passive or submissive partner is called 'fem.' No such terms are available for two male partners engaged in homosexuality. Homosexual partners may change their roles from time to time, or may continue to be perennially dominant or perennially submissive.

Of Forster's homosexuality we are interested especially in three questions: how strong was his homosexual drive? was his role in homosexual partnership active or passive? and what was the probable aetiology of his homosexuality? To answer the last question first, it is very difficult to definitely say what actually causes an individual to be homosexual; recent researches tell us that homosexuality does not depend on a single factor but on a group of factors. Before we briefly discuss those factors we should answer yet another question: why should we be so interested in the homosexuality of our novelist—Forster? We have already said that one reason of our being interested in the homosexuality of Forster is that it would help us understand the man, and the artist, Forster better. Here we may further say that we can never better understand a homosexual writer, such as Oscar Wilde, W. Somerset Maugham, Plato, Sappho (lesbian), Walt Whitman and W.H. Auden, without going into his homosexual drive and its relation with his work, because the works of a homosexual writer invariably reflects his particular sexual behavior. Somerset Maugham (1874-1965), Forster contemporary writer—and a novelist like him—is a case in point. In many places of Maugham's works, particularly in some of his novels, say in, especially, *The Razors's Edge, The Narrow Corner, Of Human Bondage, The Circle,* etc. there are subtle homosexual references. The homosexual, due to his being what he is, has his particular and peculiar (in the sense of not falling in the general line) *Weltanschauung* and aesthetic sense, which of course will cast their shadows over his works. So the understanding of the homosexual life of a homosexual writer is almost a *sine qua non* for understanding his works. And so we are legitimately interested in the homosexual life not only of Forster but of all homosexual writers. In fact, not only the homosexual drive but the general sexual drive of the writer is proximately or distantly, overtly or covertly, related to his works. However much we may despise sex, may be ashamed of it, sex is of immense importance in the sphere of art and aesthetic sentiment. Richard von Krafft-Ebing, one of the great sexual psychologists, in his *Psychopathia Sexualis,* writes: "Sexual influence is just [as] potent in the awakening of aesthetic sentiments. What other foundation is there for plastic art or poetry? From (sensual) love arises that warmth of fancy which alone can inspire the creative mind, and the fire of sensual feeling kindles and preserves the glow and fervour of art. This explains the sensual natures of great poets and artists. The world of fancy keeps pace with the development of sexual power. Whoever during that period cannot be animated by the ideals of all that is great, noble and beautiful remains a 'Philistine' all his life. Even the dolt tries his hand at poetry when in love" (Krafft-Ebing, 11).

Now, to probe into the aetiology of homosexuality. Homosexuality is certainly not a rare phenomenon: it is and was prevalent in the four corners of the world since forgotten times. The population of homosexuals is also not so negligible. According to one 'admittedly biased source,' homosexuality is practised, wrote Benjamin Kleinmuntz in 1980, "by no less than 20 million Americans" (Kleinmuntz, 348). This number may seem fantastic, but it perhaps is not so, for H. Maisch wrote in *Encyclopedia of Psychology* in 1972, that "In the USA, about 4% of adult white males have only homosexual contacts; after puberty about 37% had at least one homosexual experience leading to orgasm. The incidence was much rarer among women (Kinsey, 1948)" (Eysenck, I, 462). Homosexuality is present not only in America or among the Americans but has been in existence in all countries and in all races, though the frequencies of homosexual incidents vary from one country to another and from one people to another. Reference to homosexuality is available even in the Bible: "'You shall not be with a man as with a woman: that is an abomination'" (Kleinmuntz, 348). Inspite of the moral disenfranchisements of all the religions, homosexuality has been continuing to remain in force down the ages. Not only this, of recent times, it has been growing in prevalence, so much so that in America several provincial governments have been forced to change laws relating to homosexuality. Benjamin Kleinmuntz writes: "...in 1969 Connecticut amended its criminal statutes and now does not treat adult, private, and consensual homosexual acts as crimes. Similar changes have been made in the laws of Illinois and California" (*op. cit.,* 348-49).

Homosexuality is not simply frottage, i.e. rubbing genitals against someone else's body for obtaining pleasure, but it also entails love—love for the frotteur's own self and not for the person against whose body the frottage is done. Therefore, "According to Freud (1914), homosexual love differs from heterosexual love in being narcissistic (...) since the object is loved on account of its similarity to what the subject is, once was, or hopes some time to become, as opposed to heterosexual love, which is anaclitic, being dependent on the object providing what the subject cannot himself be" (Rycroft, 62). It is interesting to know that homosexuality and heterosexuality do not absolutely depend on the nature of the gonads or sex glands. Psychologists say that at the beginning both the male gonads and the female gonads remain bisexual, i.e. these give pleasure whenever they are stimulated, irrespective of who stimulates and how stimulates. This means that each and every individual begins to sexually grow up as a hermaphrodite, but then when the individual gradually gets aculturised or socialised, and the society expects the individual to assume one single and particular sexual role (shading off the previous bisexuality or hermaphroditism) for life, commensurate with the manifest nature of the gonads, the individual slowly psychologically becomes a male or a female. Therefore it is not predetermined whether an individual will be heterosexual or homosexual.

But this in no way negates the fact that the gonads are a potent factor in determining the sexual behaviour of an individual. Eviration is a case in point: it has been observed that after the male gonads are surgically removed or they are somehow considerably damaged, the individual tends to show the traits of opposite sex. Richard von Krafft-Ebing writes: "...eviration induces a desire for the passive *role,* and, further, for (passive) pederasty. It makes a deeper impress on the character. The character becomes feminine" (Krafft-Ebing, 302). Krafft-Ebing further writes: "*Herodotus* already describes a peculiar disease which frequently affected the Scythians. The disease consisted in this: that men became effeminate in character, put on female garments, did the work of women, and even became effeminate in appearance. As an explanation of this insanity of the Scythians, *Herodotus* relates the myth that the goddess Venus angered by the plundering of the temple at Ascalon by the Scythians, had made women of these plunderers and their posterity. "*Hippocrates,* not believing in supernatural diseases, recognised that impotence was here a causative factor, and explained it, though incorrectly, as due to the custom of the Scythians to have themselves bled behind the ears in order to cure disease superinduced by constant horse-back riding. He thought that these veins were of great importance in the preservation of the sexual powers, and that when they were severed, impotence was induced. Since the Scythians considered their impotence due to divine punishment and incurable, they put on the clothing of females, and lived as women among women" (*op. cit,* 302-03). The explanations of Herodotus and Hippocrates may be incorrect, but their belief that impotency in the male leads to effemination is certainly correct, that is gonads are somehow related to a male's being effeminate.

The real causes of homosexuality are not yet identified. H. Maisch, however, says that at present there are three theories as to the development of homosexuality. Maisch writes: "The causes of homosexuality are still open to question. At present there are three theories concerning the origins of homosexuality, (a) Biologically oriented theory: homosexuality is dependent on biological factors which are not influenced by experience; (b) Psycho-socially oriented theory: homosexuality is conditioned by the environment, i.e. dependent on experience, and acquired (psychoanalytical theory and learning theory); (c) Convergence theory: homosexuality stems from a biological (learning) disposition; its occurrence in an individual is, however, dependent on environmental influence" (Eysenck, 463). If we consider these three theories, we may say that environmental factors at least play a vital role in the development of homosexuality. Confirmation of this opinion may be found in Kleinmuntz who tells us that "Homosexuality is common among male adults whose access to the opposite sex is limited for any reason" (Kleinmuntz, 348).

Now, what may have been the causes of Forster's being a homosexual? Biological causes, if there be any, we cannot ferret out now, but we have some reasons to believe that Forster was environmentally predisposed to be a homosexual. Firstly, his father died when he was just a baby, and so when he grew up as a boy and when the other boys, in their teens, found their fathers for 'identification,' Forster had to vacantly and despairingly wait for a surrogate father (a substitute for father) for 'identification,' and due to his intellectual immaturity at this stage, in the extremely affectionate and protective circle of his mother, he rather unconsciously identified himself with his mother and thus developed some covert feminine traits, such as shyness, timidity, etc. Secondly, since when he was a little boy of around five years, for a couple of years, Lily sometimes used to dress him in female clothes, like a girl. Forster's photograph (with Lily) when he was five years old is a proof of this—in the photograph he, with his long hair, and in frock, does not look like a boy, but like a girl. Such a treatment perhaps made him think that he was rather a girl than a boy. Thirdly, Lily was over-protective about her son, for which reason Forster could not mix with other boys and emulate their masculine roles, but had to remain confined within the narrow circle of Lily and one or two other women, and thus unconsciously imbibed feminine manners. Fourthly and lastly, even while he was growing up to be an adult, he had no access to any one of the fair sex, and thus he was deprived of any physical or mental stimulation for the growth of his normal sex, and consequently he had an inverted sex.

Our first question now: how strong was Forster's homosexual inclination? Forster had homosexual relationship not with one or two persons, which generally happens, but with more than half a dozen 'minorites' or homosexuals: Masood, Kanaya, Sebastian Sprott, Achille (French sailor),

Mohammed el Adl, Albert, Bob Buckingham *et al.* Some of these persons, for instances Masood, Kanaya and Achille, were initiated into the cult of homosexuality by Forster himself. Forster was so enamoured of, and enthusiastic about, homosexuality that he wished the Queen became a boy. In 1953, he received the appellation C.H. (Companion of Honour) from the Queen, as the New Year's Honour, and "returned to Cambridge in a glow of loyalty, declaring that if the Queen had been a boy he would have fallen in love with her" (Furbank, II, 289). His homosexual life spanned a long time: he was perhaps first oriented with homosexual life when he was at King's College, Cambridge, for the college was a den or breeding ground of homosexuals, and continued to remain a homosexual till his end. He was also a secret preacher of homosexualism; throughout his long literary career he, from time to time, as opportunities presented themselves, made subtle and votive references to homosexual orientation in his creative works. In his collection of short stories, *The Life to Come,* and in his novel *Maurice,* he maintained no secrecy about his support for homosexual life, but only kept the manuscripts of these works in secrecy for probable posthumous publication. Forster was a millenniarian as regards homosexualism.

The second, or the last, question is difficult to answer authoritatively: was Forster an active, or a passive, homosexual co-partner? was he a 'butch' or a 'fem?' Psychologists are now telling us with more and more authenticity that not only homosexuals but even normal human beings are "a mixture of 'male' and 'female'" (Kleinmuntz, 347). So it is only natural that homosexuals will also be hermaphrodite or bisexual. According to Laud Humphreys, male homosexuals fall into four categories. Benjamin Kleinmuntz writes: "Four types of male homosexuals were described by sociologist Laud Humphreys in a study described in his book, *Tearoom trade: Impersonal Sex in Public Places* (1970). These categories, which use the argot of the male homosexual sub-culture, are *trades, ambisexuals, gays,* and *closet queens.* The trades are mostly unhappily married men, blue-collar or clerical workers, who, according to Humphreys, may be further described as follows (...): *They are almost uniformly lonely and isolated; lacking success in their marriage bed or work, unable to discuss their three best friends (because they don't have three), enroute from the din of factories to the clamor of children, they slip off the freeways for a few moments of impersonal sex in a toilet stall.*

"The ambisexuals are less confined than the trades to tearooms, are less likely to be fleeing from an unhappy and loveless home life, and are more candid in their recognition of homosexuality as a lifestyle. They tend also to read extensively about homosexuality and discuss it with their friends. The third type, the so-called 'gay' homosexuals, are usually single and are open participants in a male homosexual subculture. They are also often supported by older male lovers, have a median age of 24 (the range is from 19-50), are well-educated, have effeminate mannerisms, are careful of their appearance, and keep immaculate and well-furnished apartment houses. They speak of marrying the men they love and, Humphreys reports (...), 'in a surprising number of cases they take their lovers 'home to meet mother."' "The closet queens, so-named because they keep their orientation hidden, are parallel to the trades in that they have blue-collar and clerical jobs, and are lonely and less educated than ambisexuals or gays. Their distinguishing feature is that they prefer teenage boys as sex objects and frequently cruise the streets in search for boys thumbing rides home from school. Among the bar set of the homosexual subculture, 'closet queen' is a pejorative term because their activities frequently result in the sort of scandal feared by the gay community" (*op. cit.,* 348-349). (In the homosexual argot, the term 'tearooms' means public restrooms, and the term 'trade' implies agreements between consenting partners.) The case of Forster as a homosexual seems refractory to fall into any one of the fore-mentioned four categories. Nevertheless, we may hazard, from what we know of him, that he was either a 'trade' or an 'ambisexual'—the second alternative being more likely.

As we have said, homosexuals generally change their roles (the role of the 'butch' and that of the 'fem') between themselves, and, perhaps, the case of Forster was not different. While engaged in homosexual activities with his partner, Forster perhaps assumed both the active and dominant (sadistic) role and the passive and submissive (mesochaistic) role alternately. To Masood and Buckingham, for instance, he was probably most of the time passive and submissive, for we know that he oftentimes marvelled at the beautiful musculature and the maleness of the two co-partners. He was attracted by the maleness of the males, and, on the other hand, he was unmanlikely shy, pusillanimous, prone to inwardness, and rather overly sensitive—all indicative of femininity. In most of his novels, predominance of femininity is noticeable—so much so that, for instance, immediately after the publication *of Howards End,* "... Mrs Dawson Scott, the novelist who was later to found PEN, remarked that she had 'just read *Howards End* by Miss Forster" (Beauman, 224). On the other hand, Forster's relationship with the young barber Kanaya seems to be paederastic, on his part; here Forster appears to be the 'butch': Kanaya, on the arrangement made by the Maharaja of Dewas (Sr), "paid a second visit, and on this occasion, as he was shaving Forster, the latter drew K—[Kanaya] to him and kissed him. He took it with the greatest calm, and Forster proceeded to bolt the door" (Furbank, II, 84). However, the slur of Forster's homosexuality has already cost him much in regard to his appreciation; it is time now to retrieve him from the shadow of ignominy, for human beings without frailties we cannot conceive of, and Forster is no ordinary human being.

The Short Stories

3

GENERAL INTRODUCTION TO THE SHORT STORIES

Forster wrote dozens of short stories and during his lifetime published two collections of short stories: *The Celestial Omnibus and Other Stories* (1911) and *Eternal Moment and Other Stories* (1928). In 1947, Sidgwick and Jackson published these two Collections in a single volume with the title *E.M. Forster: Collected Short Stories*. Alter his death another collection of short stories was published in 1972 with the title *The Life to Come and Other Stories*. But these three collections certainly do not contain all the short stories that Forster wrote, some he himself destroyed, particularly those having homosexual under-tow, and a few are yet untraced. *The Celestial Omnibus and Other Stories* contains six short stories: 'The Story of a Panic,' 'The Other Side of the Hedge,' 'The Celestial Omnibus,' 'Other Kingdom,' 'The Curate's Friend' and 'The Road From Colonus.' *The Eternal Moment* contains the same number of short stories: 'The Machine Stops,' 'The Point of It,' 'Mr Andrews,' 'Co-ordination,' 'The Story of the Siren' and 'The Eternal Moment.' The third and posthumous collection of short stories *The Life to Come and Other Stories* contains 14 stories, of which 10 are blatantly homosexual in purport. The 14 stories are: 'Ansell,' 'Albergo Empedocle,' 'The Helping Hand,' 'The Rock,' 'Three Courses and a Desert,' 'Where is Another,' 'The Life to Come,' 'The Obelisk,' 'Dr Woolacott,' 'Arthur Snatchfold,' 'What Does It Matter? A Morality,' 'The Classical Annex,' 'The Torque' and 'The Other Boat.' However, in this chapter we shall engage ourselves only in the discussion of the 12 short stories of *E.M. Forster: Collected Short Stories* first published in 1947.

It is interesting to know that Forster's first published creative work was not a novel but a short story—'The Story of a Panic' that was first published in 1904 (his first novel *Where Angels Fear to Tread* was published in 1905). But here is a puzzle or a muddle. In fact, his first published short story was 'Albergo Empedocle,' but long afterwards he claimed that not this story but 'The Story of a Panic' was his first published story. Nichola Beauman writes: "'Albergo Empedocle' was later to be ignored by Morgan [Forster]; although his first story to be published,... he later disclaimed it as his first piece of fiction. This distinction he was to give, after forty-five years, to another story called 'The Story of a Panic'" (Beauman, 109-110). One reason of Forster misguiding us here may be the blatant homosexual overtone of 'Albergo Empedocle:' he wanted to hide his antipathic sex from the very beginning. 'Albergo Empedocle' was posthumously published in *The Life to Come and Other Stories* (1972).

As all the novels of Forster are realistic social comedies, barring only *Maurice*, so all his short stories are fantasies. In the Introduction to the 1947 publication of his stories, *E.M. Forster: Collected Short Stories,* Forster himself called his stories 'fantasies.' He meticulously kept the two genres quite separate from one another. In his stories he took flight on the wings of imagination, as in his novels he quietly sat under the glow of rationality to analyse social and cultural phenomena like a social scientist. His stories are mythological, alogical and amoral, having no ulterior suggestions beyond mere enjoyment; but his novels are artistically discursive, and they deal with the problematics of morality, having in perspective a resolution of those problematics. The fundamental dichotomy between short story and novel is undeniable, and they differ from one another in many points. Firstly, short story deals with episode or episodes, while novel deals with 'histories' (Merson, ix). Secondly, in novel the 'story' is of insignificant importance, but in short story the attention of the reader is drawn principally to the 'story.' Elizabeth Bowen very rightly says: "'A story must *be* a story'" (Hudson, ix). Thirdly, the point of characterisation—of developing a character or characters—is poorly taken notice of in short story, but it is of prime importance in novel. Fourthly, due to its short length, short story cannot provide adequate space for development of plot, but development of plot is of immense importance in novel. Fifthly, the Aristotlean three unities are not well regarded in novel-writing, but the nature of short story generally requires adherence to them as far as possible. And lastly, short story is rather short and novel is rather long. But how far is short story short? This is a very puzzling question, and all do not agree as to the answer to it. Short story is of course much shorter than novel, but how much short is short story? "D.H. Lawrence's *The Fox* (1923) is about 30,000 words; Kleist's ghost story *Das Bettetweib von Locarno* (1810) is only 800 words. In his preface to his *Complete Short Stories* Somerset Maugham remarks that the shortest item [story] runs to about 1,600 words and the longest to about 20,000 words. The vast majority of short stories would fall somewhere between the two" (Cuddon, 815). However, Forster has his own opinion about the length of a short story. In the concluding sentence of his short story 'The Curate's Friend,' the narrator tells the reader "that this is a short story, suitable for reading in the train." Forster's longest short story 'The Machine Stops' runs upto about 38 pages. Inspite of all these parameters, it is very difficult to identify a short story; so elusive it is.

The generally admitted differences between short stories and novels hold good in the case of Forster's short stories and novels as well; but, nevertheless, there is a striking similarity between his short stories and his novels: *travel* is a central theme in both the categories; not just physical movement through geographical space but also mental peregrination through thickets of experiences, or orders of *vecu* (lived, authentic, realistic) experiences. As a result of the protagonists' or chief characters' *vecu* experiences they get mentally transmogrified. In all Forster's novels, travel or journey is a common ingredient: the principal characters move from one country to another, or from one psychological space to another (in *The Longest Journey)*. In *Where Angels Fear to Tread,* Lilia Herriton, a rather young widow with a child, travels to Italy to spend there a year, and falls in love with and marries the gawky and gauche Gino Carella, engendering disagreeable consequences which lead to new experiences and reconstruct her perception of life in its totality. The same thing happens to Lucy Honeychurch in *A Room with a View.* She also goes to Italy, falls in love with the roughshod and uncultured George, but leaving him behind comes back to England and marries the cultured and gentlemanly Cecil Vyse. After the marriage, she discovers that—and this is her new experience—that she loves not Cecil but George, and marries him. In *The Longest Journey* there is no geographical travel, so to say, but then there is a journey nevertheless: a journey through the endless highway of life. Rickie is the traveller, and his journey procures him bitter knowledge of life. The Wilcox family and the Schlegel family, in *Howards End,* go to Germany from England for vacationing, and both Margaret Schlegel and Helen Schlegel gather the new experience that mere intellect is not enough for life and that one also needs emitional responses. In *A Passage to India*, Adela Quested and Mrs Moore come from England to India, and while Mrs Moore's angle of perception is enlarged by her Indian experiences, Adela's experiences in India only narrows and blurs her view. In most of *Maurice,* there is no travel, but at the end of it Clive leaves England for Greece to regain health, and Alec sails for Southampton to stay there, where Maurice decides to join Alec for enjoying unending homosexual love.

In most of Forster's short stories also the principal characters undertake journeys and through the journeys they come across new experiences that modify their visions of life. John Sayre Martin writes in this regard: "Like his novels, most of Forster's short stories turn on the exposure of one or more characters, generally through travel, to a new order of experience. A group of English tourists encounters in Italy the great god Pan; an elderly Englishman experiences an 'eternal moment' in a grove of plane trees in Greece; a small boy goes to Heaven in a celestial omnibus; a Roman youth, conducting his sister on a difficult journey, is raped by a Goth in the woods; an army captain en route to India has a disastrous affair with a half-caste native; and so on. Some of the travellers are revitalized by their encounters; some are frightened; some are destroyed. But whatever the final result, their outlook is likely to be transformed" (Martin, 48). Besides travels, in many of Forster's short stories we come across picnics or picnic-like situations, like in some of his novels (for instance, the picnic in the Marabar Hills in *A Passage to India)*. There are picnics or picnic-like situations in 'The Story of a Panic,' 'The Road from Colonus' and 'The Curate's Friend' and other short stories. Tea is also not very infrequently served in the short stories, as in the novels. Picnics and tea are therefore two points where Forster's stories and his novels converge.

The point of divergence between Forster's short stories and his novels, as we have already mentioned, is that while the stories are fantasies, or rather, escape fantasies, the novels are obviously realistic. But though the stories are escape literature, they give us an impression of magic realism. In magic realism, fact and fiction are mingled or juxtaposed in such a convincing way that the fiction appears to be fact, and our disbelief is suspended, for the moment we are negotiating with a piece of magic-realistic literature. The psychology behind magic realism is that truth or reality is not absolute but relative, and depends upon the individual's perspective or angle of view. The term 'magic realism' was coined in 1925 by Franz Ron, and till now the technique of magic realism has been adopted by many creative writers, including George Saiko (1892-1962), Luis Borges (1899-1988), Alejo Carpentier (1904-80), John Fowles (1926-), Gunter Grass (1927-), Gabriel Garcia Marquez (1928-) and Salman Rushdie (1947-). Some of the principal characteristic features of the fictions of magic realism are "the mingling and juxtaposition of the realistic and the fantastic or bizarre, skilful time shifts, convoluted and even labyrinthine narratives and plots, miscellaneous use of dreams, myths and fairy stories, expressionistic and even surrealistic description, arcane erudition, the element of surprise or abrupt shock, the horrific and the inexplicable" (Cuddon, 488).

According to *The Wordsworth Companion to Literature in English*, the term 'magic realism' "originated in the question posed by the Cuban novelist Alejo Carpentier: 'What is the story of Latin America if not a chronicle of the marvellous in the real?' It was first employed as a literary definition by the

American critic Alastair Reid, and referred then to the large body of spectacular, fantastic fiction produced in South American countries after World War II. This powerful and fecund outpouring of a nascent literary autonomy paralleled such nations' newly-own political independence, and came to be known as 'el bourn'..." The genre [magic realism] is characterized by the juxtaposition of apparently reliable, realistic reportage and extravagant fantasy: Marquez's novel will at one moment narrate the building of a new banana-processing plant, at another describe a woman visibly ascending to heaven. While there is a certain inscrutable playfulness to magic realism (Marquez is recorded as proposing that "you can get people believe anything if you tell it convincingly enough) its method was first conceived, more importantly, as a response to the nature of South American reality.... Indeed, the genre's further assumption...is that truth is best viewed as a communal, collaborative construct, rather than as residing in the integrity of individual perceptions, whose authority tends merely to that of caprice and rumour. Such emphasis, implying the limitation of individual responsibility and the quixotic unpredictability of fate, makes magic realism an essentially comic genre" (Qusby, 584). Forster's such short stories as 'The Story of a Panic,' 'The Celestial Omnibus' and 'The Machine Stops' smack of magic realism.

It is interesting that in the Introduction to the 1947 publication of his short stories (which were earlier published in two separate volumes: *The Celestial Omnibus* and *The Eternal Moment)* in a single volume with the title *E.M. Forster: Collected Short Stories,* Forster re-dedicated the collection to the Greek god Hermes Psychopompus: "should they [the collected short stories] be dedicated anew? Perhaps, and perhaps to a god. Hermes Psychopompus suggests himself, who came to my mind at the beginning of this introduction. He can anyhow stand in the prow and watch the disintegrating sea" (Forster, 1947, 7). The god Hermes Psychopompus differs from Hermes, to some extent, and has been variously conceived: he has had no fixed identity. Hermes Psychopompus has been conceived as the god of the sky, of the cloud, of twilight, and of wind. Hermes Psychopompus, though he differs from

Hermes, originated in the conception of Hermes and has retained many of the attributes that were comprised in the conception of Hermes. However, "Hermes was above all thought of as the god of travellers, whom he guided on their perilous ways [see Forster's 're-dedication:' Hermes 'can anyhow stand in the prow and watch the disintegrating sea.']. His images were placed where country roads branched and at crossroads in towns. It is without doubt a natural extension of this role that Hermes was also charged with conducting the souls of the dead to the underworld [hence, from Hermes to Hermes Psychopompus]. Unless, indeed, this *Hermes Psychopompus* (conductor of souls), who is sometimes differentiated from the celestial Hermes, was not a substitute for some older subterranean divinity, a kind of *Zeus Plutos*" (*New Larousse Encyclopedia of Mythology*, 123). Forster's dedication, or rather re-dedication, perhaps signifies this that like Hermes Psychopompus he is going to guide us in our travels, through his short stories, to fantastic regions. The re-dedication, additionally, may have an allusion to homosexuality. This hazard rests on the emphasis placed on the (male) beauty of Hermes. As the myth of Hermes gradually developed, the god was becoming "the idealized type of the *ephebe* or young gymnast, with lithe and graceful body. His hair is short and crisp, his features fine," *(ibid.)*. It may be noted here that Hermes is seductively beautiful: he has an admirable physical beauty—a beauty that Forster himself found in Masood and in the punkhah-puller in the trial scene of *A Passage to India,* or Lilia, in *Where Angels Fear to Trade,* found in Gino Carella; or Lucy Honeychurch, in *A Room With a View,* found in George Emerson.

Another special feature of many of Forster's short stories is that in them he has either introduced, or alluded to, a good number of mythological figures, as nowhere else in his other creative writings—such mythological figures (most of them gods) as Pan ('The Story of a Panic' and 'The Other Kingdom'); Oreads, Sirens, Tritons, Nereids, Naiads, Satyrs, Fauns, Dryads, Croesus, Midas, Jupiter, Venus, Juno ('The Other Kingdom'); etc. However, with so much for our Introduction, let us take up the stories themselves. We will deal not with all of Forster's stories but only with the dozen stories that are there in *E.M. Forster: Collected Short Stories,* first published in 1947. We will first succinctly tell the tales, one after another, noting a few observations of critics and some other things relating to each particular story at the end of it, and then engage ourselves in a general discussion about all Forster's short stories, particularly about the twelve stories we are going to take up just now.

2

'THE STORY OF A PANIC'

'The Story of a Panic' has a history. In 1902, Forster and Lily were touring over Italy and Sicily. In May of that year, they returned from Sicily to southern Italy, and were staying at the Hotel-Pension Palumbo at Ravello. Forster felt satiated of his hunger for sight-seeing, and Lily noticed that he was gaining in health, but was unexpectedly and abnormally quieter. Perhaps it was Forster's literary gestation period, for sometime afterwards—in June of the same year—he was 'most anxious to get some real work to do.' It was at Ravello, and during this time, that he got the inspiration to write 'The Story of a Panic.' Forster himself wrote about the genesis of this short story: "'I think it was in May of 1902 that I took a walk near Ravello. I sat down in a valley, a few miles above the town, and suddenly the first chapter of the story rushed into my mind as if it had waited for me there. I received it as an entity and wrote it out as soon as I returned to the hotel'" (Beauman, 112). A few days afterwards, the story, as it was already written down (i.e. the first part or section of the story in its present length), seemed to him inadequate or unfinished, and so he "added some more until it was three times as long" (Furbank, I, 92).

Forster said that 'The Story of a Panic' was his first story, though we know that, in fact, as we have already said, 'Albergo Empedocle' was his first story. 'The Story of a Panic' was first published in the *Independent Review* in 1904. Subsequently, it was included, in 1911, in the collection of short stories entitled *The Celestial Omnibus;* and in 1947 it was included in the collection of short stories entitled *E.M. Forster: Collected Short Stories*. The locale of the story is Ravello in Italy, and the narrator of it is one Mr Tytler. The story is about some incidents that happened eight years ago, says Mr Tytler, who is a persona of Forster himself. John Sayre Martin summarises the story of 'The Story of a Panic' thus: "In 'The Story of a Panic'—one of the best of the fantasies [Forster's fantastic stories]—a party of English tourists go for a picnic to a secluded valley near Ravello and there encounter the spirit of Pan. The great god, long presumed dead, appears as a mysterious 'catspaw of wind' which strikes panic into the hearts of the adults, who flee at its approach. Only Eustace, a repressed and moody boy of fourteen, is exhilarated by the encounter; and he in fact is permanently transformed. That night he escapes from his hotel bedroom into the courtyard below, where, to the astonishment of Mr Tytler, the complacent and snobbish narrator, and the other awakened adults, he proceeds grandiloquently to expatiate on 'the great forces and manifestations of Nature.' He is returned to his room; but later, with the help of Gennaro, a sympathetic young waiter, he escapes again. Together they leap from a second-floor window into the courtyard. The fall kills Gennaro, but Eustace, uninjured, climbs over the garden wall, swings down from an olive tree, and escapes, presumably forever. 'Signora Scafetti [the landlady] bursts into screams at the sight of the dead body, and, far down the valley towards the sea, there still resounded the shouts and the laughter of the escaping boy'" (Martin, 48-49).

A couple of Miss Robinsons; their fourteen-year-old nephew Eustace; Mr Sandbach, the ex-curator, and the would-be-artist Mr Leyland had come from England and put up in a delightful little hotel in Ravello. There were also Signora Scafetti, the nice landlady; Mr Tytler, the narrator; and Mr Tytler's wife and two daughters. The English-speaking waiter, Emmanuele, was away from the hotel for visiting his sick father. As the Robinsons, along with their nephew Eustace were stopping at the hotel for about six weeks, Mr Sandbach voluntarily took the charge of educating Eustace.

The narrator did not like Leyland, because he was 'conceited and odius,' and also Eustace, because he was 'repellent.' Eustace was of 'delicate' constitution. 'That memorable day' they all went out for a picnic, except Jenet Robinson. They climbed upto Vallone Fontana Caroso, a valley which seemed 'a vast hollow, shaped like a cup, into which radiated ravines from the precipitous hills around. Both the valley and the ravines and the ribs of hill that divided the ravines were covered with leafy chestnut, so that the general appearance was that of a many-fingered green hand, palm upwards, which was clutching convulsively to keep us in its grasp.' From there they could see Ravello (river) and the sea—'the only sign of another world.' The narrator's younger daughter Rose, Miss Mary Robinson and Mr Sandbach were charmed by the beauty of the surrounding landscape, but Mr Leyland could not appreciate it, and the narrator remained noncommittal about it.

When it was time for lunch, Miss Mary Robinson called out for Eustace for helping her in arranging the lunch, and when Eustace appeared it was found that he had made a whistle with wood and was blowing it. After lunch Eustace disappeared into the woods. Deforestation was going on there, and so Leyland burst out: 'All poetry is going from Nature.' He said, "we are all hopelessly steeped in vulgarity. I do not except myself. It is through us, and to our shame, that the Nereids have left the waters and the Oreads the mountains, that the woods no longer give shelter to Pan." Mr Sandbach said: 'Pan is dead. That is why the woods do not shelter him.' Leyland agreed.

After the noises from the forest and chatterings died down, a lull prevailed over the area—the innocuous lull that was going to be followed by a fearful surprise, because suddenly an 'excruciating noise' come from Eustace's whistle. All were startled, but silence once again settled. The narrator then saw 'a cat's-paw of wind that was running down one of the ridges opposite, turning the light green to dark as it travelled.' He felt it was a foreboding, and saw that all others were also watching the 'cat's-paw.' All were terrified and ran away helter-skelter. It was not a 'spiritual fear' but a brutal 'physical fear.' The narrator was also panicky, but in a peculiar way: 'I had been afraid, not as a man, but as a beast' (section I).

The fear soon went away from all, and most of them sustained only minor physical wounds for running frantically. Miss Ribinson now shrieked: 'Oh, merciful heavens! where is Eustace?' But Eustace was not to be found. After a while, when they were returning by climbing down the slope, they saw that 'at the farther side, were the remains of our lunch, and close to them, lying motionless on his back, was Eustace.' He did not care to respond to their calls, and when they approached near him they 'saw one of those green lizards dart out from under his shirt-cuff.' Miss Robinson closed towards him and 'touched his hand' and only then Eustace 'opened his eyes and smiled.' His aunt, Mrs Tytler, 'showered kisses on him,' but he remained passive. She asked him what he had so long been doing, but without answering her question he only said; 'I have been very happy.' The narrator then saw some footprints of goats and asked Eustace if he knew that goats grazed there. On hearing of the footprints Eustace rushed to the spot of the footprints and 'lay down and rolled on them, as a dog rolls in dart.' Mr Sandbach announced: 'The Evil One has been very near us in bodily form.' He and others therefore knelt down to pray, and Eustace also, at their bidding. Rising from prayer, Eustace was ferreting out for his whistle which Mr Leyland presently broke, perhaps thinking that it was the source of the Evil. The narrator thought the thought of the Evil was a superstition. Miss Rose asked Eustace to say what went wrong (behind his wallowing on the footprints), but he remained silent. The narrator noticed that 'Eustace was at last taking some pride in his personal appearance.' Mr Sandbach said Eustace should thenceforth be observed carefully, but the narrator found 'nothing wrong with Eustace.' The narrator said: 'Our experiences are mysterious, not his [Eustace]. He was astonished at our sudden departure, that's why he was so strange when he returned. He is right enough—improved, if anything.' Mr Leyland wondered at this: 'And is the worship of athletics, the cult of insensate activity, to be counted as an improvement?' And: 'The passionate desire to rend from

Nature the few beauties that have been still left her—that is to be counted as an improvement too?'

However, while returning to the hotel, they were discussing the queer behaviour of Eustace (whether his behaviour was right or wrong, normal or abnormal), but Eustace was indifferent to their discussion and was only frolicking about in the woods on the right side of the hotel. He expressed his desire to meet Gennaro, the stop-gap waiter of the hotel (in lieu of Emmanuele), who was 'a clumsy, impertinent fisher-lad.' When asked why he wanted to meet Gennaro, Eustace said: 'Because, because I do, I do; because, because I do.' He was dancing in the wood to the tune of his words. Whenever Eustace went to the wood, he came back prancing like 'a wild Indian' or 'a dog.' Once he came back 'with a poor dazed hare, too frightened to move, sitting on his arm' and at another time he came back bounding like a goat.

The 'next extraordinary incident of this extraordinary day occurred' 'where the staircase path debouches on the white high road.' The narrator tells us: 'Three old women were standing by the wayside. They, like ourselves, had come down from the woods, and they were resting their heavy bundles of fuel on the low parapet of the road. Eustace stopped in front of them, and, after a moment's deliberation, stepped forward and—kissed the left-hand one on the cheek!' Mr Sandbach said to Eustace: 'are you quite crazy?' But the old woman received the offer of some flowers from Eustace, and blessed him.

Coming back to the Piazza near the hotel, Eustace cried out at Gennaro. The landlady (of the hotel) told the narrator about Gennaro that 'however much she superintended his toilette, he always managed to introduce something incongruous into it before he had finished.' When, however, Gennaro came out to the call of Eustace, 'Eustace sprang to meet him, and leapt right up into his arms, and put his own arms round his neck.' And this he did before a number of persons. The narrator, Mr Tytler, once wanted to talk to Eustace seriously on 'the subject of intercourse with social inferiors' but this did not happen. 'Meanwhile, Gennaro...carried Eustace into the house, as if it was the most natural thing in the world.' While he was carrying Eustace into the house, Gennaro (presumably to answer the call of Eustace) cried out: 'Ho capito' (which Italian expression means 'I have undestood'). Everybody there was bewildered at Eustace's behaviour, but none was outspoken. Mr Sandbach thought of 'the possibility of infernal influences' on Eustace, that required the services of a doctor, but Mr Leyland thought that Eustace was an 'unspeakable Philistine.' On the other hand, Miss Rose supposed that Eustace's behaviour was 'excusable.' But Mr Tytler, the narrator, was of the opinion that Eustace needed 'a sound thrashing.' Miss Robinson followed the middle path: she conceived of stern supervision over the boy.

During dinner Gennaro addressed Eustace as 'Tu' (Italian second person singular), which means close familiarity, before all around the table. The irate Mr Tytler cautioned Gennaro and asked him to use respectable forms—'Lei' or 'Voi.' Gennaro told him that if Eustazio (Eustace) asked him to call him 'Voi' only then he would call him so, otherwise not (Section II).

At night the narrator woke up to 'a noise in the garden' and a 'cold terrible fear seized me [the narrator]—not a fear of something that was happening, like the fear in the wood, but fear of something that might happen.' He saw through the window that Eustace 'had got out of bed' and gone down to the terrace below, which was covered with vine and roses. Mr Tytler went near the terrace below and sternly asked Eustace to come back. Eustace 'stopped his antics' and said; 'I hate my bedroom. I could not stop in it, it is too small.' Mr Tytler warned him that he would bring him by force, but, undaunted, Eustace 'began singing and chattering to himself in a most alarming way.' Mr Sandbach told Mr Tytler that Eustace's case was one for the doctor, for Eustace now began singing wildly snatches from every category of songs. All importuned Eustace to come from the wood and stay at the hotel, but he did not come, and continued singing and talking madly and aloud. He was singing about themes which the greatest poets have found almost beyond their power.' 'Eustace Robinson, aged fourteen, was standing in the nightshirt saluting, praising, and blessing the great forces and manifestations of Nature.' He delivered a high faluting and long lecture on all the things and creatures of Nature, from fireflies to rain and wind. Mr Tytler thought that Mr Leyland was perhaps thinking Eustace's speech to be 'a diabolical caricature' and so was feeling a drive to kick Eustace off.

After some time, Eustace calmed down, and all attempted to catch hold of him; but he turned round after running a distance and began to cry. All then left Eustace to his madness, only 'Rose had an inspiration' from him. Rose announced that Gennaro might have caught him, and so his service was deployed. He had been sleeping in a charcoal-bin from where Signora Scafetti, the landlady, called him out. He appeared in abject dress, and was ordered to fetch Eustace. At this, Gennaro flew into a rage, because he thought Eustace was well where he was, and expressed his violent anger in Italian, which none could follow. Mr Tytler offered Gennaro rewards of money to fetch Eustace, but he declined the offer saying 'I do not desire them. Eustazio is my friend.' Ultimately, on further persuasions, Gennaro submitted and went to find out Eustace, found him, and 'had his arm round Eustace's neck.' Eustace, the 'grotesque figure,' told the slim Gennaro: 'The trees, hills, stars, water, I can see all. But isn't it odd! I can't make out men a bit. Do you know what I mean?' Gennaro replied: Ho capito'.

Eustace was brought before Mr Tytler, Mr Leyland and Mr Sandbach. When they were expressing their dissatisfaction with him, Eustace heard a paper note of money cracle in the pocket of Mr Tytler and snatched it away. But he was instantaneously apprehended by them and was being forcefully drawn into the house (hotel), when Eustace gave out a scream and showers of rose petals fell on the truant boy. In the house, Eustace cried profusely, and defiantly said that he would not enter into his room because 'It is too small.' But force was applied on him to lay him on the bed. He was sobbing and saying: 'I nearly saw everything, and now I can see nothing at all.' Signora Scafetti was then found conversing with Gennaro in a subdued voice, perhaps about the eerie behaviour of

Eustace, and Mr Sandbach was writing to a doctor at Naples about Eustace. Mr Tytler now offered Gennaro the money he promised him for fetching Eustace, and Gennaro 'grabbed' the money forthwith. Mr Leyland asked Gennaro what he understood when Eustace said that 'he could not make out men a bit.' Gennaro replied that though he understood the meaning of what Eustace said, he could not explain it. And then realising that he was being held responsible for the incident (of Eustace's going into the wood), Gennaro said: 'What has happened is very sad. But what can I do? I am poor. It is not I.' He held all, including himself, responsible for the sad incident: 'It is you, it is I. It is all in this house, and many outside it. If he [Eustace] wishes for mirth, we discomfort him. If he asks to be alone, we disturb him. He longed for a friend, and found none for fifteen years. Then he found me, and the first night I—I who have been in the woods and understood things too—betray him to you and send him in to die. But what could I do?' Gennaro concluded: 'Oh, assuredly he will die.' Mr Sandbach said he would be taking care of Eustace, sitting all along by him. But Gennaro told him that he would be of no avail to him, and then narrated to him the story of Filomena Giusti and Caterina: 'Filomena Giusti sat all night with Caterina, but Caterina was dead in the morning....' He told Mr Sandbach the central point of his biography: 'And I am alive now,' he went on, 'because I had neither parents nor relatives nor friends, so that, when the first night came, I could run through the woods, and climb the rocks, and plunge into the water, until I had accomplished my desire!'

Just at that moment a distressful cry came out from Eustace's room—'a faint but steady sound, like the sound of wind in a distant wood heard by one standing in tranquility.' Gennaro said that it 'was the last noise of Caterina. I was hanging on to her window then, and it blew out past me.' Then he began to curse Mr Sandbach, Mr Leyland, the narrator Mr Tytler and also Fate, because Eustace was going to die in the upper room. At this moment the foolish Mr Leyland 'upset the lamp with his elbow,' drowning the room in darkness, and 'the mere physical change from light to darkness had more power over the ignorant animal nature of Gennaro than the most obvious dictates of logic and reason.' A hurry-scurry ensued to make light, and in the melee Gennaro was carrying Eustace down and off, but their passage was blocked on the landing. So they, in their perplexity, 'retreated to the upper landing.' A scream now came from the room of the narrator Mr Tytler's wife—Gennaro and Eustace 'had leapt out of her window.' Mr Tytler saw Eustace climbing down a tree and then disappearing among the trees below. He heard Gennaro cry aloud that Eustace now 'has understood and he is saved' and that 'Now, instead of dying he will live!' Then Mr Tytler demanded the money, that Gennaro snatched from him, back. But Gennaro clandestinely replied that the money now belonged to him, and not to Mr Tytler, and saying this he took to his heels. But he 'fell upon his face on the path' and he was dead.' 'The morning was still far off, but the morning breeze had began, and rose leaves fell on us as we carried him in. Signora Scafetti burst into screams at the sight of the dead body, and, far down the valley towards the sea, there still resounded the shouts and the laughter of the escaping boy' (Section III).

'The Story of a Panic' is of great moment, because it may be taken to be the key or the prolegomena to all other creative works of Forster, and very appropriately this story preceeds, in time, all his other creative works, it being written in 1902 and published in 1904. The story turns on a theme on which Forster wrote over and over again—wrote his major novels, in particular. Nicola Beauman very aptly writes that in this story Forster "found his theme: in all essentials he would never need to search for another" (Beauman, 112). Beauman has expatiated a bit on this point of his: "The idea [behind this story] that came to Morgan's [Forster's] mind was that he 'would bring some middle-class Britishers to picnic in this remote spot. I [Forster] would expose their vulgarity. I would cause them to be terribly frightened they knew not why and I would make it clear by subsequent events that they had encountered and offended the Great God Pan.' Here [in this story] were all the elements of the future *oeuvre*: the English middle classes exposed to something other (a foreign country, an expedition away from their normal territory), who are mocked for their insularity and obtuseness, who then encounter something so disconcerting that they are forced to realise, even if subconsciously, that they have confronted something vaster than themselves; at the end they are either saved—or not" (*ibid.*).

Some of the points of similarity between this story and Forster's novels are obvious. In most of his novels, the plot develops around a travel to a foreign country: in the two Italian novels, *Where Angels Fear to Tread* and *A Room With A View,* in *Howards End,* and in *A Passage to India*. In 'The Story of a Panic,' some Britishers—Miss Robinsons, Mr Sandbach, Mr Leyland, Mr and Mrs Tytler and their two daughters (one being Rose), and Eustace—went to Italy. Whatever happened in Ravello in Italy, would not have happened had they not taken on a journey. In most of the novels, travels lead to interactions among members of small groups of travellers, and these, in turn, are followed by *unsuccessful* picnics, resulting in reformations of the perspectives, or widening of the perspectives, of the chief characters. And this, as well, we also see in 'The Story of a Panic.' It may be that picnic or picnic-like situation which shifts the perspectives brings in the unexpectedly new experiences for the chief characters. Picnic is present, for instances, in *A Room With A View* (chapter 7) and in *A Passage to India* (chapter 16). In the picnics, the chief characters encounter strange experiences by which their perspectives are altered and they are re-educated, in a sense. In the case of 'The Story of a Panic' Forster himself has told us, as mentioned earlier, that it was his deliberate motive to 'bring some middle-class Britishers to picnic' with the objective of exposing 'their vulgarity,' which would be a sort of re-education for them.

But the re-education (or enlargement of the perspective) is not intended merely for its own sake; the re-education, said Forster, must lead to salvation—salvation, not in the religious sense exactly, but in the temporal. Salvation, in the temporal sense, means escape from the conventionality, traditionality or the mores of the society, all that are internalised by the individual during the course of his socialisation. Salvation means freedom of the soul from the circumspection of conventionality, and conventionality means repetition of the same social behaviour—a sort of echo. Forster believed that individuals normally revolve in the same perennial social vortex, like etherised patients, and to bring them to consciousness a sharp jolt was necessary—to take them, for instance, out of the Tonbridge School moral regimentation and introduce them to the moral freedom of Cambridge a sudden and phenomenal shift in the circumstantiality was necessary. Forster believed that in the modern civilisation, with its absolute predominance of rationality and nullity of emotion or passion, the individual remains insulated, and is a sort of split personality—in the sense that his rational and emotional components are disjunct, while in a whole and normal person the two are compact. The split personality is a suffering being; he needs to be salvaged; and he can achieve salvation only if his rational component is conjoined with his emotional component. This is what Forster meant when he wrote in the twenty-second chapter of *Howards End*: 'Only connect!' In this a novel Mr Wilcox is a split personality of sorts and Margaret Schlegel wants to help him: "She would only point out the salvation that was latent in his soul, and in the soul of every man. Only connect! That was the whole of her sermon. Only connect the prose and the passion, and both will be exalted, and human love will be seen at its highest. Live in fragments no longer. Only connect, and the beast and the monk, robbed of their isolation that is life to either, will die."

Rationality is the foundation of civilisation, and emotion or passion is the *elan vital* of the non-civilised social organisation. Should we be able to conjoin the two contrary components of us, we shall be able to convert strangers into friends, to a man, and then lead a happy life—everything else is non-essential. In 'The Story of a Panic' also Forster has occasioned a clash, a concussion, between the civilised, mechanised, echoing, dull, and spiritually void Britishers and their counterparts—uncivilised, non-mechanised, non-echoing, but passionate and spiritual—represented singly by the simpleton Gennaro. It may be pointed out here that Forster deliberately chose the name Gennaro and Eustace. 'Gennaro' means January (month) or the beginning of things (in Italian), or 'noble, well-born' (in Greek: from 'Eugene'). Gennaro may be physically ignoble, but spiritually he is certainly noble, thought Forster, because he was endowed with the heavenly attribute of being passionate. The name 'Eustace' means 'inflamed' or 'fruitful'; and it may allude to St Eustace who 'was a patron saint of huntsmen.' Eustace, previous to his coming to Ravello, Italy, was dull and repellant, and so was not a desirable boy for the (Tonbridge-type) public education in England, and this was why Mr Sandbach temporarily took the charge of preparing him for such an education, while in the hotel in Ravello. However, the narrator of 'The Story of a Panic' describes Eustace, before his salvation or spiritualisation under the informing influence of the 'noble' and 'spiritualised' Gennaro thus: 'I would not have minded so much if he had been a really studious boy, but he neither played hard nor worked hard. His favourite occupations were lounging on the terrace in an easy chair and loafing along the high road, with his feet shuffling up the dust and his shoulders forward. Naturally enough, his features were pale, his chest contracted, and his muscles underdeveloped. His aunts thought him delicate; what he really needed was discipline. But, no, he did not, in fact, want discipline; he needed only spiritual energising, the infusion of a doze of passion into his blood-stream, which the civilised parts of the world would not allow him to get. Eustace was pale, dull, insulated from the outer world—he was living in the cocoon of his own self. If he wanted anything, it was salvation, i.e., freedom from all social, moral and ideological constraints—all that raised a high-rise and hard wall all around him. The spirit that was there in him, therefore, was atrophied, cribbed. Eustace, so, required to be salvaged from all his constraints, so that he could develop into a fully formed human being.

In 'The Story of a Panic,' as in most of his novels, Forster has arranged picnics or picnic-like situations for the salvation of the chief characters, as we have told earlier. Through a picnic a man must come into closest contact (physical and psychological) with another, be locked in real friendship with him and thereby get his soul enlarged, to have the wider perspective of life and thus be salvaged. When he will be affronted by the newer or wider perspective of life, he may be suddenly affrighted or confounded, but he will certainly soon recognise the wider perspective as the truth. This is Forster's philosophy of life and the creation. Picnic is there in *A Passage to India* (chapter 16) and in *A Room with a View* (chapter 7), as we have said, and in both the cases this mechanism of salvation is operative. A panic episode was also there in *The Longest Journey,* but before the novel was published, Forster extrapolated the panic chapter from it. In that chapter, the Pan-like Stephen behaved like Eustace. Nicola Beauman writes that Forster "had cut a 'Panic' chapter from *The Longest Journey,* in which a Pan-like Stephen bounds about naked" (Beauman, 193). The picnic and the panic are not disjointed phenomena in a Forsterian novel, but are correlated to each other: the picnic is the occasion and the panic is the shock-evoked emotion generated out of the wider perspective of life. The god Pan is present in 'The Story of a Panic' and some Forsterian novels. In chapter 7 of *A Room with a View* we come across Pan: 'Pan had been amongst them—not the great god Pan, who has been buried these two thousand years [due to the introduction of Christianity into England?], but the little god Pan, who presides over social contretemps and unsuccessful picnics.'

Pan was the god of the inexplicable, of panic. He was half-man in his upper part, and half-goat in his lower, and he lived in pastoral regions, in wildernesses, and in caves. 'Pan was ithyphallic [meaning 'bearing an erect penis'], lascivious and debauched. He was most comfortable in the possessions of Dionysus, where he added his own form of madness. He was constantly pursuing nymphs who would flee in terror. Caves rang with the cries which escaped from their lips in the course of some furtive coupling with the god. However, Pan was no less interested in boys who often satisfied his needs.... "He was in love with the nymph Echo, who had rejected him..."Perhaps it was Pan's rages—like the singing, cries and noises which surrounded him and the caves where he took refuge, all slightly irrational things—which led him to be considered responsible for the uncontrollable 'panics' experienced by the

Greeks of antiquity. He was the god of the inexplicable" (Comte, 156-57). Forster had utilised the myth of Pan at many places of his creative works. Pan had two versions, so to say, the comic and mischievous Pan, and the frightening, and panicking Pan. In *A Room with a View,* Pan is only comically mischievous, but in *A Passage to India* he is frightening and panicking, and this Pan Adela encounters in the Marabar cave. Pan is not explicitly stated in the Marabar cave episode, but the cave, the echo, the panic, etc. point to the god Pan. In 'The Story of a Panic,' Eustace is *panoleptic,* i.e. charmed by Pan—is possessed of Pan, and that is why he wallows on the footprints of goats, does bestiality, and behaves inexplicably. Besides bestiality, there is a suggestion in the story that Gennaro and Eustace committed mutual homosexuality. Though Forster denied the presence of any homosexual or even sexual imagery or suggestion in the story, when, in 1904, it was published, Charles Sayle, Assistant Librarian in the University of Cambridge, interpreted the behaviour of Eustace to the famous economist Maynard Keynes thus: "having had an unnatural act performed upon him by a waiter at the hotel, Eustace commits bestiality with a goat, then when he has told the waiter how nice it all has been, they try it on each other again" (Furbank, I, 113-14). The dull Eustace was ignited, 'inflamed' (recall 'Eustace' means 'inflamed') by his brief physical association with Gennaro, and consequently there grew in him a burning desire to break open the cocoon of conventions in which he was forcefully kept confined. He wanted to be a free soul, a free spirit, an independent judge of his own free will. He wanted to make Gennaro his model, and actually did—he made him his friend, after his physical contact with him. Nicola Beauman writes: "Eustace's afternoon in the woods ('racing about, like a real boy') makes him long to be free of the stifling conventions that have surrounded him all his life. He manages it although at the expense of the newly-beloved friend, the waiter Gennaro" (Beauman, 113).

As we have said, Forster got the inspiration to write 'The Story of a Panic' when he was touring over Italy with his mother. Then, one day, when he was sitting meditatively on the bank of the river Ravello, suddenly the idea of the story came to his mind, and almost forthwith he wrote down the first section of the story. Forster arrogated the generation of the idea of the story to the *genius locus* of Ravello. He believed that a particular place with particular distinctive features may provide one with a sort of inspiration to think creatively—to free oneself from conventions and imagine freely, which is the *sine qua non* of creative writings. In the case of Eustace, the *locus* is Ravello and its pastoral and arborous surround. The *genius locus* of Ravello shook the trammels of conventions off the mind of Eustace and thus his soul was salvaged. In the same way Figsbury Rings was the *genius locus* for writing *The Longest Journey.*

On 3rd February, 1915, in a letter written for Forster, D.H. Lawrence expressed his opinion about 'The Story of a Panic:' "...I have just read the Story of a Panic. You with your 'Only Connect' motto, I must say that you reach the limit of splitness here. You are bumping your nose on the end of the cul de sac. 'My angels & devils are nothing compared with your Pan. Don't you see Pan is the undifferentiated root & stem drawing out of unfathomable darkness, & my Angels & Devils are old-fashioned symbols for the flower into which we strive to burst, Now no plant can live towards the root. That is the most split, perverse thing of all. 'You see I know all about your Pan. He is not dead, he is the same forever. But you should not confuse him with universal love, as you tend to do. You are very confused. You give Pan great attributes of Christ. 'All that dark, concentrated, complete, all-containing surge of which I am the fountain, and of which the well-head is my loins, is surging forward, like a plant to flower or a fountain to its parabola. And my angels and devils are a sort of old-fashioned flowering. I am just in love with medieval terms, that is all—& Fra Angelico & Cimabue & the Saints. 'But your Pan is a stooping back to the well-head, a perverse pushing back the waters to their source, & saying the source is everything. Which is stupid & an annihilation—but very stupid...you are intentional and perverse & not vitally interesting. One must live from the source, through all the racings & heats of Pan, and on to my beloved angels & devils, with their aureoles & their feet upon the flowers of lights, &

with their red-mouthed despairs and destructions'" (Furbank, II, 8). Lawrence is perhaps quite right: Pan cannot be the end of everything; Pan has to be transmuted, if not sublimated. Lawrence is also very perceptive when he says that the force of Pan cannot generate universal and authentic love.

John Sayre Martin, in his *E.M. Forster: The Endless Journey,* very rightly interprets the story and comments upon it: "The story's considerable impact stems in great measure from Forster's care in delineating the setting and characters. Like several other epiphanous spots in his fiction (for example, the dell at Madingley, the Cadbury Rings, the Marabar Caves, the grove of plane trees at Plataniste), the valley where 'Pan' appears is cut off from the rest of the world and seems to possess a peculiarly retentive power.... The adults who choose this site for their picnic are well contrasted: but they have one thing in common, they are ill attuned to the unseen. Besides Tytler, the most notable are Mr Leyland, a would-be artist and sentimental aesthete, and Mr Sandbach, a pontifical clergyman who has undertaken to tutor Eustace. Principally through these three characters, Forster cleverly prepares for the first of the story's two climaxes. As they admire the scenery, Leyland laments that. 'All the poetry is going from Nature...her lakes and marshes are drained, her seas banked up, her forests cut down. Everywhere we see the vulgarity of desolation spreading.' Taking a more practical and economic view, Tytler defends the cutting of trees and the right of landlords to make money from their land. But the woods, Leyland reminds everyone, 'no longer give shelter to Pan'; and when Mr Sandbach remarks that that is because 'Pan is dead...the great God is dead,' Leyland abandons himself 'to that mock misery in which artistic people are so fond of indulging.' To Leyland, Pan is, of course, the benevolent guardian of sheep—"Pan ovium custos"—not the sinister deity equally known to literature and mythology. The nature that all of the adults admire is Arcadian. Consequently, they are unprepared for the 'catspaw of wind' that races mysteriously up the ridge on which they are standing. Their inability to cope with the wind signifies spiritual failure. They cannot cope with it because, as representative adults, they have repressed their emotional and instinctive drives. The wind, which is unexpected and inexplicable, corresponds to their repressed unconscious, to what Jung calls the shadow. 'If we step through the door of the shadow,' he writes, 'we discover with terror that we are the objects of unseen factors. To know this is decidedly unpleasant.... It can even give rise to primitive panic.' Only Eustace, who, as a boy, still communes with his 'shadow,' is exhilarated by the encounter, and is drawn to worship 'Pan' as an all embracing power. Only he appears to be saved from the emotionally inhibiting forces of adult life.

"But how saved is Eustace? Not, one suspects, completely. Certainly it is a salvation unlikely to win much sympathy form the average reader, for Eustace remains to the end an unappealing boy, moody, selfish, and secretive. His attachment too is a 'natural' and as much of a misfit as a waiter as Eustace seems to be a boy; but that Eustace's feeling for him is too self-seeking to be called love is underlined by the waiter's death and the boy's carefree escape from all human concern and responsibility. Eustace's natural piety, in fact, cannot embrace the human, as he himself declares when, praising the great forces and manifestations of nature, he adds, 'and then there are men, but I can't make them out so well.' Accordingly, he escapes from humanity; but in Forster's ethic, a salvation that evades the human is an ambiguous one at best" (Martin, 49-51).

3

'THE OTHER SIDE OF THE HEDGE'

This story was written in the early autumn of 1904 and was first published in *The Independent* in November of the same year. Subsequently it was included in *The Celestial Omnibus and Other Stories* which appeared in 1911. The story is, as Forster admitted in 1944, a 'fantasy, with few pretensions to reality.' Forster delighted in playing with fantasy and in writing about it. He said: "'I like the idea of fantasy, of muddling up the actual and impossible until the reader isn't sure which is which'" (Beauman, 158). Nicola Beauman writes about the fantasy involved in the story: "The impossible in this story is a young man who finds himself in a dream-like utopia which he cannot understand; it appears to him to be a prison, whereas in fact he had *been* in prison, 'the other side of the hedge.' The actual is obviously recognisable setting of the two concentric circles at Figsbury Rings, allegorically the outside where one is imprisoned and the inside where one is timeless and free. At the end of the story the narrator sees a man 'returning for the night to the hills, with a scythe over his soldier' and 'I saw that he was my brother.' It would be the theme of *The Longest Journey*; here, in fantastical form, Morgan (Forster) was trying it out" (*ibid.*).

This fantastical story appears to be a fable, but it is more than a fable; it is allegorical. It is a 'story about a young man escaping a materialistic society for a pastoral community.' The pedometer ('an instrument for counting paces and so approximately measuring distance walked') of the narrator of the story indicated that he had walked twenty-five miles. He therefore felt tired, and to take rest sat on a milestone on one side of the road. People passed by jeering at him; even Miss Dimbleby, a great educationist, did so. The narrator's brother, earlier, wasted his energy by singing and helping others, and died two years ago and was buried by the side of that road. On either side of the dusty road there were 'brown crackling hedges.' The road was strewn with left out things of travellers, and the things, being covered with thick films of dust, looked like stones. As the narrator was dog-tired, he 'lay there prostrate,' 'praying that I might give up.' Presently a puff of fresh air from the hedge at a distance on the other side of the road revived him, and then he became curious to see what was there 'on the other side' of the road. Accordingly, he pushed forward to 'the other side' of the road through thorns, etc. that made him so ragged that he felt he would 'perish in the undergrowth.' On his way through, the narrator suddenly fell into a deep pool and was trying to scramble out of it, when someone on the opposite bank of the pool shouted 'Another!' and rescued him. Coming out of the pool, the narrator asked his rescuer: 'Where does this place lead to?' The rescuer, a man of fifty or sixty, laughingly replied: 'Nowhere, thank the Lord!' The rescuer showed no anxiety, and his voice was like that of a boy of eighteen.' The narrator corrected him: "But it must lead somewhere!" At this the rescuer shouted to someone else on the hillside and told him that the narrator wanted to know where that particular path led to. Then the two men—the rescuer and the other man—laughed and 'waved their caps' at the narrator.

The narrator then understood that the pool was actually a moat running along the hedge. He found there a beautiful natural scenario in which happy men and women were, but the place appeared to him to be a prison, for all that. The narrator and his rescuer moved away from the place. The narrator told him that their walking there was 'terrible,' because none of them, could 'advance' or 'progress' inspite of walking. The narrator said that men were supposed to advance continually: 'We are always learning, expanding, developing. Why, even in my short life I have seen a great deal of advance—the Transvaal War, the Fiscal Question, Christian Science, Radium. Here for example—.' But suddenly he saw that his pedometer 'still marked twenty-five, not a degree more.' The narrator thought that his pedometer stopped, and the rescuer told him that Many things don't work in here.' The narrator thought that the water of the moat in which he fell must be the cause of the pedometer's stopping. He told the rescuer: 'The laws of science are universal in their application. It must be the water in the moat that injured the machinery. In normal conditions everything works. Science and the spirit of emulation—those are the forces that have made us what we are.'

In that particular spot, the narrator saw people busy in divers occupations and evocations, such as singing and gardening, and found them all happy. He said that he also could be happy if he could forget that 'the place led to nowhere.' He was suddenly startled by the approach of a young man who ran along and then 'plunged into a lake, across which he began to swim.' He wondered at the 'true energy' of that young man. Then he found a girl singing. He wondered at 'the waste in production'—the production of many varied creatures which do not lend a hand in developing.

He said: '...Every achievement is worthless unless it is a link in the chain of development....' The narrator now wanted to part company with the rescuer, and with that objective in view he wanted to mend his pedometer, but the rescuer urged him to see the unused gate. The rescuer showed him the gate over a long bridge from which another road began. Seeing that second road, the narrator cried out: "That's my road!"

The rescuer told the narrator that the gate was not his (the narrator's) 'part of the road' and that 'It is through this gate that humanity went out countless ages ago, when it was first seized with the desire to walk.' The narrator could not agree with him because, he said, the earlier road was two miles off from this second road. He continued: 'It is the same road. This is the beginning, and though it seems to run straight away from us, it doubles so often that it is never far from our boundary and sometimes it touches it.' The rescuer said that he did not know where the road did end—it might be the sky or the sea, which allured men to run on, some striving to excel others in running on. Then the narrator exclaimed to see Miss Eliza Dimbleby standing at a distance 'with her feet in the fountain!' The rescuer agreed. But then the narrator disagreed because, he recalled, she was 'due to lecture this evening at Tunbridge Wells.' The rescuer philosophised: 'People always are astonished at meeting each other. All kinds come through the hedge, and come at all times—when they are drawing ahead in the race, when they are lagging behind, when they are left for dead. I often stand near the boundary listening to the sounds of the road—you know what they are—and wonder if anyone will turn aside. It is my great happiness to help someone out of the moat, as I helped you. For our country fills up slowly, though it was meant for all mankind.' The narrator told him that 'Mankind have other aims' than just walking, and that he must join those who had been proceeding through that road. But the rescuer, an old man, physically barred him from going away, and so the narrator had to go with the rescuer to the latter's country where there were some sights about which the rescuer was worried: the rescuer saw that the people of his country had been sleeping like cattle. Apprehensive, the narrator kept awake all night and did not receive any food, though hungry, from the people of the rescuer's country, and murmured 'indomitably, to the rescuer: 'Give me life, with its struggles and victories, with its failures and hatreds, with its deep moral meaning and its unknown goal!'

At last the two men came across another gate on another bridge over the 'encircling moat.' This gate was different from the previous one. The narrator, 'in the waning light,' saw that another road (the third road), which was like the former (the second) dusty and monotonous one and which issued from that gate. At the sight of the last road, the narrator was disquieted, and lost self-control. Now he saw a man returning for the night to the hills, with a scythe and 'a can of liquid in his hand.' He tells us: 'I forgot the destiny of our race. I forgot the road that lay before my eyes, and I sprang at him, wrenched the can out of his hand, and began to drink.' The drink sent the narrator to a hypnagogic state in which he saw, as if in a dream, that the 'old man,' who was returning to the hills, shut the gate. The old man told the narrator: "'This is where your road ends, and through this gate humanity—all that is left of it—will come in to us.'" Though the senses of the narrator were now sinking into oblivion, due to the drink, he saw human beings multiplying before reaching the end of the road. He saw that they 'perceived the magic song of nightingales, and the odour of invisible hay, and stars piercing the fading sky.' The old man, whose beer the narrator had stolen, laid him (the narrator) down to sleep, and, says the narrator, "'as he did so, I saw that he was my brother.'"

As told earlier, 'The Other Side of the Hedge' is allegorical; it has a definite meaning or message behind its fable, and the meaning or message is that love and friendship can grow only in bucolic environments, and that salvation can be achieved through love and friendship. Like 'The Story of a Panic,' 'The Other Side of the Hedge' is also a story of salvation. According to John Sayre Martin, 'The Other Side of the Hedge' is rather a 'straight-forward' story of salvation through escape. Martin interprets the story thus: "The hedge divides the winding, dusty road of life down which mankind is hurrying to who knows where, from the earthly paradise. After crawling exhausted through a gap in the hedge and being rescued from drowning in the surrounding moat, the narrator finds himself in a pastoral country whose inhabitants, as he learns from his rescuer and guide, are unprogressive and agricultural. Lovely as it all is, the traveller feels that nevertheless he might like to rejoin the rat race, for, after all, as his pedometer has told him, he is only twenty-five. But, after a bit more sight-seeing, he is tired and thirsty—so thirsty that he steals a can of beer from a passer-by. Drinking, he sinks into oblivion, but discovers just before doing so that the man whose beer he has taken and who is now lowering him gently to sleep off its effects is his long-forsaken brother. Unlike Eustace who escaped from humanity, the present traveller escapes into it" (Martia, 51). And, by escaping into humanity he gets salvaged. The meeting with, and recognition of, the traveller's brother at the end of the story is a striking pre-figuring of Rickie's meeting with, and recognition of, his half-brother Stephen Wonham in *The Longest Journey*.

4

'THE CELESTIAL OMNIBUS'

The two most important events in the life of Forster that happened in 1908 were the publication of his short story 'The Celestial Omnibus' in January in the *Albany Review* and the crystallisation of what was to become his fourth novel, *Howards End*. At the time of the publication of this story Forster wrote: "'the only thing that I am wanting to publish at present is some short stories'" (Beauman, 215). In 1911, 'The Celestial Omnibus' was again published, this time as the little story of a collection of six stories. Forster persuaded Messrs Sidgwick and Jackson to accept a volume of short stories, and submitted ten stories for the volume, but Frank Sidgwick "had decided on a selection of six only, all in Forster's fantastic vein—there being just then a vogue for mythological fantasy" (Furbank, I, 199). Sidgwick took the fancy of printing an illustration on the cover of the volume, at which Forster vexedly wondered. Ultimately Roger Fry "turned out enthusiastic and, after much procrastination, produced a woodcut design to illustrate the little-story, depicting a rainbow, sunset, and Valhallan crags overtopping the terraces of Surbiton. In the foreground of Fry's cover-design stand two billboards bearing the legends 'Practical Culture' and 'Imperial Culture'—presumably Fry's own contribution to the story's indictment of culture-snobbery" *(ibid.)*. The volume of six stories, *The Celestial Omnibus,* came out of the press in the spring of 1911, and Forster apostrophised: "'O lovely Spring!'" *(ibid.)*.

Forster was influenced by his reading of Samuel Butler's *Erewhon* which was published in 1872. "Erewhon (an anagram of 'nowhere') is discovered by Higgs, the narrator, on the far side of a chain of unexplored mountains in a remote colony. His [Higgs's] description embodies Butler's attack on the mental and moral stagnation and hypocrisy he found in England, and his society's attitudes to crime, religion and the rearing of children. Higgs escapes from Erewbon in a balloon he constructed himself, accompanied by a girl with whom he was fallen in love" (Ousby, 305). The idea of escaping with a balloon Forster perhaps got from Butler's *Erewhon.* The second source of the idea of 'The Celestial Omnibus,' or rather the anti-machine stance of the story was his cynical response to H.G. Wells's scientific 'utopian visions' (for instance, in his *The Time Machine)*. The immediate stimulus to write the story was Forster's reaction to the news circulated in January 1908 that a man had been able to fly in an air machine for 'one and half minutes.' Forster recorded his reaction to this news on 27 January, 1908, in *Notebook Journal*: "'It's coming quickly, and if I live to be old I shall see the sky as pestilential as the roads. It really is a new civilization. I have been born at the end of the age of peace and can't expect to feel anything but despair. Science, instead of freeing man—the Greeks nearly freed him by right feeling—is enslaving him to machines. Nationality will go, but the brotherhood of man will not come. No doubt the men of the past were mistaken in thinking 'dulce et decorum est pro patria mori' but the war of the future will make no pretence of beauty or of being the conflict of ideas. God what a prospect! The little houses that I am used to will be swept away, the fields will stink of petrol, and the air will shatter the stars. Man may get a new and perhaps a greater soul for the new conditions. But such a soul as mine will be crushed out'" (Beauman, 214).

Like Samuel Butler's *Erewhon,* his *The Way of All Flesh* also has influenced Forster's 'The Celestial Omnibus.' The condition of the life of the boy in the story, before his escaping flight, is not very different from that of the young Ernest Pontifex, the hero of *The Way of All Flesh*. Pontifex 'endures an unhappy upbringing in the Evangelical parsonage at Battersby,' and the boy in 'The Celestial Omnibus' was frequently being scathed with belittling jokes by his unsympathetic mother and others. When once the boy asked about the sign-post, his mother did not at all entertain his question, and so did Mr Bons who said that it was 'the joke of a person named Shelley,' In fact, like *The Longest Journey* 'The Celestial Omnibus' is also Forster's compliment to Shelley. However, 'The Celestial Omnibus' is the story 'about a small boy's attempt to escape his parent's suburban home by taking an omnibus to heaven.' There was an old sign-post, which read 'To Heaven,' in Buckingham Park Road in Surbiton. A boy, a resident of Agathox Lodge at 28, Buckingham Park Road, Surbiton, being puzzled by the signpost, asked his mother about the meaning it bore, and the mother summarily explained it away as a joke. Mr Bons, who 'was probably the wisest person alive' and who came for afternoon tea with his daughter to the house of the boy, also opined that 'the sign-post was a joke—the joke of a person named Shelley.' The tea over, the boy, at the bidding of his mother, saw off the Bonses, walking with them upto the end of the road. The beautiful scenario of the place, in the afternoon saffron glow of the sun, caught the imagination of the boy. Seeing, the guest a off, the boy 'slipped across the road towards the sign-post and began to run up the blank valley.' He attentively examined the sign-post and exclaimed: "'I'd like to kick that Shelley.'" Casually, he saw a slip of paper pasted on the sign-post. From that slip of paper he came to understand that a certain travel company, 'S. and C.R.C.C. was providing journeys, presently by only one category of vehicles, named 'Sunrise and Sunset Omnibuses.' The Company warned possible travellers that it would not 'be responsible for any negligence or stupidity on the part of Passengers, nor for Hailstorms, Lightning, Loss of Tickets, nor for any Act of God.' The Company advertised that for the first time it was going to issue 'Return Tickets,' available for only one day's journey, and that such tickets could be had of the driver. It cautioned that tickets were not available at the other end of the journey.

The boy could not understand where the omnibuses were bound for, nor could he make out the meaning of the abbreviated expression, 'S. and C.R.C.C.' He thought S. was for Surbiton and R.C.C. was for 'Road Car Company,' but he failed to understand the meaning of the last C. He hazarded that the last C. might be 'Coombe' or 'City,' but he was not confident. Everything there seemed to him to be a hoax, for there he neither found nor heard of any omnibuses. Howbeit, at last the boy emerged from the alley and met his father at the other end of it, his father laughing all the while. His mother also laughed when she heard of what the boy had been doing and thinking in the alley. And the father and the mother cut a few jokes at him.

At night, in his dream, the boy saw the hoax about the omnibuses came to be true. In his dream he saw that he himself was driving the omnibus and that the real Surbiton was a hoax. He also saw, in his dream, his destination. He woke up from dream crying, half an hour before sunrise, dressed up, and determined to settle which was real and which a hoax—the omnibus he drove or the Surbiton street he drove through, in his dream. He was afraid to go into that alley, but seeing a policeman nearby undaunted he went. It was then pitch dark around the alley thanks to the heavy fog. He found there only nothingness and decided to tell his mother about the hoax. While coming back, he suddenly saw that his watch was fast and that the sun would not rise for two minutes, and so he went back to the alley and there found the omnibus! (section 1).

The boy saw the two horses of the omnibus, 'whose sides were still smoking from their journey,' and also the two lamps of it, which were still shining through the fog. He also saw the driver, and was imagining 'how he would drive out.' The boy took the driver to be a pirate, for, he thought, none else would drive out at 'such odd places and at such odd hours.' However, after a brief conversation with the driver, the boy jumped into the omnibus and the driver drove it off, just before dawn. The boy was the only passenger. Suddenly he discovered that he was without his purse, and so shouted out at the driver to stop: 'Mr Browne! stop; oh, do please stop!' But the driver did not stop, and so the boy offered him his watch for a ticket. The driver told him that the ticket of the omnibus could not be purchased with earthly coins, and that the 'chronometer [the watch], though it had solaced the vigils of Charlemagne or measured the slumbers of Laura, can acquire by no mutation the double cake that charms the fangless Cerberus of Heaven!' Then the driver gave the boy a ticket *gratis,* and said that he was Sir Thomas Browne. The boy wondered that if passengers were allowed to travel *gratis* then the omnibus company would be a losing concern. But the driver told him that the omnibus was not intended for profit-making. The driver, Sir Browne, described the omnibus to the boy: 'Many are the faults of my equipage; it is compounded too curiously of foreign woods; its cushions tickle erudition rather than promote repose; and my horses are nourished not on the ever-green pastures of the moment, but on the dried bents and clovers of Latinity. But that it pays!—that error at all events was never intended and never attained.' The boy felt sorry at his words, and the driver now seated the boy beside himself and drove on.

The driver told the boy that he had been a physician, not so much of the body as of the soul—'healer of the spirit.' He would administer 'cunning goblets' to cure 'the queasy soul.' He informed the boy that, like himself, (P.B.) Shelley was also a driver in the Company, with his own carriage. He and the boy were now ascending in their carriage, but on a sudden the carriage was struck by a thunder-bolt, and there were echoes from the surrounding hills. The boy recalled his father and mother, and 'saw them sitting down to sausages and listening to the storm.' He wished to be back home with presents for the parents. But there was the second thunder-bolt which broke the clouds into smithereens. He of course was not daunted though a shade perplexed. He asked the driver to listen to the sound of the exploded thunder: "Oh, listen, Sir Thomas Browne! No, I mean look; we shall get a view at last. No, I mean listen; that sounds like a rainbow!' The sound metamorphosed into a murmur, and the murmur grew and widened in widening curves of a rainbow spreading from the horses's 'feet into the dissolving mists.' The boy wondered at the colour and the sound that 'grew together' and formed the shape of a solid rainbow of enormous span. He cried out: 'what is that out there?' and 'What does it rest on, out at the other end?'

As the morning broke out there appeared something like a precipice or a castle on the far end of the rainbow, and the driver and the boy 'set their feet upon the rainbow.' They saw waves above and below the rainbow, and they saw people and trees and the 'flames of the rainbow that licked against their wheels.' And as the sunbeams appeared, they saw below three maidens rise to the surface of the pool, singing, and playing with something that glistened like a ring.' The driver and the boy were high up and the maidens were below. Now a music was being played—music that said: '...Truth in the depth, truth on the height.' The driver told the boy that the maidens were sporting 'in the mancipiary ['manus' meaning 'hand,' and 'capare' meaning 'take'] possession of their gold.' Meanwhile, the omnibus arrived back at Surbiton (section 2).

The boy now found himself in disgrace, for he found him locked up in the nursery of Agathox Lodge, learning poetry for a punishment.' Further, his father cudgeled him severely for his truancy, saying: 'There is no omnibus, no driver, no bridge, no mountain; you are a *truant,* a *gutter-snipe,* a *liar.*' But inspite of all that, to the boy, it 'was the greatest day of his life.' The boy was taken back from the fateful alley to his house, after a gap of only three hours, by a serving maid. The maid talked to the boy about omnibuses, barouches (double-seated four-wheeled carriages with falling tops) and landaus. The boy was surprised that the present voice of the maid was quite different from the one that he heard while in the region of the rainbow, and this change occurred within only three hours! The mother of the boy now asked him to bring his poetry (which he was supposedly reading before his imaginary journey to heaven). The boy found that a party was given in their house, in which Mr Bons was present. His father introduced him to Mr Bons, saying: 'Here is the great traveller!' and 'Here is the young gentleman who drives in an omnibus over rainbows, while young ladies sing to him.' The father was pleased over the wit of the boy. Mr Bons said about the journey of the boy that after all 'there is something a little like it in Wagner. It is odd how in quite illiterate minds, you will find glimmers of Artistic Truth.... We have all romanced in our time, haven't we?' The father now asked the boy to recite the poem, and the boy stood still and began: "'Standing aloof in giant ignorance'" (from Keats). The father became disgusted with the recitation of the boy and went in to bring whisky, handing over the boy to Mr Bons for the boy's poetic exercises. Mr Bons took up his charge, and the boy continued: "'Standing aloof in giant ignorance, of thee I dream and of the Cyclades, as one who sits ashore and longs perchance to visit—.'" Mr Bons asked him: '...To visit what?' The boy replied: "'To visit dolphin coral in deep seas'." And then he burst into tears. Mr Bons asked why he was crying, and the boy said: 'Because—because all those words that only rhymed before, now that I've come they're me.'

Mr Bons was befuddled; he asked the boy how the sonnet of Keats (from which the lines were recited) could be he. Mr Bons doubted the truth of poetry. The boy asked him to look to the distance, and then said to him: 'Yes—and further on: "Aye, on the shores of darkness there is light, and precipices show untrodden green." It is so, sir. All these things are true.' Mr Bons now agreed with the boy that there is 'the essential truth of Poetry,' but he did not believe in the details and ornamentations of the poet, or in the omnibus, the driver, and the storm that the boy perceived. The boy insisted that whatever he had seen were all true: ...There is light upon the shores of darkness. I have seen it coming. Light and wind.' Yet Mr Bons could not believe even a shade of any one of those things. The boy told him that he was so pleased to see all those things that he did not want to come back from that celestial sphere, but for his father and mother. The boy disclosed to Mr Bons that earlier his parents told him that as he (Mr Bons) was a scholar, he would not believe in his (the boy's) yarn (fantastic story). Mr Bons was certain that the boy had been suffering from some sort of delusion or hallucination, and assured him (the boy) that he would cure him. Mr Bons gave him word that he would take him to that alley (to show him that there were no such things as the omnibus and all that), but, contrarily, he (the boy) thought that now Mr Bons believed everything about his omnibus journey, and so he was bounding in joy.

Next evening Mr Bons came and took the boy to that alley (to show him that there was no omnibus and such other things), and to his wonderment he found a different omnibus in the glow of the setting sun. This omnibus had three horses, instead of two—'black, grey, and white, the grey being the finest.' Mr Bons seemed to recognise the driver of the omnibus—'a sallow man with terrifying jaws and sunken eyes'—and was violently trembling, supposedly in fear. The boy jumped into the omnibus named 'Dan someone,' and asked Mr Bons to go in as well. Aghast, Mr Bons cried out: "'Is the impossible possible?" Nonetheless, Mr Bons also boarded the vehicle. A gust of wind shut the door and the windows of the vehicle, and the vehicle moved away. The boy uttered at the top of his voice: "'Hooray!'" It was now night and so the inside of the omnibus was dark, Mr Bons felt the journey 'A strange, a memorable adventure'.

Over the door of the omnibus was written: 'Lasciate ogni baldanza voi che entrate.' The boy asked the driver—the cadaverous driver—for two tickets and the tickets were given to him with any money in return. Mr Bons could recognise the driver in the faded star-light as none else than 'impossible' (personified). He said it was the man who wrote the 'vellum books.' His boy sat still and was wondering if he would be able to meet Mrs Gamp (a character in one of Dickens' novels) and Mrs Harris whom he much liked. He said that he met a man, in the past, "'who took me out beyond to a race-course.

You run, and there are dolphins out at sea.'" Mr Bons asked him the name of the man, and the boy replied: "'Achilles. No; he was later. Tom Jones.'" Mr Bons told him that he (the boy) was making a mess of all the characters (of the fictions), and that cultured people knew all the characters quite well, including the characters created by Homer and Shakespeare, and also that cultured people were not fidgety, like him. Seeing the boy restless, Mr Bons asked him to give him the two tickets, lest he lost them, and the boy obeyed.

For some time past, it was raining, but now rain stopped, and the moonlight entered into the omnibus through the cracks in the windows, The boy recognised that it was night, and so wondered: "'how is there to be a rainbow?'" But seeing Mr Bons very cultured, vowed to himself to remain gentle. Now, as soon as the blind of the window was lifted up by a gust of wind, the boy saw 'the summit of a moonlit hill' up there, and water and camp-fires below, and was prattling about them. Mr Bons snubbed him, saying all those he was talking about were not real, were nonsensical. Then the boy peeped out and saw the rainbow, the finest one he ever yet saw, but did not tell Mr Bons about it, because, he thought, Mr Bons would think also of it as nonsense; and so he rather began to sing to 'the tune that rose from the sleeping waters' below. Mr Bons also looked out of the window, and seeing something fell down on the floor of the omnibus, and began to writhe, his face turning green. He now wanted to return, but the driver would not let him to. At this moment, the boy announced that they were about to reach their destination, and that the creatures of the place, they were moving towards, were then asleep. The omnibus ran over the 'lunar rainbow,' which was gradually tapering behind its wheels. The night was still. The boy cried out: "'I am returning—I, the boy.'"

Someone saw the boy and Mr Bons returning, and then others, but none uttered a word; there was prevailing profound silence. Achilles, young and wonderfully armed with shield, stood sentry 'on the rocky causeway.' Mr Bons wanted to go where he and the boy started from. 'The last fragment of the rainbow melted, the wheels (of the omnibus) sang upon the living rock, the door of the omnibus burst open.' The boy landed and accosted Achilles who lifted the boy up on his shield, and the boy 'crouched on the wonderful shield, on heroes and burning cities, on vineyards graven in gold, on every dear passion, every joy, on the entire image of the Mountain that he had discovered, like it, with an everlasting stream.' He implored Achilles to lift up Mr Bons, too. Mr Bons was whimpering (in fear). Achilles commanded him to stand up on the shield. To pacify Mr Bons the boy told him that there nothing to fear, because there was only the great Achilles whom he (Mr Bons) knew. But Mr Bons continued to scream: "'I see no one. I see nothing, I want to go back. Then he cried to the driver, "Save me! Let me stop in your chariot. I have honoured you. I have quoted you. I have bound you in vellum. Take me back to your world.'" The driver replied, "I am the means and not the end. I am the food and not the life. Stand by yourself, as that boy has stood. I cannot save you. For poetry is spirit; and they that would worship it must worship in spirit and in truth." Mr Bons was imbued with the spirit of the speech of the driver and slowly emerged out of the omnibus, but accidentally fell on the hard rock with a shriek of "I see London," and dead he was. People came in a procession to honour him with music and torches. They showered 'fresh leaves on his forehead,' and somebody placed on his head a crown with the engraving 'TELOS'.

The *Kingston Gazette, Surbiton Times* and *Raynes Park Observer* published the obituary of Mr Bons, which read thus: 'The body of Mr Septimus Bons has been found in a shockingly mutilated condition in the vicinity of the Bermondsey gas-works. The deceased's pockets contained a sovereign-purse, a silver cigar-case, a bijou pronouncing dictionary, and a couple of omnibus tickets. The unfortunate gentleman had apparently been hurled from a considerable height. Foul play is suspected, and thorough investigation is pending by the authorities' (section 3).

This is also a fantasy and escape story suffused with wit and imagination. It sufficiently demonstrates Forster's *tour de force* of story-telling. The subject-matter of the story is quite thin and light, and yet it occupies about eighteen interesting pages (divided into three sections). John Sayre Martin summarises the story thus: "In 'The Celestial Omnibus,' the boy escapes from a dreary suburb and a couple of dreary parents to heaven. The suburb is gray and monotonous; the parents are facetious and superficial; their friend Mr Bons is pompous fraud—a literate who collects books ('I believe we have seven Shelleys') as some people collect art, and who patronises the boy. But the boy, just because he is a boy, is nearer the celestial light than his elders. Hence be ascends to heaven—not, however, on the wings of poesy but in a horse-drawn celestial omnibus piloted, on three separate occasions, by Sir Thomas Browne, Jane Austen and Dante. And the heaven to which he goes, together with Mr Bons, is a romantic fantasy of heights and depths, swirling clouds, Rhine maidens, heroes, and eminent authors. The boy remains in heaven, but Mr Bons, who quotes poetry without having proved it upon his pulses, crashes down to a horrible death" (Martin, 51-52).

According to Nicola Beauman, 'The Celestial Omnibus' is, in a sense, a homage of Forster to Samuel Butler's (1835-1902) *The Way of All Flesh* (Beauman, 200). In this novel Butler took cudgel against the Victorian moral hypocrisy and advocated liberation or freedom of will as the source of happiness. The hero of the novel. Ernest Pontifex, was a victim of parental tyranny, and he wanted to escape from it. Through a chain of *faux pases* and new experiences, he could free himself from the atrophying Victorian morality and achieve liberation, to his utmost satisfaction. The condition of the 'boy' of 'The Celestial Omnibus' before his liberation is not different from that of the pre-liberated Ernest Pontifex. Nicola Beauman writes about the condition from which the 'boy' escaped into heaven: "He is submissive and dutiful, yet his mother and father 'though very kind, always laughed at him;' they punish him brutally when they decide he is lying, and are implacably convinced of their own rightness" (*ibid.).* That Butler's *The Way of All Flesh* informed the theme of the story is evident from what Nicola Beauman writes: "In September [1909], possibly because the boy in the story was in part inspired by *The Way of All Flesh's* Ernest, who 'writhes under the paternal lash, he is stifled by the maternal embrace,' Morgan [Forster] re-read Butler's other great novel, *Erewhon*. He had first read it rather unenthusiastically at Nassenheide, and may have been reminded of it by Elizabeth on their caravan trip the month before; this time he was greatly impressed. 'It's the human race re-made,' he told Trevy, adding: 'It will help us among the planets when we're dead'" (*op.cit,* 201).

'The Celestial Omnibus' is obviously an escape story; but escape from what? In 'The Celestial Omnibus' the escape, ultimately, is from culture put on wrong track, or culture that does not further humanness but hinders it. Forster was always spiteful towards culture put on wrong track, or culture that hinders the development of man's innate humanness. The 'boy' of the story was vexed by the stifling condition or the atrophying culture of his parents and of Mr Bons, and so he wanted to get liberated from such a culture and fly away somewhere, where liberation is unlimited, on the wings of his imagination. P.N. Furbank writes about Forster's preoccupation about wrong culture: "Culture put to the wrong end was, as we know, a major preoccupation in all his early novels. He had identified various versions; the use of culture as an escape, as with Philip Herriton; the use of it to bolster one's superiority, as with Cecil Vyse; the use of it as a conspicuous possession, as with Mr Bons in 'The Celestial Omnibus.' All these were abuses, in his view, cutting culture off from what gave it its value, the furthering of humanness generally" (Furbank, I, 173). The 'conspicuous possession' of Mr Bons is his anti-imaginative, anti-romantic and materialistic cultural hypocrisy. Mr Bons does not believe in any value other than materialistic value; he cannot conceive of any truth beyond the mundane. He is not at all acquainted with literature, he has no sense of it; but despite of this he is an eager collector of literary curiosities: he is a literary hypocrat. Literary hypocrisy is his 'conspicuous possession' and his culture put on wrong track.

The 'boy' of 'The Celestial Omnibus' wanted to escape from this pseud-culture of mindless sticking to blind tradition of materialism, and achieve freedom of imagination and will, and actually he did escape over the rainbow region. The name of the driver of the vehicle by which he made his escape bears significance—it is Sir Thomas Browne. Sir Browne (1605-82), an M.D. and a religious writer, is the author of two important works—*Religio Medici* and *Urn Burial.* In the former work he has dwelt mainly on the ingeniousness of God's creation, and in the second on the ephemerality of earthly life. The basic belief of his was spirituality and anti-materialism. Forster expropriated this spirituality of Sir Browne in 'The Celestial Omnibus.' Sir Browne was the driver of the flying vehicle because he had spirituality (though not in the religious sense) and this spirituality is wanting both in Mr Bons and in the culture in which he lives. The name of another driver of the vehicle is Shelley or P.B. Shelley (1792-1822), the most ebullient of the great romantic poets of England, and the most virulent advocate of freedom and spirituality (not in the religious sense). The following lines from Shelley's 'Ode to the West Wind' may illustrate the nature of his spirituality:

Make me thy lyre, even as the forest is,
  What if my leaves are falling like its own!
The tumult of thy mighty harmonies,
  Will take from both a deep, autumnal tone,
Sweet though in sadness. Be thou, spirit fierce,
  My spirit! Be thou me, impetuous one.

Shelley wanted to escape this insensate earth on the wings of the West Wind as the 'boy' wanted to flee from his oppressive and opprobrious parents. Allusion to Keats is also there in the story: the 'boy' was ordered by his parents to memorise Keats' sonnet 'To Homer.' The 'boy' recites only the beginning three and a quarter lines from the sonnet once and two other more lines from it at another time. The full-length sonnet is being cited below:

Standing aloof in giant ignorance,
  Of thee I hear and of the Cyclades,
As one who sits ashore and longs perchance
  To visit dolphin-coral in deep seas;
So thou wast blind;—but then the veil was rent,
  For Jove uncurtain'd Heaven to let thee live,

And Neptune made for thee a spumy tent,
    And Pan made sing for thee his forest-hive;
Aye on the shores of darkness there is light,
    And precipices show untrodden green,
There is a budding morrow in midnight,
    There is a triple sight in blindness keen;
Such seeing hadst thou, as it once befel
To Dian, Queen of Earth, and Heaven, and Hell.

In this sonnet Keats hears of Homer, from afar, and likewise the 'boy' in 'The Celestial Omnibus' hears the call of the region of freedom, which is the virtual heaven to him,--the region over the rainbow. Keats' poem 'Fancy' may also have some influence on the idea of the story. The beginning and the ending couplets of the poem may be cited below to prove the point. The beginning couplet runs thus: "Let the winged Fancy roam, /Pleasure is never at home." And the concluding couplet reads thus: "Ever let the fancy roam, / Pleasure is never at home." The refrain of the poem, "Pleasure is never at home," dovetails with the theme of the story. However, John Sayre Martin says that the story is 'encumbered with incidents' and is infused with an overdoze of sentimentality. But, says Martin, these two potential drawbacks are aptly managed by "Forster's wit and lightness of touch" (Martin, 52). When the volume *The Celestial Omnibus,* which included this present story, was first published, the main burden of the objections of reviewers was that Forster "wrote them [the six stories contained in that volume] for himself rather than for his readers" (Beauman, 244). According to Nicola Beauman, "this was true," for, says Beauman, Forster "inhabited the world of his stories" *(ibid.).*

5

'OTHER KINGDOM'

'Other Kingdom' is the fourth story in the collection of short stories, entitled *The Celestial Omnibus.* As in the immediately preceding story 'The Celestial Omnibus' the 'boy' wanted to escape, so in this story the 'heroine' Evelyn needs to be escaped. As an escape story, 'Other Kingdom' is certainly better than 'The Celestial Omnibus.' According to John Sayre

Martin, "'Other Kingdom' is one of Forster's best stories. Carefully and dramatically structured, it is a sustained comedy generated by the confrontation of opposites: the civilized and the natural, the sham and the true, the ugly and the beautiful, the dead and the vital" (Martin, 56). In 'Other Kingdom,' Forster wants to establish one of his fundamental beliefs that the free spirit cannot be shackled or attenuated or encompassed; and that the spirit of man is his overlord; and also that the proper habitation of the spirit is nature, not the city. The "heroine' of this story, Miss Evelyn Beaumont, represents Forster and his attitude towards spirit, nature and humanity; and, in this sense, this story has kinship with *Howards End* and *The Longest Journey.*

As the story begins to unfold, we see Miss Evelyn Beaumont, Mrs Worters and Mr Inskip (the narrator of the story) engaged in a debate among themselves as to whether gods dwelt in the waters or in the woods or in the sky, Mr Ford remaining present there but taking no part in the debate. Mrs Worters opined that gods always resided in the sky; Mr Inskip agreed with her; but Miss Beaumont objected: "'Not always.'" Consulting her note-book, Miss Beaumont said that the chief deities lived on Mount Olimpus; Pan lived in most places: Oreads over mountains: Sirens, Tritons and Nereids in salty waters; Naiads in fresh waters; Satyrs, Fauns, etc. in woods; and Dryads in trees. The narrator, Mr Inskip, now asked Miss Beaumont: "'Well, dear, you have learnt a lot. And will you now tell me what good it has done you?'" Like the narrator, Miss Beaumont was also deeply interested and vastly learned in the classics, and yet she fumbled. At this moment Mr Ford came to her rescue. He said that classics are full of tips with which one can dodge things—one can mean one thing or the other, depending on one's intention.

Meantime, the word 'dodge' acquired prominence, and began to be used as an instrument of teasing to the Regius Professor Jack Ford. Ford told Miss Beaumont that Midas was a god who did never dodge; if Midas would ever touch her, for instance, she would become a golden lady for sure—there would be no dodging. Miss Beaumont insisted that Midas would not touch her, but Ford was certain that Midas would touch her. To put the conversation back on the right track, Mrs Worters repeated the former question to Miss Beaumont, *mutatis mutandis*: '...What good has Latin done you?' At this moment, the narrator was readying to go out for tea. Before he went out, Mrs Worters raised the question of the importance of Latin other than passing an examination. Jack and Miss Beaumont had to pass their entrance examination in which Latin was one of the subjects, so the tongue was important for Jack, but it was of no worth to Miss Beaumont—said Mrs Worters. The narrator objected. He said that Miss Meaumont was also taking the examination, like Jack, and so Latin was also important to her. Further, the new civilization into which she was entering required the knowledge of Latin. The narrator further said that classical education was not as valueless as dreams. Just at this moment Mr Harcourt Worters, who was Mrs Worters' son and Miss Beaumont's *fiance* and Ford's guardian and the narrator's employer, joined the conversation by gate-crashing. He heard only the word 'dreams' of the on-going conversation and ejaculated: 'Let us cherish our dreams!' Mr Worters then sat on a chair in the lawn and took Miss Beaumont's hand into his. He had recently bought Other Kingdom Copse, in Hertfordshire, of which the beech-trees are very fine. Mr Worters told Miss Beaumont about the purchase of Other Kingdom: 'The purchase will be drawn up in your name. You will sign the deed. Receive the wood, with my love. It is a second engagement ring.' Miss Beaumont was filled with joy to the brim; she kissed Mr Worters and Mrs Worters. She was possessed by the joy of possession. She was to possess Other Kingdom for ninety-nine years! To Ford ninety-nine years meant eternity, and yet Miss Beaumont felt disappointed because she knew she would not live as long as ninety-nine years. Meanwhile, tea came and Mr Worters jumped to it, along with the two ladies, and all of them were soon joined by a hive of ladies who emerged from the house, with excitement of joy over the purchase of Other Kingdom. But Ford could not be joyous; he was musing over the worth of the patch of earth newly bought by Mr Worters. He thought that

Mr Worters was dreaming 'of the tangible and the actual: robust dreams, which take him, not to heaven, but to another earth.' But Mr Worters sat cozily, and was trying to construe the meaning of Virgil's Eclogues and was searching for the value of his newly bought Other Kingdom (section 1).

Suddenly Miss Beaumont proposed a visit by cycling to Other Kingdom which had no speciality but that it was just filled with beech-trees and that a stream ran in front of it. Miss Beaumont next modified her proposal and said that it would not be simply a visit but a picnic; and according to this proposal, a procession of eight persons, including the sisters of Mrs Worters and Mrs Osgood, and the narrator, proceeded towards Other Kingdom in a single file led by herself (Miss Beaumont). Miss Beaumont became so excited with joy that she spoke some irrelevant things; for instance, she asked Harcourt Worters to throw 'to the Naiad a pinch of tea. She has a headache. She has had a headache for nineteen hundred years.' She also absurdly asked Inskip, the narrator, to sing. The narrator tells us: 'I was not surprised that Harcourt had picked her [Miss Beaumont] out of "Ireland" and had brought her home, without money, without connexions, almost without antecedents, to be his bride. It was daring of him, but he knew himself to be a daring fellow.' Harcourt 'had so vast a surplus of spiritual and commercial good' to satisfy Miss Beaumont.

However, when all reached the wood of Other Kingdom, Miss Beaumont cried out: 'Stop singing!' All sat down according to their individual choices of places—Ruth, Mrs Osgood, Anna, the weakling bookworm Jack, and others. Discrete points of conversation went by, and then a debate ensued on the cognate earlier topic: if the classics are of any worth beyond their mere beauty. Miss Beaumont expressed her opinion that the classics were 'Just writing down things.' The narrator disagreed with her, and said: 'But the classics have their poetry as well as their prose. They're more than a record of facts.' 'Harcourt supported Miss Beaumont: '...The classics are not everything. We owe them an enormous debt; I am the last to undervalue it; ...They are full of elegance and beauty. But they are not everything. They were written before men began to really feel.' He concluded: "Hence, the chilliness of classical art—its lack of—of a something.' At this point the narrator tells us that Miss Beaumont 'also lacks something. She has not yet developed her soul.'

Refreshment was now served, and everybody laughed and talked. The air was that of frivolity in the open air; so much frivolous was it that at one time Mrs Worters 'expectorated her flies with a smile.' Miss Beaumont was appreciating the muscular and 'chivalrous figure of Ford'; she 'chaffed him and licked his ankles and calves,' and said 'this is nice' and 'I am happy.' Mr Worters accosted the young Ford and 'slipped his hand up round the boy's [Ford's] ankles,' and Ford cried out in distress and fell down. Miss Beaumont was spiteful towards Mr Worters, at this, and said: "Don't hurt my wood!' Mr Worters then withdrew his hand and exclaimed: 'Victory!' Miss Beaumont then left the place, presumably with disgust, and then the party broke into small splinter groups.

Mr Worters told Mr Inskip that Miss Beaumont was 'practically a child' and that she 'has everything to learn.' Mr Worters further told him that 'Her new life is so different—so strange. Our habits—our thoughts—she has to be initiated into them all.' Miss Beaumont came back and reported to Harcourt that there were in the wood seventyeight trees in all, and that she was very pleased with them. The narrator here describes the person of Harcourt. He tells us that he was 'tall and handsome, with a strong chin and liquid brown eyes, and a high forehead and hair not at all grey.' Harcourt told Miss Beaumont that he would put a fence along the edge of Other Kingdom to prevent anyone's coming in from outside, and the boys cutting initials, and within the fence only they two would exist. Harcourt further told her that he would make an asphalt path and a bridge for coming to the wold. Miss Beaumont objected to all these plans. She said: 'I'd rather always come [to the wold] as we came to-day. And I don't mind the boys and their initials. They and the girls have always come up to Other Kingdom and cut their names together in the bark. It's called the Fourth Time of Asking. I don't want it to stop.' Harcourt, looking at 'a large heart transfixed by an arrow' in the bark of a tree out there, felt a qualm inside his heart. Miss Beaumont continued: 'They cut their names and go away, and when the first child is born they come again and deepen the cuts. So for each child. That's how you know: the initials that go right through the wood are the fathers and mothers of large families, and the scratches on the bark that soon close up are boys and girls who were never married at all.' She stopped by expressing her wish: 'And, Harcourt, I don't want this to stop.' Harcourt became persuasive:

'My dear girl, the villagers will find other trees!
There's nothing particular in Other Kingdom.'
'But———,'
'Other Kingdom shall be for us. You and I alone.
Our initials only.'

Yet, Miss Beaumont would not melt. She rather protested: 'Oh, fence me out, if you like! Fence me out as much as you like! But never in. Oh, Harcourt, never in. I must be on the outside, I must be where anyone can reach me. Year by year—while the initials deepen—the only thing worth feeling—and at last they close up—but one has felt them.' Harcourt took out his pen-knife to engrave into the bark of 'an unsullied tree' murmuring to himself the following: 'E.B. [Evelyn Beaumont], Eternal Blessing. Mine! Mine! My haven from the world! My temple of purity. Oh, the spiritual exaltation—you cannot understand it, but you will! Oh, the seclusion of Paradise. Year after year alone together, all in all to each other—year after year, soul to soul, E.B. Everlasting Bliss!' Harcourt now 'stretched out his hand to cut the initials.' 'As he did so she seemed to awake from a dream. She cried out: 'Harcourt! What's that? What's that red stuff on your finger and thumb?' (section 2).

But all this was but a dream of Miss Beaumont. Actually, Harcourt was just reading from the (amorously or libidinally) 'inflammatory' passages of Ford's note-book. After the incident of Mr Worters' violent emotion (leading to engraving in the bark Miss Beaumont's and his names), Ford felt ashamed because he held himself responsible for that incident. However,

Mr Worters decided to make both the bridge and the fence, and this aggrieved Miss Beaumont, though once 'she gave her Harcourt permission to do what he liked.' The narrator understood that Mr Worters was too much emotionally wafted in the wood, while Miss Beaumont was beside him, because he read what was written in Ford's note-book, and so Ford was responsible for the measureless expression of Mr Worters' emotion. The narrator therefore asked Ford to apologize to Mr Worters, warning him that if he did not obey he would have to quit Mr Worters' home and in that case he would have no place to go to. Ford only succinctly replied that in that case he would go 'To an aunt at Pechham.' At this moment Miss Beaumont came there and wanted to see Ford's note-book though 'She had no "proper feeling" of any kind.' Ford was a apprehensive that Harcourt would somehow punish him because he laughed at him (tongue in cheek). But Miss Beaumont told Ford that Harcourt would not punish him because Harcourt was large-hearted. Ford now pleaded not for him but for Harcourt; he said that Harcourt had the right to demand apology from him. At this Miss Beaumont became cross: 'Right? What's a right? You use too many words. "Rights"—"appologies"—"society"—"position"—I don't follow it. What are we all here for, anyhow?' She went further and said that Harcourt 'soars above conventions. He does not care about "rights" and "apologies." He knows that all laughter is nice, and that the other nice things are money and soul and so on.' The narrator was aghast to hear of 'soul.' Miss Beaumont almost snubbed Ford by telling him that it was simply nonsense if all only 'kept taking offence and apologizing.' She wondered with disgust that 'Forty million people in England and all of them touchy!' Meanwhile, Ford was perhaps crying, keeping his head down between his knees. Miss Beaumont tapped his hair with her mallet, and called him a 'Cry-baby,' and then went into the distance, saying that she was going to speak to Harcourt.

After going into the distance, Miss Beaumont became her normal self—the self she brought with her from Ireland: crude, unsophisticated, beautiful, ludicrous in the extreme, and 'extremely pathetic.' The narrator first saw her in the distance, hanging on the arms of Harcourt, and then saw 'Their two little figures parted and met and parted again, she gesticulating, he most pompous and calm. She pleaded, she argued and—if satire can carry half a mile—she tried to be satirical. To enforce one of her childish points she made two steps back. Splash! She was floundering in the little stream.' This was the *denouement* of the comedy enacted by Harcourt and Miss Beaumont. However, Harcourt rescued her from the pool while a crowd was gathering there. Many came forward for the girl's comfort and safety from influenza, and ultimately she was led to bed for rest. There was terror and bewilderment in the girl's eyes. She said: 'I've failed with Harcourt. He's offended. He won't laugh. He won't let me do what I want...I wanted to know about gods and heroes and he wouldn't let me: then I wanted no fence round Other Kingdom and no bridge and no path—and look!' She now wanted Ford go away from the house of the Worters (section 3).

Ford had actually departed, and the bridge was built, and the fence finished, and Other Kingdom surrounded by asphalt path—keeping Other Kingdom shut off from the world. Miss Beaumont was now dressed in green but in brown, and Harcourt was now repentant for Other Kingdom being secluded. He begged forgiveness to the girl who told him: 'Anything, Harcourt, that pleases you, is certain to please me.' Harcourt told her that when the wind go down the wood, he would go there, along with others. And actually they all went there. When it was lunch time, the wind blew fiercely like a tornado—leaves and twigs flew past them, and a good-sized bough fell on the asphalt path. Miss Beaumont rushed to the bough and touched it. She was elated, and called out to Harcourt: 'mightn't we go up to the copse after lunch, you and I?' In fact, all went—Mrs Worters, Anna, Ruth, Mrs Osgood, Mr Inskip (the narrator), Mr Harcourt Worters and Miss Beaumont. All went lugubriously. As soon as they started going there, the wind fell and calm prevailed. Miss Beaumont told Harcourt 'some gracious and alluring thing,' and then Harcourt asked her to come nearer and give him a kiss. She obeyed and then ran away to invite his passion, and the on-lookers enjoyed the romance. Miss Beaumont cried out:

'Oh, I am so happy!' and 'I think I've everything I want in all the world. Oh dear, those last few days indoors! But oh, I am so happy now!' Then she replaced her brown dress by her former flowing green, and she danced uninhibitedly, unstoppably, to the song of an invisible bird. Her hair, limbs and the other parts of her body now seemed to be transformed into a virtual tree. Harcourt sprang to her to 'inarm' her, crying: 'Evelyn! Eternal Bliss! Mine to eternity! Mine!' But Miss Beaumont slipped away from him, singing: 'Oh Ford! Oh Ford, among all these Worters, I am coming through to you to my Kingdom. Oh Ford, my lover while I was a woman, I will never forget you, never, as long as I have branches to shade you from the sun.' And then she crossed the stream, singing all the while.

Harcourt Worters, in deep passion, ran on after her and repeatedly tried to catch hold of her, but she escaped into the shadow of the trees. Harcourt entered the shadow and cried: 'Evelyn!' But Evelyn ensconced herself cleverly, not to be discovered. Others also searched for the girl but in vain. The wind once again began to blow fiercely, this time with showers. Everyone now thought that Miss Beaumont must be returning, but she did not. Then everyone thought that she had eloped with Ford. Harcourt became venomous; he called Miss Beaumont 'a treacherous woman.' He said: '...I found her no better than a savage, I trained her, I educated her. But I will break them both. I can do that; I will break them soul and body.' The narrator believed that none could now break Ford, and he was trembling for fear of the fate of Miss Beaumont.

The party could not return to London because it missed the train, and so it, rending no other way, went to the suburban home of Ford's, in which Ford was reading Sophocles' *Oedipus Colonus*. Harcourt shouted at Ford: '...You've got Miss Beaumont with you, and I know it.' Ford retorted: 'No such luck.' Harcourt was infuriated at this, and stammeringly asked Inskip, the narrator to repeat the words of Miss Beaumont's song to prove that she was with Ford, Inskip pronounced the words of the girl's song: 'Oh Ford! Oh Ford, among all these Worters, I am coming through to you to my

Kingdom. Oh Ford, my lover while I was a woman, I will never forget you, never, as long as I have branches to shade you from the sun.' Harcourt said that 'on another occasion' Miss Beaumont 'sent a message of similar effect' (to Ford), and from all these Ford was to "guess" something (that she had forsook Harcourt).' Ford told Harcourt that he had already guessed something. Harcourt was astonished: 'So you practically—' Ford told him: 'Oh, no, Mr Worters, you mistake me. I have not practically guessed. I have guessed. I could tell you if I chose, but it would be no good, for she has not practically escaped you. She has escaped you absolutely, for ever and ever, as long as there are branches to shade men from the sun.'

'Other Kingdom' is undoubtedly one of Forster's best short stories. It is also an escape story—the story of the escape of an *ingenue* from the clutch of an extremely possessive man, a story like that of the frightened Daphne running away from the pursuing Apollo. John Sayre Martin, in his *E.M. Forster: The Endless Journey,* has discussed the story at some length, and his discussion is very illuminating. Let us therefore profitably quote his discussion almost in full. Martin begins his discussion comparing. 'Other Kingdom' with 'The Celestial Omnibus'—both escape stories. Martin writes: "'Other Kingdom' is another escapist fantasy, but a better one. The conflict between Harcourt Worters and Evelyn Beaumont, his fiancee, who runs away from him and turns into a tree, is treated in a spirit of Meredithian comedy. The situation in fact recalls *The Egoist.* Like Sir Willoughby Patteme, Harcourt is handsome, virile, and rich, and lives in a big country house surrounded by a worshipful family, including his mother, two maiden sisters (Sir Willoughby has two maiden aunts), an impecunious young ward Jack Ford (compare Crossjay Patteme), his ward's Latin tutor Mr Inskip (compare Vernon Whitford), and a retinue of servants. A successful and not over scrupulous businessman, Harcourt resembles Sir Willoughby in his egoism. He can enjoy only what he possesses, and like Sir Willoughby he wants to possess his wife. Evelyn Beaumont is as unsuited to be married to such a man as Clara Middleton was to Sir Willoughby. In fact, she recalls Meredith's heroine in temperament and circumstance, for she is gay and impulsive, a psychologically free spirit whose inexperience and naivety have engaged her to the wrong kind of man.

Their story [the story of Miss Beaumont and Harcourt Worters] is told by Mr Inskip, whose sycophantic regard for Harcourt, appreciation for classical myth and literature, and failure to understand the crucial events to which he contributes enhances the irony. Sensitive and self-deceiving, he can communicate the superior values of the 'other kingdom' while subscribing, out of material self-regard, to the inferior ones of this. He can enjoy Evelyn's impulsive gaiety and admire Ford's idealism, yet Harcourt is his man; for a Latin teacher without independent means must, as Jane Austen might have said, be in need of a rich employer.

The crisis is broached by Harcourt's purchase of Other Kingdom, an adjacent copse, as a wedding present for Evelyn. True to his nature, Harcourt wants to fence it off from the outside world and build an asphalt path between it and his house. But Evelyn will not hear of a fence or path. 'I don't want to be fenced in...I hate fences. And bridges. And all paths.' Furthermore, she values just what Harcourt cannot abide—the tact that the boys and girls of the village have for ages come to Other Kingdom and cut their initials in the trees: 'They cut their names and go away, and when the first child is born they come again and deepen the cuts. So for each child. That's how you know the initials that go right through to the wood are the fathers and mothers of large families, and the scratches in the bark that soon close up are boys and girls who were never married at all.' In her wish to preserve the copse in its natural state, Evelyn obviously speaks for Forster. The passage looks forward to similar ones in *Howards End* commemorating the life of tradition as nurtured by the country and the folklore associated with the wych-elm. Evelyn's feeling, too, that the outside world should not be excluded from Other Kingdom is in keeping with Forster's visionary humanism. On the other hand, there is an ideal realm, harmonious and self-contained, as projected in vision and realized in art; on the other, there is humanity and the world of daily life with which the novelist and humanist must concern himself. Forster's belief in art for art's sake because it 'creates little worlds of his own' testifies to his sympathy with what is beyond the human; whereas his fiction and social criticism amply testify to his concern with humanity. Just so, in *The Longest Journey,* Rickie Elliot, the character who most intimately speaks for Forster, realizes that, for all its beauty and seclusion, the dell at Madingley must be available to all. He did not love the vulgar herd, but he knew that his own vulgarity would be greater if he forbade it ingress, and that it was not by preciosity that he would attain to the ultimate spirit of the dell.' It is Harcourt, then, intent like Sir Willoughby in keeping the outer world without, who is vulgar; and Evelyn, willing to admit others into her kingdom, who possesses aristocracy of spirit that he can only ape.

"Their conflict comes to a head when Harcourt gets hold of Ford's 'practically private notebook,' reads in it the latter's love poems to Evelyn, and perhaps sees the picture of himself blushing 'like a boiled lobster.' For this piece of treachery Ford must be expelled. Evelyn, after all, is his, Harcourt's property—'My haven from the world! My temple of purity.' Evelyn, for her part, cannot believe that Harcourt would be so ungracious, but, finding that he is, finally manages her escape, though not before Harcourt has had his way with Other Kingdom. 'The bridge is built, the fence finished, and Other Kingdom lies tethered by a ribbon of asphalt to our front door.' The climactic scene, with Evelyn running towards Other Kingdom and Harcourt hot in pursuit, parodies the legend of Daphne and Apollo (although the tempest that precedes and follows Evelyn's disappearance may have been borrowed from *The Egoist:* Clara Middleton flees during a thunder-storm.) Evelyn's feeling for myth and folklore, as expressed in the Latin lesson that begins the story and in her reference to the initials that the boys and girls have cut in the beech barks, has prepared us for her role. Her transformation has also been foreshadowed when, in playful appreciation of Harcourt's purchase, she tries to imitate a beech, 'She flung her arms up above her head...like the layers of a beech.' Now as she flees, Evelyn assumes mythic dimensions. She represents freedom and nature, the antithesis to Harcourt's sham world with its machinery of servants, fences, and asphalt paths, and its pretension to claims, position, and rights: 'She danced to the song of a bird that sang passionately in Other Kingdom, and the river held back its waves to watch her (one might have supposed), and the winds lay spellbound in their cavern, and the great clouds spellbound in the sky. She danced away from our society and our life, back, back, through the centuries till houses and fences fell and the earth lay wild to the sun. Her garment was as foliage upon her, the strength of her limbs as boughs, her throat the smooth upper branch that salutes the morning or glistens to the rain. The leaves move, leaves hide it as hers was hidden by the motion of her hair. Leaves move again and it is ours, as her throat was ours again when, parting the tangle, she faced us crying, 'Oh!' crying 'Oh Harcourt! I never was so happy. I have all that there is in the world.' Her only human rapport is with Ford; for the youth, in his quietly enigmatic way, has stood for the simple and natural: "He cannot, understand the footman and the solid silver kettle-stand. They make him cross. For he had dreams—not exactly spiritual dreams: Mr Worters is the man for those—but dreams of the tangible and the actual: robust dreams, which take him, not to heaven, but to another earth. There are no footmen in this other earth, and the kettle-stands, I suppose, will not be made of silver, and I know that everything is to be itself, and not practically something else.' Studious, clear-sighted, witty, rather detached yet able to love. Ford is temperamentally closer to Forster than to Crossjoy Patterne, his counterpart in *The Egoist.* With the notebook in which he writes, he is an artist-figure, and it is due to him and his poetry that Evelyn escapes. Supported, in other words, though he is by a tasteless materialism, he is the means through which the visionary ideal is realized. And the vision repays the debt just as he once, during the picnic at Other Kingdom, blocked Evelyn's view of Harcourt's ugly house, so now she will screen Ford from the withering character of Harcourt's influence. 'Oh Ford! Oh Ford, among all these Worters, I am coming through you to my Kingdom. Oh Ford, my lover while I was a woman, I will never forget you, never, as long as I have branches to shade you from the sun.' The story ends with Ford in exile in a 'squalid suburb,' ironically engrossed, when Harcourt and Inskip enter his room in pursuit of Evelyn, in the 'Oedipus Coloneus' of Sophocles. Solitary and self-contained, he sees what Harcourt never see, that the free spirit cannot be fenced and possessed as Harcourt possesses his property. 'She has escaped you absolutely, for ever and ever, as long as there are branches to shade men from the sun'" (Martin, 52-56).

We know that Forster was greatly influenced by Jane Austen (1775-1817) and George Meredith (1828-1909) in his conception of the novel and in his style of narration. In 'Other Kingdom' Meredith's influence is obvious, particularly in the depiction of the characters of Harcourt Worters and Miss Beaumont. Meredith's conception of human evolution, and the associated impediments to the evolution, expressed in the contrary attitudes of man and woman towards each other, quite dovetails with the mutually contrary relationships between Harcourt Worters and Miss Beaumont of 'Other Kingdom,' Meredith championed freedom of women as a precondition of the advent of the superman in the sustained course of evolution. He believed that the human evolution is directed towards the absolute realisation of the spirit that is innately dormant in human beings. Diana Neill writes about Meredith's conception of 'spiritual evolution:' "Meredith's conception of this purpose [in human evolution—the 'spiritual evolution'] was not unlike the gospel of vitalism Bernard Shaw preached in *Back to Methuselah*. Man, he believed, was on earth in order to transcend himself, to create the superman. To accomplish this purpose he needed a fit mate, and the laws that governed social life impeded this purpose by setting up the wrong ideals of womanhood. Meredith's championship of woman, his demand for her emancipation, his respect for her intelligence, hinged upon what he considered to be her significant role in bringing into existence a more glorious race. 'Are they not of [a] nature warriors, like men?—men's mates to bear them heroes instead of puppets? But the devouring male Egoist prefers them as inanimate, overwrought polished pure-metal precious vessels, fresh from the hands of the artificer, for him to walk away with hugging, call all his own, drink of, and fill and drink of, and forget that he stole them" (Neill, 247). Whether Forster believed in the spiritual evolution of humanity is a different question, but he certainly believed in the emancipation of women and disliked man's possessiveness over womankind, and this attitude of his towards man and woman has found expression in 'Other Kingdom.' Miss Beaumont, the independent-minded and freedom-loving spiritual girl escapes from the cruel possessiveness of the materialistic Harcourt Worters. She escapes by transmogrifying herself into a tree in the green wood of Other Kingdom; and this is Wordsworthian, pure and simple.

Lionel Trilling found in Miss Beaumont Forster's prototype of sadistic woman, and partially sadistic female characters are not too rare in his novels. Lucy Honeychurch, Lilia Herriton and even Adela Quested, though all of them are passionate enough, hardly feel any compunction when they part with the men with whom they once had been in close intimacy. Perhaps Forster was more interested in manly woman who would not be enslaved by any man, who could easily disengage herself from the possessive lime of a man. He would in his fancy see her somehow enjoy her freedom. Miss Beaumont's character is illustrative of this point. She is the prototype of Forster's freedom-loving woman, as well, and this prototype Forster borrowed, according to Lionel Trilling, from George Meredith. Trilling writes that in 'The Eternal Moment' Forster has sketched 'the type of the wise and gentle heroine.' Trilling writes about the other type of Forster's heroine (represented by Miss Beaumont): "One other feminine type must be mentioned, the heroine that Forster seems to have taken over from Meredith. Appearing first as Evelyn Beaumont of 'Other Kingdom'...who turns into a tree to escape her stuffy, possessive lover—she will recur as Lucy Honeychurch of *A Room with a View* and, somewhat modified, as Helen Schlegel of *Howards End*. Wholly feminine, natural, simple, passionate, right, this is the heroine trapped and in the need of rescue by a man" (Trilling, 43-44).

'Other Kingdom,' like very few of Forster's short stories, is redolent of mythology; the story refers to more than a dozen kinds of, and individual, mythological figures—Pan, Oreads, Sirens, Tritons, Nereids, Satyrs, Fauns, Dryads, Croesus, Midas, Jupiter, Venus and Juno. Pan is the god of 'shepherds and flocks, of nature and wild beasts' and the 'god of animal instinct.' "Pan, the god of woods and fields, of flocks and shepherds, dwelt in grottos, wandered on the mountains and in valleys, and amused himself with the chase or in leading the dances of the nymphs. He was fond of music, and,...the inventor of the syrinx, or shepherd's pipe, which he himself played in a masterly manner" (Bulfinch, 206). The Naiads, 'who presided over brooks and fountains,' the Oreads, who were 'nymphs of mountains and grottos,' and the Nereids, who were 'sea nymphs,' were all partners in Pan's dances. Sirens were maidens who allured mariners to their destruction by their captivating songs. Tritons are sea gods that blow shell or conch. They are like fishes below the waist and like men above the waist. Satyrs are "Lesser gods of the forest with bodies of men, legs and feet of goats, hair over all their bodies and short horns on their heads. Attendants of Dionysos, they represented the vital forces of nature, and were famous for their lust. Nowadays, satyr is another term for a lecher" (*op. cit.,* 196-97). Faunus (from which Fauns) is a "Roman god of nature and fertility, identified with the Greek Pan.... Fauns were minor rural deities represented as men with ears, horns, tails and hind legs of goats. They are identified with the Greek satyrs" (Lass, 77). Dryads were "tree nymphs (also called 'hamadryads') of Greek mythology, specifically nymphs of the oak tree (*drys* meaning 'oak' or 'tree') but later generalized; they died with the trees they lived in" (*op. cit.,* 65). Midas was "a legendary monarch of Phrygia in Asia Minor, who, in return for his hospitality to Silenus, was granted a wish. He wished that everything that he touched would to gold" (*op. cit.,* 146). Croesus was the "king of Lydia (fl. 550 B. C.) who was fabled for his great wealth" (*op. cit.,* 50). Jupiter is identical with Zeus, and was the most powerful god of the Greeks. He was the ruler of the heavens. Juno (also called Hera) was the sister and wife of Jupiter. And Venus (also called Aphrodite) was the Roman goddess of love. The objective of this rather long catalogue of mythological figures is to show that the theme of

'Other Kingdom' hinges on the antagonism between the natural, instinctual and uninhibited amorous drive of Miss Beaumont and the Croesusian wealth-mongering and possessiveness *sans amor* of Harcourt Worters in the pastoral and arboreal tableau of the Other Kingdom.

Forster's Wordsworthian attitude is expressed through Miss Beaumont, when she tells Mr Inskip that 'gods live in woods.' Miss Beaumont is so much romantically and spiritually attached to nature that when she finally escapes Harcourt's possessive grip she transforms herself into a tree. One of Forster's fundamental premises for happiness is to connect rationality and instinct or emotion, and Harcourt and Miss Beaumont are, as if, the two contrary terms of the premise—Harcourt representing rationality or civilization or order or tradition, and Miss Beaumont representing native instinct or nature, or, in short, the uninhibited enlargement of the spirit that dwells in every human heart. Unlike the foregoing three short stories of Forster, 'Other Kingdom' is a story told in a relaxed mood: there is no urgency or anxiety, and no tensed suspense. Even the love-triangle among Harcourt, Ford, and Miss Beaumont does not disturb us. Really, 'Other Kingdom' is a fine examplar of Forster as a story-teller of supreme excellence. However, according to John Sayre Martin, this story is "clever and entertaining rather than profound, it is because it primarily deals with manners and conduct rather than with the attitudes and impulses that help guide them" (Martin, 56).

6

'THE CURATE'S FRIEND'

This is the fifth story in the collection of short stories first published in 1911 with the title *The Celestial Omnibus and Other Stories*. According to John Sayre Martin, it "is a much slighter tale" (Martin, 56) than 'Other Kingdom,' and yet it is much entertaining thanks to the story-telling artistry of Forster. Sexual suggestion, not infrequent in Forster's short stories (and in his novels), is obvious in 'The Curate's Friend.' The Roman god of nature and fertility, Faun, whom we met in the immediately preceding story, appears just in the beginning sentence of 'The Curate's Friend,' prefiguring the sexual element of the story. Unlike most of Forster's stories, 'The Curate's Friend' is not divided into sections: it starts and finishes non-stop. The narrator tells us that the Roman god Faun perhaps came to Wiltshire with the 'Roman legionaries'—Faun about whom we read in (Shakespeare's) *Tempest* and in *Benedicite*. Faun, he says, likes 'truthfulness' and 'animal spirit'—the two things he himself possesses. The narrator says that he foolishly gave sermons to Emily, the faithful wife to another person, over practical matters. Emily was serious about sermons, but she could laugh heartily also. However, Emily's mother, the other day, arranged for a 'tea-ing out' over the chalk down. The narrator, Emily's mother, Emily, and her young friend, who was 'full of intelligence and poetry', went, for the 'tea-ing out,' into the distance, where the young friend 'longed to wrest earth's secret from her.'

Emily's mother was glad when the narrator asked her to 'prepare the cup that cheers.' Emily always wished to live a simple life, and this was why the simple and silent spot over the down attracted her. But there was 'a little cry, faint but distinct as of something in pain.' The narrator, Mr Harry, felt that there was noise, and that it came from beside Emily. The noise seemed to him to be, as if, that of a great party. At this point the narrator tells us that 'the Faun is of the kind who capers upon the neo-Attic reliefs, and if you do not notice his ears and see his tail, you take him for a man and are horrified.' Then the narrator, Mr Harry, really saw a tail, as he was proceeding towards the bathing place through the wood, and 'uttered a wild shriek and fled into the beech copse behind.' There in the copse he was hearing 'multitude of voices' and was troubled: 'Already in the wood I was troubled by a multitude of voices—the voices of the hill beneath me, of the trees over my head, of the very insects in the bark of the tree....' The voices or noises were not loud, at least not louder than the sound of the flight of a bee. Superceeding those noises, the Faun told the narrator: 'Dear priest, be placid, be placid; why are you frightened?' The narrator was not actually frightened; he was only aggrieved of being 'disgraced in the presence of ladies' by the Faun.

The Faun told the narrator that nobody else but only be (the narrator) saw him, and that he (the Faun) had been loving children for years but he was sorry to see that as soon as they grew up they forgot him. The Faun assured the narrator that he would continue to be attracted to him till his (the narrator's) death. After this the Faun told the narrator: '...Now I begin to make you happy: lie upon your back or run races, or climb trees, or shall I get you black-berries, or hare-bells, or wives—.' The narrator, in turn, told the Faun that he was more happy to give happiness to others than to receive it, and that his was the life of self-denial. Just at this moment the hill told the narrator that he was able to 'reach' the Faun. But, instead, the narrator told the hill that he wanted to 'touch' him (the hill). The hill then told the narrator that he (the narrator) had already 'touched' the Faun. The Faun once again assured him that he would never leave him. The narrator then begged to Faun to help him so that he (the narrator) might make others happy.' But the Faun could not understand why the narrator should make people happy, and why he (the Faun) should help him (the narrator) make people happy—people whom he (the Faun) never saw and who never saw him. At this moment the narrator told the Faun that on that hill there was a 'young lady' for whom he had great respect. He asked the Faun to 'Commence with her.' But the Faun seemed shy and defeated. At this the narrator told him that he (the Faun) was good for nothing, because he '*cannot* do anything.' And now the Faun told him that he could make that young lady happy.

Emily's mother now started for home, and Emily and her 'little friend'—the apparition-like small 'creature'—'sat beside the tea-things—she in her white pique dress and biscuit dress, he in his rough but well-cut summer suit. His great pagan figure of the Faun towered insolently above them.' The little friend asked Emily: "'And have you never felt the appalling loneliness of a crowd?'" Emily replied she did. 'Then the Faun laid his hands upon them. They, who had only intended a little cultured flirtation, resisted him as long as they could, but were gradually urged into each other's arms, and embraced with passion.' The narrator rebuked the 'little friend,' but the 'little friend' told him that "'...In the great solitude we [he and Emily] have found ourselves at last.'" The narrator then asked the Faun to remove his hand from them (to remove them from paganism and to let them get back to civilization), and the Faun obeyed. The 'little friend' then told the narrator: "'It is idle to chide. What should you know, poor clerical creature, of the mystery of love of the eternal man and the eternal woman, of the self-effectuation of a soul?'" Emily accorded with the 'little friend,' and told Harry, the narrator, that he would never be able to give her happiness. She further told him: "'...I must be treated seriously: I must see infinities broadening around me as I rise. You may not approve of it, but so I am. In the great solitude I have found myself at last.'" After this, the 'little friend' led Emily away, and the narrator despaired and denounced the 'little friend' as devil ('D'). But the 'little friend' was only hilarious at this.

There fell a great silence then, and the narrator suffered from his 'injured pride' due to his losing of Emily. That evening the narrator, for the first time, 'heard the chalk downs singing to each other across the valleys, as they often do when the air is quiet and they have had a comfortable day.' The Faun was sitting comfortably before the beech copse, and as the night came, the Faun, the hills and everything else fell asleep, except the stream which rather became more vocal. The narrator, Mr Harry, the curate (i.e., the clergyman who assists a rector or vicar), would never forget the happiness of that evening. He remembers the incident of that evening as he now ascends the pulpit or sits in his 'comfortable bachelor rectory' or while he is engaged in the works of the church. But he cannot tell anyone how he came by that happy incident, because if he told anybody even a single word about how he came by that happy incident, he would be driven out of his parish, and people would curse him. And this is the reason why he has moulded his experience of that incident in the shape of this innocuous short story.

What John Sayre Martin writes about this story, in his *E.M. Forster: The Endless Journey*, is perhaps enough aid in following the tenor and meaning of it. So we may here quote fully what he writes: The Curate's Friend is a much slighter tale [compared to 'Other Kingdom,' as we have said]. Yet it has an amusing twist. It shows how a not-too-humble curate is led by a spiritual encounter to worldly success. The curate is a callow and histrionic youth who one day, while picnicking with his fiancee, her mother, and another young man, encounters a faun. The creature offers to make him wealthy; but scorning the offer, the curate tells him to make others happy instead. 'On this very hill sits a young lady for whom I have high regard. Commence with her. Aha! your face falls. I thought as much. *You cannot do anything.* Here is the conclusion of the whole matter!' But the Faun takes up the challenge, and when the curate returns to the picnic spot, it is to find his fiancee and the other young man locked in each other's arms. Scornfully the curate dismisses them and then, in solitude, faces the facts. 'I thought of my injured pride, of my baffled unselfishness, of Emily, whom I was losing through no fault of her own, of the little friend, who just then slipped beneath the heavy tea basket, and that decided me, and I laughed.' No more wanting to marry Emily, as he now realizes, than she him, he settles into a bachelor's life and becomes a happy, worldly, and respected curate. His encounter with pagan nature has helped him to contribute to the happiness of his Christian parishioners, who in turn reward him materially and spiritually. But he dares not tell them the source of his joy, 'for if I breathed one word of that, my present life, so agreeable and profitable, would come to an end, my congregation would depart, and so should I, and instead of being an asset to my parish, I might find myself an expense to the nation' (...). "The connection implied between spiritual enlightenment and material success may seem oddly un-Forsterian: but it is not. Forster's spiritually enlightened characters are seldom hard-up, and three of them, Miss Raby, Margaret Schlegel, and Mrs Wilcox, are conspicuously well-off. Like Shaw and Butler, Forster seems to feel that money and comfort are highly desirable spiritual props" (Martin, 56-57).

We know that tea, picnic, journey, etc. are stock elements in Forster's novels as well as in many of his short stories. In 'The Curate's Friend' also tea-things and picnic and associated journey are present. Further, there seems to be a faint echo of the following passage of this story in the cave incident of *A Passage to India* (ch. 14):

> "There was a little cry, faint but distinct, as of something in pain.
>
> 'How silent it all is up here!' said Emily.
>
> I dropped a lighted match on the grass, and again I heard the little cry.
>
> 'What is that?' I asked.
>
> 'I only said it was so silent,' said Emily.
>
> 'Silent, indeed,' echoed the little friend.
>
> Silent! the place was full of noises. If the match had fallen in a drawing-room it could not have been worse, and the loudest noise came from beside Emily herself. I had exactly the sensation of going to a great party, of waiting to be announced in the echoing hall, where I could hear the voices of the guests but could not yet see their faces. It is a nervous moment for a self-conscious man, especially if all the voices should be strange to him and he has never met his host."

7

'THE ROAD FROM COLONUS'

The title of this short story refers to a place or locale away from the city of Colonus near Athens—an idyllic place full of anemones and asphodels, an ideal place for picnics, as according to Forster. The title of this story may remind one of Sophocles' (c. 496—406 B.C.) last and greatest tragedy *Oedipus at Colonus* in which the aged, blind, helpless and tragic king Oedipus arrives at the city of Colonus where his 'mysterious apotheosis takes place.' The reason of Forster's going away from Colonus is that the protagonist of his story is not a king but a common man, supposed to be dwelling in the country. But, all the same, there is a similitude between Sophocles' Oedipus and Forster's 'Oedipus,' i.e. Mr. Lucas, for both the once-magnificent characters are now, in the play and in the story, broken, jaded, and ruined souls. 'The Road From Colonus' was first published in the *Independent* in June 1904, before being included in *The Celestial Omnibus* in 1911. When the story was republished in the second collection of Forster's short stories in 1920, his mother Lily read delightfully all the stories, and said that this story was "'one of my favourites, though it always makes me very sad because it is so true to life—written sometime ago...but my darling [Forster] was always observant'" (Beauman, 281). P.N. Furbank writes that many of Forster's plots originated in his own travels and that the plot (in the wider sense of the term, for a short story does not deal with a plot but with an episode or incident) of 'The Road From Colonus' also originated in a travel undertaken by Forster: "The actual pattern of the plot, evidently suggested by Forster's own recent travel experiences, was an important invention for him too. The jaded traveller Mr Lucas [of 'The Road From Colonus'], for whom the world has lost its colours (or he wonders if it ever had them), and who asks himself why he bothered to come abroad at all, for it all seems just like England—but who unknown to himself, is rearing a confrontation with the powers of death and life—this became a favourite opening *motif* in Forster's stories. It reappears in the jaded Lucy, with her viewless room at the Pension Bertolini and again with the jaded Mrs Moore and Adela at the opening of *A Passage to India*" (Furbank, I, 103).

The old Mr Lucas rode ahead of the party, and reached the slope of the hill where there were many plane trees and banks of anemones and asphodels in the wide green edged by a stream. This was the spot where the party was to take lunch. It was April, and the trees here in Greece seemed more glorious than those in England. The Khan or country inn stood tiny and frail, near which a pig was devouring orange peel and grimy and dusty children were playing arcane games while their mothers were making gruel. Mrs Forman and the fastidious Mr Lucas were glad that they had not to have their lunch in the lowly eatery as they brought their meal with them. Mr Lucas felt relieved that Mrs Forman's daughter, Miss Ethel, was not present there. Miss Ethel 'was unselfish and affectionate, and it was generally understood that she was to devote her life to her father and to be the comfort of his old age.' Mrs Forman (for this reason) used to call her Antigone. Mr Lucas tried to assume the role of Oedipus; and actually there were similarities between Mr Lucas and the ancient Greek character, for Mr Lucas was old, and bore all the syndromes of senescence. One especial characteristic of his was that he was fond of Hellenism. But after he had come to Greece, his illusions about Hellenism almost went away because he now found no difference between the dust and wet of England and those of Greece. So he was discontented, but his discontentment somehow produced *vivre* in him. He was now possessed by a strange desire to die fighting. Greece he knew to be the land for young people, but he resolved thus: "'I will enter into it, I will possess it. Leaves shall be green again, water shall be sweet, the sky shall be blue. They were so forty years ago, and I will win them back. I do mind being old, but I will pretend no longer.'"

Mr Lucas 'took two steps forward' and saw 'an impetuous spring' gushing out of the hollow bole of the plane tree, in which bole a shrine was cut, wherein there were a lamp, a little picture of the Virgin—the 'inheritor of the Naiad's and Dryad's joint abode.' The shrine in the trunk of the tree appeared to Mr Lucas marvellous, and there in him an urge to possess the place (of the shrine) grew. And he actually sprinted to the place, while a torrent of gushing water from inside the tree formed a 'wonderful amber pool.' Mr Lucas sipped of the water and found it sweet. He looked through the burnt out hollow trunk of the tree and saw the sky blue. He also saw some green leaves. And then 'another of his thoughts' came to him.

There were fastened to the bark of the plane tree some votive items, such as 'tiny arms and legs and eyes in tin, grotesque models of the brain or the heart—all tokens of some recovery of strength or wisdom or love.' The narrator tells us 'that there was no solitude in that part of nature, for, as it appeared from those votive things fastened to the tree, 'the sorrows and joys of humanity had pressed even into the bosom of a tree.' Mr Lucas reclined against the tree and closed his eyes, and was strangely feeling like the swimmer who 'after long struggling with chopping seas, finds that after all the tide will sweep him to his goal.' Mr Lucas remained motionless, in this way, aware only of 'the stream below his feet' and meditating that 'all things were a stream, in which he was moving.' Suddenly he was roused by the presence of 'something unimagined, indefinable' that 'had passed over all things, and made them intelligible and good.' He now saw intelligibility and goodness in everything and in every movement of the world: the stooping of the old woman, a young man singing while on a mule's back, the patterns of the sun-rays, and in the nodding of the asphodel.

Now, Miss Ethel, Mrs Forman, Mr Graham and the English-speaking dragoman arrived near Mr Lucas. Ethel wondered that her father was 'playing at being Merlin.' On the other hand, to Mr Lucas, all of them seemed unreal phenomena. Ethel provided Mr Lucas with dry socks and boots, instead of his wet ones, and then went with others to 'explore the grove.' They came back with enthusiasm, but Mr Lucas noticed that their enthusiasm was 'superficial, commonplace, and spasmodic,' and that they failed to perceive the 'coherent beauty that was flowing around them.' And he tried to explain his current feelings to them. He said that he was simply spell-bound by the beauty of the place. Mrs Forman superceded him in praising the beauty of the place: "'I could live and die here! I really would stop if I had not to be back at Athens! It reminds me of the Colonus of Sophocles.'" Dittoing Mrs Forman, Ethel said that she must, positively must, stop there. Mr Lucas was resolute on the strength of Ethel's flint-like determination: "'Yes, do! You and your father! Antigone and Oedipus. Of course you must stop at Colonus!'"

Mr Lucas was in uncontrollable joy in the shade of the wood, but he was apprehensive that no sooner would he return to the Khan than his 'old thoughts, old weariness' would again visit him, and yet he expressed his wish: "'I should be willing to put in a night here.'" Ethel told her father that she wished to stop there for a week, and Mr Lucas irritatedly (for perhaps he did not want anybody stayed there with him) but joyfully agreed with her. During lunch in the wood near the Khan, Mr Lucas hardly spoke to anybody. After the lunch, Mrs Forman urged all to go back, saying "'...The best things must end'"—meaning that best things cannot last upto eternity. Mr Lucas was visualising, sitting on a rug, that going back Mrs Forman and others would pray in the shrine and put offerings. He was so absorbed in his vision that he was unaware of the surrounding. Mr Graham reminded him that the rug was to rolled. Mr Lucas got up and told Ethel that he would first go to bed and then put his offerings (before the shrine), only because he had to. Ethel patted on his cheek and told him that the mules, on whose backs they went there, were all ready for the journey back. Mr Lucas lost his head. He asked Ethel: "'Mules? What mules?'" He was forgetful of everything. Ethel reminded him that they were to travel to Olimpia that night on mules' backs. Mr Lucas, in turn, reminded her that according to her own plan they were to stop there for a week. Ethel retorted that she was just cutting a joke with him. But he would not yield to her: he would not go to Olimpia, and even back to England. Ultimately, finding her refractory, she devised to inject a doze of humour into his sagged soul, and to this objective she drove him, along with the dragoman, to the Khan, thinking that the Khan and its environ might cheer him up.

The old woman and the young man, in the Khan, gave them a warm welcome. The others of the party were, after sometime, waiting for Mr Lucas and Ethel to return, i.e., to come out of the Khan which they entered into. After a while, Ethel really came out of the Khan, and also the dragoman, with a little pig that he bought from inside the Khan. Before coming out of the Khan, Ethel warned her father that the innumerable fleas inside it might prove deadly and so he should accompany them out of the Khan. But Mr Lucas resolutely told Ethel: Ethel, you go on. I do not want you. I do not know why I ever consulted you. I shall stop here alone. Ethel in an angry voice reminded her father of the list of his duties and hazards at home in England, such as getting his meals and baths at his advanced age, answering letters, etc., and Mr Graham warned him that he might have been knifed at that place of a foreign land. But neither the force of Ethel's arguments nor the fear of Mr Graham's knife could bend Mr Lucas' resolution to stay there. Mr Lucas' resolution was fortified by the warm, friendly, generous, innocent and appealing behaviour of the Greek folk. For such behaviour Mr Lucas seemed to have both mentally and physically regressed in age: 'he had regained youth or seen beauty or found happiness, but because in that place and with those people a supreme event was awaiting him which would transfigure the face of the world. The moment was so tremendous that he abandoned words and arguments as useless, and rested on the strength of his mighty unrevealed allies: silent men, murmuring water, and whispering trees.'

Failing to persuade her father, Ethel sought the help of Mr Graham who advised her to bring the mule for Mr Lucas, and drag him away and set him on the back of the animal. Ethel managed to do so, and Mr Lucas submitted to the violators. When the mule was carrying Mr Lucas away, the little boy and the little girl were pelting Mr Graham. Then a young Greek (brother to the boy and the girl) desperately stopped the small cavalcade, when Mr Graham's musculature vanquished and thrown him in the thick of the asphodels to clear the path. Mr Graham explained to Ethel that those savage people would cut the purse of her father had he remained in their house. Ethel thanked Mr Graham for his good service. After some time she begged pardon of her father for imposing her own will on him, and told him that she now felt relieved, because 'you are your old self again.' Mr Lucas remained mute. Behind the little cavalcade the 'eventful place' was invisible, but yet 'a faint cry of defiance or farewell' was travelling after them. When they reached their appointed rented house in Olimpia, Mr Lucas resignedly got down from the mule's back, and was affectionately led by Ethel into it. Looking back one could now no more see the 'picnic' place near the Khan because of the 'spur of the hill' (section 1).

In Olimpia, Mr Lucas could not sleep well that night. Next morning, when fog spread all around, he sat by the breakfast table, and Ethel, who was going 'to be married in a few weeks,' was listening to him. He said his sleep was enormously disturbed throughout the night: "'First the door bell rang, then you came back from the theatre. Then the dog started, and after the dog the cat. And at three in the morning a young hooligan passed by singing. Oh yes; then there was the water gurgling in the pipe above my head.' He wanted to leave the house and go elsewhere, and told Ethel during breakfast:'" The reason I am giving up the house is this: it is perfectly impossible to sleep in it. Ethel did not lose her aplomb; she asked him: "'Some more toast, father?'" Mr Lucas told her that he was not going to tolerate any noise in the new house wherever they were going to live next. At this moment a parcel arrived, which was but 'some asphodel bulbs...wrapped up in Greek newspapers' sent by Mrs Forman for planting in the conservatory. Ethel tried to read aloud from the newspaper to the hearing of her father. The newspaper bore the sad news of the death of five persons, belonging to the little Khan at Plataniste, in the province of Messenia, under the impact of the fall of a big tree blown down during night. Hearing this, Mr Lucas faintly and mournfully recalled the memory of the place where they took their lunch and from where the dragoman bought the pig. There was coming in a noise from the next door, and Mr Lucas wore a sorry mien. Ethel was touched. To buoy up her father, she told him that it was just a piece of old newspaper and that the sorry incident occurred just in the night that followed the evening in which they left the place. Ethel told him that "'...All those people, those poor half savage people, tried to keep you, and they are dead. The whole place, it [the newspaper] says, is in ruins, and even the stream has changed its course. Father dear, if it had not been for me, and if Arthur [Graham] had not helped me, you must have been killed.'" Mr Lucas felt irritated and avoided the point of Ethel's good service of saving his life. He rather told her that he would write to the landlord of the present house the reasons of their leaving it: "'the dog barks, the chickens next door are intolerable, and I cannot stand the noise of running water.'" Ethel showed no concern about what he said; she was only wonderfully thinking about the deadly close shave her father had had by leaving the Khan at Plataniste, and then concluded that such incidents as the narrow escape of her father were a pointer to the existence of the Providence (section 2).

The story 'The Road From Colonus' unwinds itself around the character of Mr Lucas, who in the story may seem a shabby, swarthy, uncouth, and half-aboriginal human being with a leaning towards what the civilised man would like to call nastiness and vernacularity, but—and this is important—Forster very significantly called him 'Lucas.' The name 'Lucas' derives from Latin *lucus* which means 'sacred grove, woods.' Nicola Beauman writes that the name 'Lucas' "derives, as does the name Lucy, from *lux* = light and *luceo* = to shine, hence it means a clearing in the woods" (Beauman, 134, f.n.). In the story, Forster perhaps has used the name 'Lucas' in the primary sense of 'sacredness' or 'spirituality,' and in the secondary sense of 'purity' or 'naturalness.' Sophocles' Oedipus found solace and spiritual boosting up, in his wretched old age, in the affectionate attendance of his two daughters (particularly of Antigone), and likewise, Forster's Mr Lucas, alter ego of Oedipus, so to say, found, in his senility, the much-needed spiritual prop in the soothing bosom of nature—in a place far from the maddening crowd of the city-dwellers, in a place where men are perfectly aligned with nature. Forster may be bracketed with Wordsworth and Hardy as regards his love of nature and naturalness, which is manifest in this story as in most of his other short stories. Mr Lucas was not loath to the Khan and its surround inspite of the innumerable flies and the pigs, as Ethel and Mr Graham were, because there he found the appropriate environment for his spiritual life—the environment in which he found the solitude and the beauty of nature, and the condition for the unstinted and free expression of his mind.

John Sayre Martin has beautifully explained, and commented upon, this story at some length in his *E.M. Forster: The Endless Journey,* which is perhaps enough to understand the meaning of the story and to evaluate it. So let us quote in full what he has written in his book, though such long quotations are oftentimes disagreeable. Martin writes: "The title of Forster's (next) story,' The Road From Colonus',—and it is one of his two best—ironically recalls Sophocles' great play. Forster's 'Oedipus' is an aging, querulous Englishman, Mr Lucas, who accompanied by his daughter Ethel, a young Mr Graham, and a Mrs Forman, is fulfilling a lifetime wish to visit Greece. But it is not until Mr Lucas visits an out-of-the-way settlement mainly consisting of a Khan (inn) and grove of plane trees that he sees 'the real Greece.' Up to this point the country had proved disappointing. 'Athens had been dusty, Delphi wet, Thermopylae flat, and he had listened with amazement and cynicism to the rapturous exclamations of his companions.' (...) Plataniste, however, enchants him. Though the surrounding country is hot and dry, here there is shade, and even a stream, which issues mysteriously from the hollowed-out trunk of a plane tree in which the local inhabitants have hung votive offerings. Mr Lucas, who has ridden ahead of his companions ('he was perhaps reaching the age at which independence becomes valuable, because it is so soon to be lost'), enters the tree trunk and allows the water, which wells up from subterraneous depths, to bathe his ankles. And for him at this point, the world of time is invaded by eternity. 'His eyes closed, and he had the strange feeling of one who is moving, yet at peace—the feeling of the swimmer, who, after long struggling with chopping seas, finds that after all the tide will sweep him to his goal. So he lay motionless, conscious only of the stream below his feet, and that all things were a stream, in which he was moving.' Opening his eyes, he sees for the first time a coherent world in which all things have meaning. 'There was meaning in the stoop of the old woman over her work, and in the quick motions of the little pig, and in her diminishing globe of wool. A young man came singing over the streams on a mule, and there was beauty in his pose and sincerity in his greeting. The sun made no accidental patterns upon the spreading roots of the trees, and there was intention in the nodding clumps of asphodel, and in the music of the water. To Mr Lucas, who, in a brief space of time, had discovered not only Greece, but England and all the world and life, there seemed nothing ludicrous in the desire to hang within the tree another votive offering—a little model of an entire man (...).

"Mr Lucas' reverie is rudely shattered by the arrival of his companions, oo-ing and aah-ing with sentimental hyperbole over the beauty of the surroundings; to which Mr Lucas, rendered inexpressive by deep feeling, can only reply that the place 'impresses me very favourably' and other words to that effect. The place in fact impresses Mr Lucas so favourably that like Oedipus at Colonus, he wants to stop there, at least for one night. 'To sleep in the Khan with the gracious, kind-eyed country people, to watch the bats flit about within the globe of shade, and see the moon turn the golden patterns into silver—one such night would place him beyond relapse, and confirm him for ever in the kingdom he had regained. (...)' To humour him, his companions at first pretend that they would like nothing letter; but it soon becomes apparent to Mr Lucas that, they have no such intention. Where he has responded to the eternal, they know only the world of time. There are schedules to meet and places to get to. 'Enroute!' says the shrill voice of Mrs Forman, 'Ethel! Mr Graham! The best of things must come to an end.' (...) And so the place becomes a battle ground with Mr Lucas, morally and physically supported by the inhabitants of the Khan, trying to stay, and his companions, by trickery and physical force, finally forcing him to leave.

The last part of the story finds Mr Lucas back in his London house with his daughter Ethel. Old and fretful he has nothing to look forward to but the arrival of his sister, whom he hates, to keep house for him. Everything upsets him—the street noises, the piano next door, and especially the sound of water gurgling through an overhead pipe. 'There's nothing I dislike more than running water.' The morning's mail brings a parcel from Mrs Forman in Greece—asphodel bulbs wrapped in a Greek newspaper. And one of the papers contains news of 'a rural disaster.' Ethel proceeds to read it aloud. A tree blew down at Plataniste, crashing to death the five occupants of the Khan. And from the date of the paper, the accident clearly happened the day that Mr Lucas and his companions left. Ethel's response to the news is the crowning irony. 'She was aghast at the narrowness of the escape, and for a long time kept silence. At last she said: "Such marvellous deliverance does make one believe in Providence." (...) But Mr Lucas is only concerned with the present. Without replying, he proceeds to compose a letter of complaint to his landlord.

The story's strength depends in part on the character of Mr Lucas. Touchy and self-centred, yet with a desire and potentiality for self-transcendence, he is both individual and archetypal. Forster's rendition of his 'eternal moment' is psychologically realistic. He gives us an inside view of it rather than an external, mytliologized one as in 'The Story of a Panic' and 'Other Kingdom,' and faces, too, its psychological implications. Intense and compelling as the moment is, it is also, we realize, only for one time one place. Far from being able to 'transfigure the face of the world,' it cannot even withstand the impact of everyday life—the arrival of Mrs Forman and others, and the impress of London with its cacophony of sounds and endless series of petty irritants. Like Mrs Moore who, in *A Passage to India,* enjoys a similar moment of mystical rapture, Mr Lucas declines into apathy and inertia. He cannot connect the poetry of life with its prose, and finally the prose engulfs him. Eliot's 'Prufrock' might supply his epitaph: 'Till human voices wake us and we drown.'

"As for the windstorm that destroys the Khan and all its inhabitants on the very day of Mr Lucas's visit, one may, I think, justly accuse Forster of indulging in a facile coincidence in order to end the story with an ironic punch. Nevertheless, the windstorm also underscores the temporal and psychological character of Mr Lucas's vision. The peace and harmony that he felt within the plane-tree grove was inspired by the character of the scene at that particular time. But nature can also be violent, destructive, chaotic. Order and meaning can collapse in an instant. Within the grove, Mr Lucas is, as it were, for perhaps the only time in his life, an artist, endowing with unity and meaning the diverse elements in the surrounding landscape. He is a surrogate for Forster who, as a novelist, strives to give form and meaning to the raw material of experience; for art, as Forster declares in 'Art for Art's Sake,' is the only object in an essentially chaotic universe to possess internal order. Hence the windstorm at Plataniste. Embodying the spirit of chaos, it is an implicit comment on the temporal and psychological character of Mr Lucas's vision, just as in *A Passage to India* the Marabar Caves afford a similar comment on Mrs Moore's erstwhile mystical sense of oneness with the universe. Visionary truth and objective reality, the story suggests, may be irreconcilable. Art is one thing, life another. Unable to connect the two elements of his experience, Mr Lucas loses the vision and succumbs to actuality. But Forster, a tougher, more gifted man, conveys through art his double commitment to vision and actuality and his desire to fuse them" (Martin, 57-60).

Forster has demonstrated two sorts of women—the meek, submissive and sentimental women, who may be represented by Adela Quested of *A Passage to India*; and the strong, domineering and practical women, who may be represented by Ethel Lucas of 'The Road From Colonus.' The women in the second category may be called sadistic, in different degrees. Lionel Trilling writes in this regard: "'The Eternal Moment' first sketches the type of the wise and gentle heroine who is to descend from Miss Raby; 'The Road From Colonus' gives us our first example of the woman who is to be contrasted with her. Ethel Lucas, when her father is lifted on to his saddle by a Mr Graham of the party, sighs that she 'admires strength;' she is the progenitor of Forster's sadistic women" (Trilling, 43).

8

'THE MACHINE STOPS'

This story is a science fiction of sorts, and, unlike his other stories in the volumes of short stories, *The Celestial Omnibus* and *The Eternal Moment,* this story was written with a definite objective. Forster was not very happy with the prevailing credo for science and technology, which, he thought, was gradually attenuating the mind and the body of man, and was surreptitiously enslaving man to machine. Long ago Mary Wollstonecraft Shelley (1797-1851), wife of P.B. Shelley, saw, as if in a vision, the flip-side of science, and wrote a superb gothic ghost story, based on mindless scientific discoveries and consequent marginalisation of humanness of man, and called it *Frankenstein, or the Modern Prometheus* (1818). In it, Frankenstein creates a robot-like machine—a monster. The monster receives some Shelleyan and Godwinian ideas of freedom and humanism through study, and then is greatly influenced by the sorrows of Werther after reading Goethe's *Die Leiden des jungen Werthers,* and ultimately, in vengence of being enslaved by his creator, destroys Frankenstein himself. Mrs Shelley was no scientist, and yet she could visualise the impending danger of giving a free rein to science. Years afterwards, H.G. Wells (1866-1946), a scientist in the academic sense, contradicted Mrs Shelley. Wells passionately believed 'in the perfectibility of mankind through scientific advance,' and to propound his belief into theory wrote such novels as *In the Days of the Comet, The Shape of Things to Come* and *The Time Machine.* Forster was dissatisfied with Wells's extreme trust in science, and this story, 'The Machine Stops,' is his broadside against him.

But the proximate stimulus for Forster to write this story was not the battle of books but an actual incident. "On 13 January 1908 Henri Farman won a contest, in France, for the flying of a heavier-than-air machine over a kilometre circuit" (Furbank, I, 161 f.n.). At that time, Forster was thinking on the future of humanity in the nascent twentieth century. When he heard that Farman "flew a heavier-than-air machine over a three-quarter mile circuit in one and a half minutes" (*op. cit.,* I, 161), Forster could not join the bandwagon in applausing the scientific wizardry; instead, he became disappointed, and wrote: "'if I live to be old I shall see the sky as pestilential as the roads. It really is a new civilisation. I have been at the end of the age of peace and can't expect to feel anything but despair. Science, instead of freeing man—the Greek nearly freed him by right feeling—is enslaving him to machine. Nationality will go, but the brotherhood of man will not come.... God what a prospect! The little houses that I am used to will be swept away, the fields will stink of petrol, and the airships will shatter the stars. Man may get a new and perhaps a greater soul for the new condition. But such a soul as mine will be crushed out'" (*op. cit.,* I, 161-62). The flight of Farman was a confirmation of Wells's optimism, but Wells's optimism seemed dark pessimism to Forster. Forster believed that only science—or logic or head—could not make man happy, and that only the harmonious co-operation between science and aesthetics—or passion or heart—could. Therefore, to Wells's scientific treatise-novels, particularly to his *The Time Machine* and *In the Days of the Comet* Forster sharply reacted: "'Passion is necessary—only Wells's comet is not enough'" (*op. cit.,* I, 162). "His [Forster's] gloomy reflections on the Farman flight bore fruit later in the year [1908] in his story 'The Machine Stops,' described by him as 'a reaction against one of the earlier heavens of H.G. Wells.' It pictures humanity as it might be after the final triumph of the machine: hairless, toothless, muscleless, living in air-conditioned underground cells, exchanging, by a sort of television, the 'last sloth stirrings' of a spirit that had once grasped the stars. In the story, the rebel hero Kuno escapes for a day to the surface of the earth, and his last glimpse of hope and freedom, before recapture by the Machine, is the constellation of Orion. Seeing it, he feels—the words recall those earlier in Forster's diary—as if 'a man of my own sort lived in the sky.' The thought grew to be a favourite with Forster and became his formula for religion. 'London is religion's opportunity,' he was to write in *Howards End,* 'not the decorous religion of theologians, but anthropomorphic, crude. Yes, the continuous flow would be tolerable if a man of our own sort—not anyone pompous or tearful—were caring for us up in the sky'" (*ibid.*).

'The Machine Stops' is divided into three parts or sections, each part having a sub-title—the first part 'The Air-ship,' the second 'The Mending Apparatus,' and the third 'The Homeless.' The story is around 38 pages long, and is perhaps the longest of all Forster's short stories, 'The Eternal Moment' being the second longest, running upto about 35 pages. The story opens with a description of the room or, rather, machine of a woman 'about five feet high, with a face as white as fungus' and 'without teeth or hair.' The room is small and is hexagonal in shape like the cell of a bee. It is lighted neither by window nor by lamp, yet it is filled with a soft radiance, there is no aperture for ventilation, yet the air is fresh. There are no musical instruments, and yet, ...this room is throbbing with melodious sounds. An armchair in the centre, by its side a reading-desk—that is all the furniture.' The woman, Vasti by name, was talking to her son, Kuno, who was residing in the 'island in the northern hemisphere' on the antipode of the place where she had been. Kuno told her that he was desirous of seeing his *real* mother and not her picture on the plate-like screen of his sort of videophone in his narrow cabin-like machine (the son and the mother did never see each other face to face, in reality, just since Kuno's birth, but only communicated with each other through videophones in their respective machines). Vasti was persuading her son to take her picture on the screen as his real mother. She also told him that she was so busy that she could allow him to see even her picture on the screen only for five minutes, and that it would not be possible for her to meet him in reality by the air-ship. Kuno told her that the machine could not replace man, and that "'Men made it [the machine]...Great men, but men.'"

Kuno was so much disgusted and disgruntled with his machine, and at the same time so much attracted by (real) human beings that when he looked at the starry sky, he could figure out human beings in the firmament. He was, supposedly, pining for real human expressions and intercourses, but the machine could not transmit *nuances* of expression. The machine could only give a 'general idea of people' and Vashti thought it was 'good enough for all practical purposes.' 'The imponderable bloom, declared by a discredited philosophy to be the actual essence of intercourse, was rightly ignored by the Machine, just as the imponderable bloom of the grape was ignored by the manufacturers of artificial fruit. Something "good enough" had long since been accepted by our race.' However, Kuno told his mother that he only wanted to see the stars, standing on the earth, like our ancestors did. But his mother informed him that the surface of the earth was only full of dust and mud, and that there was no life on it. She also told him that his wish was against the spirit of the age. In anguish, Kuno switched off his end of the videophone system, and so Vashti could no more see his image on the plate of her videophone. But before that Vashti warned him that should he ever stand on the earth (to see the stars) he must be equipped with a respirator. Vashti then switched on a button and her crib-like room was flooded with light. There were a number of buttons in the room (of the machine): 'buttons to call for food, for music, for clothing. There was the hot-bath button, by pressure of which a basin of marble rose out of the floor, filled to the brim with warm deodorised liquid. There was a cold-bath button. There was the button that produced literature. And there were of course the buttons by which she communicated with her friends. The room, though it contained nothing, was in touch with all that she cared for in the world.' She communicated with her friends who were also living, like herself, in crib-like mechanical rooms, with divers fittings for various services, needing no services from the real world outside. The most astonishing thing of Vashti's machine-like room was that there was a mechanism for getting ideas 'from the sea.' There was only one very fat book in the room which contained instructions for manipulating that machine-like room, during its normal functioning and during its mal-functioning. Vashti greatly admired the machine-like room or machine: "'O Machine! O Machine!'" The machine-like room 'hummed eternally; she did not notice the noise, for she had been born with it in her ears.'

Failing to communicate with her son, because he switched off the button of his machine-like room deciding that he would not talk to her until she meet him personally (in reality), Vashti pressed on an 'unfamiliar' button, and the walls of her room 'swang apart' and she was frightened to see a tunnel revealing itself. Through the tunnel she could reach the air-ship station on her way to her son. This new system of commutation belonged to that civilisation that preferred 'bringing people to things, instead of bringing things to people." However, through the videophonic system, opened once again, she told her son that as she was not well she would not be able to go to him. As soon as she said this 'an enormous apparatus fell on to her out of the ceiling, a thermometer was automatically inserted between her lips, a stethoscope was automatically laid upon her heart. She lay powerless. Cool pads soothed her forehead. Kuno had telegraphed to her doctor.' 'Vashti drank the medicine that the doctor projected into her mouth, and the machinery retired into the ceiling.' She now felt better. Here the narrator tells us that in this way 'human passions still blundered up and down in the Machine.'

Kuno was Vashti's latest issue, whom she ceased to physically see since 'the Machine' [of Vashti] 'assigned him a room on the other side of the earth.' Considering Kuno's importunity for her visiting him, Vashti now consulted the only book (of guidance) in the Machine or her machine-like room to know about parents' duty to a son. The book said that the duties of parents 'cease at the moment of birth.' She learnt this from the entry 'Parents' duties' at page No. 422327483 of the book. Nevertheless, she decided to go to her son, and for that matter she pressed the 'unfamiliar' button and the walls of the Machine fell apart. She then summoned a car and got into it to journey to the northern hemisphere, the walls of the Machine reunited behind her. After a few moments, she came out of the car, after reaching a distance, and entered into the lift or the air-ship, in which she found only one other passenger. The narrator tells us that the dearth of passengers in the lift was due to the fact that 'thanks to the advance of science, the earth was exactly alike all over' and so people were not interested in seeing sights. The people's 'all unrest was concentrated in the soul.' 'The air-ship service was a relic from the former age.'

The air-ship (Vashti in it) flew over and across Brazil, the Alps and other places. From the airship Vashti had to walk to the lift, again, through the gangway. In the gangway a man, who was also walking to the lift, in front of her, 'dropped his Book.' He did not find it necessary to pick up the Book; instead, he 'felt the muscles of his arm to see how they failed him'—he examined how de-energised and debilitated they had become thanks to his continual existence in the Machine of his own.' Vashti now entered into the lift, and in it she saw innumerable rooms, one upon another or one beside another, but all huddling together (indication of congested areas of high-rise buildings of the modern metropolises)—resembling a hive. Vashti entered into her own room and 'caressed her Book, and was comforted.' Then 'the air-ship, issuing from its tunnel, soared above the waters of a tropical ocean,' in the night, and edging along the coast of Sumatra, veered westward and then eastward, and thus circumnavigated the earth. The people on the earth applauded the flight, but the Committee of the Machine found wrong with the flight, for the air-ship encountered 'horrible accidents,' and threatened the crew with the punishment of making them suffer Homelessness. Vashti was annoyed, in the air-ship, when her cabin was intruded by a beam of rosy light from the sun, and to avoid it she tucked hard the blind. And yet the sunlight flooded her cabin, and so she cried out in horror. The attendant rushed to her and steadied her hand for her safety, at which Vashti rebuked him saying that "'People [now] never touched one another. The custom had become obsolete, owing to the Machine.'" However, the air-ship continued to fly over Asia—over Simla, the Himalayas, the 'Kinchinjunga,' etc.—over the Caucasus and Greece. But at no spot below (i.e. on the earth) could Vashti find any source of ideas (because the machine age had already marred the earth as a source of ideas) (section 1).

At last Vashti met Kuno in his cabin-like machine that resembled hers. She narrated to him her gruelling journey and expressed her disgust at the sunlight in the air-ship. Kuno told her that the Committee of the Machine threatened him with 'Homelessness'—which meant 'death' because he had gone out of his cabin or machine without Egression-permit and because he had wanted 'irreligiously' to find out his own way. At this his mother became angry with him and plainly and summarily told him that he was legally threatened. But Kuno did not agree with her and spitefully told her that she was beginning to worship the Machine and that all religions and all superstitions had been destroyed by it. He also told her that the Book was not authentic, because, contrary to the instructions of it, he could go out of his machine and stand on his own feet. Kuno possessed some physical strength, but this was a wrong on his part, because in the age of the Machine physical strength was looked down upon. In that age each baby at birth would be examined and the strong ones would be destroyed. Kuno said that man's sense of space had been obliterated. He believed that "'Man is the measure [of all things]'" and that man's "'body is the measure for all that is lovable and desirable and strong.'" Kuno said that he acquired the sense of space by walking. He said: "'I seemed to hear the spirits of those dead workmen who had returned each evening to the starlight and to their wives.'" Lately, he expressed his desire to be a father but the Committee refused his request because it did not consider it wise to beget children of such a person as he was. Vashti now felt miserable at what Kuno told her, because she thought he was spurning away 'civilisation.' Kuno felt that humanity had been essentially 'naked.' He said: "'I felt that humanity existed, and that it existed without clothes. How can I possibly explain this? I was naked, humanity seemed naked, all these tubes and buttons and machineries neither come into the world with us, nor will they follow us out, nor do they matter supremely while we are here.'" Kuno thought that the 'humanity' of (the Machine) perhaps entered into the blood-stream of human beings and guided men's thought-processes. He went beyond the humming (of the Machine) and found there silence, and from the silence came to him voices which gave him energy. Vashti also heard the voices and sighed. One voice, he told her, asked him to jump, and said: "'Come to us your own way.'" And he jumped. Saying thus far Kuno paused, and 'Tears gathered in his mother's eyes.'

Kuno's mother was really full of pity and shame, for him. Pity, because she thought he was fated to die, for there 'was not room for such a person in the world [of the Machine). And shame, because such a worthless boy, as Kuno, had been born to her. Vashti found that hair had grown around his lips, and from this she concluded that he had been reverting to some savage type. Kuno did not stop but continued telling the tale of his adventure to his mother. He told her that after he had jumped through the hollow (of the Machine), he fell down and found himself in a grassy patch of land in Wessex (in England), forgetting everything about the Machine. In Wessex he saw the 'low colourless hills' which seemed to him living. He told her: "'...to me they [the low hills] were living and the turf that covered them was a skin, under which their muscles rippled, and I felt that those hills had called with incalculable force to men in the past, and that men had loved them. Now they sleep—perhaps for ever. They commune with humanity in dreams. Happy the man, happy the woman, who awakes the hills of Wessex. For though they sleep, they will never die.'" Kuno's voice then 'rose passionately': "'Cannot you see, cannot all you lecturers see, that it is we that are dying, and that down here the only thing that really lives is the Machine? We created the Machine, to our will, but we cannot make it do our will now.'" Kuno stopped, but his mother urged him to talk on. Kuno told her that he could talk on, but he would not. Saying so he bade good-bye to his mother. 'Vashti stood irresolute. All her nerves were tingling with blemishes. But she was also inquisitive.' So, Kuno, before actually departing, told her more. He said mat every action of everyone in that civilisation (of the Machine) would be reported to the Central Committee. Kuno told his mother that once he got down to the grass in the dell (coming out of the Machine) but was entwined around his ankle by a long white worm—such worms are plenty in the grass, he said. He was afraid and cried for help, and none but a woman came to his dire need. But the woman herself was entwined by another long and white worm, which killed her. Vashti gloomily told him that he was fated to become Homeless. She said that those who rebelled against the rule of the Machine in the past, had to face their deaths (had to become Homeless). She assured him that "'...The surface of the earth supports life no longer.'" Thinking that Kuno had become mattoid, Vashti departed, never to see his face again (section 2).

After Kuno escaped the Machine or his machine-like-crib, two 'important developments took place.' One, the respirators were abolished, and also terrestrial motors. The advanced thinkers conceived that first-hand ideas or knowledge, even of the earth, could well be spumed, because previously recorded experiences would do. Actually, first-hand experiences of the earth, they thought, were vitiated by love and fear, while knowledge must be pure and rarefied. For instance, instead of actual experience of the French Revolution, one should learn what others thought about it. Generation after generation such knowledge would percolate downwards, and thus in course of time man would become 'seraphically free' from the 'taint of personality'. The second development was the re-establishment of religion. It was the religion (the "'word 'religion' was sedulously avoided'") of the Machine (in which the Machine supplanted God). All the people praised the Machine and prayed to it, taking it to be divine. But all the people did not worship it in unison, or taking it as a whole: different persons worshipped the different parts of the Machine. For instance, some worshipped the optic plates, some others the mending apparatus, and so on. However, these two developments were announced by the Central Committee, and everyone accepted them under pressure. It was a 'progress' (of the Machine age). Each person was occupied with a particular part of the Machine, and none knew of the whole of it—'the monster as a whole' (the Machine). And 'No one confessed that the Machine was out of hand. Year by year it was served with increased efficiency and decreased intelligence.' The narrator here tells us that '.... Humanity, in its desire for comfort, had overreached itself. It had exploited the riches of nature too far. Quietly and complacently, it was sinking into decadence, and progress had come to mean the progress of the Machine.'

Vashti went on living quietly and peacefully. She kept on communicating with her innumerable friends through her cinematophote (inside her Machine or machine-like room), as she had earlier been doing. Being oppressed by pains, mental and physical, she once desired to resort to Euthanasia, but the Machine refused, because it would not allow the death-rate to exceed the birth-rate. However, Vashti did not communicate any more with her son, though she knew that he was alive. But one day she was astonished to receive a message from her son to the effect that due to his 'misbehaviour' he was transferred from the northern pole to the south. He told her that he was allotted a room not far from hers. Vashti communicated with him and wanted to see the image of his face in the plate of her machine-like room. But from his end Kuno told his mother: "'The Machine stops.'" Vashti was astonished to hear this. Kuno again told her: "'The Machine is stopping, I know it, I know the signs.'" She laughed aloud at the 'nonsense' he spoke about and Kuno became angry at her laughter. They ceased communicating with each other. Afterwards, Vashti told a friend of hers that it was absurd that the Machine had been stopping, as her son told her. That friend was astonished to hear this. Then Vashti and her friend began to talk about music which now appeared to be the sound one makes while in pain. Vashti did not forget Kuno's speech: "'The Machine stops.'" She felt irritated at the unusual sound of the music, and complained to the Committee of the Mending Apparatus. The Committee told her that the defect in the music would shortly be mended. Another friend of Vashti also complained about the defect in the music, but due to the delay-dallying of the Committee the defect was not mended; in course of time, however, all got used to that defect in the music, such that the defect no more seemed to be a defect at all. In this way, all got used to all defects—that of the bath water, that of the artificial fruit, that of the poetry machine, and so on.

But the thing was otherwise with the sleeping apparatus: 'the beds, when summoned by their tired owners, failed to appear. So the people got irritated, 'for mankind was not yet sufficiently adapted to do without sleeping.' A complaint was lodged with the Committee, which interpreted the complaint as an attempt by someone to introduce 'the personal element' in the Machine (sleep is a personal element or matter, of course), and thought of punishing the truant with Homelessness. Taking the complaint as a portent, the Committee became overactive to save the Machine from possible harm and to that effect urged all to kill the man who lodged the complaint. However, ultimately the Committee 'confessed that the Mending Apparatus was itself in need of repair.' Meanwhile, a lecturer, on behalf of the Committee, persuaded all to do without beds (i.e. without sleep), and announced that the Mending Apparatus would automatically get repaired.' Thousands of miles away his audience applauded. And all accepted the proposal of the lecturer with equanimity and without grudging, and all 'clothed their thoughts in one garment of subserviency.' But the old ones were disgruntled because they heard 'that Euthanasia, too, was out of order, and that pain had reappeared among men.' While the lecturer was still delivering his lecture, troubles multiplied: air got polluted; but, most damn of all, light dimmed. Undaunted, the lecturer, in a heroic fashion, harangued: 'Courage! Courage! What matter so long as the Machine goes on? To it darkness and light are one.' At that time, talks about 'measures' and 'provisional dictatorship' were being heard. But a day, afterwards, came, without any premonition or sign, when the whole communication system broke down, and 'the world, as they understood it ended.' Vashti was lecturing at that time, and at the end of her lecture all fell fast asleep. She recalled her son's remark: "'The Machine stops.'" But she soon thought that even if Eternity went wrong, it could again be set aright. As long as the Book existed, there was no need of unnecessary alarm. She then stopped lecturing and merged into profound silence mixed with horror, which almost killed her and which earlier killed thousands overnight. However, after some time she pressed the unfamiliar button, and the door of her cell or machine-like room opened.

When the door opened, Vashti 'saw the dim tunnel that curved far away towards freedom.' She found that the tunnel was full of people, and that she was the last person in the queue. People were scampering, clambering, huddling and pushing things in the darkness to come out of the tunnel, and were 'blaspheming the Machine.' Some were gasping for breath. There was a tremendous uproar in the tunnel, but above it there was profound silence—'the silence which is the voice of the earth and of the generations who have gone.' Vashti now became frantic to save herself: she was 'Kissing the Book, pressing button after button,' but she knew that civilization's long day was closing.' However, ultimately she was successful to somehow come out, and she escaped into 'spirit.' But, actually, she could not fully and finally escape, because 'she was facing the tunnel again.' She saw that people 'were dying by hundreds out in the dark.' 'She burst into tears.' 'Tears answered her.' Tears wept for humanity, because they could not bear that 'Man, the flower of all flesh, the noblest of all creatures visible, man who had once made god in Ins image, and had mirrored his strength on the constellations, beautiful naked man was dying, strangled in the garments he had woven.' They wept for the 'sin against the body' done by the Machine, and they wept for the disregard shown to the soul by the Machine.

Vashti asked her son: "'Is there any hope, Kuno?'" Kuno replied that there was no hope at least for them two. She then crawled towards her son, over dead bodies, and found his body spurting out blood—she found him dying. When she neared him, he kissed and told her: "'We have come back to our own. We die, but we have recaptured life, as it was in Wessex, when Aelfrid overthrew the Danes. We know what they know outside, they who dwelt in the cloud that is the colour of a pearl.'" Vashti enquired whether there were still men on the surface of the earth. Kuno assured her there were. He told her that though they were then Homeless, in the near future they would not be Homeless for sure. She was apprehensive; she thought that in the near future "'some fool will start the Machine again".' Kuno assured her that that was not going to be, because "'...Humanity has learnt its lesson.'" Then the 'whole city' (of the Machine, or of innumerable machines or machine-like rooms) broke down into smithereens, and also the air-ship. Vashti and Kuno, for a couple of moments, 'saw the nations of the dead,' but before their own imminent deaths they saw patches of 'the untainted sky.'

The story clearly is a science fiction—Forster's only science fiction—on the theme of escape—his stock theme in almost all of his major or first-rate short stories. In 'The Machine Stops,' the escape is made from the overlordship and tyranny of modern science and technology to the world of 'spirit'—of freedom and liberty. That Forster, in this story, is despising the mindless and reckless scientific credo is obvious from his satirical description of the machine-like rooms of Vashti and Kuno, with all sorts of facilities for physical sedentary comfort and virtual or surrogate communications with the other people, but without any provision for the sustenance and growth of body and mind, in the story, the body and the mind or spirit of the human being were dwindling for lack of commerce with the real world, but the gubernatorial officials of the Machine (or the machine age) would not take this as a fault or a sign of decadence, because they were interested only in 'science and habit.' They believed that science was the lodestar, the guide, the ideal, and that habit or repeated exercise could turn any disagreeableness into agreeableness, any discomfort into comfort, any false-knowledge into knowledge. They were striving to fit the man into the machine, instead of the other way round. As a result of their very draconian and procrastinate scientific regimen, both Vashti and Kuno, supposedly like the other people, lost their hair and teeth. The officials feared personal liberty and personal relation, and so arranged that each and every one had to remain confined within the narrow space inside his or her particular machine, and was allowed to communicate with others only through the videophote fitted inside the machine. In fact, our contemporary fellows of the scientifically and economically very advanced countries are living in a state not very different from that Vashti and Kuno and others were forced to live in, and who knows in the long course of time their far descendants also will not lose their hair and teeth? The vision of the future civilisation, as experienced by Forster is perhaps not very far from truth.

We have said that Forster wrote this story with at least one objective in view—to counter the optimism of H.G. Wells particularly in his *The Time Machine*. In this novelette Wells spoke of the bright future science (like Prometheus) was going to bring in for every benefit of man. Wells was inordinately optimistic, as Forster supposed, and Wells was hoping that man could do without the unscientific emotions and affections man was heir to, again as Forster supposed. But, perhaps, Forster's study of Wells was not all correct: Wells was never a blind millenarian and he did not quite forget the intrinsic value of human passions. For instance, in the 'Epilogue' of *The Time Machine,* he says about the Time Traveller and the condition of man in the distant future: "He [the Time Traveller], I know—for the question had been discussed among us long before the Time Machine was made—thought but cheerlessly of the Advancement of Mankind, and saw in the growing pile of civilization only a foolish heaping that must inevitably fall back upon and destroy its makers in the end. If that is so, it remains for us to live as though it were not so. But to me the future is still black and blank—is a vast ignorance, lit at a few casual places by the memory of his story. And I have by me, for my comfort, two strange white flowers—shrivelled now, and brown and flat and brittle—to witness that even when mind and strength had gone, gratitude and mutual tenderness still lived on in the heart of man."

However, John Sayre Martin writes that Forster's 'The Machine Stops' is his "only piece of science fiction, a pre-Orwellian prophecy of things to come. Human beings are living in isolation in a subterranean hell. Each one lives in his separate compartment, his entire life governed by the Machine, his needs and wants limited to what the Machine can provide. Thanks to the marvels of the Machine, he can talk to others, listen to lectures and music, have all his physical needs catered for—all without leaving his cell. There are two characters, Vashti, an elderly woman with 'advanced' ideas, who is completely attuned to her environment, and Kuno her reactionary son, who is sufficiently maladjusted to his to escape by way of a ventilator shaft to the earth's surface (Wessex), which he enjoys for a few hours until he is recaptured by the horrible wormlike 'Mending Apparatus' and returned to his cell. Kuno, who speaks for Forster, yearns for direct human contact: man to him, not the Machine, must be the measure of things. Vashti, on the other hand, prefers 'ideas' to direct experience, and is content to communicate through the Machine. She is one of Forster's unmaternal, detached woman. The climax comes when the Machine breaks down. Chaos and Ancient Night reclaim the world, and everyone dies in the accompanying panic. But before death overtakes Kuno and Vashti, they enjoy a brief sympathetic reunion during which Kuno, who has seen human beings on the earth's surface, predicts that they will rebuild civilisation without use of a Machine. "Humanity has learnt its lesson." As a story 'The Machine Stops' is second-rate science fiction. It is too long and discursive, and its setting is interesting than the characters. As a prognosis, however, it seems remarkably on target. If Forster had written the story in 1970 rather than sixty years ago, there would be few of its details that he might wish to change" (Martin, 60-61).

Lionel Trilling says that in Forster's fictions there are two sorts of mother-son relationships: one, son rejects mother, for instance, in *A Passage to India* Ronny rejects Mrs Moore; and two, mother rejects son, for instance, in 'The Machine Stops' Vasti rejects Kuno. About 'The Machine Stops,' Trilling writes: "In the counter-Wellsian fantasy of the future life, 'The Machine Stops,' it is the son who sins against the mechanical dispensation by discovering the forbidden filial affection; his mother does not match it with maternal feeling, This remote quality in Forster's elder heroines must check our natural tendency to find in them a symbol of the Earth which man has deserted (although the Earth-Mother identification is explicit in 'The Machine Stops') (Trilling, 42-43). 'The Machine Stops' is obviously an attack by Forster on the present machine age. Forster was, as we have said, very much Wordsworthian; he protested against deforestation and mechanisation of the modem world—against the mindless scientific credo that has denuded the earth, obliterated the heavens, insulated man and swept away all passion from the surface of the earth. Forster always pined for the Wessexian greenery and the passion of the bygone days, as in 'The Machine Stops,' Kuno represents

Forster in detesting the Machine and pining for his mother's personal touch.

9

THE POINT OF IT

Forster wrote this disturbing and confusing story in March, 1911, and got it published in the *English Review* in November of the same year. While he was writing it, he was, all at the same time, gestating the plot of his projected but unfinished novel 'Aretic Summer' and writing his unpublished play 'The Heart of Bosnia.' In 'The Point of It,' Forster strives to show the state of Edwardian rational liberalism vis-a-vis passionate liberalism where imagination plays a great part, through the life and the after-life of the protagonist Michael. The story has three parts: part one narrates the events in the life of Michael, and the rest two parts tell us what happened in the after-life of the protagonist.

Two youngsters, Michael (Micky) and Harold were rowing near some estuary when the tide was strong, after they had spent a long time in the house on the sandy beach. At that time Harold was an invalid and so was recruiting. While rowing, Michael was full of beans. When their boat reached the channel, it hung motionless in the calmer waters, and Michael became madly romantic and recited staves of poetry:

> It may be that the gulfs will wash us down.
> It may be we shall touch the Happy Isles,
> And see the great Achilles, whom we know.

Harold played the second fiddle by shouting out, inspite of his weakness. Michael strove to stoke Harold's sagging fire, and Harold himself garnered all the little spirit that was there in him.

Michael's imagination caught fire. Looking up at the farm house, that wore a celestial screen, he was ebullient with joy: 'He looked at the flaming windows and fancied that the farm was a star and the boat its attendant satellite. Then the tide was the rushing ether stream of the universe, the interstellar surge that beats for ever. How jolly! He did not formulate his joys, after the weary fashion of older people. He was far too happy to be thankful.' Sea gulls were hovering over them and lurks were setting tunes to their songs. Just at this moment Michael noticed the vehicle of Harold's doctor approaching the farm, obviously for attending to his patient Harold. Michael told Harold that he did not see any meaning in Harold's being treated by a doctor (because Harold was already in high spirits). He said: "'...I don't see the point of it.'" Harold told Michael that though now he (Michael) may not be in need of a doctor, but some day in future he must be. However, when Harold started to get down from the boat, he 'fell heavily against the rowlock' and 'strained his heart,' and then died in the farm. Michael despaired at the sudden halting of his romantic flight (part 1).

All this happened when Michael was twenty-two, and he never expected to come across such a joy as on that boat. The doctor held Michael responsible for Harold's terminally mortal condition. Harold's parents came, and also came the curate who said that Harold was in communion with the 'unseen.' All these added to Michael's repentance, so much so that he could not expect to live long to be over seventy. He, afterwards, always remembered Harold's last dying gesture, and his last words: "'Don't you see the point of it? Well, you will some day.'" The words stuck to Michael's brain fixedly; but after thirty years he forgot the origin of the words in his brain. The memory of Harold's 'athletics and good temper' also faded. Michael had no poetic gift to immortalise himself, but he had enough practical intellect to make him 'worthy of life' in the civilised world. "Love, the love of humanity, warmed him; and even when he was thinking of other matters, was looking at Orion perhaps in the cold winter evenings, a pang of joy, too sweet for description, would thrill him, and he would feel sure that our highest impulses have some eternal value, and will be completed hereafter. So full a nature could not brood over death."

Soon after the tragic death of Harold, when he himself was recruiting during his convalescence, Michael met 'the woman who was to become his helpmate through life—Janet.

Earlier, he did not like her, when she was engaged to another man, for her hardness of sentiment; but now he discovered that 'her hardness sprang from a morality that he himself lacked.' There was actually a great divergence between Michael and Janet: 'he believed in love, Janet believed in truth.' Janet detested sentimentality, and believed that each of us should have a 'profession,' for better, the profession of not feeling for others but making others better. And she urged Michael to adopt such a profession, and consequently he was perfectly modified. The 'beauty of honest work' dawned upon Michael, and brushing aside sentimentality he 'entered the Home Civil Service—the British Museum.' For helping others—for making them 'better'—Michael overworked with his native tact, and he was rising worldly. After ten years since then, Janet and Michael got married to each other. But before they married, Janet had been suffering much from pain because Michael 'had proved unworthy of her.' Though they were contrasting characters (now in a different way, for now she wanted love and he wanted truth, unlike previously), the marriage 'proved durable and sufficiently happy.' Michael was growing more and more tolerant and sympathetic and official as regards adjustment. He was desiring to have a greater outlook which could accommodate divergent views, and with this objective in mind he turned to literature. He began writing. His second book was 'The Confessions of a Middle-aged Man,' in which he tried to teach that experience 'is the only humanizer; sympathy, balance and many-sidedness cannot come to a man until he is elderly.' Janet was not interested in Michael being an author; she 'restrained him from writing anything that he did not sincerely feel.'

Meanwhile, Henry, Catherine and Adam were born to Janet and Michael, and all of them were a 'happy family.' And 'At home, as in his work, Michael was more successful than most men.' Michael was now fifty, and he now inherited his father's house in the Surrey hills, where Janet became interested in horticulture. Janet was growing more and more fierce in manner and advanced in apparent age than Michael. On the other hand, Michael was developing more and more pliancy in him as he was nearing to be a valetudinarian. He became bald and mentally timid, though physically he kept rather stout. He ceased conversing unnecessarily with others, but he loved his children and sometimes mediated between Janet and the three issues to maintain peace in the family. Meantime, Catherine got married and thus got over her fussiness. She had been her father's 'chief support.' However, two troubles now befell Michael's lot. One, after Janet died, Michael, who was now made a knight, thought that 'he should not survive her.' But things did not happen according to his wish; when she died he was sixty and he continued to live beyond seventy. The second trouble was that, after 'a brutal scene,' Adam left home and went to Argentine, but soon wrote from there that he was sorry for leaving home, and that he 'wanted to start for himself.' Hearing this Michael said: "'I don't see the point of it.'" He said this because he did never stop anybody from starting, and because he had given Adam all freedom.

Sir Michael (for he was knighted) now retired and wrote some further literature and some soft criticism of the 'Established Church.' Further than all this, he stopped speculating or meditating. 'The experience of years disposed him to accept the experience of centuries and to merge his feeble personal note in the great voice of tradition.' His was in 'a serene and dignified old age.' He became quite free from any bias, had no ulterior motive, and had a pure heart. 'He could look back on failures and mistakes, and he had not carried out the ideals of his youth. Who has?' Sir Michael did not die by now; he was only preparing himself for death. He was sometimes 'bestially afraid' of death and sometimes indifferent to death, because experiences of a long life prepare one for death: 'Those who live longest are consequently the best prepared.' However, at last Sir Michael really died—died of an accident. One day he was passing by some women who were quarrelling among themselves over a fish, when the women appealed to him for justice. He 'advised them to lay the fish aside for twenty-four hours, which annoyed them, and one of the women, being drunk, 'slapped him with the fish in the face.' As a consequence of this, he ceased to respond to anybody's call, and then died.

Henry, Catherine and Adam gathered round the dying Sir Michael. Adam fiercely censured Sir Michael: "'He never did anything since mother died, and damned little before. They've forgotten his books because they aren't first-hand; they're rearranging the cases he arranged in the British Museum. That's the lot. What else has he done except tell people to dress warmly but not too warm?'" Adam further said: "'It's because nobody speaks up that men of the old man's type get famous. It's a sign of our sloppy civilization. You're all afraid...of originality, afraid of work, afraid of hurting one another's feelings. You let anyone come to the top who doesn't frighten you, and as soon as he dies you forget him and knight some other figurehead instead.'" Catherine told Adam that, his returning home was a relief to her, and before long they went out leaving behind Michael in the empty room. Sir Michael, at the negligence shown to him by Adam and Catherine, became ascorbic and exacerbated: 'Sir Michael grew cold with rage. This was life, this was what the younger generation had been thinking. Adam he ignored, but at the recollection of Henry and Catherine he determined to die.... The immense and superhuman cynicism that is latent in all of us came out last to the top and transformed him. He saw the absurdity of love, and the vision so tickled him that he began to 'laugh.' The nurse called an old man for help, and the old man came and bent over Sir Michael. The two boys—one of them Catherine's issue—entered the sickroom. Catherine's son enquired of the nurse about their grandfather's condition. The nurse told him that Sir Michael was not well, and then Henry's son said to the other boy: "'Come along, let's cut.'" Catherine's son replied: "'But they told us not to.'"

"'Why should we do what old people tell us? Dad's pretty well played out, and so's your mother.'" "'Shocking; be off with you both," said the nurse; and, with a little croon of admiration, Catherine's boy followed his cousin out of the room. Their grandfather's mirth increased. He rolled about in the bed; and, just as he was grasping the full irony of the situation, he died, and pursued it into the unknown' (Part 2).

After his (real) death, Sir Michael, in his after-life, found himself lying in an illimitable desert plain, where nothing moved except a few sand-pillars, and where there was no wind or noise. He lay there perhaps for years, 'long before death perhaps, while his body seemed to be walking among men.' The narrator here Platonically tries to prove the immortality of soul: 'Life is so short and trivial, that who knows whether we arrive for it entirely, whether more than a fraction of the soul is aroused to put on flesh? The bud and the blossom perish in a moment, the husk endures, and may not the soul be a husk?' Sir Michael was meditating on the irony of life, and he realised that he was in Hell, surrounded by other souls, for a little mistake of his while alive. His mistake was that he had appreciated beauty and 'the bad and mediocre upon earth,' and for this he was suffering from pain He had however a little happiness, nevertheless, because his soul itself did not commit those sins he himself committed. Sir Michael told the other soul, which was nearest him, that he would tike to enjoy his present state in Hell than 'what men miscall life.' He said he preferred the 'goodness and mercy' of Hell to the restlessness of life. He regretted his being influenced by the warmth of the sun and Orion's call to adventure, during his youth. The soul to whom he was speaking said that he was afraid of the love between the brothers, Castor and Pollux.

Though it was really Hell, to Sir Michael it seemed a heaven. The other soul informed him that there were two grades of heaven: the heaven of the soft (or of the passionate), in which they were abiding, and the heaven of the hard (or of the pursuers of truth). Sir Michael saw Janet in the heaven of the hard, in the distance. He understood that she was not saved, and he saw her surrounded by rocky hills and in the company of 'the reformers and ascetics and all sword-like souls.' On the other hand, Sir Michael's heaven was in the waste of dunes, in which he lay with 'the sentimentalists, the conciliators, the peacemakers, the humanists.' Sir Michael was on the side of love as Janet was on the side of truth. Sir Michael understood that 'Love and Truth, who seem to contend for our souls like angels, hold each the seeds of our decay.' The other soul told him that the young were neither in the hard nor in the soft heavens. But what was the point or meaning in young people dying was not clear.

Sir Michael now began to take stock of his works on earth. 'He traced his decomposition—his work had been soft [passionate], his books soft, he had softened his relations with other men. He had been good in everything, and this is itself a sign of decay. Whatever occurred he had been appreciative, tolerant, pliant. Consequently he had been a success; Adam was right; it was the moment in civilization for his type.' But later on his books were forgotten and his works suspended. Sir Michael said: "'This is the whole of my life.'" He thought there had been 'an illusive joy' in life, which was absent where he was, and this thought gave him pain, in Hell one should 'eternally oscillate between disgust and desire,' but the two were only the creations of imagination, because in Hell there was nothing having ontological existence.

"'A pillar of sand,'" said one spirit at that moment. Another spirit said that it was coming from the river. Sir Michael asked: "'What river?'" He was told that it was a swift and very broad river, and that the spirits of the damned dwelt over it and crossed it now and again. The damned spirits used to harm the dwellers of the soft (passionate) heaven with light and song, and by reminding the past life on earth. The burden of the song was: "'truth was love.'" At this moment a sand-pillar fell and a 'senile weeping' (of Sir Michael) was heard. Then some shades or spirits said that the place of Hell was death, and that there darkness was God. And then death came (to Sir Michael)—real death, and not 'a dream or a forgetting' because "'There is no abiding home for strength and beauty among men. The flower fades, the seas dry up in the sun, the sun and all the stars fade as a flower.'" But, yet, the soul or personality or 'I' has been eternally desiring: "'But the desire for such things, that is eternal, that can abide, and he who desires me is I.'" The real death now really came and Sir Michael died a second (and real) death, 'through terrible pain.' Yet, at the time of his death he uttered: 'I do desire.' It was all but a dream, and when the dream vanished, 'he

[Sir Michael] came to the bank of the infernal stream' and there he stumbled over a piece of wood (boat) which 'had once belonged to a tree.' Due to the impact of the stumbling, water gushed out (in a stream and made a river). Sir Michael boarded the boat and someone invisible began to row. When the boat neared the mid-channel, it went more slowly, and Sir Michael knew that 'once carried out he would be lost eternally, there was no second hope of salvation.' His heart was beating with the rapids of the oars. 'Hell made her last effort, and all that is evil in creation, all the distortions of love and truth by which we are vexed, came surging down the estuary, and the boat hung motionless.' Sir Michael 'heard a voice say, "The point of it..." and a weight fell off his body and he crossed mid-stream. 'It was a glorious evening.' And the boat 'sped without prelude into sunshine' (Part 3).

John Sayre Martin, in his *E.M. Forster: The Endless Journey,* has discussed this short story at some length. According to him, this short story reflects Forster's vision of the Edwardian liberal humanism and of the kind of public reception it got later on, or, rather, Forster's perception of the proximate fate of Edwardian liberal humanism. Let us here profitably fully quote Martin's explanation of the short story and his evaluation of it from that book of his. Martin writes that this story is 'more interesting' than 'The Machine Stops,' though it is 'not a completely successful one.' He writes: Michael, its protagonist, is an Edwardian liberal. He loves humanity and wants to serve it; he is tolerant, sympathetic, broad-minded, gentle. And because it was 'the moment in civilization for his type,' he becomes a success, rising to a high post with the British Museum and earning a knighthood. But Michael's liberalism, the story suggests, is a tame substitute for his 'eternal moment.' That moment with which the story begins, occurred in his youth when he was in a boat with his friend Harold and urged Harold to row with all his might. Since Harold had a weak heart and Michael was expected to help take care of him, the urging was injudicious. But 'the point of it' is that, as never again, Michael was joyously, spontaneously, alive. His mind and heart were united in a common cause. Scene and action cohered in a magical unity. 'He looked at the flaming windows and fancied that the farm was a star and the boat its attendant satellite. Then the tide was the rushing ether stream of the universe, the interstellar surge that beats for ever. How jolly! He did not formulate his joys, after the weary fashion of older people. He was far too happy to be thankful. (...).' But Michael's happiness leads to Harold's death. 'I—don't see the point of it,' Michael had nervously exclaimed at the sudden sense that his friend was overdoing it. 'Don't you?' replies Harold. 'Well, you will some day.' But Harold dies 'half in the boat and half out of it' before they can reach the shore.

"The remainder of the story is taken up with Michael's later life and after-life. Comforting himself that he was after all 'worthier of life, and of whatever may come after it' than Harold, having been born of 'a more intellectual stock,' he proceeds to cultivate his love of humanity (...). Janet, his wife, has the starch that he lacks, for she is ruled by the head rather than the heart, and unlike Michael prefers truth to tolerance. Michael's mildness facilitates his professional advancement but finally proves his undoing. Asked in his old age to adjudicate a dispute among a group of women over a fish, Michael replies 'that he had not sufficient data to judge on' and advises them 'to lay the fish aside for twenty-four hours.' One of the women, 'the worse for drink,' slaps him in the face with the fish, he falls, and never recovers (...). On his deathbed, he overhears his children condemn the mediocrity of his life; and at that, 'the immense and superhuman cynicism that is latent in all of us came at last to the top and transformed him. He saw the absurdity of love, and the vision so tickled him that he began to laugh," (...).

But his cynicism is insufficient to comfort him in the after-life. After dying, he finds himself sunk in a vast sandy desert, which is, as be learns, the 'heaven of the soft.' With him lie 'the sentimentalists, the conciliators, the peace-makers, the humanists, and all who have trusted the warmer vision' (...). Such a hell perhaps implies the lack of a strong spiritual foundation for modern liberalism. Compare Fielding's comment on *A Passage to India,* 'We all build upon sand, and the more modern the country gets, the worse'll be the crash.' Michael's wife, who predeceased him, must surely, he feels, be in the 'heaven of the hard,' a range of stony mountains that he can see in. the distance. An eternity in either place would be hell indeed. But Michael, at any rate, is to be spared. He is spared not because of what he has done (for it is Forster's point that Michael's kind of liberalism cannot do much) but because of what he desires. Lying in the sand, he hears a voice 'inexpressively sweet,' the voice of the transcendent spirit that had once 'transfigured the world' and that still governs the years between childhood and maturity. It is the spirit that had possessed Michael when he was in the boat with Harold. Again he desires it, and since 'desire is enough,' he is saved. Dying a second death, he finds himself once more being rowed in a boat in an estuary. 'Hell made her last effort, arid all that is *evil* in creation, all the distortions of love and truth by which we are vexed, came surging down the estuary, and the boat hung motionless' (...). Once again he hears the words 'The point of it...' as the boat speeds into the sunshine.

"As a critique of liberalism 'The Point of It' is not without interest, but it is weakened by a lack of dramatic force and an incoherence of aim. Most of the dramatic interest comes at the beginning and end of the story, while the middle consists of a long, discursive account of Michael's career and is over-encumbered with characters. As for the story's aim, Forster's double desire to damn Michael and save him (a desire that probably reflects Forster's ambivalence towards Edwardian liberalism) may have been what provoked his Bloomsbury friends to ask, 'What is the point of it?' (Introduction, *Collected Tales*, viii). If, as the story asserts, 'there is nothing ultimate in Hell' and man 'will not lay aside all hope on entering if, Michael should be no more saveable than anyone else. Forster's uncertain perspective is reflected in his tone, which shifts from irony to sentimentality. Compare the following sneer at Michael's youthful belief in eternity with the lyrical treatment accorded his ultimate salvation: 'Love, the love of humanity, warmed him; and even when he was thinking of other matters, was looking at Orion perhaps in the cold winter evenings, a pang of joy, too sweet for description, would thrill him, and he would feel sure that our highest impulses have some eternal value, and will be completed hereafter. So full a nature could not brood over death. (...)' But what, after all, does the story show if not that Michael's 'highest impulses' did indeed have 'some eternal value? And why should he brood over death if, as the story suggests, the hereafter may consist of a pleasant boat tide? The 'point of it' may after all be that Forster wanted to throw out his cake and eat it too" (Martin, 61-64).

It is very difficult to have a consensus opinion about the quality of this story, because even the 'point' of the story is not quite clear to us, and Forster himself was aware of this. In his Introduction to the 1947 collection of his short stories he wrote about this story: "As for 'The Point of It', it was ill-liked when it came out by my Bloomsbury friends. 'What is the point of it?' they queried thinly, nor did I know how to reply." Forster himself, P.N. Furbank informs us, thought the story 'inferior' (Furbank, I, 196). But, in his diary entry on the New Year's Eve of 1912, Forster called 'The Point of It' a 'good story.' However, we may perhaps say that the story begins very smoothly and enjoyably and thus runs well to the middle of it, say upto section 2 of it, but then only drags on, loosing progressively all the while the amount of interest it generated at the outset, and finishes itself as a mediocre and puzzling fiction.

10

'MR ANDREWS'

Like 'The Point of It,' 'Mr Andrews' was first published in the collection of short stories entitled *The Eternal Moment,* and was, in 1947, published in the *Collected Short Stories* of Forster. And like 'The Point of It,' 'Mr Andrews' is also perhaps a 'self-indulgence' of Forster. However, 'Mr Andrews' is the shortest story in Forster's *Collected Short Stories,* comprising only five pages.

The soul of Mr Andrews, a Christian, and that of a Moslem Turk, were rising upwards, hand in hand, towards the

Judgement Seat and the Gate of Heaven, being pressed on every side by the world soul, 'just as the atmosphere presses upon rising bubbles.' The world soul was 'striving to vanquish them, to break their thin envelope of personality, to mingle their virtue with its own.' But the two souls resisted, 'remembering their glorious individual life on earth, and hoping for an individual life to come.' The ascent was a long way. Mr Andrews was conscious of his faith in God and humility and love of humanity, and so he was hopeful of salvation. Mr Andrews told the moslem Turk: "'I was born of a decent middle-class family, and had my education at Winchester and Oxford. I thought of becoming a missionary, but I was offered a post in the Board of Trade, which I accepted. At thirty-two I married, and had four children, two of whom have died. My wife survives me. If I had lived a little longer I should have been knighted.'" Then the Turk told his own story to Mr Andrews: "'Now I will relate my career. I was never sure of my father, and my mother does not signify. I grew up in the slums of Salonika. Then I joined a band and we plundered the villages of the infidel. I prospered and had three wives, all of whom survive me. Had I lived a little longer I should have had a band of my own.'" Mr Andrews told The Turk: "'A son of mine was killed travelling in Macedonia. Perhaps you killed him.'" The Turk replied: "'It is very possible.'"

The Turk was godless, lawless, cruel and lustful, and yet he believed that he would be rewarded in Heaven with 'a place full of the crude pleasures of a ruffian's life on earth!' Mr Andrews, however, 'longed to save the man [the Moslem Turk:].' When they reached the Gate of Heaven, both of them sought permission to enter not for himself but for the other. Their prayer was granted, but they were asked: "'In what clothes will you enter?'" the Turk replied that he would enter in his best clothes that he had stolen, and he got attired—'he clad himself in splendid turban and a waistcoat embroidered with silver, and baggy trousers, and a great belt in which were stuck pipes and pistoles and knives.' Mr Andrews thought of wearing his best clothes to enter Heaven, but he felt no inclination to wear them. He said he would wear his white robes. He was immediately given white robes and was asked what else he did desire to have. Mr Andrews said that he desired to have a small harp, and he was given a 'small gold harp.' He refused the offer of a palm, which signified martyrdom, and followed the Turk into Heaven.

As Mr Andrews passed into Heaven, a man, dressed in white robe, passed out of it 'with gesture of despair.' Mr Andrews asked him why he was in despair, but received no reply. He again asked: "'And who are all those figures, seated inside on thrones and mountains? Why are some of them terrible, and sad, and ugly?'" And again he received no reply. On entering Heaven, Mr Andrews discovered that those seated figures were gods 'who were then being worshipped on the earth.' Then a 'group of souls stood round each [of the gods], singing his praises. But the gods paid no heed, for they were listening to the prayers of living men, which alone brought them nourishment.' Mr Andrews saw that sometimes the faith of the worshippers changed from mildness to ferocity, from universal love to specific hatred, and from latitudinarianism to orthodoxy, and that the features of the gods also concomitantly changed. He saw there Buddha, Vishnu, Allah, Jehovah, Elohim and other gods, and also some ugly and vulgar gods worshipped by savages. He saw that there was no unfulfilled human aspirations—divine or diabolic.

Mr Andrews did not play on his harp for long, instead he hunted for 'one of his dead friends.' He found that 'though souls were continually entering Heaven, it still seemed curiously empty, though he had all that he expected, he was conscious of no great happiness, no mystic contemplation of beauty, no mystic union with good.' He found in Heaven nothing good and beautiful, as he saw outside it. At last he saw the Turk and 'hailed him with a cry of human joy.' 'The Turk was seated in thought, and round him, by sevens, sat the virgins who are promised in the Koran.' He called out to Mr Andrews to come to him and share his pleasures. He asked: "'Where are my other friends? Where are the men whom I love, or whom I have killed?'" Mr Andrews replied that he found none else but only him (the Turk). Mr Andrews sat beside the Turk and ogled at the virgins with 'coal black eyes.' The Turk told him that though he found in Heaven everything that he expected he had no great happiness; he had far less happiness in Heaven than outside it. He said that though the virgins were beautiful and good, he wished them better. And the Turk so wished: 'the forms of the virgins became more rounded, and their eyes grew larger and blacker than before.' Mr Andrews, on the other hand, wished his garments to be more pure and soft, and they became so. He also wished his harp to be more glittering, and it became so. It all so happened because in Heaven one's expectations were certainly fulfilled, but not one's hopes.

At last Mr Andrews decided to come out of Heaven, because, said he, there it was not possible to desire or imagine infinity. He said: "'I have never imagined anything infinitely good or beautiful excepting in my dreams.'" The Turk decided to accompany him while coming out of Heaven. At the entrance gate 'the Turk parted with his virgins and his best clothes, and Mr Andrews cast away his robes and his harp.' As soon as they came out of Heaven, 'they felt again the pressure of the world soul.' 'For a moment they stood hand in hand resisting it. Then they suffered it to break in upon them, and they, and all the experiences they had gained, and all the love and wisdom they had generated, passed into it, and made it better.

Forster's objective, in this story, was to ironically expose the sham morality of a particular Christian and a particular Moslem. From this story it should not be supposed that his objective was to vilify the Christian or the Moslem moral doctrines. The theme is very lightly but enjoyably handled. John Sayre Martin writes about this story: "'Mr Andrews,' which concerns the ascent of two departed souls, a Christian and a Turk, to Heaven and their experience there, is a pleasant blend of comedy and pathos. Into a very short story, Forster manages to contrast with amusing irony the morality of a Christian and a Moslem and their expectations of the after-life, and to introduce a spoof on the vicissitudes of religious faith" (Martin, 64).

11

'CO-ORDINATION'

This story is a reflection of Forster's disgust at the attempt at introducing mechanical drilling and at bringing in uniformity in human behaviour, which he first experienced, and that very painfully, at Tonbridge school. It first appeared in Foster's second published collection of short stories, *The Eternal Moment,* before being published in his *Collected Short Stories* (1947). In the story, Mildred and Ellen, Rose and Enid, Margaret and Jane, and Dolores and Violet played duets, in succession, in the school's music class from 4:00 to 4:45, while, in all the cases of the duets, Miss Haddon acted as the conductor. All those students, except Dolores and Violet played better than Ellen. At 4:45 the Principal of the school explained to all the pupils that she wanted them to learn the same duet, and that 'it was part of her new co-ordinative system.' Along with other things of the curriculum, the pupils were learning Beethoven's 'Erotica' Symphony in honour of the Emperor. Many mistresses of the school 'exclaimed that they loved co-ordinating, and that it was a lovely system.' But Miss Haddon, the music mistress, could not understand the value of co-ordination, and, being conscious of her advanced age, wished to be soon cashiered by the Principal.

Meanwhile high up in heaven Beethoven sat, and all around him, ranged on small clouds, sat his clerks. The clerks were recording the events of the duets (performed by the students, in twos) in the ledger under the rubric 'Erotica.' Beethoven asked who Miss Haddon was and who were in the orchestra, and he received the answer that Miss Haddon interrupted him (Beethoven) for many years, and the maidens of the middle class constituted the orchestra and they performed the 'Erotica' every day before miss Haddon. Beethoven also asked if the maidens performed with insight. One clerk answered that they performed with 'most intimate insight.' Hearing this Beethoven approved the performance, and decreed, as a token of his approval, "'that Miss Haddon and her orchestra and all in their house shall this very evening hear a perfect performance of my A minor quartette.'"

While this decree of Beethoven was being written down (in the ledger), 'in another part of the empyrean' Napoleon was surrounded by innumerable clerks who were sitting on 'cirro-cumuli clouds.' The clerks were busy in recording the 'references made on earth,' and every few moments Napoleon asked: "'And what is our latest phase?'" The clerks, who kept the ledger, entitled 'hommages de Wordsworth,' informed him that at five-o-clock Mildred, Ellen, Rose, Enid, Margaret and Jane recited the sonnet 'Once did she hold the gorgeous East in fee.' But Dolores and Violet failed, though they attempted, to recite the sonnet. Emperor Napoleon said that the poet in the 'gorgeous East' (Italy?) celebrated his conquest of the Venetian Republic. He further said that the greatness of the sonnet overcame Dolores and Violet, and so they failed to recite the sonnet. Napoleon then asked what the next phase was, and another clerk informed the Emperor that Mildred and her company were 'sketching in the left front leg of Pauline Bonaparte's couch' and that 'Dolores and Violet are still learning their sonnet'. Hearing this and the report of another clerk, the Emperor said: "'I approve.'"

At 5:30 a fourth clerk told the Emperor that all of the students, excepting Dolores and Violet, were singing 'Marseillaise.' Rising to his feet, the Emperor now decreed: "'—I decree in response that they and all their house shall participate to-morrow morning in the victory of Austerlitz.'" And the decree was entered in the ledger. It was now 7:30 and the girls (Mildred *et al.*) were heavily despairing over the new system (of co-ordinative association). Just at that moment, wonderfully, a 'regiment of cavalry rode past the school, headed by the most spiffing band!' 'The girls went off their heads with joy. 'But Miss Haddon remained gloomy as usual, and thought about herself: "'I am stupid and tired and odd; I wish that I was dead.'" Saying this she lifted to her ear the shell, which was being used as a paper-weight, and at first heard the sound of the sea, and then 'heard the sea itself, and knew that it was hers for ever.'

The Principal asked Miss Haddon why she was not supervising the girls. Miss Haddon removed the shell from her ear, and faced the Principal 'with a growing determination.' Miss Haddon said that she could hear the voice of Ellen through the shell, though Ellen was at the other side of the house. The Principal asked her to put down the shell and go to her duties, and then herself took the shell from Miss Haddon and raised it to her own ear. She (the Principal) heard through the shell the rustling of trees and the soft conversation, through horns, of some familiar persons who were riding along the trees. While she was listening to these with one ear, Miss Haddon told her through her other ear that she would not resume her duties (of supervising the music of girls, etc.), because she was not actually 'musical' and acted as a music teacher only to earn a living. She told the Principal that she was going to give the notice of her resignation. Unexpectedly, the Principal was not angry at this, but was surprised. She asked Miss Haddon not to resign, but, instead, to lie down in her sitting room, while she (the Principal) would be preparing herself, because she (the Principal) delighted in being with girls. So Miss Haddon lay down and 'dozed the soul of the sea returned to her.' The Principal's head was 'full of forest murmurs.' After reading herself, the Principal opened the door. Meantime, the cavalry once again passed off by the school. However, in the next morning Miss Haddon told the Principal that she had received 'some extraordinary news.' She said: "'Many years ago my father saved a man from drowning. That man has just died, and he has left me a cottage by the edge of the sea, and money to live in it.'" She further said that she only waited till that day (for going to live in that sea-side cottage). The Principal then kissed Miss Haddon and expressed her intention to accompany her (Miss Haddon) towards the sea-side cottage, declaring a whole holiday for the school.

The Principal then addressed the students, gave them her (future) address at that cottage in the sea-side, and invited them to visit her at that cottage. The mistresses were asked to do different extracurricular activities (with the students) instead of engaging themselves in teaching works, and the mistresses and the students did those things without any co-ordination among them. Ellen, for instance composed a poem without co-ordination, and the small girls 'sang it without stopping for three hours.' The following was the song of Ellen:

Silly old Boney
Sat on his Pony,
Eating his Christmas Pie,
He put in his thumb
And pulled out a plum,
And said, What a good boy am I,

At the end of the day the Principal gathered the girls around herself, Miss Haddon being present there, and asked them if they did value her co-ordinative system. The girls rather said that they did not or that they did little. Then the Principal herself confessed that she herself did not really value it, and that she was obliged to value it because that type of thing impresses the Board of Education. At this all the mistresses and all the girls laughed. But this 'discreditable affair did not escape the attention of Mephistopheles.' He instantaneously 'sought the Judgement Seat' with 'an immense scroll inscribed 'J' accuse!' Then, flying up a lot, he met the angel Raphael who asked Mephistopheles to show him the new case (of the school) for adjudication. Raphael reminded Mephistopheles that he 'had such a disappointment over Job' and that his (Mephistopheles') verdict on Faust was ultimately against himself. But Mephistopheles did not give ear to Raphael, he rather told Raphael: "'...I can prove the futility of genius. Great men think that they are understood, and are not; men think that they understand them, and do not.'" Hearing this, Raphael told him that if he could prove that then he (Mephistopheles) had really a case. Raphael further told him: "'For this universe is supposed to rest on co-ordination, all creatures coordinating according to their powers.'" Mephistopheles said: "'The genius and the ordinary man have never co-ordinated once since Abel was killed by Cain.'" Then Raphael cried out to him: "'Oh, candid if infernal soul. Go back to the earth, and walk up and down it again. For these people have co-ordinated, Mephistopheles. They have co-ordinated through the central sources of Melody and Victory.'"

This story is not up to the mark; it is over-written and full of useless details, which come in the way of the story's sustained interest The theme of the story is simple: freedom and spontaneity are preferable to co-ordinated and mechanical drilling. But Forster has blown it too far, has complicated it too much, and that very unnecessarily. However, John Sayre Martin writes about this story: "'Co-ordination' expresses Forster's well-marked preference for freedom and spontaneity to external control. Two old-maid schoolteachers, Miss Haddon and her Principal, have been 'co-ordinating' the studies of their little girl pupils in order to please the Board of Education but to the intense boredom of the title girls themselves. Happening to pick up a seashell, Miss Haddon hears in it the sounds of the sea; the Principal, listening too, hears the sounds of a hunting party in a forest. Both are sounds of an 'other kingdom,' spelling freedom and truth to the teachers and momentarily delivering them from the bondage of time. Converted by their experience, they declare an end to co-ordination and a school holiday during which their charges play happy, disorganized games. For all its humour, the story is more encumbered and less forceful than 'Mr Andrews.' Not content to let it speak for itself, Forster introduces a bit of a celestial whimsy, with 'Beethoven,' 'Napoleon,' and other heavenly figures commenting on the 'co-ordination' below. The mixture does not jell" (Martin, 64) (Victory of Austerlitz is the victory of Napoleon in the decisive battle of war, fought between he, on the one hand, and the coalition between the Russians and the Austrians, on the other, on 2 December, 1805, in Moravia).

12

'THE STORY OF THE SIREN'

Forster wrote this story in 1904, the year in which he also wrote 'The Purple Envelope.' It is 'The Story of the Siren' where Forster, for the first time, wrote about his curious idea of 'falling books.' In this story, the narrator's note-book fell into the waters of the Mediterranean. The idea of 'falling books' later recurred in *A Room with a View, The Longest*

Journey, and *Howards End*. In the first novel, Miss Lavish is said to have lost a manuscript; in the second, Rickie's 'box of books' falls irrevocably down a ravine; and in the third, Leonard Bast is killed by 'falling books.' Nicola Beauman writes that this story was based perhaps, on a memory of an expedition to Sorrento in May 1902 when a 'mad' boatman distressed Lily [Forster's mother] because he 'groaned and muttered to himself' in the grottoes, it was a mysterious fantasy on the theme of salvation and showed Morgan [Forster] in a new light, unafraid of using the methods of mysticism and at the same time political. He appears to be inveighing against both the tyranny of organised Christianity and the tyranny of the State: and he contrasted both to Ancient Greek freedom from repression—of which he was...so envious. After the Sicilian boatman has related 'the story of the siren' he concludes: "'Silence and loneliness cannot last for ever. It may be a hundred or a thousand years, but the sea lasts longer, and she [the siren] shall come out of it and sing'" (Beauman, 145).

'The Story of the Siren' begins with the falling of the narrator's beautiful notebook, with pale green pages, on the 'Deist Controversy', into the waters of the Mediterranean sea. The notebook was quiveringly going downwards towards the bottom of the sea, showing itself to be 'a piece of magical India-rubber stretching out to infinity', and sometimes showing itself to be a book of knowledge. Ultimately, the notebook settled down in the sand at the bottom of the sea, and the sand prevented the notebook from being seen. But, after some time, the notebook was seen to be resting on its spine, and it was seen that some unseen fingers were browsing the pages of the notebook—the notebook which was necessary to the narrator for his Fellowship Dissertation. One of the boatmen got ready to dive into the waters to retrieve the notebook. The boatmen landed the narrator and a certain Sicilian near the Blue Grotto at Capri and went to a little distance, having made their boat thus lighter. Here the narrator tells us that the blue colour of the Grotto and the spirit of it 'is the heritage of every cave in the Mediterranean into which the sun can shine and the sea flow.'

When the boat went off, the Sicilian said to the narrator: "'Go to the end of the Grotto, and I will show you something beautiful.'" Then the Sicilian denuded himself, climbed up to the summit of the entrance rock, and then dived into the water to fetch the notebook. The narrator says that the notebook was 'wonderful' but the beauty of the naked Sicilian was 'past all description'. He tells us about the Sicilian: 'His effect was that of a silver statue, alive beneath the sea, through whom life throbbed in blue and green. Something infinitely happy, infinitely wise.' The sight was extremely attractive. The Sicilian told the narrator: "'In a place like this one might see the Siren.'" The surround was a magic world—'a world of blue whose floor was the sea and whose walls and roof of rock trembled with the sea's reflections'. In such a fantastic place, the narrator emphatically supported the words of the Sicilian: "'One might easily see the Siren.'"

The narrator was 'parting the sticky leaves of the notebook' which the Sicilian retrieved from under the water of the sea, sitting on the sand. The Sicilian was glad that the Siren (which belonged to their country) also could give pleasure to foreigners, like the narrator. The narrator, who afterwards read about the Siren in a little book, asked the Sicilian if the Siren used to come out of that blue water to sit 'on the rock at the entrance [of the grotto], combing her hair.' The Sicilian did not answer, and suddenly became grave and then asked the narrator if he had ever seen the Siren. The narrator said that he had, and that frequently. The Sicilian said that he had never seen the Siren. The narrator then asked the him if he ever heard the song of the Siren. Putting on his coat, the Sicilian replied that it was impossible for the Siren to sing under water. The narrator suggested that the Siren might have climbed upto the top of the rock and then might have sung. But the Sicilian angrily told him that the Siren could not breathe in the air or sit on the rock, because the air and the rock were blessed by priest. He said that the Siren could live only in the sea which was not blessed, because the sea was enormously vast and was always changing. The narrator understood the Sicilian, and kept silent.

After a little while the Sicilian became suave in face and told the narrator that "'As a rule only good people see the Siren.'" He said that this was a 'strange thing,' and that even the priests could not explain this 'strange thing.' The thing was strange because the Siren herself was wicked. The Sicilian further said that those who were faithful Christians, and even those who were 'merely good in daily life' were in the danger of the Siren, though for the last two generations nobody of the village saw the Siren. He told the narrator that Giuseppe was safe from the Siren, for he was good and he loved them (the Sicilian and some others) as friends. The narrator was not acquainted with Giuseppe, and so he asked of the Sicilian who Giuseppe was.

The Sicilian did not directly reply to the narrator's inquiry, but related an incident that took place in the past, and in the course of his narrative he suggested that Giuseppe was his (elder) brother. He said that the incident took place when he was seventeen and Giuseppe was twenty. It was the year when foreigners (the British colonisers), who later improved the condition of the village, first began to come in. One day he and Giuseppe took a high-born British lady and her friends to their boat to show them the grottoes. He caught a crab, tore off its claws, and then offered it to the lady as a curiosity. The lady groaned, but a gentleman, her friend, was pleased and offered him some money. But he refused the money saying that his (the gentleman's) pleasure was enough reward for him. At this, Giuseppe became angry and dealt blows and kicks at him, making bruises on his person. The Sicilian later heard that the ladies then, out of pity for him, wanted to take him away and make a waiter of him. But that did not come to pass. However, when they reached the big grotto at a distance, the gentleman was anxious to see one of the two brothers (the Sicilian and Giuseppe) dive for money, and the ladies consented. Giuseppe would not dive without receiving a silver coin, and so the gentleman gave him a two-lira piece. With that coin Giuseppe dived into the water, and saw the Siren. After some time, the dead body of Giuseppe came to the surface of the water, and there was no coin with him. At this point, the narrator asked the Sicilian about Giuseppe: "'He was drowned, then?'" The Sicilian replied that Giuseppe was not drownd; he only saw the Siren.

The narrator wanted to know from the Sicilian what Giuseppe did look like. The Sicilian said that Giuseppe was like anyone who saw the Siren. He further said that Giuseppe was "'Unhappy, unhappy because he knew everything. Every living thing made him unhappy because he knew it would die. And all he cared to do was sleep.'" Giuseppe would not work, forget to eat, forget if he had clothes on. He was robust in health, and not dull in his eyes. He would feel pity for a new-born child, and would be frightened to see a married couple. He was afraid of marriage, because he had tasted the married life with Maria. They loved each other, of course, but, said the Sicilian, 'Love is nothing,' because, after some time, Maria left him. Thus Giuseppe was tricked by the woman. Hearing so far, the narrator for a moment felt pity for Giuseppe. The Sicilian told him that Maria was big with child, and for this the people at first were glad, but later they rumoured that the would-be-born child of Maria would be an Antichrist. However the child was never born.

An old witch prophesied that, after being born, the child "'would always be speaking and laughing and perverting, and last of all would go into the sea and fetch up the Siren into the air, and all the world would see her and hear her sing. As soon as she sang, the seven Vials would be opened and the Pope would die and Mongibello flame, and the veil of Santa Agata would be burned. Then the boy and the Siren would marry, and together they would rule the world, for ever and ever...'" However, people "'decided that Giuseppe and the girl [Maria] must be sent inland until the child was born, and they subscribed the money. The night before they were to start there was a full moon and wind from the east, and all along the coast the sea shot up over the cliffs in silver clouds. It was a wonderful sight, and Maria said she must see it once more.'" Giuseppe warned her not to go to see the beautiful scenario, because the priest and the hotel-keepers would not like her loiter outside. But Maria would not stop going; she said the sea was wonderfully stormy, which she might not chance to feel again. And she went to the sea, alone.

The Sicilian was sitting beside Giuseppe for a long while. Then the door suddenly flew open, and wind and moonlight rushed into the room, and a child's voice laughingly said: "'They have pushed her over the cliffs into the sea.'" The Sicilian wanted to take revenge on them, with his knife, but Giuseppe restrained him by saying that if Maria was dead, there was no point in forcing them to death, but the Sicilian said that he could guess who it was that pushed her to death, and that he was determined to kill the criminal. But Giuseppe briskly applied adequate force to restrain him, so that he (the Sicilian) got fainted, and then Giuseppe went away, never to reappear in his (the Sicilian's) sight.

Hearing the story about Giuseppe, the narrator became disgusted with him. The Sicilian believed that Giuseppe, though he was wicked (and though the wicked would not be able to see the Siren), actually saw the Siren, but that only for once. The narrator asked the Sicilian if Giuseppe was wicked then why he did love him. The Sicilian made no answer, but only laughed, and that he did for the first time. The Sicilian now disclosed that he did never kill the murderer of Maria, who was a priest and who went to America after the murder. Giuseppe, on the other hand, had gone 'all over the world...looking for someone else who had seen the Siren' and at last went to Liverpool (in England), where he died of tuberculosis. The Sicilian told the narrator that seldom had more than a single man or woman seen the Siren, and that never in his lifetime will he see that child (Antichrist) born to a man and a woman—the child who would "'fetch up the Siren from the sea, and destroy silence, and save the world!'" The narrator exclaimed at the words 'save the world.' The Sicilian leaned against the rock and breathed deeply, and put on 'colour.' The narrator heard him say: "'Silence and loneliness cannot last for ever. It may be a hundred or a thousand years, but the sea lasts longer, and she [the Siren] shall come out of it and sing.'" The narrator wanted to know more from the Sicilian, but the cave was getting darker and the boat was returning through the narrow entrance, and so he preferred to foster silence.

This story is unique among Forster's collected stories, in the sense that only in this story has Forster vehemently shown the nullity and acerbity of the perception of transcendental truth and beauty. The sense of nullity of life was a central element in Forster's vision of life—the sense of nullity that Mrs Moore in *A Passage to India* earned in India. The pull or attraction of the transcendental truth and beauty is irresistible, like the sweet melody of the mythological woman-bird Siren, but the pull ultimately destroys its prey. "The Sirens were daughters of the Muse Melpomene and the god Achelous and were also the companions of Persephone. When Persephone was carried off by Hades, they asked the gods if they could have wings so that they could go and look for her. That is why the Sirens were half woman, half bird (...). There were three Sirens: Pisinoe, Aglaope and Thelxiope, also called Parthenope, Leucosia, and Ligia. One held a lyre, the second sang and the third played the flute. Their singing was very harmonious. "They lived on an island, using their voices to enchant sailors to the point of shipwreck. They then devoured them. The Argonauts sailed past that way, but the singing of Orpheus triumphed over that of the Sirens. Ulysses asked his sailors to stop their ears with wax. As for himself, not wanting to miss such a beautiful melody, he had himself tied firmly to ship's mast" (Comte, 190). In 'The Story of the (or a) Siren,' Forster has Leucosia in mind.

However, for a good comprehension and evaluation of this story what John Sayre Martin has to say about it is of great help. Martin says about the story 'The Story of the Siren:' Combining Christian and classic myth, it is a dark tale of spiritual suffering and the only one of Forster's in which a transcendent vision of truth and beauty is more of a curse than a blessing. Giuseppe, who after brutally beating his brother for refusing money from a party of tourists dives for money himself and sees the Siren, is haunted forever by a sense of nullity of human life and action, in the depths of the sea, he finds a potentially fertilizing force, powerless to be reborn.

Returning to land, he finds a spiritual desert. The effect of his experience on him is not unlike Mrs Moore's response to life after her visit to the Marabar Caves. Both suffer from spiritual exhaustion and sense the ultimate futility of human action. 'He would stand in the street looking at people, and the more he looked at them the more unhappy he became. When a child was born he would cover his face with his hands. If any one was married—he was terrible then, and would frighten them as they came out of church. (...)' His marriage to Maria, who has also according to rumour 'gone mad through bathing in the sea,' fails to alleviate his misery. The villagers dislike them, partly at least because they seem bad for the tourist business. When Maria becomes pregnant, she and Giuseppe are to be sent inland, like Mary and Joseph [see the similitude between the pronunciations of the names 'Maria' and 'Mary' and that between the pronunciations of the names 'Joseph' and 'Giuseppe'] before them; for the child, it is feared, will be the Antichrist, who will some day marry the Siren. But Maria is murdered instead, apparently by a priest. Giuseppe, alone and miserable, wanders about the world looking for someone else who has seen the Siren, and finally dies of tuberculosis in Liverpool. 'Never in my life,' asserts his brother, will there be both a man and woman from whom that child can be born, who will fetch up the Siren from the sea, and destroy silence, and save the world!' Eventually, however, the Siren will come up from the sea and sing, for 'silence and loneliness cannot last forever' (...).

To link the story's sensationalism and fantasy to the everyday world, Forster has provided a framework and a narrator. His narrator, an English tourist at Capri, hears it from Giuseppe's brother in the Blue Grotto, where they have been temporarily dropped by the narrator's boating party so that the young Italian might dive into the water and retrieve the narrator's dissertation on the Deist Controversy, which had accidentally fallen overboard. After retrieving the book, the brother proceeds to tell his story. When he has finished, the boating party returns. The narrator, who mediates between the world of the brother's story and the ordinary world, is carefully drawn. Susceptible to beauty and fantasy, he is nevertheless a rationalist who takes for granted the solid, familiar realities of his own world. Confronted with his companion's assertions about the Siren, he is naturally sceptical, a bit facetious, but curious. Whether the bent of his mind is suggested by his interest in deism may be open to question. In any event, his amusingly elaborate description of the dissertation sinking into the blue depths of the Mediterranean and assuming as it sinks all sorts of fantastic shapes, foreshadows his mind's submergence in the heady brew of the brother's story. That he hears the story in the Blue Grotto predisposes him to respond to it, for the Grotto appeals to him as 'a magic world, apart from all the commonplaces that are called reality,' a 'world of blue' where 'only the fantastic would be tolerable' (...). The fantastic turns out to be more than tolerable, it is compelling: before the brother has finished his tale, the narrator has been led implicitly to question the nature of reality, and whether his own familiar world, so seemingly sure in its grasp offset, is so very sure after all. 'The story of Giuseppe,' he remarks, 'for all its absurdity and superstition, came nearer to reality than anything I had known before' (...). Like Coleridge's wedding guest, he becomes, for the time being at least, both sadder and wiser. I don't know why, but it [the story] filled me with desire to help others—the greatest of all our desires, I suppose, and the most fruitless. The desire soon passed. With the return of his companions, he will go back to the everyday world and presumably finish his book on the Deist Controversy, for he seems too shallow to be permanently changed by what he has heard. But the world to which he returns, as the story makes clear, is another 'heaven of the soft,' a desert lacking secure spiritual foundations—an anticipation of Eliot's *The Waste Land*. If the Siren will ever return to sing to it, it will probably be, to cite from *A Passage to India,* "not yet...not there."

"While Forster's device of framing the story of Giuseppe and the Siren and supplying a narrator relates it to the everyday world, it also entails a liability. To hear story from someone who hears it from someone who was himself little more than a passive witness to the crucial events almost inevitably entails a loss of immediacy of impact. As for Giuseppe, he emerges as a well-drawn Italian type, not as a rounded human being. Maria is totally undeveloped. Furthermore, because of the framing, our interest is necessarily shifted from the crucial events and the two characters most concerned with them to the narrator's response to the story. And since the narrator is a peripheral character who never sufficiently engages our sympathies, the story's impact is weakened" (Martin, 64-67).

13

'THE ETERNAL MOMENT'

'The Eternal Moment' was written in 1904, and the story was published in the *Independent* the same year in three installments—in June, July and August. The same year, Forster wrote the short story 'Cnidus', and at the end of that year was expecting advance copies of *Where Angels Fear to Tread* (published in 1905). 1904 was really a very productive year for Forster. There is a striking similitude between 'The Eternal Moment' and *Where Angels Fear to Tread:* in both an English tourist does a *mesalliance* with an Italian. The central character of 'The Eternal Moment,' Miss Raby, reappears in *Where Angels Fear to Tread* as Caroline Abbott, and both the ladies are "sexually frustrated yet redeemed through the power of love" (Beauman, 139). 'The Eternal Moment,' the longest of all Forster's short stories, was published in 1928 in his second collection of short stories, as the title story. It is a short story of course, but it may be deemed to be a novella, (*op. cit.*, 138). The story was set in Cortina ('Vorta'), Italy. It was an obsessive intention of Forster to bring some so-called civilized English people into the so-called uncivilized milieu, preferably in some Mediterranean country, and expose the superficial and hypocratic 'civilization' of the English people, which 'civilization' he could never absorb or emulate. Such a refractory aspect of Forster is revealed in 'The Eternal Moment.' 'The Eternal Moment' and 'The Story of a Panic' are perhaps Forster's two best and the most representative short stories.

'The Eternal Moment' is a story of 'self-delusion and subsequent self-knowledge.' Miss Raby, an 'eccentric' lady of advanced age with grey hair on her head, her ward-like young lady Elizabeth, and an elderly retired army personnel Colonel Leyland have come to Vorta on a tourist enterprise. Miss Raby told Colonel Leyland that some twenty years ago a young man fell in love with her on the not-so-distant mountain, and that the incident was very gratifying to her to remember. The young man was a porter or concierge who was hired by her to carry luggage. The young porter carried luggage after Miss Raby for half a mile over the mountainous region, and then she scrambled and fell and sprained her ankle. Miss Raby had previously hired the same porter on another expedition over the same region. At that time Mrs Harbottle had warned Miss Raby about that porter well ahead of her former expedition. But neither in the former nor in the latter (or present) expedition did the porter insult Miss Raby (She only wistfully thought of being 'insulted,' or amorously approached by that porter). And so she thanked him. She told Leyland that the porter had been handsome and agreeable, and that he had worn beautiful clothes. In that (previous) expeditious tour, she had 'encouraged' the porter, and had 'greatly preferred him to Mrs Harbottle'—Mrs Harbottle having been one of Miss Raby's tourist party. Perhaps as a consequence of all this, the porter had picked flowers for Miss Raby and had extended the flowers towards her and she had held out her hand to receive the spray of flowers, but the porter had seized her hand and had 'delivered a love oration which he had prepared out of *I Promessi Sposi*.' Meantime, the carriage, in which Miss Raby, Elizabeth and Colonel Leyland were travelling, was crossing the frontier over the 'notorious mountain.' Miss Raby concluded the description of her (imaginary) incident or episode with the porter, saying that she would like to be made a fool by that porter instead of taking him to be a fool.

Leyland now suddenly changed the subject of the conversation, putting in that German was the coming language, because all important books were written in German. But Miss Raby contradicted him, saying that all important books were written in Italian. Elizabeth, who like her mistress Miss Raby was a novelist, did not participate in the debate. Miss Raby had become famous with her novel 'The Eternal Moment.' There was a mention of the place known as Vorta in the novel, and as a result of the mention the place became a tourist spot. The carriage of the tourist party, that include Miss Raby, Elizabeth and Leyland, now proceeded towards Vorta, where they had planned to stop at Grand Hotel des Alpes. Leyland now introduced a new topic of conversation—'human relations.' He said that throughout his life he was never interested in 'human relations,' but only in commanding other men. Miss Raby told him that he should not take the whole world to be an army. She further told him that kindness and money one could easily part with, and that the only one thing that was the most precious in the whole world was giving oneself away to someone else. She then asked him if he had ever given himself away to another person, that is, if he had ever made himself a fool before his inferior. Leyland told her that he did that frequently, but never intentionally. He of course understood what she was driving him at. 'It was her pleasure to pretend that such self-exposure was the only possible basis of true intercourse, the only gate in the spiritual barrier that divided class from class. One of her books had dealt with the subject; and very agreeable reading it made.'

The driver of their carriage suddenly announced that they had reached 'the top of the hill' at Vorta. 'The black woods ceased; and they emerged into a valley whose sides were emerald lawns, rippling and doubling and merging each into each, yet always with an upward trend, so that it was 2000 feet to where the rock burst out of the grass and made great mountains, whose pinnacles were delicate in the purity of evening.' 'Far up the valley was a large white village, tossing on undulating meadows like a ship in the sea, and at its prow, breasting a sharp incline, stood a majestic tower of new grey stone. As they looked at the tower it became vocal and spoke magnificently to the mountains, who replied.' The place was a village called Vorta. Colonel Leyland and Miss Raby approached the beautiful place, while other tourists took them to be 'a well-matched couple.' 'They did very well for a cultured and refined husband and wife, who had spent their lives admiring the beautiful things with which the world is filled.' As they advanced further, they met with a number of divers churches, bells from each of which were heard; and then they proceeded even further, leaving the churches behind, and they heard dressing-gongs. At last Grand Hotel des Alpes, their destination, showed itself before their view. Miss Raby immediately felt disgusted at the sight of the hotel and the behaviour of its people.

'The Grand Hotel des Alpes was an enormous building, which being made of wood, suggested a distended chalet. But this impression was corrected by a costly and magnificent view-terrace, the squared stones of which were visible for miles, and from which, as from some great reservoir, asphalt paths trickled over the adjacent country.' The carriage, that carried Miss Raby, Elizabeth and Leyland, ultimately drew up under the vaulted portico of the hotel. Inside the hotel they saw 'a whirl of officials—men with gold braid, smarter men with more gold braid, men smarter still with no gold braid.' Immediately after reaching the hotel, Elizabeth 'assumed an arrogant air,' Colonel Leyland 'became every inch a soldier', and Miss Raby only flew to occupy an expensive bedroom. Miss Raby then saw the dining room filled with English French and German people. 'She liked company, but to-night she was curiously depressed. She seemed to be confronted with an unpleasing vision, the outlines of which were still obscure.' In the plushy hotel that Grand Hotel des Alpes was Miss Raby could not think of people like Signor Cantu 'with his china-bowled pipe' and Signora Cantu 'with her snuff-coloured shawl.' When the waiter brought her diner to her room, Miss Raby asked after her host and hostess, and when they arrived, she came to know from them that only poor people went to the hotel named *Biscione,* and that Signora Cantu lived there. Miss Raby immediately announced her intention to leave her present posh hotel, Grand Hotel des Alpes, and go to the other hotel, *Biscione,* which was rather nondescript.

Miss Raby, with her huge luggage, ran to the door to leave for *Biscione*. Colonel Leyland perplexedly ran after her and asked if she was not comfortable there. She said that *Grand Hotel des Alpes* belonged to the son (Signer Cantu) and so she would not stay there and must move to *Biscione* (which belonged to the mother, Signora Cantu). Leyland did everything to persuade her not to leave *Grand Hotel,* but she would not be dissuaded from leaving. She said: "'I am too old to be a tragedy queen as well as an evil genius.'" After she went away, Leyland received a letter from his sister Nelly. Addressing Leyland as Edwin in the letter, Nelly asked her brother Leyland if he had really been engaged with Miss Raby. In feet, Nelly would not like Miss Raby as the wife to Leyland, because, she thought, "'Literary people are always unpractical....'" But Leyland only could not resist 'the peculiar charm of the relations between himself and Miss Raby.' The relation between them was really extraordinary: 'There had never been a word of marriage, and would probably never be a word of love. If, instead of seeing each other frequently, they should come to see each other always it would be as sage companions, familiar with life, not as egoistic lovers, craving for infinities of passion which they had no right to demand and no power to supply. Neither professed to be a virgin soul, or to be ignorant of the other's limitations and inconsistencies. They scarcely even made allowances for each other.' 'Colonel Leyland had courage of no mean order: he cared little for the opinion of people whom he understood...Miss Raby was an authoress, a kind of Radical; he a soldier, a kind of aristocrat. But the time of their activities was passing; he was ceasing to fight, she to write.'

Leyland tore off Nelly's letter, and was thinking of Miss Raby. He was ofcourse desirous of marrying her, who earned two thousand pounds a year, but he would not admit of his own desire even to himself. However, Leyland was now thinking about Miss Raby, who had already gone to *Biscione*. Miss Raby always tried to 'put right what never was right', only causing unhappiness to herself. Leyland was sorry for her, because people would not understand her. He was musing on the torn fragments of his sister Nelly's letter. Presently, in the valley the campanile appeared, rising out of wisps of silvery vapour.' Leyland whispered to himself 'Dear lady!', and then made 'towards the village [i.e. the village of Vorta, where Miss Raby stopped] a little movement with his hands' (section 1).

The setting of Miss Raby's first and ambitious novel 'The Eternal Moment' was the village Vorta. The novel was 'written round the idea that man does not live by time alone, that an evening gone may become like a thousand ages in the courts of heaven—the idea was afterwards expounded more philosophically by Maeterlinck.' But later on she was not happy with her novel: she called it tiresome and affected. But 'By a strange fate, the book made a great sensation, especially in unimaginative circles. Idle people interpreted it to mean that there was no harm in wasting time, vulgar people that there was no harm in being fickle, pious people interpreted it as an attack upon morality. The authoress became well known in society, where her enthusiasm for the lower classes only lent her an additional charm.' Vorta, the village where Miss Raby now put up, due to its being mentioned in her novel 'The Eternal Moment,' became a famous tourist spot. The novel was based on Miss Raby's previous expeditious tour over Vorta along with Leyland and Elizabeth.

Her present adventure to the village of Vorta made Miss Raby saddened. She detested the posh ambience of the Grand Hotel des Alpes. 'She was not enthusiastic over the progress of civilization, knowing by Eastern experiences that civilization rarely puts her best foot foremost, and is apt to make the barbarians immoral and vicious before her compensating qualities arrive. And here there was no question of progress: the world had more to learn from the village than the village from the world.' The Grand Hotel des Alpes was the symbol of aristocracy. Miss Raby disgustedly recalled her visits to dukes in that hotel, in the previous occasion. She recalled that 'Through this cleanly, gracious dwelling there had once moved Signor Cantu with his china-bowled pipe, Signora

Cantu in her snuff-coloured shawl, and Bartolommeo Cantu, now proprietor of the Grand Hotel des Alpes.'

Next morning Miss Raby sat, in a bad mood, in the hotel *Biscione,* 'opposite the famous fresco, which formed the only decoration of the room,' for her breakfast. The working men and women of the hotel were bent on showing their readiness to please the English tourists, who delighted in frightening the natives. Miss Raby liked coming here herself, she said; but she hardly liked to recommend it to her friends: it was the kind of hotel one felt like that about. Males were rare, and in great demand. A youngster was describing, amid fits of laughter, the steps he had taken to astonish the natives. 'The fresco, opposite which Miss Raby sat, consisted of four figures of sibyls holding prophecies of the Nativity.' An American lady told Miss Raby that the four sibyls seemed cunning. The lady's father made some derogatory remarks about the sibyls, perhaps because the lady and her father had been cheated in the Holy Land where they had recently gone. Miss Raby only said that the saints were sibyls. And to this remark of Miss Raby, the father sadly added his own remark that priests were invented to deceive the peasantry. The lady complained that her father, who had been suffering from insomnia, was being disturbed by the six-o-clock bell from the church. On the other hand, English and American tourists felt disturbed by the behaviour of the peasants (of Vorta). About the peasants they complained: 'Every week they got drunk and sang till two.' Miss Raby left the place, expressing her opinion that 'a new universal religion of the open air' was necessary. The father (of the lady) remained there, and now 'Over his head stood the four sibyls, gracious for all their clumsiness and crudity, each proffering a tablet inscribed with concise promise of redemption.' Miss Raby was perching in the evening on the wooden balustrade, where people of low classes used to eat. This seemed awkward to the German waitress, who came and civilly asked her to go into the drawing-room of the hotel. Miss Raby strongly refused to leave the place and indignantly asked the waitress: "'for how many years have you classified your guests according to their birth?'" Next came a grey-haired lady 'shading her eyes from the sun, and crackling *The Morning Post.*' She 'blew her nose', apologized for speaking, and then said to Miss Raby mat that evening "'there is a concert in aid of stained-glass windows for the English Church. May I persuade you to take tickets? As has been said, it is so important that English people should have a rallying point, is it not?'" Miss Raby told her "'but I wish the rallying point could be in England.'" The ticket-selling lady felt humiliated, and departed.

After the departure of the ticket-selling lady, Miss Raby felt sorry for behaving rudely with her. Miss Raby's life 'had been successful, and on the whole happy. She was accustomed to that mood, which is termed depressed, but which certainty gives visions of wider, if greyer, horizons.' 'That morning her outlook altered. She walked through the village, scarcely noticing the mountains by which it was still surrounded or the altered radiance of its sun. But she was fully conscious of something new; of the indefinable corruption which is produced by the passage of a large number of people.' The village of Vorta was surrounded by hills, but it was a bad season for climbing. The village was once always 'full of virility and power', and was happy with its hard-working people. It had dignity, kindliness and love. 'Civilization did not relax these energies, but it had diverted them; and all the precious qualities, which might have helped to heal the world, had been destroyed. The family affection, the affection for the commune, the sane pastoral virtues—all had perished while the campanile which was to embody them was being built. No villain had done this thing; it was the work of ladies and gentlemen who were good and rich and often clever—who, if they thought about the matter at all, thought that they were conferring a benefit, moral as well as commercial, on any place in which they chose to stop.' Miss Raby was thinking about all these—about such a 'universal misdoing'—while walking across the village, and then returned, shattered and exhausted.

Returning to the hotel *Biscione,* Miss Raby was in conversation with Signora Cantu. 'The two women had little in common; for Signora Cantu was an inflexible aristocrat.'

Signora Cantu said that she believed in fate. She then began to describe her own misfortunes, beginning with a landslip which destroyed her farm. But Miss Raby could not show sympathy to her. Nevertheless, from the misfortune due to the landslip, Signora Cantu went to her other grievances. She said that servants of her hotel did not understand the guests, and the guests did not understand the servants. She was therefore advised to employ a concierge. But, thought she, concierges were there in all hotels; so what was the good of keeping a concierge? At last the Signora came to the point of Grand Hotel des Alpes which her son owned. She said that her son persuaded guests to avoid her hotel and to go to his, with all tricks and slanders. Miss Raby requested her not to be so angry with her son, and to remember all her complaints against her son in her orisons. On the suggestion of orison, Signora Cantu suddenly became aware that she was a Christian (and so she should have forgiveness), and yet she cursed her son's hotel. But Miss Raby showed her catholicity and said that 'there is not much wickedness in the world. Most of the evil we see is the result of little faults—of stupidity or vanity.'

Their conversation was 'interrupted by an uproar in the street. Miss Raby opened the window; and a cloud of dust, heavy with petrol, entered. A passing motor-car had twitched over a table. Much beer had been spilt, and a little blood.' Signora Cantu exhausted her ill temper, and remained motionless. Miss Raby had it in her mind to touchingly and dramatically persuade Signora Cantu to forgive those who were responsible for the untoward incident that occurred outside, but the staid frame and closed eyes of Signora Cantu prevented her. She felt that her life ended in her conversation with Signora Cantu. Now, 'Before her eyes there arose the pleasant face of Colonel Leyland, with whom she might harmlessly conclude her days. He would not be stimulating, but it did not seem desirable that she should be stimulated.... For the first time in her life, she was tempted to become old.' Signora Cantu did not actually cease to narrate the list of allegations against her son; after a while she again continued her cant. She spoke about her son's wife's vulgarity and her son's concierge's ingratitude. Signora Cantu told her that the concierge, Feo Ginori, once came to her as an obscure boy, and used to carry luggage, and that it was due to her charity that he had a rather comfortable position. 'Now he had sided against her. Such was the reward of charity.' At this moment from a distant campanile 'a flood of sound' entered into the room and shook the copper vessels. The heavy sound compelled Miss Raby to lift her hands and close her eyes with them. 'In her enfeebled state, the throbbing note of the bell had the curious effect of blood returning into frozen veins' "'I remember that man perfectly', she said at last: 'and I shall see him this afternoon'" (section 2).

Miss Raby and Elizabeth came to Grand Hotel des Alpes to see Colonel Leyland, and were waiting in the lounge for him. But Leyland had gone to *Biscione* to meet them, which they did not know. In the lounge Miss Raby was killing time on tea, and Elizabeth on ice. From the lounge Miss Raby could see the great precipices in the distance, and beyond them Italy. The evening sun magically transfigured everything. Miss Raby persuaded Elizabeth to find a friend for herself and go out with that friend (to enjoy the evening). She asked Elizabeth to tell Leyland, should she met him, that she (Miss Raby) was waiting there. Elizabeth noticed that Miss Raby did not look well: 'Possibly the course of love was running roughly.' Those who occupied the lounge slowly moved out, leaving behind only Miss Raby, the Russian Prince, and the concierge (Feo Ginori). It seemed that the concierge had once been muscular, but his face was hard to read. He was busy dusting, tidying, and doing all such 'unquestioning' things. He picked up Miss Raby's handkerchief with a genteel bow, pronouncing 'Excuse me, madam!', and returned the handkerchief to her. 'The gesture with which he returned the handkerchief troubled her with vague memories.'

The concierge was talking to a guide about his percentage. Miss Raby enquired about the percentage 'with the definite intention of disconcerting him [the concierge], not because she was unkind but because she wished to discover what qualities, if any, lurked beneath that civil, efficient exterior [of his]. And the spirit of her enquiry was sentimental rather than scientific.' The concierge was uncouth, devoid of logic. To Miss Raby's question "'And what is the percentage?'", he illogically replied: "'Yes, madam! this is perfect weather, both for our visitors and for the hay'." 'This was the man [the concierge] who had talked of love to her [Miss Raby] upon the mountains. But hitherto he had only revealed his identity by chance gestures bequeathed to him at birth. Intercourse with gentle classes had required new qualities—civility, omniscience, imperturbability. It was the old answer: the gentle classes were responsible for him. It is inevitable, as well as desirable, that we should bear each other's burdens.' That concierge was Feo—Feo Ginori.

'It was absurd to blame Feo for his worldliness—for his essential vulgarity. He had not made himself. It was even absurd to regret his transformation from an athlete: his greasy stoutness, his big black kiss-curl, his waxed moustache, his chin which was dividing and propagating itself tike some primitive form of life. In England, nearly twenty years before, she had altered his figure as well as his character. He was one of the products of 'The Eternal Moment.' 'Miss Raby felt sympathetic towards Feo Ginori whom she had altered: 'A great tenderness overcame her—the sadness of an unskilful demiurge, who makes a world and beholds that it is bad. She desired to ask pardon of her creatures, even though they were too poorly formed to grant it. The longing to confess, which she had suppressed that morning beside the bed of Signora Cantu, broke out again with the violence of a physical desire. When the bishop had gone she renewed the conversation, though on different lines, saying: "'Yes, it is beautiful weather. I have just been enjoying a walk up from the *Biscione*. I am stopping there!'"

Feo understood that Miss Raby was eager to go on conversing with him. He told her that when he was a mere lad, Vorta was a poor but pleasant place. Miss Raby now felt the impulse of disclosing the secret to him that they had, in the past, met with each other. 'All day she had sought for a spark of life, and it might be summoned by pointing to that other fire which she discerned, far back in the travelled distance, high up in the mountains of youth. What he would do, if he also discerned it, she did not know; but she hoped that he would become alive, that he at all events would escape the general doom which she had prepared for the place and the people. And what she would do, during their joint contemplation, she did not even consider. 'She would hardly have ventured if the sufferings of the day had not hardened her. After much pain, respectability becomes ludicrous. And she had only to overcome the difficulty of Feo's being a man, not the difficulty of his being a concierge. She had never observed that spiritual reticence towards social inferiors which is usual at the present day.'

Miss Raby boldly told Feo that it was her second visit to *Biscione,* that she first came to *Biscione* twenty years ago. Feo showed signs of emotion and annoyance. Miss Raby told him that she was told that she would find him there in *Biscione* (and that was why she went there), and that she remembered him well, and also that he used to take her and others over the passes. Hearing this, Feo took off his peaked hat and exclaimed: "'I remember you perfectly, madam. What a pleasure, if I may say so, to meet you again!'" Feo also recalled the memory of Mrs Harbottle. Miss Raby looked up at him. 'He was standing near an open window, and the whole of fairyland stretched behind him.' Her sanity forsook her, and she said gently: "'Will you misunderstand me, if I say that I have never forgotten your kindness either?'" Feo replied: "'The kindness was yours, madam; I only did my duty.'" Miss Raby exclaimed: "'Duty?'" She could not understand how what he did could be duty. Feo explained: "'You and Mrs Harbottle were such generous ladies. I well remember how grateful I was: you always paid me above the tariff fare—'". But Miss Raby promptly realised that Feo actually remembered nothing. She told him that he had never been polite, as now he was. She showed him the mountain at a distance and the flower-decked road over it, and then told him: "'...It was there [on the road] that you once gave yourself away.'" Feo was nonplussed, gasped, trepidated. It was at that moment that Colonel Leyland returned.

Miss Raby coloured at the sight of Leyland, but introduced Feo to him, saying: "'The man who fell in love with me when I was young.'" Feo, in fear, protested, saying it was false. He told Leyland: "'I shall lose my place, sir, and I have a wife and children. I shall be ruined.'" Leyland assured him that Miss Raby would in no case ruin him. Miss Raby apologetically asked him not to misunderstand her. Then Leyland told Miss Raby that they both were unlucky, missing each other. He asked her if she would walk a little distance before diner. Miss Raby did not attend to his proposal, but was intently watching Feo whose 'alarm had subsided; and he revealed a new emotion, even less agreeable to her. His shoulders straightened, he developed an irresistible smile, and, when he saw that she was looking and that Colonel Leyland was not, he winked at her.'

'It was a ghastly sight, perhaps the most hopelessly depressing of all the things she had seen at Vorta. But its effect on her was memorable, it evoked a complete vision of that same mass as he had been twenty years before. She could see him to the smallest detail of his clothes or his hair, the flowers in his hand, the graze on his wrist, the heavy bundle that he had loosed from his back, so that he might speak as a freeman. She could hear his voice, neither insolent nor diffident, never threatening, never apologizing, urging her first in the studied phrases he had learnt from books, then, as his passion grew, becoming incoherent, crying that she must believe him, that she must love him in return, that she must fly with him to Italy, where they would live for ever, always happy, always young. She had cried out then, as a young lady should, and had thanked him not to insult her. And now, in her middle age, she cried out again, because the sudden shock and the contrast had worked a revelation. "Don't think I'm in love with you now!" she cried.

'For she realized that only now was she not in love with him: that the incident upon the mountain had been one of the great moments of her life—perhaps the greatest, certainly the most enduring: that she had drawn unacknowledged power and inspiration from it, just as trees draw vigour from a subterranean spring. Never again could she think of it as a half-humorous episode in her development. There was more reality in it than in all the years of success and varied achievement which had followed, and which it had rendered possible. For all her correct behaviour and lady-like display, she had been in love with Feo, and she had never loved so greatly again. A presumptuous boy had taken her to the gates of heaven; and, though she would not enter with him, the eternal remembrance of the vision had made life seem endurable and good.'

Leyland was only noticing the loss of respectability and growth of foolishness on the part of Miss Raby before the lowly Feo. He was frightened by the last sentence of Miss Raby to Feo: "'Don't think I'm in love with you now!'" She obviously babbled: "'I never knew till now that I had loved him and that it was a mere chance—a little catch, a kink—that I never told him so.'" 'She was still detached, looking back at a fire upon the mountains, marvelling at its increased radiance, but too far off to feel its heat. She told Feo that if she could confess her love for him to someone and if he could understand her, she could be happier. Feo greatly wondered and Leyland felt unbearably irritated. She told Feo that she, ultimately, decided to confess before him her love for him, expecting that he would understand her. She reminded him that once he was gracious—"'yes gracious: there is no other word'"—to her. But as she had done harm to him, could he understand her? Feo told her that he understood her perfectly, and that she did not harm him; she rather benefited him. After her book (on Vorta: 'The Eternal Moment') was published, tourists began to come there in flocks, and consequently Vorta benefited, everyone of Vorta benefited, he benefited. Now he could sustain his wife and three sons.

Learning that Feo had three sons, Miss Raby urged upon him to give her the youngest son who was five years old. She was persuading him thus: "'...I will bring him up. He shall live among rich people. He shall see that they are not the vile creatures he supposes, always clamouring for respect and deference and trying to buy them with money. Rich people are good: they are capable of sympathy and love: they are fond of the truth; and when they are with each other they are clever. Your boy shall learn this, and he shall try to teach it to you. And when he grows up, if God is good to him he shall teach the rich: he shall teach them not to be stupid to the poor. I have tried myself, and people buy my books and say that they are good, and smile and lay them down. But I know this: so long as the stupidity exists, not only our charities and missions and schools, but the whole of our civilization, are vain.'"

Miss Raby's words were nauseating to Leyland, but she continued her prayer to Feo importunately, resistlessly. She requested him to give her a son of his, because she had been tired of recalling the sweet memories of her affair with him (Feo). She wanted a son, a 'living boy', as a vignette or memento of her affair with him. And after so much so, she desperately asked Feo whether that day (on which she had an affair with him) he truly told her that he had loved her. Feo did not answer, nor did he try to, he only 'saw again that he was menaced by an ugly, withered, elderly woman, who was trying to destroy his reputation and his domestic peace.' In a faultering and submissive manner he told her that his wife would not allow his son to be given to her. At this stage Leyland thought that Miss Raby was being insulted (by Feo), and so shouted and 'made a chivalrous movement of attack'. But Miss Raby told Leyland about Feo: "'He will never think me respectable.'" Saying this, she looked 'at the dishevelled Feo, fat, perspiring, and unattractive, and smiled sadly at her own stupidity, not at his.' Feo was, as if, reduced to a frightened rabbit.

Miss Raby now looked at Leyland, and apologised to him for 'vexing' him so long by taking no notice of him. Leyland was well born and well educated, and thought that he had insight and knowledge and culture. But at this crucial moment he thought himself equivalent to Feo: 'he had proved himself to be at the exact spiritual level of the man [Feo] who had no advantages, who was poor and had been made vulgar, whose early virtue had been destroyed by circumstance, whose manliness and simplicity had perished in serving the rich.' If

Colonel Leyland also believed that she [Miss Raby] was now in love with Feo, she would not exert himself to undeceive him. Nor indeed would she have found it possible.'

At this moment the 'first strong singing note' came from the campanile, and the note was reverberated by the mountains. Feo said that a certain gentleman believed that the land under that campanile would slip and that campanile would fall down as a consequence thereof. Miss Raby now took up her *Baedeker* [a guide-book for tourists] and went away 'with no tragic gesture. 'In that moment of final failure, there had been vouchsafed to her a vision of herself, and she saw that she had lived worthily. She was conscious of a triumph over experience and earthly facts, a triumph magnificent, cold, hardly human, whose existence no one but herself would ever surmise.' To Miss Raby, it seemed that the valley, near where she had been enduring, receded, and was existing in a distant star. She said to herself: "'I suppose this is old age.'" When she was moving away, nobody called her from behind. Leyland would not call her for she had hurt him much: she had discovered the 'nakedness' of the people of his class to Feo, who was an alien.

Dinner and concert were being readied in the hotel. People were busy dressing themselves. A stream of servants was in hot pursuits, it was impossible to pretend that nothing had happened. The scandal would be immense, and must be diminished as it best might.' Leyland took Feo by the arm, 'and then quickly raised his finger to his forehead.' "'Exactly, sir,'" whispered the concierge [Feo]. "'Of course we understand—Oh, thank you, sir, thank you very much: thank you very much indeed!'"

'The Eternal Moment' is the best among the six stories in the collection of short stories entitled *The Eternal Moment,* and is one of the two or three best stories of Forster. In his Introduction to the 1947 publication of his collected short stories, Forster wrote: "The Eternal Moment, though almost an honest-to-God yarn, is a meditation on Cortina d' Ampezzo." Forster actually first visited Cortina (the Vorta of the story) about a year before he wrote this short story. The planning of the story was done when he was in Cortina for the second time, and the execution of the plan was done after his returning to England from Cortina. Nicola Beauman writes: "Returning a year after the previous visit gave an extra impetus to the story: he imagined what it would have been like if a novelist had published a book based upon Cortina and then returned to view the book's effect upon its real-life setting. He wondered, too, whether and how an incipient romance might have been affected by the novelist's departure, fame and return; and he used as a heroine a Miss Lavish figure whom he had already used in 'Old Lucy' and who was to reappear the following winter of 1903-4 in 'New Lucy'; she would be finally perfected in *A Room with a View*" (Beauman, 138).

'The Eternal Moment' has a two-fold theme: 'self-delusion and subsequent self-knowledge' and 'artist's responsibility.' Nicola Beauman writes: "Miss Raby in 'The Eternal Moment' has come back to Cortina ('Vorta') after twenty years and tells her companions that an Italian porter had fallen in love with her during a mountain expedition. Of course he had not, and one of the themes of the story is Miss Raby's self-delusion and subsequent self-knowledge. The other theme is the exploitation of Vorta consequent on her book and, by corollary, the artist's responsibility. Miss Raby had not only been the cause of the large pompous hotels and fashionable pursuits and the changes in the village, she had exploited her Italian by putting him in her book. Here was Morgan (Forster) discussing, in fictional form, ...the aesthetic impulse and his justification for submitting to it...he was exploring the moral dilemma inherent in 'using' the places and people he saw around him; he realised that if he continued as he had began he was in danger of exploiting them as unscrupulously as Miss Raby" (*op. cit.*, 139). Nicola Beauman is of the opinion that 'The Eternal Moment' is a document of Forster's absolute belief in the immense power of love. Beauman writes: "Having reminded the now-concierge of her declaration two decades before, and after receiving his inexpressibly coarse wink, Miss Raby has a revelation. It is Morgan's [Forster's] first expression of the belief, with which his work was to be through and through imbued, in the vast and enduring power of love" *(ibid.)*. Beauman is quite right, because Miss Raby realised that "'the incident upon the mountain had been one of the great moments of her life—perhaps the greatest, certainly the most enduring: that she had drawn unacknowledged power and inspiration from it.... A presumptuous boy had taken her to the gates of heaven; and, though she would not enter with him, the eternal remembrance of the vision had made life seem endurable and good'" *(ibid.)*.

John Sayre Martin's explication of the story 'The Eternal Moment' and his comments on it, in his book *E.M. Forster: The Endless Journey,* may here be quoted wholly for understanding the story better. Martin writes: 'The Eternal Moment', although a comparatively early tale, is one of Forster's most richly satisfying. Miss Raby, who in her middle age returns to the village near which she had once experienced on 'eternal moment', is a convincing combination of honesty, self-deceptiveness, naivety, warmth and detachment. She has mind and heart, she has the gift of friendship, and yet she is also, one feels, essentially solitary. Twenty years ago, when she was a girl, she had visited Vorta, near the Italian-Austrian border, and one day, while on a walk, had been amorously accosted by the young porter assigned to carry her things. Alarmed but not really displeased, she had repelled him, and only much later realized that the situation had constituted her 'eternal moment.' She had based a novel on it; the novel had put Vorta, then unspoiled, on the map—and spoiled it. Tourists came in, big hotels went up, commerce thrived. Now, accompanied by her friend Colonel Leyland and her maid, she returns to see how the place has changed.

Two changes are especially significant. The Albergo Biscione where she had stayed, and to which she returns, has been superseded in public favour by grander and more commercial establishments, in particular by the Grand Hotel des Alpes, which is owned by the son of Signora Cantu, who owns the Biscione. The second and more significant change is in the handsome young porter who had tried to make love to her. He is now the stout, greasy, and middle-aged concierge of the Grand Hotel des Alpes.

A well-intentioned, democratic woman, Miss Raby has thus managed, as she realizes, to cause grave social harm. To make partial restitution for the damage and assuage her conscience, she approaches Feo Ginori, the concierge, in order to recall him, if possible, to their eternal moment. The eternal moment for her was life: 'she had drawn unacknowledged power and inspiration from it, just as trees graw vigour from a subterranean spring' (...). Vorta, on the other hand, spells death. The hordes of tourists, the shopkeepers, the big hotels, have all but crushed the essential life of the place; and Feo, with his oily servility and professional smoothness, is the primary embodiment of the new Vorta, a kind of life-in-death. If, as Miss Raby feels, she can recall him to their supreme moment, she can save him. And she can also save herself, for she stands at the brink of old age and spiritual death. Her inspection of Vorta and her meeting with Signora Cantu, the refined owner of the now shabby Biscione, have made her feel that her life has been misspent, and that all that remains to her is to 'fold her hands and to wait, till her ugliness and her incompetence went the way of beauty and strength.' (...) But upon learning from the Signora that the concierge of the Grand Hotel des Alpes is the very man who tried to make love to her on the mountainside, she suddenly revives, determined to see him that very afternoon.

Her sense of responsibility for Vorta and Feo is of course misguided. It is as absurd for her to blame herself for their 'destruction' as for the assassin of the Archduke Ferdinand to blame himself for the First World War and its aftermath. Feo, in any case, as the ensuing interview comically reveals, has not the slightest wish to be 'saved' by Miss Raby or anyone else. And Miss Raby is, to say the least, presumptions in trying to use Feo in order to mitigate her exaggerated sense of guilt.

The story comes to a head in a superb blend of comedy and pathos on the balcony of the Grand Hotel, with Miss Raby trying to confront Feo with the facts of their common past. At first he remembers nothing, for this particular past is buried deep in his subconscious, just as the town's agrarian past is buried beneath its later-day commercialism. When at last, through Miss Raby's persistent prompting, he does recall their meeting, it is with horror. What, he wonders, can be her motive in reminding him of it? Is she trying to ruin him professionally? Or is she—heaven forbid—in love with him? This last possibility flatters his vanity, but not enough to dispel his fear. She wants to save his soul, but he only wants to save his face. To Colonel Leyland who appears in the course of the scene, it looks, as it does to Feo, as if a frustrated spinster is trying to stoke a dead furnace. To the hotel guests lucky enough to overhear, however imperfectly, the colloquy, it looks as if 'an Englishman had surprised his wife making love to the concierge.' As for Miss Raby, she is guilty of the very stupidity she deplores. If she cannot redeem Feo, perhaps at least, she suggests, he would let her adopt his youngest child.... Such a combination of self-seeking and self-deception is worthy of Mrs Herriton or Herbert Pembroke, two of the prime goats in Forster's fiction; but that a woman as fundamentally frank and generous as Miss Raby should be guilty of it is the story's crowning irony.

Finally, realizing the hopelessness of her effort, she desists. Feo is too much the official to be brought back to 'life', and Colonel Leyland too much the fool to see the truth. 'If Colonel Leyland also believed that she was now in love with Feo, she would not exert herself to undeceive him' (...). Accordingly, she withdraws from the pair of them, leaving them, spiritually akin for all their difference in class, to contemplate her behaviour and scandal that will certainly ensue.

"But despite her failure to 'save' Feo, Miss Raby feels—and Forster apparently would have us believe—that she has at least 'lived worthily.' She has transformed her experience into art and thereby, in a sense, triumphed over it. She has also tried, whatever the results, to live honestly. She has 'given herself away'—intentionally risked making a fool of herself—in order to break down the barriers that divide class from class and restore a fellow human being to 'life.' It is a final irony that her very failure holds a qualified success: Leyland and Feo, divided though they are by class, feel a kinship. 'Much as

Colonel Leyland disliked touching people he took Feo by the arm, and then quickly raised his finger to his forehead. 'Exactly, sir,' whispered the concierge. 'Of course we understand—Oh, thank you, sir, thank you very much: thank you very much indeed!'"

The story's effectiveness does not depend on Miss Raby alone. Colonel Leyland and Feo, both of whom might have stepped from a nineteenth-century farce, comparatively simple, but well drawn. The Colonel, stiff, class-conscious, morally unimaginative, and not unmindful of Miss Raby's wealth ('it lent an unacknowledged perfume to his thoughts') is humanized by his affection for her.... Feo is the essence of the deferential petty official. With a sharp eye for the revealing gesture, Forster sets him before us.... A flat character incapable of surprising us, Feo is comic in his rigidity, in his wholesale commitment to his role.

Another important factor in the story's success is Vorta itself. Once an agricultural village 'full of virility and power,' it has become a miniature megalopolis destructive to human relationships. Its anomalous mixture of teutonic and latin culture, its hordes of tourists, its dedication to commerce and money, its vulgarity and pretentiousness, epitomise all that Forster dislikes about urban life. Only the new campanile in Vorta is beautiful. A symbolic reminder of the past and of transcendent aspiration, it nevertheless shares in the rootlessness of the town; for it has been built, as Feo points out, on a landslip, and will eventually fall.

"What, finally, makes 'The Eternal Moment' superior to most of Forster's other stories is its moral and psychological complexity. Unlike some of the stories, it implies no pat moral judgements. It does not suggest that eternal moments are inevitably good, or that Miss Raby as a girl should have followed her instincts and run off with the porter, or that, returning to Vorta in her middle-age, she should have left well alone. Rather, it shows how intertwined in this world of ours good and evil can be. Miss Raby's moment, life-giving to her (because she did not follow her instinct), spells spiritual death to the town and the man she loved. And the town's present condition and the man's were promoted by 'ladies and gentlemen who were good and rich and often clever—who, if they thought about the matter at all, thought that they were conferring a benefit, moral as well as commercial, on any place in which they chose to stop' (...). Miss Raby's attempt to undo some of the damage she has inadvertently helped to create only embarrasses Feo and the Colonel and leads to her social and psychological isolation. If there is, then, a moral, it is, as Lionel Trilling pointed out in connection with Forster's fiction as a whole, that any attempt to live morally is full of pitfalls. But Forster's primary concern is not moral judgment but psychological exploration. To this end, he has eschewed the use of mythology—of pans, fauns, sirens, magic seashells and haunted copses—for such devices inevitably emphasize wonder and mystery at the expense of the psychological. Instead he reveals the workings of Miss Raby's mind, and explores, ironically and dramatically, the clash between that mind and others. As a result, Miss Raby emerges as one of the most subtly drawn and convincing characters in Forster's fiction" (Martin, 67-72).

'The Eternal Moment' does have one or two peccadilloes. For one thing, the character of Colonel Leyland is not sufficiently developed, and that of Elizabeth is only a cypher. Secondly, R.C. Trevelyan, to whom Forster first sent this short story for his opinion, found 'facetiousness in the style', which Forster seemed to naively admit: "Soon after his return to London, Forster sent 'The Eternal Moment' to Trevelyan, who admired it but objected to a certain facetiousness in the style. This came home to Forster, who replied: 'I wish you had told me where are the facetiae; they are a most certain fault, and my taste doesn't guide me. Someone told me, many years ago, that I was amusing, and I have never quite recovered from the effects'" (Furbank, I, 113).

14

A SHORT STORY OF SHORT STORY

Short story or short-story has always eluded all attempts at defining it. In his *Aspects of the Novel* Forster has called short story "the chopped-off length of the tape-worm of time" (Pelican Books, 1966, 93). A short story must be carefully differentiated from what we call, in a drama or a novel or even a poem, 'story,' because while a short story is a literary piece which can independently stand on its own feet, the 'story' of a drama, novel, or poem is not even an independent thing, but is an aspect or element of a drama, novel or poem, let alone the question of its standing on its own feet. Further, and for the reason of that, literary terminology does not generally recognise the word 'story' as a technical term in the sense of its being a simple linear narrative of multiple episodes, but employ the term 'tale' for that. So a story that is brief is not a short story, for a story, short or long, generally constitutes a component of a larger literary piece—a drama, a novel, or a poem—, and for a short story may not even contain what we generally know to be a 'story'—for instances, James Joyce's *The Dead* and Somerset Maugham's *The Pacific*.

The definition of short story given by Forster, and cited above, is, in fact, no definition of it. Forster has never tried to define short story, and that very wisely, because, as we have said, short story defies defining. Yet, Edgar Allan Poe came forward to define short story. He said that a short story is "a prose narrative (of indeterminate length) requiring anything from half an hour to one or two hours in its 'perusal'; a story that concentrates on a unique or single effect and one in which the totality of effect is the main objective" (Cuddon, 817). Poe, who is supposed by many critics to be the originator or innovator of short story, called short story the 'prose tale,' but a short story is not a tale because a tale is "written in the tone of voice of someone speaking" (Cuddon, 899) which tone we, as if, hear, but a short story we merely read. Short story is also to be differentiated from fable, for while the objective of fable is to preach or teach morals, short story aims at giving a reader a momentary pleasure. Short story, further, is different both from tale and fable in that while tale and fable may appear both in prose and verse, short story appears only in prose. Failing to define short story, some critics have attempted to describe it with the help of its length. They say that short story is shorter than *novella* or short novel. J.A. Cuddon writes that "In athletic terms, if we take the *novella* (...) as a 'middle-distance' book/story, then the short story comes into 100/200 metre class. Nevertheless, there are very long short-stories and short ones. D.H. Lawrence's *The Fox* (1923) is about 30,000 words; Kleist's ghost story *Das Bettelweib von Locarno* (1810) is only 800 words.... The vast majority of short stories would fall somewhere between the two" (Cuddon, 815). But a short story may be as short as not to go beyond a hundred words. J.A. Cuddon writes that some of the Czech writer Franz Kafka's short stories are "barely a hundred words long" (*op. cit.,* 821). Further, Cuddon writes that some of Kafka's short stories "include fable, parable, sketch, report, letter, dialogue, dramatic dialogue and essay, but all qualify as short stories" (*ibid.).* This means that short story is very difficult to define.

Instead of defining short story, Austin M. Wright speaks of three tendencies of short story: "(1) The short story tends to be between five hundred words long and the length of Joyce's' 'The Dead' [around fifty pages] (...). (2) It tends to deal with character and action in its fictional world (...). (3) This action tends to be externally simple with few developed episodes and no subplots or secondary lines of action" (Lohafer and Clarey, 51). M.H. Abrams has found that short story "organizes the action, thought, and interactions of its characters into the artful pattern of a *plot,* which has a beginning and develops through a middle to some sort of denouement at the end" (Abrams, 157). It is for this reason that A.S. Collins has said that "the short story (which) is a novel in brief" (Collins, 262). But the plot of short story is a thing which modern short story writers are fiercely striving to eschew. Austin M. Wright writes: "that the 'short-story' have [*sic.*] a plot did not stand up well in the early twentieth century, when everybody—the short story writer especially—was trying to get rid of plot" (Lohafer and Clarey, 46). However, we may stop trying to define short story following what Dominic Head, in his *The Modernist Short Story: A Study in Theory and Practice,* writes about the nature of short story: "The short story,... involves only 'one dramatic event,' with other subordinate events which 'facilitate the understanding of the main event'" (Head, 5). A.S. Collins' opinion that short story 'is a novel in brief' is, perhaps, not folly tenable; 'a novel in brief' may be called a *novella* or novelette but not a short story. Short story is certainly at a remove from novel, though the distance is small. Thomas M. Leitch is of the opinion that the two are nearest neighbours, and that short story has contributed to the development of modern novel: "Of course, the novel has been and continues to be the dominant literary narrative in terms of economics and prestige. But the short story, far from defining itself purely in contradistinction to the novel, has established formal patterns which have been crucial to the development of the modern novel" (Lohafer and Clarey, 146). Short story, however, may be said to deffer from novel in that, unlike in novel, there is generally a single episode or very few episodes in short story; and in that short story, compared to novel, is far more compact, tightly woven, concentrated, and is shorn of elaboration and digression.

Though we have not been able to define short story, we may observe a few more or less common elements in short stories. Like drame and novel, short story also have a trajectory of progression, which is somewhat like Gustav Freytag's pyramid-like diagram of the five acts of a drama. Short story has an originary incident or situation which starts the movement or unfolding of the story. The movement, touched off by the originary situation, next, gathers momentum and gets complicated in course of time, and then reaches the climax where the generated emotion is the most intense. The climactic point automatically or naturally restructures the situation and thereby begins to provide for the abatement of the crisis, and ultimately the crisis is somehow dissolved, when the story ends. All these elements of short story may not be found in all short stories, because short story has inconceivably various modes or manifestations. We can only say that short story is a short fiction in narrative prose that has close affinity or kinship with novel or novelette.

It is very difficult to say when exactly short story came into being. According to J.A. Cuddon, the 'forefathers' of short story were the following: "myth, legend, parable, fairy tale, fable, anecdote, *exemplum,* essay, character study and *Marchen,* plus *loi,* the *fabliau* and even the ballad" (Cuddon, 816). Cuddon further writes: "The term 'short story' has relatives in the shape of the French *conte* and *nouvelle,* the Spanish *novella,* the Italian *novella,* the German *Novella* and *Kurzgeschichte* (a word used to translate the English 'short story'), the yarn, the sketch, the tale and the Russian *skaz.*" *(ibid.).* If we ignore for the moment the fact that short story is prose fiction (not fiction in verse), we may even deem the stories contained in the verse narratives in Chaucer's *Canterbury Tales* to be some things approaching short story, like the tales or stories in Boccaccio's *Decameron* (c. 1349-51).

Short story was tardy to grow in the soil of England, and it grew there after it flourished in France, Germany, Russia and America. Short story is believed by some to have been born in America at the hand of Edgar Allan Poe (1809-49), who was greatly influenced by the German romantics. But, in fact, American short story was earlier ushered into existence chiefly by Washington Irving (1783-1859) and Nathaniel Hawthorne (1804-1864), ofcourse Poe gave it a fillip towards perfection. Poe's "'Metzgerenstein' published in the Philadelphia 'Saturday Courier' on 14th January, 1832, is the first American example of the successful utilization of the technique of single effect on which modern short story is based" (Chatterjee, 27-28). "In France the short story was established in 1829-31 with the publication of a dozen *contes* [tales or stories] by Prosper Merimee, Balzac and Gautier" (Cuddon, 818). Since then the French short story developed considerably at the hands of Alphonse Daudet, Gustav Flaubert, Alfred de Vigny, Jules Barbey d' Aurevilly, Arthur de Gobineau, Auguste Villiers, Anatole France, and such others. Among all the French short story writers, Maupassant is generally recognised as the foremost, as among all the Russian short story writers Chekhov (1860-1904) is generally thought to be the best. Realistic Russian short stories touched the high water-mark of perfection in the

1830s at the hand of Alexander Pushkin (1799-1837). Some of the great Russian short story writers are: Nikolay Vasilievich Gogol' (1809-1852), the author of the very famous short story *Shinel* or *The Overcoat,* Ivan Turgenev (1818—1883) whom Henry James honoured with the title of 'beautiful genius'; Leo Tolstoy (1828-1910), the author of the famous novel *Voyna i mir* or *War and Peace;* and Maxim Gorky (pseudonym of Aleksey Mikhaylovich Peshkov: 1868-1936), the author of *Mat* or *Mother.* Gogol's short story 'The Overcoat' was the harbinger of modernism in Russian short stories.

Among the great European short story writers, Franz Kafka (1883-1924), the Austrian existentialist novelist and short story writer, stands out unique, because of his point of view about reality and the individual's shifting and incomprehensible condition in it. Kafka's nearly eighty short stories "display a remarkable variety of length, style, theme and technique" (Cuddon, 821). Several Irish writers have to their credit a good number of short stories, each one of them. Such short story writers are: James Joyce (1882-1941), Sean O' Faolain (b. 1900), Liam O' Flaherty (b. 1897), Frank O' Connor (1903-66), Oscar Wilde (1854-1900), and such others. In Germany, in the twentieth century, short story had its heyday, and phenomenal physical and qualitative advancement at the hands of Anna Seghers, Luise Rinser, Heinrich Boll and such others. Short story also got a shot in the arm in Italy and Spain and some other European countries, in the twentieth century.

England was conspicuously late in joining the race: the English community of creative writers turned their attention towards short story being attracted by the phenomenal successes of the short story writers of France, Russia and America. In the beginning of the development of short story in England, Thomas Hardy (1840-1928) made a great contribution to its development with his four main collections of short stories: *Wessex Tales* (1888), *A Group of Noble Dames* (1891), *Life's Little Ironies* (1894) and *A Changed Man and Other Stories* (1913). In the last decade of the 19th century and at the beginning of the 20th century a band of English short story writers came up, the band including, among many others, Anthony Trollope (1815-82), R.L. Stevenson (1850-94), Joseph Conrad (1857-1924), Rudyard Kipling (1865-1936), W.W. Jacobs (1863-1943), 'Saki' (H.H. Munro: 1870-1916), John Galsworthy (1867-1933), D.H. Lawrence (1885-1930), Oscar Wilde (1854-1900), Katherine Mansfield (1888-1923), William Somerset Maugham (1874-1965) and Elizabeth Bowen (1899-1973). Katherine Mansfield was the rare writer who wrote only short stories and yet became famous, and first made short story an 'independent' genre in England: before her short story was rather a by-product of novel. Hardy, Conrad, D.H. Lawrence, Kipling, Wilde, Forster, *et al.* used to write short stories at spare times or intervals between bouts of novel writings.

In the twentieth century, short story had undergone enthusiastic experimentations, as a result of which various sorts of short stories have cropped up, such as 'sensation short story,' 'romance short story,' 'comic short story,' 'ghost or horror short story,' 'detective short story,' etc. The latest kind of short story is the 'aesthetic short story' which is now an in-thing in English literature. Suzanne Ferguson writes in this regard: "Emerging in the last two decades of the [twentieth] century, the aesthetic story put the finishing touches on the restyling of the English short story for modern tastes. Another variation of the romance [romance short story], this type utilized the descriptive techniques and gradual heightening of psychological tension of the sensation story and the concealment of meaning associated with the detective story, along with 'fine writing,' to make an overt bid for high-prestige. Its preoccupation with its own precosity, together with its frequently morbid themes, earned it the epithet 'decadent' as well as 'aesthetic.' Writers and critics began to claim this type of story to be superior to the novel in artistry because the short story was more controlled, intense, and, finally, reflective of life itself" (Lohafer and Clarey, 189).

Recently critics have much interested themselves in short story, as in novel, and consequently they have been trying to define short story in clearer terms and to identify the dividing line between short story and novel. William O' Rourke, in his article 'Morphological Metaphors for the Short Story: Matters of Production, Reproduction, and Consumption', says how Alberto Moravia differentiated between novel and short story: Holding that a novel has a skeletal structure, is not, of course, a new concept. Alberto Moravia, in his essay 'The Short Story and the Novel,' speaks of a novel's 'ideology, that is the skeleton of the theme from which the flesh of the story takes its form.' He also claims that "'the novel has a bone structure holding it together from top to toe, whereas the short story is, so to speak, boneless.' It is this 'absence of bone structure that makes a short story not a novel'" (*op. cit.,* 193). To differentiate between short story and novel, William O' Rourke, in the same article, further writes: "A novel's vertebrate structure is necessarily interior, whereas its flesh, its text, is exterior. A novel is wrapped around its structure, stretched around it, as a canvas is fastened on its frame. But a short story's text is its structure and its structure is its text" (*op. cit.,* 194). O' Rourke says that "A story, because of its size, is always (like a piece of sculpture) held in view; but it is difficult to see a whole novel (with all its parts), just as it is difficult to take in an entire painting at once" (*ibid.).*

The birth of modern short story, into which category Forster's short stories fall, happened during the period from 1880 to 1900. Since then short story has stolen the thunder of novel, or is about to steal it, because "the short story encapsulates the essence of literary modernism, and has an enduring ability to capture the episodic nature of twentieth-century experience" (Head, 1). Short story has been a major literary genre in our times, and has been undergoing both critical attention, and innovative experimentation as regards its form and content. Critics are also engaged in finding out short story's generic identity and its phenotypic variations to ascertain its real identity. But what short stories actually are is still an open question. However, we may accept, for the time being, as short story's identifying features what Dominic Head lists in the Preface to his *The Modernist Short Story:* "What *does* emerge from existing short story theory, such as it is, is a static notion of the genre's unity—its supposed reliance on certain unifying devices, such as a single event, straightforward characterization, a coherent 'moment of revelation' from which an easily identifiable 'point' can be recognized" (*op. cit,* X). However, as signs are rife, short story, in the very near future, may be expected to have achieved the status, that novel has already been enjoying, in the emerging literary world of modern times, as once it has become modern in its style, congruent with modern literary spirit. Modern short story reveals certain recognisable special features. For one thing, modern short story generally generates some sort of tension which pushes the story forward till its resolution. Secondly, modern short story writers are not plain-spoken; they do not make clear statements, but statements that mean more than what they are normally expected to mean. Thirdly, in modern short story the 'story' occupies a relatively subordinate status, the principal emphasis falling on the 'pick moment' or on the 'significant moment.' The writer of modern short story is most concerned with his fictionally created demanding impression of the moment, which he is anxious to deliver to the reader raw without even the least elaboration or ornamentation. This, in fact, means that the writer wants to present the reader with a select slice of life or a select slice of his lived *(vecu)* experience unalloyed, unadulterated. And lastly, modern short story is designed to meet the intellectual need of the *avant garde* readers. A.S. Collins very justly writes: "The 'modern' short story, often very far from being a story in the normal sense, was not for all, and it appealed naturally rather to the younger readers than to their elders and to the literary than to the average reader" (Collins, 265).

(15)

FORSTER AS A SHORT STORY WRITER

Even when he was an undergraduate at Cambridge, Forster was a big noise as a short-story writer. In his *Notebook Journal* he wrote on 16 March, 1904, about his fame as a short story writer, while at Cambridge: "'instead of an undergraduate, I was famous [as a short-story writer]: those who had read my story liked it'" (Beauman, 166). In fact, Forster began his career of fiction-writer not with a novel, like William Somerset Maugham, but with a handful of short stories. All the short stories that Forster wrote have not come down to us, because some of them he himself destroyed, even though a few of their 'focuses' he liked, the reason behind his doing this being still *incognito*. Again, some of his short stories he did not (or could not) publish during his life-time. However, two of his early short stories are: 'The Helping Hand' and 'A Day Off.' The latter, a very short story, is about "two German tourists who came across a bizarre 'brood of seventeen magenta-coloured chickens' and was published in the *Pilot* for May, 1904" (*op. cit.,* 148). The other early short story is 'The Helping hand,' whose focus Forster liked and so inspite of its obvious weaknesses he did not destroy it. This story is also, like the previous one, based on a visit—his own visit to Milan. We shall see, later on, that in most of his fictional works, both novels and short stories, Forster employed visits, tours and journeys as central components of the plots. He wrote only one ghost story: 'The Purple Envelope.' P.N. Furbank writes about the plot of this story: "The plot concerns an old man who commits a crime, from high-minded motives, and then, for complex reasons, feels compelled to reveal it, and is finally shot in the head by an unknown assassin, in mistake for a wild duck" (Furbank, I, 121). The story came a cropper after it failed to find a publisher, and so Forster came to the perhaps illegitimate conviction that he was "too refined to write a ghost story" (*ibid.*).

Forster's short stories may be divided into three categories: most of his short stories are fantasies; more than a dozen are erotic stories; and only one is ghost story, 'The Purple Envelope.' His erotic stories were posthumously published under the rubric *The Life to Come and Other Stories*. This collection contains 14 short stories, out of which ten are overtly homosexual. Forster is famous as a short-story writer chiefly for his twelve fantastic short stories, contained in his *Collected Short Stories*, first published in 1947 by Sidgwick and Jackson. As we have already said, his short stories are fantasies, as his novels are quite realistic. He has drawn his experiences of the real world and the real world itself in his novels, as in most of his short stories he has drawn his world of fancy. But, then, the world of fancy and the world of reality are not conceptually or experientially poles apart, because they sometimes close ranks and overlaps each other, though sometimes they develop a chasm between them, because our fancy does not grow out of a vacuum but out of our *vecu* experiences. Fyodor Dostoevsky believed that the reality itself is fantastical: "...What can be more fantastic and more unexpected than reality? What can sometimes be even more improbable than reality? The novelist can never imagine such impossibilities that reality confronts us with every day in their thousands in the shape of the most ordinary things. Reality stands above everything else" (Kashina, 29). The fantastic is the absurd, and the absurd is the fantastic, and, according to Dostoevsky, the absurd, which is the fantastic, is a systemic component of what life is. So, even fantastic short stories are somehow and somewhat related to the reality, and, therefore, are, at least partially, authentic: no normal human being can think of absolutely absurd or fantastical things. Dostoevsky voiced his view of the necessity of the absurd or the fantastic through the mouth of one of his characters, thus: "'...Absurdities are too necessary. The world is based on absurdities, and without them nothing perhaps could have happened'" (*op. cit.,* 44). Is man contented only with his begotten reality and does he not need to create beyond that reality? No, man is not satisfied with the reality; rather, sometimes the reality hangs heavy on his shoulder. T.S. Eliot, in his play *Murder in the Cathedral,* has very justly expressed his opinion that the reality is sometimes insufficient and sometimes burdensome: "Human beings cannot bear/Very much reality." Really, man is a mysterious being. Dostoevsky was again quite right when he wrote: "'Man is a mystery which has to be unravelled'" (*op. cit.,* 47).

Though they are fantasies, some of Forster's short stories, such as 'The Celestial Omnibus,' 'The Other Side of the Hedge,' 'The Machine Stops,' 'Co-ordination,' 'The Eternal Moment,' may be said to have some resemblance with magic realistic fictions. The term 'magic realism' is of recent origin. According to *The Wordsworth Companion to Literature in English,* "The exact provenance of the term is disputed, but it probably originated in the question posed by the Cuban novelist Alejo Carpentier: 'What is the story of Latin America if not a chronicle of the marvellous in the real?' It was first employed as a literary definition by the American critic Alastair Reid, and referred then to the large body of spectacular, fantastic fiction produced in South American countries after World War II" (Ousby, 584). J.A. Cuddon, who is a little at variance with the immediately foregoing, as to the origin of the term 'magic realism,' writes about it: "This term was coined by Franz Roh and used in the title of his book *Nach-expressionismus, magischer Realismus: Probleme der neusten europaischer Malerei* (1925). He was concerned with the characteristics and tendencies discernible in the work of certain German painters of the period [the first quarter of the 20th century], especially the *neue Sachlichkeit* (...) artists of Munich. Their work was marked by the use of still, sharply defined, smoothly painted images of figures and objects depicted in a somewhat surrealistic manner. The theme and subjects were often imaginary, somewhat outlandish and fantastic and with a certain dream-tike quality" (Cuddon, 487). In the 1940s the term 'magic realism' came to be associated with certain kinds of fiction. "Some of the characteristic features of this kind of fiction are the mingling and juxtaposition of the realistic and the fantastic or bizarre, skilful time shifts, convoluted and even labyrinthine narratives and plots, miscellaneous use of dreams, myths and fairy stories, expressionistic and even surrealistic description, arcane erudition, the element of surprise or abrupt shock, the horrific and the inexplicable" (*op. cit.,* 488). Gabriel Gàrcia Màrquèz has, for instance, blended the real and the fantastic in his novels and short stories in a unique and stunning way. In 1982, he received the Nobel Prize for Literature, when the Citation said that he was being awarded the Prize "'for his novels and short stories, in which the fantastic and the realistic are combined in a richly composed world of imagination, reflecting a continent life and conflicts'"

(Allen, 9). And Màrquèz called the American novelist William Faulkner his 'master'—Faulkner from whom he received the idea of making an ersatz of the real and the fantastic.

Some of Forster's short stories may, perhaps, be called 'escape literature.' Aristophanes' play, *Frogs,* has been dubbed by some critics as the ever first piece of escape literature. In escape literature the writer (and the reader) wants to symbolically escape from his unbearably sour atmosphere or condition of life. Aristophanes (from 450 to 385 B.C.) wrote *Frogs* for entertaining the people of Athens who had been leading a despicably penurious and straitened condition that arose out of the Peloponnesian Wars between the Athenians and the Spartans, for 27 years (from 431 to 404 B.C.). So in the entertainment that Aristophanes provided for the Athenians during that period through *Frogs* the Athenians found an escape route from their sour life. This is the reason why some critics have called *Frogs* an escape literature or 'escape drama.' Another 'escape drama' of Aristophanes is *Birds.* "It is an escapist fantasy in which two Athenians, Pisthetaerus and Euelpides, dissatisfied with Athens, go in search of somewhere better, they join forces with the birds, the original lords of creation, and build a new city, Cloudcuckooland, in mid-air. They soon dominate mankind, and by cutting off the nourishing steam of sacrifices force the gods to surrender Zeus's sceptre to the birds and his colleague Basileia ('Sovereignty') as a bride for the exultant Pisthetaerus" (Dudley and Lang, 32).

Escape literature or literature of escape had its resurgence in the 20th century, especially since the First World War, and a spat of pieces of escape literature were written. J.A. Cuddon, in his *The Penguin Dictionary of Literary Terms and Literary Theory,* writes about literature of escape: "From the First and the Second World Wars came many books about escaping—mostly from prisoner-of-war camps. They form almost a minor genre of their own, and many of them, apart from being very exciting, are well written. Well-known examples from the First World War are: H.E. Hervey's *Cagebirds;* H.G. Durnford's *The Tunnellers of Holzminden; Escapers All* by various contributors; and *The Escaping Club.* Probably the most famous from the Second World War is *The Wooden Horse* (1949) by Eric Williams. There have been many others..." (Cuddon, 473). In many of Forster's short stories the principal characters escape from their unhappy conditions or atmospheres: for instance, in 'The Story of a Panic' Eustace escapes from the grips of his guardians in the hotel and escapes into Gennaro's arms (the story ends with the overjoyed laughter of Eustace—the 'escaping boy'); in 'The Celestial Omnibus' the little boy escapes from the tyrannous behaviour of his father and mother and escapes into the region of the rainbow, in the celestial omnibus; in 'Co-ordination' Miss Haddon and the Principal escape from mechanical co-ordination and draconian discipline and escape into the freedom in the sea-side; and in 'The Eternal Moment' Miss Raby escapes into the region of fantasy from the world of the reality. So we may, perhaps, call some of Forster's short stories escape literature.

Forster has freely employed ancient Greek mythological figures in some of his short stories. For instance, in 'The Story of a Panic' we read about Pan, Oreads, Nereids and Fate; in 'The Road From Colonus' we come across Naiad, Dryad, the Virgin and Merlin; and in 'The Eternal Moment' we hear about sibyls. Hindu, Jewish and Moslem Gods and gods are cited in the short story 'Mr Andrews': there are 'Buddha, and Vishnu, and Allah, and Jehovah, and the Elohim.' In the region of the fantastic mythological figures are appropriately expected to haunt as legends are appropriately expected to float around it, and in this regard Forster's fantasies are veritable fantasies. When we wish to escape from the reality, we want to escape into a fairy land or into a land where fairies might have trodden, i.e., we wish to escape into some bucolic or pastoral or arboral corner of the world where we might meet the paradisical beauty of nature. Forster was a great devotee of nature; had he not been a novelist, he might have become a Wordsworthian poet. In many of his short stories, more than in his novels, he has found opportunities to draw the immaculate beauty of nature, and has expressed his deep love for nature. In such short stories as 'The Story of a Panic,' 'The Other Side of the Hedge,' 'Other Kingdom,' 'The Story of the Siren' and 'The Eternal Moment' he has very beautifully painted the various aspects of nature.

Perhaps the most important thing of Forster's short stories is that though they are fantasies, unlike his novels which are realistic, there are a few similarities between some of the short stories and a few of the novels. For one thing, in most, or rather all, of his novels the plots weave around travels or journeys, and travels and journeys we also come across in some, or rather most, of his short stories. Journeys are there, for instance, in 'The Story of a Panic,' 'The Machine Stops,' 'The Celestial Omnibus,' 'The Eternal Moment' and 'Other Kingdom.' The journeys are undertaken mostly for picnics, and in the picnics, as elsewhere, tea and tea-things are rather frequently mentioned. Journeys, again, are done to pastoral, arboral or bucolic scenarios—scenarios which are simply romantic. Forster's blatantly erotic stories appear in *The Life to Come,* but many of his short stories outside that volume also bear suggestions to carnal amour, illicit love and homosexuality. Echoes from the short stories of Forster are heard especially in his *A Passage to India,* and the two short stories of his from where the echoes arrive are 'The Story of a Panic' and 'The Eternal Moment.' The 'panic' in 'The Story of a Panic' is a parallel to Adela's 'panic' in the Marabar caves in *A Passage to India,* and Miss Raby's imaginary love affair with Feo Ginori in 'The Eternal Moment' is echoed in Adela's wishfulfilment of being raped by Aziz in the Marabar cave. Further parallelism is not hard to descry between the novel and the two short stories. We may here recall that Forster published short stories earlier than novels. Though he began his actual career of a writer, after leaving Cambridge, with exercises in novel writing, as we may recall, he had been a short story writer of some standing even while he had been at Cambridge. This means that his short-story writing preceded his novel writing, and so his short-story writing was a sort of apprenticeship in novel writing.

Forster is an *avant garde* writer in his novels and he is no different in his short stories. He is never anxious about making things clearer to the reader, and his readers are never the general rung of readers. He never cares if some unclear spots are left across a story. His suggestions and innuendoes are witty and facetious. He hardly repeats proper names, and employs pronouns instead, or such devices as 'the other person', 'the other,' etc., or leaves the reader to guess who the speaker is, which is sometimes a little difficult for the common reader. However, unlike in James Joyce's short story, 'The Dead,' or in William Somerset Maugham's short story, 'The Atlantic,' there is always a story (as well as a plot) in the short story of Forster. In his novels Forster's attitude is satiric, but in his short stories his attitude is comic; but underneath both his satiric and comic attitudes there always pervades a serious meaning.

Forster as a Novelist

4

Not many novelists have been blessed, like Forster, by being given a secure and permanent place in the history of English novel for producing novels, which can be counted on fingertips, of well moderate lengths (150 to 300 pages). He was a short-story writer of first water, a learned critic, and a theorist of the novel of considerable standing, but above all he was a great novelist. Loud acclaims have been made for Forster, the novelist and writer, by great critics and men of letters. Let us cite only a couple of instances. "In 1943 the influential American critic Lionel Trilling published a book on Forster. It made large and persuasive claims for him. Forster, he said, was for him 'the only living novelist who can be read again and again and who, after each reading, gives me what few writers can give us after our first days of novel-reading, the sensation of having learned something" (Trilling, 9). Nicola Beauman a biographer of Forster, records Stephen Spender's very high opinion of Forster as a novelist: "Spender, who considered Morgan [E.M. Forster] 'the best English novelist of this [20th] century,' said that he 'found the effect of knowing Forster was that he became a kind of supplementary conscience tacked on to my own and bringing what I imagine to be Forsterian scruples to bear on my conduct'" (Beauman, 363).

Elizabeth (Dorothea Cole) Bowen (1899-1973), herself a novelist and a short-story writer of considerable standing (her best known novels include *The Death of the Heart* and *The Heat of the Day*), in her article 'A Passage to Forster,' has given an idea of the considerable influence on her development as a novelist. She was being influenced by Forster's short stories and novels since she was a schoolgirl. She was first attracted by the lucidity of Forster's writing: "The lucidity of

Forster's writing was, I suppose, what attracted me first of all" (Edward Arnold, 2). She says she developed a "passion for Forster novels" (*ibid.*), and she praises his rare *métier* of telling a tale (particularly in the short-stories): "No, the magic was not in the matter but in the manner, the telling, the creation of a peculiar, electric climate in which *anything* might happen. In itself, the writing acted on me as an aesthetic shock" (*op. cit.*, 4).

Forster was a liberal humanist in thought and actions, and so naturally his novels anywhere and every where breathe liberal humanism. The term 'liberal humanism' is a compound of the two terms 'liberalism' and 'humanism.' Roger Scruton, in his *A Dictionary of Political Thought,* has elucidated the meaning of the term 'liberalism.' He says that most forms of liberalism comprise the following ideas: belief in the absolute value of the individual and his freedom and his natural rights, which rights are independent of government and ought to be protected; recognition of the supreme value of freedom; belief in the universality of the rights and duties of the individual; an anthropocentric, rather than theological view of man; toleration in matters of religion and morality etc. (Scruton, 269). And about the term 'humanism' Scruton says that the import of the term may be summed up in the epigrammatic expression of the Greek sophists, 'Man is the measure of all things,' and in Terence's dictum, *Homo sum, et nihil humanum mihi alienum puto* ('I am a man and hold nothing human alien to myself') (*op. cit.,* 209).

Liberal humanism demands a rational approach to the evaluation of human ideals, behaviour, and relationships. It supports the liberty of the individual to choose his own particular philosophy of life and value system. It advocates toleration of, and respect for, other's views about life and value system. It, on the other hand, does not recognise tradition as absolute, inviolable and sacrosanct, and it spitefully quoits away tradition where the tradition baulks the free and full spiritual, aesthetic and intellectual development of the individual. At the Tonbridge school, Forster, in his tender ages, received indelible impress of how tradition monstrously and draconically demanded conformity from each and every one of the innocent kids there—the kids who were not ready enough to decide what was wrong and what right. But when he moved to Cambridge from there, he impressionably experienced the sanative and salubrious influence of the liberal humanism that prevailed at Cambridge, and soon he adopted the philosophy of liberal humanism for life. And later on his liberal humanistic attitude was reinforced by his association with the liberal humanist philosopher G.E. Moore (1873-1958) and by the philosopher's *Principia Ethica,* and he took it upon himself as his categorical imperative to propagate this philosophy through his fictional and non-fictional works. George Sampson justly writes that Forster "is the finest survival in literature, as Bertrand Russell in philosophy, of that liberal, humanist tradition of the early twentieth century against which some of the most acute intelligences of our time have directed their powers of denigration" (Sampson, 869). And F.R. Leavis, finding the fine expression of the liberal tradition in *A Passage to India,* writes about the book: "there is a point in calling it a classic of the liberal spirit will, I suppose, be granted fairly readily, for the appropriateness of the adjective is obvious. In its touch upon racial and cultural problems, its treatment of personal relations, and in prevailing ethos the book is an expression, undeniably, of the liberal tradition; it has, as such, its fitness, its strength and its impressiveness; and it makes the achievement, the humane, decent and rational—the 'civilized'—habit, of that tradition appear the invaluable thing it is" (Leavis, 277).

In his essay 'Forster as a Humanist,' W.J.H. Sprott has written at some length about Forster's humanism. Sprott writes in that essay about Forster: "'The humanist,' he says, 'has four leading characteristics—curiosity, a free mind, belief in good taste, and belief in the human race'" (Edward Arnold, 75). Sprott then goes on to show how far Forster himself possessed these four characteristics. He says that Forster had curiosity about music, people, places, etc. and that "His range of literary criticism displays an inquiring mind" (*ibid.*). Secondly, about whether Forster had a free mind, Sprott writes: "There is no question about this qualification. Forster has a free-ranging intellect, an unfailing readiness to consider new ideas, and a complete disregard for authority" (*op. cit.,* 76). Thirdly, Forster had 'belief in good taste.' About this characteristic of his Sprott writes: "Again there is no question.... He does not say that the humanist must *have* good taste, but that he must believe in it" (*ibid.*). And lastly, Sprott says that Forster certainly had 'belief in the human race,' i.e., he believed that the human race has been and will have been able to achieve progressive refinement of a standard of moral values and production of works of art.

Forster respected rationalism, but his regard for rationalism did not debar him from believing that emotion plays a vital role in human life and that paganism is not to be altogether spurned away, because it also has value in human life. His ideal in human life was an investing mutuality between rationalism and emotionalism—he wished the two 'connected' with each other. Like Nietzsche and D.H. Lawrence, he was rather an advocate of the heart than of the head. He believed that in our crises of life we can be salvaged by the wisdom of our heart and not by the intellect of our head. Diana Neill writes in this regard: "Although a rationalist, Forster, like Lawrence and Virginia Woolf was convinced that life was something more than merely mental. A love of the bright pagan life of the senses, of impulse and spontaneous emotions, drew him to the Greeks, but his fastidious intelligence and innate dualism forced him to distrust the imaginative vision of life even while he succumbs to its inspiration. He was far from accepting Lawrence's religion of the blood and would have shrunk from a conception of human personality that was based on repulsion and attraction, violence and primitive self-assertion. He was convinced that the 'wisdom of the heart' had been too little considered in the nineteenth century, with the result that in spite of material progress there had been a weakening of human sympathy and understanding. Englishmen were especially to blame in this, since their educational system neglected the emotions and by overvaluing restraint as a means of developing character they impaired sensitivity. Hence his attack on the Public Schools" (Neill, 386).

Although he had regards for paganism, Forster was a believer in civilisation, and though he was a votary of rationalism, he believed in the necessity of imagination, besides feeling or emotion. His task ahead was therefore uphill—his task, in his novels, was to show an ideal, desirable compromise among the three recalcitrant factors working in human beings: reason, emotion, and imagination. Diana Neill further writes in this regard: "Forster, a liberal and humanist loved civilization, which he regarded as liberalism's finest achievement. But he perceived the peculiar dilemma confronting liberalism in the twentieth century. Liberalism was based on reason; it had rejected theology; its chief exponents were agnostic or vaguely pantheist. Moreover, reason which had denied the force of imagination was itself in danger of being swept away by irrational impulses the mere presence of which indicated an unadmitted hunger of the human soul for deeper satisfactions that trade, commerce and a civilized social system could provide. Reason was obviously not enough, but the alternatives were alarming and uncontrollable. Forster's problem was how to reconcile civilized order with imaginative awareness and the world of feeling" (*ibid.*). In all his novels, from *Where Angels Fear to Tread* to *A Passage to India*, Forster has arrayed a small but unforgetable gallery of characters that are preponderantly either rational or emotional, and the crises of the novels grow out of the incongruence of the two psychological extremities of the principal characters, and, withal, *a la* the Forsterian philosophy of the ideality of life, resolutions of the crises occur in the characters' recognition of their psychological inadequacy—of the absence of the other half of their souls: the rational half or the emotional.

As has just now been said, according to Forster, man is a complex being, having two vital psychological components: rationality and emotionality. Deny any one of them to a man and he is incomplete: he or she is, so to say, an one-dimensional being, and so is prone to suffer in life that demands that he or she be complete with both head and heart. The one-dimensional rational man is like Adela Quested or Helen Schlegel or Caroline Abbott or Ronny Heaslop or Cecil Vyse, and the one-dimensional emotional man is like

George Emerson or Mr Wilcox or Jacky Bast or Lilia or Aziz. In the courses of his novels, life shows these people their inadequacies and edifies them to make themselves complete or pitiably suffer. A single component individual is a sort of misanthrope. Forster has sarcastically termed the merely rational men 'crustaceans' and the only emotional men 'vitalists,' and the principal objective and the driving force of his novels was to arrange a marriage between the two groups of human beings or to show that in the absence of the marriage salvation was impossible. His teaching was that the merely rational man should learn to be emotional as well, and so should the merely emotional man inculcate into himself the virtue of being rational.

In chapter 31 of *A Passage to India* his philosophical comment that "Life is not a scientific manual" is a smashing blow of Forster on the glassy confidence of the rationalists—the 'crustaceans.' But all at the same time he cautions that extreme reliance on emotion or imagination, as against reason, will lead the 'vitalists' astray from the normal course of life. And it is here that Forster's distinction and importance as a theorist of life lies, and this theoretical position he has indefatiguably endeavoured to expound in his novels. Let us here once again quote from Diana Neill (this time also at some length): "No modern writer has so scrupulously set down the dusty answer life reserves for those who seek for certainties and expect to find clear-cut distinctions. His attitude to society provided the basis for the conflict embodied in his novels between the two ways of life—the way of the heart, which loves and understands but is often confused and misguided, and the official way that preserves order but stifles genuineness and sincerity under a pall of good form and convention. Human beings tend to fall (in Forster's world) into two main groups, the 'crustaceans' and the 'vitalists.' The former are the adherents of lifeless convention, hidebound conservatives whose responses, once conditioned in youth, are never modified by experience or understanding. They are the enemies of the idea, they destroy love because their hearts are undeveloped and they cause the delicate fibres of human relationships to wither.

Such people make admirable officials because they are rather less than human. Opposed to them are the 'vitalists,' who feel deeply and are not afraid of their feelings, who let the heart guide them in their relations with others, who take the broad view and refuse to let respect for convention stifle their generous impulses. Among the 'crustaceans' in the novels are Ronny Heaslop, Charlotte Elliot, Major Callender and the Turtons; the 'vistalists' include such characters as Fielding, Mrs. Moore and George Emerson" (Neill, 347).

John Sayre Martin would not count Forster with the other great novelists, because of his narrow range and sympathies, because some of his vital characters are not life-like but like phantoms, and because he miserably failed in the treatment of heterosexual love. About the narrowness of his range and sympathies, Martin writes: " 'I am quite sure I am not a great novelist,' Forster told an interviewer in 1959; and probably few readers would wish to dispute this claim. Well as he manages many of his effects, his range and sympathies are too narrow to class him among the Tolstoys, Dostoevskys and Prousts. His most vital characters are, generally speaking, those to whom in real life he would have probably been attracted—a varied group, to be sure, although all of them are sensitive to the needs of their inner lives. Most of them belong to the English upper-middle-class people with enough money and leisure to travel and cultivate their interests. Of these who fall outside this class, all are male and non-English: Gino, Aziz, Godbole, and perhaps Cocoanut, the half-cast native in 'The Other Boat'" (Martin, 170).

About the lack of verisimitude of some of Forster's characters, i.e. about their lifelessness Martin writes: "Into several of his important characters, Forster clearly fails to breathe life, or enough life. Stephen Wonham, George Emerson, Henry Wilcox and Alec Scudder are comparative failures. And they fail perhaps because Forster was too intent upon fixing them with certain moral and spiritual qualities rather than allowing them to grow organically. That is to say, he envisioned the qualities first, then invented the characters to fit them, and the results are thin and wooden" (*ibid.*). Martin is also not satisfied with Forster's scant and unrealistic portrayal of love between man and woman, and the reason of this is not unknown to us—Forster was a confirmed misogynist and so did never experience the beatings of his heart for a woman, and how could he, so, describe the love between the opposite sexes? Martin writes: "Forster's treatment of heterosexual love—for reasons now clear—is equally unconvincing. One need only contrast the pallid, manipulated connection between Margaret Schlegel and Henry Wilcox, or Adela Quested's equally dry engagement to Ronny Heaslop, with Maurice's passion for Clive Durham or Lionel Matches for Cocoanut, to test the validity of this judgment" (*op. cit.,* 170-171).

All the same, the same John Sayre Martin, at the same place, writes: "But the limitations and weaknesses [and they are, according to him, as have just now been shown] of Forster's fiction are minor when set against its virtues. And it is because of its virtues that his best fiction is still enjoyed" (*op. cit.,* 171). What are those virtues? Martin's brief inventory comprises four great virtues of a novelist: moral realism, psychological insight, comic vein, and the 'personal voice' of a humanist. Firstly, about Forster's moral realism, Martin writes that Forster's fiction "is morally realistic. In Forster's fictional world, as in the real one, individual actions, however well intentioned, have unpredictable consequences. The Schlegels' kindness to Leonard Bast prepares the way for his murder. The excursion to the Marabar Caves that Aziz arranges in order to entertain his English friends precipitates the death of one of them and dislocates an entire community. As Lionel Trilling long ago pointed out, Forster's novels reveal a network of moral forces in which everybody is implicated. In today's impersonal world, in which it is always tempting to blame 'the others' for overpopulation, pollution and most of our other problems, Forster's moral realism is provocative and refreshing" (*ibid.*).

Secondly, Martin says that Forster has unawares demonstrated, at many places in his novels, his 'psychological insight' into the characters. Forster, as if, enters into the being of the character, and then describes what the character perceives or feels or wills, and also forms the dialogues of the character accordingly. For instance, "Consider the realism and sensitivity with which Forster develops Maurice's passion for Clive. Or the following passage in which Aziz, looking at a photograph of his wife, tries to recollect her [in chapter 6 of *A Passage to India*]: "And unlocking a drawer, he took out his wife's photograph. He gazed at it, and tears spouted from his eyes. He thought, "How unhappy I am!" But because he really was unhappy, another emotion soon mingled with his self-pity: he desired to remember his wife and could not. Why could he remember people whom he did not love? They were always so vivid to him, whereas the more he looked at this photograph, the less he saw. She had eluded him thus, ever since they had carried her tomb. He had known that she would pass from his hands and eyes, but had thought she could live in his mind, not realizing that the very fact that we have loved the dead increases their unreality, and that the more passionately we invoke them the further they recede. A piece of brown cardboard and three children—that was all that was left of his wife. It was unbearable, and he thought again, "How unhappy I am!" and became happier. He had breathed for an instant the mortal air that surrounds Orientals and all men, and he drew back from it with a gasp, for he was young.' A lesser novelist would sentimentalize such a scene, presenting not a living heart and mind but a series of emotional cliches" (*op. cit.*, 171-172). Martin further tells us that Forster's psychological realism is also reflected in the dialogues he puts into the mouths of his characters.

Thirdly, as we have said more than once, Forster is almost constitutionally, if you like, a comic writer, occasionally employing gentle but penetrating satire. His witty comedy is built up around social phenomena that are, from his point of view, gone astray from the social norms. He was influenced in his comic attitude as a writer by Jane Austen, as he was also influenced by some other qualities of hers as a writer. But Forster's comic is not always simple and light but complex in its texture and grave in its meaning, and here it is that his comic vein is remarkably different from Austen's. Forster's comic is not elaborate but is done with a few sure strokes of the brush, as Dickens had earlier done. Martin writes: "Like Dickens, Forster can enliven a comic portrait with a few deft touches. One recalls Miss Bartlett 'talking to Mr Beebe, and as she spoke, her long narrow head drove backwards and forwards, slowly, regularly, as though she were demolishing some invisible obstacle.' Or Herbert Pembroke, who, 'though not in orders...had the air of being on the verge of them.' Or Mrs Turton, who 'was "saving herself up," as she called it—not for anything that would happen that afternoon or even that week, but for some vague future occasion when a high official might come along and tax her social strength. Most of her public appearances were marked by this air of reserve'" (*op. cit.,* 173).

And fourthly and lastly, about Forster's 'personal voice' in his novels, Martin writes that its tone is clearly sympathetic towards human beings, irrespective of creed, colour, and class. Martin writes: "A final word must be said about Forster's personal voice which marks every page of his fiction. It is the voice of a humanist—one seriously committed to human values while refusing to take himself too seriously. Its tone is enquiring, not dogmatic. It reflects a mind aware of the complexities confronting those who wish to live spiritually satisfying, morally responsible lives in a world that increasingly militates against the individual's needs. Sensitively and often profoundly, Forster's fictions explore the problems such people encounter. And for this reason it is emphatically a fiction for our time" (*op. cit.,* 174).

There has been an elaborate debate, leading to nowhere, about whether art is for its own sake or for the sake of something other than art, or whether or not art is independent of everything that is not art. Writers and critics have always remained divided on this question. Tolstoy and Shelley, for instance, were of the opinion that art cannot be independent of morals. Bernard Shaw did not feel it derogatory to declare that he produced his plays for propagandistic purposes. But Forster believed that art was independent of our quotidian necessities or worldly profits: he was a votary of the principle that art is absolutely for the sake of aesthetic enjoyment.

Forster said that art is something that has got no parallel in the universe, because art is internally organised while the things of the universe maybe organised by adventitious forces. The implication of this opinion of his is that if this is so then there cannot be any mutual benefaction between art and the universe, or art and life. In his P.E.N. speech published in *Horizon* of December, 1941, he said: "'[A work of art] is the only material object in the universe which may possess internal harmony. All the others have been pressed into shape from outside, and when their mould is removed they collapse. The work of art stands by itself, and nothing else does. It achieves something which has often been promised by society but always delusively. Ancient Athens made a mess—but the Antigone stands up. Renaissance Rome made a mess—but the ceiling of the Sistine got painted; Louis XIV made a mess—but there was Phedre; Louis XV continued it, but Voltaire got his letters written. Art for Art's sake? I should think so, and more so than ever at the present time. It is the one orderly product which our muddling race has produced'" (Trilling, 154).

Forster is not only a moral realist in his novels, but his novels are realist in all aspects. He is a marvellous fantasist in his short stories: he has created atmospheres where imagination has had its full play in leading us far away from our quotidian life. Though in his novels myths and fantasies are sparsely strewn, the novels are essentially realistic—the fantasies being, as he has called them in *Aspects of the Novel,* side-shows, that the reader may enjoy with a minimum payment, alongside the main course of the narrative. In his novels, he does not overstep the limit of probability and enter the region of the fantastic. Lionel Trilling writes that "...Forster is not bizarre. He simply has the certainty of the great novelists that any novel is a made-up thing and that a story, in order to stand firmly on reality, needs to keep no more than one foot on probability" (*op. cit.,* 11).

But probability is not reality, and so when a fiction includes probability, we may legitimately ask the question: does not the inclusion of probability destroy a fiction's claim of being realistic? No, says Robert Scholes. The concept of realism includes the concept of truth; only when a thing is true can it be real. But this definition of truth is narrow, because truth is not fact. 'Someone has an umbrella' is a fact, but 'Everybody hates the non-believers' is a truth. Truth is more general than fact. It is the task of the novelist to present some sort of truth before us, and he can do this better not always with facts but with probabilities—with made-up characters and events. Here lies the essential difference between history and fiction. Robert Scholes writes about the realist novelist: "Realism is a matter of perception. The realist presents his impressions of the world of experience.... The realistic writer seeks always to give the reader a sense of the way things are, but he feels that a made-up structure of character and event can do better justice to the way things are than any attempt to copy reality directly. The realist's truth is a bit more general and typical than the reporter's fact. It may also be more vivid and memorable" (Scholes, 9). Forster's realism in any case must be seen from this perspective as well as keeping in mind what Frank Kermode said in his 'Mary Flexner Lectureship' (1965), later on published in his book *The Sense of an Ending*: "any novel, however 'realistic,' involves some degree of alienation from 'reality'" (Kermode, 50) and "None of our fictions is a supreme fiction" (*op. cit.*, 155).

Though Forster believed in 'Art's for Art's sake,' and though his novels are in no way didactic or propagandistic, some elements of his philosophy of life and some of his views about tradition and society are reflected in his novels, as we have already hinted at. What remains here is to say is that he did not recognise the compartmentalisation of the integral life into intellectuality and emotionality, into matters of the head and the matters of the heart, and ignore either of them entirely, in which case, he believed, life would be hugely incomplete and so false. As a novelist, Forster always strived to bring together intellectuality and emotionality, or reason and emotion, or the head and the heart. Extreme rationalism as much as extreme predominance of emotion or will he decried. He believed that the devastating pugnacity of today's world is due to overmuch and tensed will of modern human beings. To do away with today's evils he therefore suggested a relaxation of will. Lionel Trilling writes in this regard: "A world at war is necessarily a world of will; in a world at war Forster reminds us of a world where the will is not everything, of a world of true order, of the necessary connection of passion and prose, and of the strange paradoxes of human being. He is one of those who raised the shield of Achilles, which is the moral intelligence of art, against the panic and emptiness which make their onset when the will is tired from its own excess" (Trilling, 157-158). This was the literary mission of Forster, if he at all had any mission, a mission at once humanitarian and apocalyptic.

As we know, Forster wrote his novels in a light, leisurely and comic manner that apparently demands no seriousness on the part of the reader, though below the surface it is grave, exerting and engagingly thought-provoking. His plots, on the other hand, are visibly simple, sharp and definite. In his plot, he always presents an encounter between two opposing forces, and tries to work out a compromise formula, but it does not work, and so some sort of confusion appears to the reader. Lionel Trilling writes: "Forster's plots are always sharp and definite, for he expresses difference by means of struggle, and struggle by means of open conflict so intense as to flare into melodrama and even into physical violence. Across each of his novels runs a barricade; the opposed forces on each side are Good and Evil in the forms of Life and Death, Light and Darkness, Fertility and Sterility, Courage and Respectability, Intelligence and Stupidity—all the great absolutes that are so dull when discussed in themselves. The comic manner, however, will not tolerate absolutes. It stands on the barricade and casts doubt on both sides. The fierce plots move forward to grand simplicities but the comic manner confuses the issues, forcing upon us the difficulties and complications of the moral fact. The plot suggests eternal division, the manner reconciliation; the plot speaks of clear certainties, the manner resolutely insists that nothing can be so quite simple. 'Wash ye, make yourselves clean,' says the plot, and the manner murmurs, 'If you can find the soap'" (*op. cit.*, 13).

As a novelist, Forster was neither an escapist nor a fatalist nor even an optimist. In his short stories, he is a fantasist, and one may infer from this that he is an escapist, but this is wrong. He accepted life as it is, not lying supine but facing it with forbearance. G.D. Klingopulos writes: "though Mr Forster has defended 'escape,' he was never a whole-hearted escapist. 'I cannot shut myself up in a Palace of Art or a Philosophic Tower and ignore the madness and misery of the world.' Nor has he been tempted to insist on optimism or fatalism or any doctrinal position which would simplify the stresses of life" (Ford, 249). But then why did Forster engage himself with his fantastic stories, and withal employ fantasies, though sparingly, in his novels? Klingopulos explains why: "His lighter works of fantasy must be regarded as attempts to organise and bring to a focus certain intuitions which at first derive from books, and later from experience and from travel. They attempt to open windows for enclosed and regimented men, and to evoke intuitive or childlike memories, as in dreams, of other levels of existence—'the magic song of nightingales, and the adour of invisible hay, and stars piercing the fading sky'" (*ibid.*). This other level of our existence is not altogether meaningless, absured, but it occupies a part of our life—never an unimportant portion of our life, of course. In a sense, there is no impervious wall between the novel and the fantasy, for every novel, however much realistic, borders on the fantastic—no novel portrays very faithfully the quotidian life we lead. "Novels, says Sartre, are not life, but they owe our power upon us, as upon himself as an infant, to the fact that they are somehow like life. In life, he once remarked, 'all ways are barred and nevertheless we must act. So we try to change the world; that is, to live *as if* the relations between things and their potentialities were governed not by deterministic processes but by magic.' The *as if* of the novel consists in a similar negation of determinism, the establishment of an accepted freedom by magic" (Kermode, 135). This at once justifies Forster's fantastic stories and the place of fantasy in his novels.

Lionel Trilling has noticed that Forster works his novels by providing his readers with occasional surprises. He is always unpredictable: he leads us through mazes, while we move smoothly, expecting naturally something to meet soon on the way, but suddenly there is a *volte face*—something else unexpectedly happens, something we did not even dream of, and this has a great charm, indeed, because the unexpected soon does not appear to be absurd but, as we change our perspective, it seems very legitimate. Trilling explains this with instances: "... Forster, as I have said, likes to work with surprises mild or great. 'Gerald died that afternoon,' is the beginning of a chapter [of *The Longest Journey*] which follows immediately upon a description of Gerald full of superabundant life.... He [Forster] is always shocking us by removing the heroism of his heroes and heroines; in *A Passage to India,* Mrs Moore, of whom we had expected high actions, lets herself be sent away from the trial at which her testimony would have been crucial; Cyril Fielding, who as a solitary man had heroically opposed official ideas, himself becomes official when he is successful and married; and Dr Aziz cannot keep to his role of the sensitive and enlightened native" (Trilling, 17).

A very vital question now arises: is Forster a Victorian novelist, or a modern? But before we try to answer the question, we should be clear about the concept of 'modernism.' Modernism is a very comprehensive and vague term to define, of it only one thing can be said definitely that it completely broke away from the past, sometime in the early years of the twentieth century, particularly after the First World War. Perhaps Virginia Woolf, in her essay 'Modern Fiction' (1919), approached nearest the mark in elucidating the term. She believed that the older-generation novelists were 'materialists,' keeping themselves concerned only with the hulk, the body, the externality, but the modern novelists probed deeper into the inner structure, the spirit, or the motive of man. She questioned the stuff of life the novels produced before modernism took hold: 'Is life like this? Must novels be like this?' And she answered, and she explained modernism in her *The Common Reader* thus: "Look within and life, it seems, is far from being 'like this.' Examine for a moment an ordinary mind on an ordinary day. The mind receives a myriad impressions—trivial, fantastic, evanescent, or engraved with the sharpness of steel. From all sides they come, an incessant shower of innumerable atoms; and as they fall, as they shape themselves into the life of Monday or Tuesday, the accent falls differently from of old; the moment of importance came not here but there; so that, if a writer were a free man and not a slave, if he could write what he choose, not what he must, if he could base his work upon his own feeling and not upon convention, there would be no plot, no comedy, no tragedy, no love interest or catastrope in the accepted style, and perhaps not a single button sewn on as the Bond Street tailors would have it. Life is not a series of gig lamps symmetrically arranged; life is a luminous halo, a semi-transparent envelope surrounding us from the beginning of consciousness to the end. Is it not the task of the novelist to convey this varying, this unknown and uncircumscribed spirit, whatever aberration or complexity it may display, with as little mixture of the alien and external as possible? We are not pleading merely for courage and sincerity; we are suggesting that the proper stuff of fiction is a little other than custom would have us believe it" (Woolf, 189). Woolf's rejection of the traditional novel and its orderliness and planning and her admission of subjectivity in the theme of novel as the basic feature of the modern fiction is evident here.

J.A. Cuddon writes not specifically about modern fiction but about modern literature in general: "As far as literature is concerned modernism reveals a breaking away from established rules, traditions and conventions, fresh ways of looking at man's position and function in the universe and many (in some cases remarkable) experiments in form and style. It is particularly concerned with language and how to use it (representationally or otherwise) and with *writing itself*" (Cuddon, 515-516). Modernism was much influenced by dadaism, surrealism, expressionism, existentialism, imagism, stream-of-consciousness theory, etc. The slogan of the dadaists is 'nothingness' and their artistic endeavour is to create 'nothingness' mostly with collage effects. Surrealism disbelieves in the world of logically categorised phenomena; the truth, it believes, is beyond all categorisation and so truth could be apprehended only non-logically, intuitively, in a dream-like state. The expressionist artists are not interested in representing the world as it is around them; they are interested in presenting their highly personalised image or view of the world. The philosophical tenet of existentialism is to concern oneself with the (helplessly directionless) situation of man in the world. Imagism is specifically a poetic cult that believes that the principal vocation of the poet is merely to create hard, clear and well-defined images in poetry. In the stream-of-consciousness method of writing the author records the non-stop kaleidoscopic experiences of characters, free from the trammel of logic or the control of consciousness. The advent of all these during the early part of the twentieth century coupled with a distaste for Victorian prudery, hypocrisy and formalism gave birth to modernism in literature.

Now the question is: is Forster a modern novelist? Barring his maverick novel, *Maurice,* which was posthumously published in 1971, and *A Passage to India,* which was published in 1924, all the other four novels of Forster were written and published during the Edwardian period, and not in the modern period: *Where Angels Fear to Tread* in 1905, *The Longest Journey* in 1907, *A Room with a View* in 1908 and *Howards End* in 1910. It may be pointed out at the very beginning of our discussion on the question of Forster's modernism that he was not a modernist novelist either as regards themes or as regards style. Forster, the liberal humanist, was, in his life as well as in his novels, pre-eminently interested in human relationship and the cultural mesh that prevents the growth of it and also in the problem of under-developed heart; he was not, like, say, James Joyce or Virginia Woolf, interested in the inner workings of the minds of his characters and in experimentations in the style of novel writing. He was not the novelist of the inwardness of man but of his externalities, and this failed him to be recognised as a modern novelist, although a great novelist nevertheless he had been. In some aspects he was a follower of Jane Austen (1775-1817) and the poet-novelist George Meredith (1825-1909). Austen drew fine characters in simple everyday language and Meredith told entertaining stories, and these Forster absorbed within himself. Forster was also benefited much by Proust's technique of elaborating or leading forth the story: the technique of opening a window which will open another and which yet another and so on. But he never followed the stream-of-consciousness method, nor was he engaged in depicting the motives of his characters. And for this, though he had been a bitter critic of the Victorian middle-class hypocritic morality, as a novelist he was definitely a Victorian, if not by choice then by native genius. Jeremy Tambling confirms that "Forster never became a modernist" (Tambling, 2). Tambling further writes: "Though *A Passage to India* is sometimes discussed as modernist, it is no more than D. H. Lawrence's novels, which remains largely realist and antagonistic to modernism's experimentation and interest in language at the level of signifier rather than at that of the signified" (*ibid.*). And, the Indian novelist, writing in English, and admirer and fictional beneficiary of Forster, Mulk Raj Anand, believes that Forster as a novelist was no modernist but was rooted in the tradition of the Edwardian and Georgian eras. Anand writes that Forster was primarily "an English novelist of the Edwardian and Georgian era, firmly rooted in the tradition of Jane Austen and George Meredith, though he extended that tradition to take in something of the detachment of Flaubert" (Naik, 22).

Forster has left behind a legacy, a heritage that has been admired by a number of novelists who have profited much from his thoughts and style: Elizabeth Bowen, Christopher Isherwood, Angus Wilson and others. Bowen is almost idolatrous of Forster, even since she was a 'schoolgirl.' She is particularly charmed by Forster's lucidity and his skill as a teller of tales. She writes: "The lucidity of Forster's writing was, I suppose, what attracted me first of all. Adult fiction had hitherto riled and bothered me by being not only elaborate, but, it seemed, fussily enigmatic.... As story-telling, the story-telling was of an adroitness which confronted no reader with hitch or obstacle. All was—one might have thought—in order" (Edward Arnold, 2-3). Malcolm Bradbury also exalts the inheritance of Forster in definite terms: "There are major writers whose work seems to us important as a contribution to the distinctive powers and dimensions of art; there are others whose work represents almost a personal appeal to value, and who therefore live—for certain of their readers, at least—with a singular force. There have not been many English novelists of our own time who have established with us the second function, but E.M. Forster is certainly one of them. He has served as an embodiment of the virtues he writes about; he has shown us their function and their destiny; he has left, for other writers and other men, a workable inheritance. Partly this is because he has always regarded art as a matter of intelligence as well as passion, honesty as well as imagination. In making such alliances he has given us a contemporary version of a once-familiar belief—that art can be a species of active virtue as well as a form of magic—and has thus sharply appealed to our sense of what man can be" (Bradbuiy, 1983, 224).

This is no mean praise of Forster as a novelist or of the virtues he high-lighted in his novels, but let us cite yet another passage where Cyril Connolly generously praises Forster's style and M.D. Zabel extols the moral virtues of his novels. J.B. Beer, in his *The Achievement of E.M. Forster,* writes that though some critics have mildly complained against the mystic tendency in Forster, Connolly hugely praises the lucidity of his style while Zabel extols the moral passion of his novels. Beer writes: "some of his [Forster's] most enthusiastic admirers have deplored his tendency towards 'mysticism.' Cyril Connolly has pointed out the pioneering importance of his style: the extreme simplicity, the absence of relative and conjunctive clauses and the choice of everyday words marking the evolution of a more radically simplified, disintegrated and colloquial form of art which appeals to the reading public of the twentieth century and has steadily ousted the 'mandarin' style of the nineteenth. M.D. Zabel, on the other hand, is more preoccupied with Forster's moral tone and describes him, with his 'English' qualities, as the greatest single influence on the writers of the thirties—'the one most clearly stamped by the peculiarly English sceptical sensibility and moral passion that has survived two wars with sanity and made possible the reassessment of the tradition and delusion that made those wars and their consequences possible in the Twentieth Century" (Beer, 30).

5 Forster as a Critic

Forster was not only a novelist and short-story writer of exceptional standing, he was also—though unfortunately, we seldom keep it in mind—a good critic. William Henry Hudson, himself a noted novelist, writes about Forster's critical acumen: "Like Virginia Woolf, E.M. Forster (...) has written literary criticism of exceptional quality, in *Abinger Harvest* and *Two Cheers for Democracy*. As the title of the latter book indicates, he is also a critic of social and political affairs, a fair-minded one with no party bias" (Hudson, William Henry, 301). As a literary critic, Forster has considered a wide range of authors including William Cowper, Sir Walter Scott, Jane Austen, George Meredith, Charlotte Brönte, Herman Melville, Edgan Allan Poe, Thomas Hardy, D.H. Lawrence, T.E. Lawrence, Joseph Conrad, Sinclair Lewis, Howard Sturgis, Marcel Proust, Roger Fry, Christopher Isherwood, Tolstoy, Dostoevsky, Virginia Woolf and even Rabindranath Tagore. His criticisms and appreciations of novels and novelists were generally done on the principles laid down in his *Aspects of the Novel*.

In his short essay 'William Cowper, an Englishman' (*The Spectator*, 16 January, 1932), Forster predicted that Cowper's fame as a poet was dated to sink because there is nothing substantial in his poetry to keep it floating: "Cowper perishes. His magic is too flimsy to preserve him, and his knowledge of human nature is too much overshadowed by fears of personal damnation to radiate far down the centuries:

> Those twinkling tiny lustres of the land
> Drop one by one from Fame's neglecting hand,

he writes, 'on observing some names of little note recorded in the *Biographia Britannica*,' and the epitaph might be his own"

(Jones, 239). In his *Aspects of the Novel,* Forster scathingly criticises the novels of Sir Walter Scott, of course admitting his métier as a teller of tales: "Scott is a novelist over whom we shall violently divide. For my part I do not care for him, and find it difficult to understand his continued reputation.... He is seen to have a trivial mind and a heavy style. He cannot construct. He has neither artistic detachment nor passion, and how can a writer who is devoid of both, create characters who will move us deeply?" (Forster, 1966, 38). A few pages afterwards in the same book, Forster copiously praises Tolstoy and his *War and Peace. War and Peace* he says 'is certainly great,' because it "emphasizes the effects of time and the waxing and waning of a generation. Tolstoy, like Bennett, has the courage to show us people getting old—the partial decay of Nicolay and Natasha is really more sinister than the complete decay of Constance and Sophia: more of our own youth seems to have perished in it. Then why is *War and Peace* not depressing? Probably because it has extended over space as well as over time, and the sense of space until it terrifies us is exhilarating, and leaves behind it an effect like music. After one has read *War and Peace* for a bit, great chords begin to sound, and we cannot say exactly what struck them (*op. cit.,* 46).

Forster praises Austen's characterisation: "She is a miniaturist, but never two-dimensional. All her characters are round, or capable of rotundity" (*op. cit.,* 82). In *Abinger Harvest,* Forster has written a short essay, 'Jane Austen,' (1932) exclusively on Jane Austen where he has uninhibitedly expressed his great admiration for her: "I am a Jane Austenite, and therefore slightly imbecile about Jane Austen.... She is my favourite author! I read and re-read, the mouth open and the mind closed. Shut up in measureless content, I greet her by the name of most kind hostess" (Forster, 1953, 172). But, while he praises the complementarity of Meredith's incidents and characters he is censorious of his plots: "Meredith's plots are not closely knit...A Meredithian plot is not a temple to the tragic or even to the comic Muse, but rather resembles a series of kiosks most artfully placed among the wooded slopes, which his people reach by their own impetus, and from which they emerge with altered aspect. Incident springs out of character, and having occurred it alters that character" (Forster, 1966, 98). Forster writes about Hardy that he "is far greater than Meredith, and yet less successful as a novelist—Thomas Hardy. Hardy seems to me essentially a poet, who conceives of his novels from an enormous height" (*op. cit.,* 100). Dostoevsky, Forster says, had prophetic vision, but not George Eliot, though both had vision (*op. cit.,* 131).

As we have seen Forster was almost idolatrous of Jane Austen, so was he an adulator of Virginia Woolf. In his brief essay 'The Early Novels of Virginia Woolf' (1925), he writes very entertainingly about the elusiveness of her novels and about her lasting contribution to the art of the novel: "It is profoundly characteristic of the art of Virginia Woolf that when I decided to write about it and had planned a suitable opening paragraph, my fountain pen should disappear. Tiresome creature! It slipped through a pocket into a seam. I could pinch it, chivy it about, make holes in the coat lining, but a layer of tailor's stuffing prevented recovery. So near, and yet so far! Which is what one feels about her art.... She has, among other achievements, made a definite contribution to the novelist's art" (Forster, 1953, 125). Forster says that *The Voyage Out* is a 'strange, tragic, inspired book', *Night and Day* 'is the simplest novel she has written, and to my mind the least successful,' and *Mrs Dalloway* 'is perhaps her masterpiece, but difficult.' He has noticed Woolf's 'visual sensitiveness' and 'remarkable intellectual powers.' About Woolf's métier of describing characters, Forster writes in the same essay of his: "It is easy for a novelist to describe what a character thinks of;... But to convey the actual process of thinking is a creative feat, and I know of no one except Virginia Woolf who has accomplished it" (*op. cit.,* 132).

Forster, after the death of his friend D.H. Lawrence, saluted him as 'the greatest imaginative novelist of our generation.' He used to keep himself abreast of the newest publications of Lawrence, and of all his novels he formed 'a preference for *The Plumed Serpent.*' He, in fact, had great 'admiration' for Lawrence, so much so that, when after

Lawrence's death in 1930 the obituary in *The Times* did not show enough respect to Lawrence in his eyes, Forster dealt a slap in the face of the newspaper. The obituary in *The Times* ran thus: "'There was that in his intellect which might have made him one of England's greatest writers, and did indeed make him the writer of some things worthy of the best of England literature. But as time went on and his disease took a firmer hold, his rage and his fear grew upon him. He confused decency with hypocrisy, and honesty with the free and public use of vulgar words. At once fascinated and horrified by physical passion, he paraded his disgust and fear in the trappings of a showy masculinity'" (Furbank, II, 163 f. n.). Forster could not keep his anger and hostility, due to this part of the obituary, buckled, and wrote to the *Nation and Athenaeum* on 29 March 1930 the following rebuff: "...Now he [Lawrence] is dead, and the low-brows whom he scandalized have united with the high-brows whom he bored to ignore his greatness. This cannot be helped; no one who alienates Mrs Grundy and Aspatia [*sic*] can hope for a good obituary press. All that we can do...is to say straight out that he was the greatest imaginative novelist of our generation. The rest must be left where he would have wished it to be left—in the hands of the young" (*ibid.*).

In chapter entitled '*Aspects of the Novel:* Forster's Theory of the Novel,' we have said that, according to Forster, a character is round if it changes or is modified in the course of the narrative, and if it does not it is flat—it is a character that will be counted as defective in a novel. Forster, in *Aspects of the Novel,* chapter IV, further says that "The test of a round character is whether it is capable of surprising in a convincing way. If it never surprises, it is flat. If it does not convince, it is flat pretending to be round. It has the incalculability of life about it—life within the pages of a book" (Forster, 1966, 85). In the same chapter of the same book, he tells us that "Dickens's people [characters] are nearly all flat;" "all Wells's characters are flat as a photograph. But the photographs are agitated with such vigour that we forget their complexities lie on the surface and would disappear if it was scratched or curled up;" and all of Austen's "characters are round, or capable of rotundity." In the same place, again, Forster gives us additional examples of round characters: "All the principal characters in *War and Peace,* all the Dostoevsky characters, and some of the Proust—for example, the old family servant, the Duchess of Guermantes, M. de Charlus, and Saint Loup; Madame Bovary—who, like Moll Flanders, has her book to herself, and can expand and secrete unchecked; some people in Thackeray—for instance, Becky and Beatrix; some in Fielding—Parson Adams, Tom Jones; and some in Charlotte Brönte, most particularly Lucy Snowe" (Allott, 289).

In chapter 7 of *Aspects of the Novel,* entitled 'Prophecy,' Forster says that Emily Brönte was a prophetess in her novels as Blake was a prophet in his poetry, of course, in both the cases, we must understand the word 'prophecy' in his sense of it. About Brönte, he says: "she was a prophetess: because what is implied is more important to her than what is said" (Forster, 1966, 148-149). But, for instance, the Noble Laureate Indian poet Tagore, is no prophet like Nietzsche or Whitman. And Forster says this while reviewing Tagore's dance-drama *Chitra.* In *Abinger Harvest,* he writes (in 1914) about *Chitra:* "The story is told with faultless delicacy and grace. Its action is no stronger than a flower, and the fragrance of blossom clings round every phrase. But, of course, there is 'something behind,' that something for which the worshipper pants. Allegories stalk in the background, not always upon all fours. The contrast between the material and the immaterial, the contrast between pleasure and action, the nature of wedded joy, which though only to be gained through youth and beauty, knows how to survive their departure—*Chritra* symbolizes all three ideas in turn. It is true that the play is not the least spoilt by the symbolism. An allegory may be as lame as it likes if it walks quietly, and Tagore's always do that. Indeed, one's enjoyment is increased by the sense of half-audible stirrings in the midst of the Jasmine bowers. But to drag the allegory from its retirement, and proclaim it has importance in itself is to brutalize the atmosphere and pay no real honour to the author. Tagore is a poet who, like any other, must contrive some sub-structure on hitch to exhibit beauty, and, being an Indian poet, he has turned to general ideas more readily than does his English brother. That is all. He is not a seer or a thinker. He is not to be classed with Nietzsche or Whitman, or others of whom he occasionally reminds us. Such, at all events, is the verdict suggested by *Chitra*'" (Forster, 1953, 364).

Forter's criticism (done in 1919) of Tagore's *The Home and the World* is harsher. Let us quote it in full: "When a writer of Tagore's genius produces such a sentence as Passion is beautiful and pure—pure as the lily that comes out of the slimy soil; it rises superior to its defilement and needs no Pears' soap to wash it clean"—he raises some interesting questions. The sentence is not attractive—in fact, it is a Babu sentence—and what does Tagore, generally so attractive, intend by it? Is he being dramatic, and providing a Babu of his creation with appropriate English, or is he being satirical, or was there some rococo charm that has vanished in the translation, or is it an experiment that has not quite come off? Probably an experiment, for throughout the book one is puzzled by bad tastes that verge upon bad taste. The theme is so beautiful; here it is, beautifully stated: 'while the day is bright and the world in the pursuit of its numberless tasks crowds around, then it seems as if my life wants nothing else. But when the colours of the sky fade away and the blinds are drawn down over the windows of heaven, then my heart tells me that evening falls just for the purpose of shutting out the world, to mark the time when the darkness must be filled with the One...that work alone cannot be the truth of life, that work is not the be-all and the end-all of man, for man is not simply a serf—even though the serfdom be of the True and the Good.'

"But when the theme is developed, one receives inappropriate emotions, and feels that the contrast is not so much between the Home and the World as between the well-bred and the ill-bred. The Home is not really a home, but a retreat for seemly meditation upon infinity. And the World—it proves to be a sphere not for 'numberless tasks,' but for a boarding-house flirtation that masks itself in mystic or patriotic talk. The action is laid in Bengal, during the Swadeshi movement, and it leads up to the theft of Rs. 6,000. How, why, and by whom were the Rs. 6,000 stolen from the safe? Tagore is scarcely at his soundest when speculating on such problems. Not here, O Nirvana, are haunts meet for thee, and we learn without emotion that they were stolen by a wife from her husband for the Cause, that they were misappropriated by an amorous and amoral Babu, and that they led to the death of another Babu, who was chivalrous and young. The tragedy is skilfully told, but it all seems to be about nothing, and this is because the contrast does not work out as the writer intends. He meant the wife to be seduced by the World, which is, with all its sins, a tremendous lover; she is actually seduced by a West Kensingtonian Babu, who addresses her as 'Queen Bee,' and in warmer moments as 'Bee.' In spite of the beautiful writing and the subtle metaphor and the noble outlook that are inseparable from Tagore's work, this strain of vulgarity persists. It is external, not essential, but it is there; the writer has been experimenting with matter whose properties he does not quite understand.

"Why should he care to experiment? Here is a more profitable but more difficult question. Having triumphed in *Chitra* or *Gitanjali,* why should he indite a 'roman a trois' with all the hackneyed situations from which novelists are trying to emancipate themselves in the West? These Bengalis—they are an extraordinary people. Probably this is the answer. They are more modern and mentally more adventurous than any of the other races in the Indian peninsula. They like trying, and failures do not discompose them, because they have interest in the constitution of the world. They have in a single generation produced Tagore and Bose, innovators both, and the people that has done that will not rest content. In literature, as in science, they must work over the results of the West on the chance of their proving of use, and one expects that the younger writers will reject the experiment of *The Home and the World,* and will adopt some freer form" (*op. cit.,* 365-367). Nevertheless, Forster had to admit Tagore's worth as a writer: "He is a good writer. All must assent to this minimum" (*op. cit.,* 363).

Howbeit, Forster expressedly had less regard for criticism than for creative works. In his Harvard Lecture (1947), entitled 'The Raison D'Etre of Criticism in the Arts,' he recognised 'many merits' of the 'critical state' of mind but all at the same time said that that state is twice removed from the creative state, and so criticism can hardly do proper justice to creative works. P.N. Furbank writes: "The 'critical state,' he [Forster] said, had many merits; it employed 'some of the highest and subtlest faculties of man'; but it was 'grotesquely remote from the state responsible for the works it affects to expound.' Criticism did not have 'spiritual parity' with creation, and 'his main conclusion on it had therefore to be unfavourable'" (Furbank, II, 272).

The question may be asked: how much worthy a critic is Forster? To Lionel Trilling, for one, he is not so good a critic, because he lacks in 'consistency.' Trilling writes that Forster "is a critic with no drive to consistency, no desire to find an architectonic for his impressions. We might say of him that he is a critic without any desire for *success*. In short, he is an impressionistic critic" (Trilling, 141). Trilling has compared between Forster and T.S. Eliot, as critics, and says that the difference between them may not be fundamental, but certainly is considerable: if between a critic like Forster and a critic like, say, Eliot, the difference is not so fundamental as at first appears, it is still considerable. For one thing, there is a great difference in aesthetic result. In Eliot the desire to make laws and the conscious effort for dignity have their unquestionable effect upon us. We respond to the effort; the form of dialectic gives us pleasure; we are connected with large issues. Literature thus acquires a magnificent importance, life seems more interesting. In such a critic we have met either an ally with whom we attack some enemy of the human spirit, or an opponent who gives us the satisfaction of conflict. Forster, on the contrary, asks us to relax. He can tell us very movingly, of the importance of literature, but he never intends to make any single literary work important. And the manner of his presentation of ideas is personal in a way that mocks the erection of laws. "Eliot of course, emerges as the better critic.

Even if we grant Forster every possible virtue of his method—and it has virtues—he is never wholly satisfactory in criticism and frequently he is frustrating" (*op. cit.*, 141-142).

****